HAMPSHIRE
COUNTY CRICKETERS

DAVE ALLEN

HAMPSHIRE
COUNTY CRICKETERS

1864–2018

DAVE ALLEN

Moyhill Publishing

Second Edition Revised 2019
ISBN 978-1-905597-89-5

First published in 2018
ISBN 978-1-905597-83-3

A CIP catalogue record for this book is available from the British Library.

Printed in UK.

—∿∿∿∿∿∿—

This Special Edition is limited to one hundred (100) numbered copies for sale, each signed by the author.

Copy Number

43

Dave Allen

Moyhill Publishing,
1965 Davenport House, 261 Bolton Rd, Bury, Gtr. Manchester BL8 2NZ. UK.

This publication is dedicated to the memory of Neil Jenkinson,
a fine Hampshire historian and my mentor and friend.

PREFACE TO THE SECOND EDITION

I published the first, paperback edition of this book during the 2018 season. Despite taking some care over the processes of proof-reading there were a number of errors, so at the very least I hope that this one will offer a correct version of the tales of the 700+ men who have played for Hampshire since that first match of the newly constituted *County Cricket Club* in 1864.

With considerable help from the Ageas Bowl shop, the first edition has pretty much disappeared – not entirely 'sold out' because I was pleased to present copies to quite a few of the men who appear between its covers – but this fact, plus the corrections seemed to justify a second edition. This one is a hardback and after some thought, it is also a limited edition, each signed and numbered. I do not anticipate a reprint, although I hope that one day someone else might update and perhaps improve this record.

I did note originally that for reasons of space I had not included a statistical summary for every player, although in many cases significant figures do appear and some have been added to, including all those who appeared in 2018. I would remind you of the excellent statistical site by our supporter 'Tigger' Miles (*http://hampshirecricket.net/*) which links directly to the *Cricinfo* site. The original Introduction and Foreword are unchanged apart from corrections and a little tidying-up.

Apart from a couple of matches in England colours for Liam Dawson, the descriptions, facts and records in this edition cease at the conclusion of the 2018 domestic season. I have however included players who joined Hampshire in the final few months of the year and are expected to play in 2019. Those men, Barker, Donald and Fuller appear in *italics*, but by the time you read this there will be others – not least the 2019 overseas players – who are not here. The additions for the 2018 first-class season were Sam Northeast, Hashim Amla, Dale Steyn, Ollie Rayner (on loan), and Oliver Soames, and there were two men who played in the T20 competition, Colin Munro and from Afghanistan, Mujeeb Zadran.

There have been some happy events over the past year, and not merely on the field with the winning of another Lord's Cup Final. In June, Dorset Cricket Society arranged a delightful surprise 90th birthday party for Alan Rayment who became, by dint of the date of his debut in 1949, Hampshire's 'Senior Pro'.

A few weeks later, Alan and I drove to Hungerford to spend an enjoyable day in the company of John Manners, and shortly after John became the first man ever to have played first-class cricket to reach his 104th birthday. A few months later he is still with us and moving towards 105!

The birthday party down in Dorset was attended by Alan's team-mate Mike Barnard, the best and bravest of men and greatly mourned when we heard of his death just before Christmas 2018. Another of Alan's colleagues, and another footballing cricketer, Ralph Prouton has also died since the first edition. If nothing else, this publication ensures that they are not forgotten, and we thank them and everyone here for enriching our lives by being Hampshire cricketers.

January 2019

FOREWORD

AWH Rayment
Hampshire CCC 1949-1958

The History of the Game of Cricket in the British Isles can be viewed as analogous to the way the Game of Life has been played, and has changed, through succeeding generations since the 18th century. All levels of British society manifested leaders who became legendary, pioneers who revolutionised industry and medicine, heroes and heroines and unsung hard working families who maintained, through wars and social upheaval, a level of relative normality whilst experimenting with futuristic possibilities until 'tomorrow became today'.

The History of Hampshire County cricket also abounds with legendary players and characters in famous teams of each era, supported by dedicated administrators and financiers, excellent writers and broadcasters, hard-working ground staff and caterers – not forgetting stalwart members and spectators who together created and maintained the Club's time line of relative normality for more than a century.

During the last forty years media generated financial abundance in the world of cricket, combined with worldwide changes in social ethics and mores – linked with an escalating public demand for rapid gratification – has revolutionised the mind-set of the game's power brokers who have, of necessity, modernised the structure of the sport.

In parallel, a burgeoning athleticism and inventive experimentation with playing techniques, together with changes in players' attitudes and expectations of financial rewards have completed an historic transformation of cricket, aligning it with the digital-media-corporate age of the 21st century. 'Yesterday is history: today is the tomorrow few dared dream of'.

Dr. Dave Allen's long, enthusiastic and creative devotion to Hampshire cricket has borne many varieties of fruit, including publications galore and several major books that have recorded and expounded upon the evolution of the Club and exploits of the players since 1863. Dave has recently devoted months of research and finger-tapping screen time to create this commendably comprehensive compilation of cricketers who have represented the County of Hampshire in one or more first-class matches. Congratulations Dave: does this excellent historical record of Hampshire players complete your collection? 'Game, set and match?' I hope not!

The A to Z of Hampshire County Cricketers will delight the game's statisticians and many a Hampshire aficionado. I am surprised to discover that since Hampshire were admitted to The County Championship in 1895, around 550 amateur and professional cricketers have represented the County in first class matches, of whom 171 were awarded a County Cap. I was privileged to be playing when sixteen colleagues, everyone a good friend, were presented with their County Cap:

> 1949: Vic Ransom; Cliff Walker; Derek Shackleton.
> 1950: Vic Cannings.
> 1951: Jimmy Gray; Leo Harrison.
> 1953: David Blake.
> 1954: Revd. John Bridger; Reg Dare.
> 1955: Peter Sainsbury; Roy Marshall; Mike Barnard;
> Henry Horton; Mervyn Burden.
> 1957: Colin Ingleby-Mackenzie; Malcolm Heath.

During the Hampshire versus Glamorgan match in July 1952 I was honoured to be presented with my County Cap by our Captain, Desmond Eager, on the field of play in front of the Members Pavilion at Dean Park, Bournemouth. A proud moment! Emotional too as I received warm wishes and hand-shakes from the skipper and members, followed by thumps on the back by jesting team mates … no hugs and tribal dances in those days. But how did this young Middlesex amateur, who had felt so at home at Lord's, become a lover of Hampshire County and of Hampshire Cricket?

The seeds of my romance with the County of Hampshire were sown in the 1930s during our family summer holidays with my Uncle Jack who lived in Ryde, Isle of Wight. The rail journey from Waterloo through the Surrey and Hampshire countryside was always exciting but rose exponentially as the hissing, rail-grinding Nelson 4-6-2 dragged its family of green coaches past the United Services Ground then snaked round the final tight bend to expire in a cloud of steam at Portsmouth Harbour Terminus. I loved Portsmouth Harbour – of being at sea aboard the paddle steamer PS Whippingham as she navigated the busy Solent to dock at Ryde's glorious pier-head – then eagerly disembarking to run the short distance into the station and stand transfixed at the sight of my beloved Puffin' Billie tank engines. Cricket on Ryde sands; fishing on the pier; rail excursions round the Island; breathing sea air; ships everywhere … *why did we have to live in London?* I expressed my affection for The Island in 'Last Peacetime Holiday, 1939': a chapter in my book of 'Early Memoirs'. Until resident in Southampton ten years later I had always thought The Island was part of Hampshire.

Nine years passed before I trod on Hampshire soil again, when in June 1948 I played for Middlesex 2nd XI against Hampshire 2nd XI at Dean Park, Bournemouth. Rain interrupted play on the first day; on the second I scored 40 in a longish innings on a turning wicket in a memorable duel with Reg Dare. Maybe that innings and my fielding impressed Arthur Holt, whom I ran out with a direct hit on the stumps from cover point. In August Desmond Eagar wrote to the Finchley Club's secretary and to my parents, requesting a meeting between his Chairman and members of the club's committee. I was not consulted or involved in person but thereafter exchanged correspondence with Desmond Eagar and was offered a two-year contract.

In September 1948 demobilisation from the RAF was postponed due to the Berlin Air Lift crisis, so I continued my role as a plotter in the Operations Room at RAF Uxbridge until the New Year. Meanwhile, in October when my bride and I were on honeymoon in Bournemouth, we travelled by train to Southampton where we were met by Arthur Holt who drove to Hampshire CCC headquarters and introduced us to Desmond Eagar. Contracts were signed; my childhood dream fulfilled. I was now a professional; *A Hampshire Cricketer*. Five pounds per week – half paid-out in rent. Married, soon to be a father, required to dress smartly and buy own kit. In that era if a young person with talent *just had to be* an actor, a classical musician, a ballet or stage dancer, or a cricketer, that person's motivation could only be love, not money.

Hampshire County and Hampshire cricket: so many wonderful memories – so few unhappy moments. Ten precious years in the classrooms of Life! In the summers learning to cope with failure and success, protocols and relationships in the enclosed world of cricket. In the winters, working hard to build a business and to fulfil my roles and responsibilities in family life and the local community. As the team travelled north, west and east I enjoyed meeting with people in all levels of society across a wide range of occupations, opinions and varieties of interest. My role: a member of a team playing a game – relatively seriously. The overall experience was a major part of my education! Thank you Hampshire CCC.

What about the players, the characters, the memorable matches? Too, too many – but here is a snapshot. I enjoyed the company of *all* the Hampshire players of my era and before – except one. In my first few seasons Arthur Holt, Gerry Hill and Neil McCorkell shepherded and encouraged me. Ralph Prouton and Jimmy Gray taught me to play golf – I was best man at Jimmy's wedding. My wife and I taught several Hampshire team mates to dance waltzes and quicksteps. Pete Sainsbury achieved a Bronze Medal.

To meet and talk with veteran Hampshire players was indeed an honour and a learning experience. They included Lord Tennyson; CB Fry; Jack Newman; Walter Livsey; Len Creese; Stuart Boyes: Dick Moore; Sam Pothecary; Lloyd Budd. In the dressing room at Dean Park I enjoyed sitting and chatting with Phil Mead, then blind, and one day – surprise – with Boris Karloff. To play with a kindly bunch of pre-war Hampshire cricket professors was invaluable: Johnny Arnold; Jim Bailey; 'Lofty' Herman; George Heath; Gerry Hill; Neil McCorkell and Arthur Holt … there was a lot of Real Hampshire character and playing experience in that group! Desmond Eagar, Captain and Club Secretary, whom I held in high regard, was the most influential person in my playing career. The President, Harry Altham and pre-war captain Cecil Paris (also my solicitor) were wise counsellors and our much-loved coach, Arthur Holt, a wise Uncle to everyone.

Lovely memories abound: of playing Club & Ground and Benefit matches against club sides all around the County, of new places and faces – some very good cricketers too, beautiful cricket grounds in glorious countryside. In September 1949, I was a member of a strong County team that toured the Isle of Wight on a goodwill mission led by Desmond Eagar. In May 1952, we played Hartley Wintney's XV during their Village Festival, with colourful bunting encircling the picturesque cricket ground ringed with hundreds of spectators. On the first-class circuit I relished playing in the traditional Bank Holiday matches against Kent, attended by large crowds, and colourful festival occasions at Bath, Eastbourne, Scarborough and Glastonbury. Many county players socialized with opponents and club members after a day's play; at Portsmouth's United Services and Bournemouth's Dean Park invitations to Mayoral and 'posh club' marquees were plentiful.

Writing this piece is akin to opening a Pandora's Box of memories. I remain truly proud to have played cricket for the County of Hampshire and the Isle of Wight where we played at Cowes against Worcestershire in 1956 (Colin Ingleby-Mackenzie scored his maiden hundred), and Nottinghamshire in 1957 (AWH scored 80). I conclude with a tale that, hopefully, 'lights up' the social environment and playing ambience of county cricket in the 1950s: this young boy's dream that unfurled in June 1953 and became a reality forever remembered.

Hampshire v the Australian Touring Team
at Northlands Road, 6, 8, 9 June 1953.

Australians: Hole, Morris, Harvey, de Courcy, Craig, Benaud, Archer, Davidson, Tallon, Hill, Johnston

Hampshire: Marshall, Gray, Walker, Rayment, Horton, Eagar, Hill, Prouton, Dare, Shackleton, Cannings

As a capped Hampshire, professional I received £7.50 per week, summer and winter, plus small end of season bonuses that included £5.0 for a win in Championship matches. Our School of Ballroom Dancing, studio adjacent to the Northlands Road cricket ground, produced a much greater income than cricket and enabled us to build a family house near the Sports Centre, about two miles from Hampshire's headquarters. First car, 1937 model, purchased later in that year.

On that momentous Saturday morning, ironed two pairs of cricket flannels and two shirts, packed them in a holdall, mounted my bicycle, pedalled down Hill Lane and then walked through 'The Cut' into Northlands Road where I was engulfed by friendly spectators who chatted away and wished me well as they hurried to the turnstiles. Having chained my bike to some old railings behind the groundsman's cottage I strolled past the nets and up the wooden steps into The Hutch: "Punchy's here … unusually early today", quipped Vic Cannings. Sunny summer's day; full house of spectators; the air vibrating with a tuneful buzz of expectation; The Australians!

The Australians win the toss and bat. I dream the scene from cover point …

Shack bowls to Graham Hole … second ball lifts alarmingly … a puff of dust rises slowly from the pitch. Skipper Desmond at short-leg stares with gloomy awe, curses and predicts loss of the third day's gate money. Insufficient rain and watering following lime dressing has caused grass roots to rot. Result: hard dry crumbling wicket, spiteful unpredictable bounce. Next scene: Vic Cannings bowls to Graham Hole who shapes to play a drive past my right at cover – ball kicks high and hits sharp corner of bat's shoulder – Reg Dare, crouching at forward short-leg doesn't move and is hit on left cheek and collapses. Bleeding profusely, Ex-Guardsman Dare is aided to 'The Hutch' and laid on the old pine table. Members and spectators a-buzz with concern for Reg – and questions about 'that pitch'. Hole holes-out to Roy Marshall: enter twenty-four-year-old Neil Harvey who, on this treacherous pitch plays one of the finest innings, in defence and attack, that I witness as a player on the field. Neil Harvey 109…Arthur Morris 55: a partnership of 124. Unforgettable!

Entering 'The Hutch' before lunch we congregated around Reg Dare who was laying on the old table wearing a bloated leech on his cheek… two more in a saucer …. he recovered to bat. First innings: Australians 268: Hampshire 131: a fat duck for Punchy who, at the end of play avoided the only bath in 'The Hutch'; a Victorian single domestic roll-top and adjacent pre-war gas boiler. A flannel wash; a half pint with Aussies Craig and Hole, and naturally, congratulations to Neil Harvey. Dirty shirts in hold-all, unchain bike, cycle home to a loving welcome from wife, and son age three, and – oh so wonderful – a hot bath!

On Monday, the Australians declared their second innings 306 runs ahead of Hampshire: the wicket like a dusty road with potholes. Batting number four, I joined Roy Marshall with the score at nine. My inimitably brilliant Test batsman partner challenged the pitch and the Australian bowlers with a glorious display of immaculately timed stroke-play: I survived to play a few drives and pulls – one from a short ball by Bill Johnstone disappeared over the boundary wall into the garden beside our dance studio … six and lost ball. Roy scored 71; I was caught & bowled by Richie Benaud on 30. We entertained for an hour.

I am sure the members and spectators were filled with long-lasting memories of the two-day Australian match – especially the batting of Neil and Roy – and the privilege of watching Aussies in their Baggies performing live on Hampshire soil. I am also sure that current and future generations of cricket lovers, young and old, will garner happy memories from watching skilled athletic men and women play the game of cricket, in all its modern colourful varieties, on the verdant acres of the Ageas Bowl, the wonderful stadium that is now The Home of Hampshire Cricket.

Finally, from the day of my debut at Cardiff sixty-nine years ago, I have always been, and remain, thankful and proud to have worn my Hampshire cap, to have played with and against unforgettable characters, and to have occasionally entertained Hampshire cricket fans on Hampshire soil.

Alan 'Punchy' Rayment
Milford-on-Sea.
April 2018.

INTRODUCTION

Exactly 60 years ago John Arlott published the first of four consecutive, annual 'Cricket Journals' documenting in this one his experience of the rather damp 1958 English season, when England hammered the New Zealanders, who struggled to cope with their first experience of five-day Test Matches in England. Arlott also reported on a variety of days watching the County Championship unfold, making little attempt to hide his excitement as *his Hampshire* threatened to depose the Champions of the previous six years, Surrey.

In the end, Hampshire and Arlott had to wait three more years, their hopes spoiled in particular by a remarkable match at Burton-on-Trent in August on a pitch that these days would have a posse of 'inspectors' calling. But things were different in 1958, entirely different, since not only did counties play for three days on 'uncovered' pitches, but they played at a variety of grounds away from their Headquarters, assuming that in every case they owned one. Apart from Northlands Road, Southampton, Hampshire went to Cowes, Isle of Wight, while in his journal, Arlott visited the Royal Navy's modest but ship-shape ground by Portsmouth's city centre and less than a quarter-of-a-mile from where I live today. He went too, to beautiful Chesterfield where I spent summer holidays as a kid, to 'Kiss Me Quick' Clacton-on-Sea, commuter-belt Guildford, the evocatively-named Wagon Works Ground at Gloucester, Gothic Cheltenham, and as a pilgrim to Canterbury for the (early) August Bank Holiday. At the end of that month, he joined the holiday-makers from up north for a week at Bournemouth, watching Yorkshire and Derbyshire, but he went also, to friendly Hove and Taunton and to the big cities Cardiff, Taunton, Manchester, Birmingham, Leeds and London.

Things were simpler then of course. Arlott devoted much time to speculating about the England side that would tour Australia in the winter and when the names were announced in late July, he observed that "no better side could be picked", adding it "must surely be the strongest sent from England for over twenty years – and a better balanced and more fully equipped party than any other cricketing country could muster today". So much for prophecy and expertise; the final Test of that winter series took place in mid-February, a little more than six months after Arlott offered his judgement, as Australia won by nine wickets to take the series 4-0. There again, they 'cheated'. They had a battery of younger fast-bowlers, some of whom seemed to deliver with a bent arm, and mostly from halfway down the pitch, dragging their back foot and exploiting the no-ball law of the time.

Was it ever thus? Perhaps it was. Arlott's journal also had a chapter on "The Wardle Affair", in which Yorkshire's slow-left-armer, selected for the tour, was told by Yorkshire there would be no new contract, withdrew from the county side, published a series of derogatory comments about his colleagues in *the Daily Mail*, was sacked with immediate effect, and so MCC (in those days, England overseas) de-selected him. Meanwhile Surrey's Yorkshireman Jim Laker, having said he would not tour, did so, but after retiring the following year, published a controversial autobiography, and both MCC and Surrey withdrew his Honorary Memberships. In this context, and with a County Championship which in the 1950s seemed to deny 16 of the 17 counties any chance of winning the one Trophy on offer, the exploits of Colin Ingleby-Mackenzie and his Hampshire team brought a lightness to the game, with his exhortation to his men to "Entertain or Perish". They, mind you were largely a bunch of tough, hardened professionals – there was to be no messing with men like Shackleton, Cannings, Gray, Harrison, Marshall, Sainsbury and the like, but they did seem to enjoy themselves at times.

Enjoying the game has been difficult to discern in the winter of 2017/18, with the Match Referee Jeff Crowe, a New Zealander, reporting that he "had never seen such animosity" as in the series between Australia and South Africa – an atmosphere that boiled over into one of the saddest episodes in cricket history. There was at least, no sense of that in Arlott's account of the 1958 season, particularly recounting his travels watching County Cricket Clubs playing in the County Championship; which was all there was as far as competitive county cricket was concerned. What they played then is simply not what they play now, over four days, in two divisions, mainly on county headquarters, with covered, often flat, pitches and good drainage. I read in a very recent publication that in 1973, Richard Gilliat was "one of only two men to lead (Hampshire) to the Division One title" but he wasn't, and neither was the other man, because there was no Division One then or for some decades to come. Apart from eleven v eleven, *everything* has changed, across the country and particularly in Hampshire. The Championship season of 2018 opened with a Hampshire side that included five men born in South Africa, one in the West Indies, one recently arrived from Kent and one 37-year-old born in Hampshire. During that season, Hampshire will not play in the Championship against some of their nearest neighbours, Middlesex, Sussex or Kent, and neither will they play at Bournemouth, Portsmouth, Cowes, or Southampton; but rather at the suburban ground which has only existed – under two names – in the twenty-first century. It is a ground that inevitably lacks memories – it is not, in the well-known words of poet Francis Thompson ('At Lord's') a field "full of shades" where "a ghostly batsman plays to the bowling of a ghost".

Perhaps that sense of having to search hard for 'history' at the modern Hampshire makes this project more urgent, although I am aware of other counties that have done similar work. In the winter before he began his journal,

Hampshire's great run-scorer Philip Mead died, and Arlott was commissioned by the BBC to broadcast a tribute from the County Ground in Northlands Road. Mead only played in 17 Tests, the last in England more than 35 years earlier, yet his achievement was such that he warranted a national radio tribute and Arlott reproduced his script in *Cricket Journal*. It began

> That monumentally reliable batsman, Philip Mead is dead. But we who were boys in Hampshire in my generation – or for that matter, in the two generations on either side of it – can never, as long as we live, see this county ground at Southampton, without remembering him.

Arlott lived to a good age, but Mead has been gone these 60 years. The only man still living who played in the same match as Mead, is Commander JE Manners whose details, like Mead's, can be found here. Even better, John Manners followed him to the crease in three Championship matches over a fortnight in late August 1936, including Mead's farewell v Yorkshire at Bournemouth (lbw Verity 52). John Manners, now the oldest-ever first-class cricketer might remember, but anyone else who saw Mead and claims to recollect his style, and strange rituals must be at least 90.

What is more, even those of us from younger generations who have fond memories of the old County Ground can no longer go there and recall 'Shack', the Marshalls, or Barry Richards. In 1958, Arlott went there to see his county play the tourists, who in those far-off days, actually *toured* the country, and wrote

> Back once more on the ground where the backways and the little odd rooms – conjured out of accidental bulges in the old pavilions – are familiar as home … the ground has an air of improvisation, of gradual growth, additions and after-thoughts merging into a unity like the photos, nick-nacks and pieces of china which, over the years, accumulated on our grandparents' mantelpieces.

It describes perfectly what is now simply a modern housing estate. I went back once to film a short piece for television, when Hampshire celebrated its 150th anniversary, but there was no sense of what had once been, while at the new home of Hampshire, Mead, who had a stand named after him on the old ground, now has a somewhat shadowy tribute, next to the lift in the Shackleton Bar. If this publication helps a little to preserve the achievements and memories of Mead, and the 720+ Hampshire's cricketers over the past 155 years, that will make it worthwhile.

We marked that 150th anniversary in 2013 in various ways, but it was in itself a slightly odd celebration which leads me to the matter of the precise title of this publication, *Hampshire County Cricketers 1864-2017/18*, which is slightly ambiguous and unwieldy. Firstly, while the majority of the players included here played for the Hampshire County Cricket Club, which was formed in the late summer of 1863, for most of this century that *Members' Club* has been replaced by a PLC which is simply known as Hampshire Cricket. This is not the place to consider the shift towards corporate identities in county cricket but it does require a recognition that things are different. As to the dates, it is 1864 rather than 1863 because that was the year when that formally constituted County Cricket Club played its first matches. There were of course, many matches played by sides called Hampshire for more than a century prior to that, and those players are only included here, if they played also in matches from 1864. I have not listed anyone who played for sides designated as Hampshire (including those of the famous 18th century Hambledon Club) prior to 1864.

More specifically, any inclusion requires that across the first hundred years, the cricketer played in first-class cricket. In the biographies that follow, there are many references to appearances in non-first-class matches, but to be listed here requires an appearance in what constitutes a first-class match at least until from 1963, when Hampshire began playing what is now known as white-ball cricket. First-class cricket includes, of course, all matches in the County Championship, which most people believe Hampshire first joined in 1895. This too is not entirely straightforward; there are distinguished cricket historians who prefer the view that the County Championship can be traced back at least to 1864; indeed, Robert Brooke (1991) offered an incomplete list of "unofficial champions", from 1826-1863, while previously, Roy Webber (1958) suggested that the "first phase" ran from 1873. This publication is content to agree with Stephen Chalke (2015) whose marvellous history of the Championship, *Summer's Crown* places the 'real' start in 1890, when matters were formalised.

Hampshire joined that competition in 1895, because in the previous five seasons their matches were still second-class; indeed, had been since 1886. During the Victorian era, Hampshire were rarely a strong side, winning a few matches here-and-there, and finishing last rather frequently as Victorians became Edwardians. To be precise, Hampshire's matches were considered first-class in 1864-1867; 1869 & 1870; 1875-1878; and 1880-1885. In the intervening years, their matches were second-class, and often scarce or, as in 1868, none at all by a team called Hampshire. But from 1895 they were playing Championship matches and occupying their often-lowly place in the published tables.

The cricketers who played in those days, in first and second-class matches, are listed on the invaluable on-line site *Cricket Archive*. This publication might have appeared without that resource, but it would have been diminished – the availability of on-line resources such as the full scorecards of every Hampshire first-class match, is of extraordinary value to those of us who research cricket history, and indeed it is so comprehensive, that its list of Hampshire cricketers includes some who do not appear in here. The first of those alphabetically is Jeffrey Charles Amherst, who died in France in 1877, before he reached his mid-30s. He had two brothers who played first-class cricket for MCC, one of them, JGH Amherst *against* Hampshire in 1866, but JC is included on *Cricket Archive* by virtue of playing for Hampshire and other sides in the county, only in non-first-class matches.

In some cases, such omissions might be considered unfortunate. By contrast, there are players included in the lists that follow, whose selection and performance are unremarkable, as well as more than one who neither batted nor bowled in their entire county careers. In other cases, the matches which qualify for inclusion are perhaps rather minor; there are players who appeared just once in an early-season friendly first-class game against one of the relatively weak university sides, matches that are nonetheless first-class, because first-class is not simply the County Championship. There are others here who have played only in T20 matches for Hampshire, and while some are overseas signings with significant careers elsewhere, some played only in that new form of the game. Anyone who has played in a competitive T20 or limited-overs match for Hampshire appears here, and a few whose only appearance was in a friendly 'white ball' game too, including for example, a number of players whose single appearance for the county was in a limited-overs match v Sri Lanka 'A' at the Ageas Bowl in August 2014, a game that lasted just 18 overs before the rain intervened.

There are unlucky players who appear here – for me, none more so than Jon Ayling – and others who do not make it. John Arlott at different times suggested that two fine Hampshire-born cricketers, Jim Bailey and Mervyn Burden were perhaps the unluckiest, but they enjoyed pretty full careers; elsewhere we might repeat the point that the relatively complete careers of Alan Castell and Richard Lewis did not warrant the award of a county cap, which in earlier years often went to amateurs for a few appearances – a habit that was repeated briefly with one or two overseas players in this century. One of the least fortunate is perhaps Brian Robbins who does appear on the Cricket Archive site but with a somewhat incomplete record of his matches for Hampshire's 2nd XI during the late-1950s and early 1960s. His greatest day is not (yet) there, a friendly 2nd XI game at Dartford in 1958, in the year before the 2nd XI Championship began, when his figures against Kent 2nd XI were 26-17-28-9 (11-68 in the match). His victims included Luckhurst, Dixon, Jones and Ufton who all enjoyed first-class careers, but Brian did not. Were a young spinner to return such figures today, he might anticipate the call.

This means that the quality control that is exercised in designating first-class matches or major limited-overs games is not infallible if we are trying to understand the standard of some cricket and more specifically, some cricketers. It is not difficult to be sure that Wynyard, Mead, Kennedy, Shackleton, Richards and many others, were the finest of cricketers and would have been at any stage in the game's history. We can state with some confidence too that men like Baldwin, Livsey, Herman, Rogers, Gray and Turner who never went beyond county cricket were the finest professionals, or indeed that the best amateurs like AJL Hill, Hesketh-Prichard, AEG Baring, and CJ Knott stood rightly alongside them. But this is not an exercise in the evaluation or comparison of quality, except to some extent, by implication through the length and nature of each story. This is a record, largely factual, although having watched Hampshire for 60 seasons, there is probably a hint of 'bias' in the writing here-and-there. The facts do not merely come from *Cricket Archive*, they come from a variety of sources and from a lifetime living and absorbing Hampshire cricket.

This is of course an exercise in looking back. Everything here has passed, while the real attraction of sport is always to wonder what might occur, today or tomorrow. We can enjoy our reminiscence as Arlott did, but it is tomorrow's game – and I am completing this Introduction on the day of Hampshire's first Championship fixture of 2018 – that counts, and there I must confess that I read with nostalgic envy of Arlott travelling the country watching Test and county cricket through the high summer of 1958. In 2018 Hampshire will play one home Championship match in normal day-time hours, between the start of May and the middle of August; the cricket I loved most is fading away, and while people will tell me we always feared that would happen in the near future, it is already happening. In 1958, Hampshire's season opened in Yorkshire on 10 May and ended at Bournemouth on 2 September. In 2018, a great deal of the Championship will occur outside those dates, if the weather permits, while the 'summer' will be occupied by 'white ball' games, that start and end on the same day.

A word in that respect about nomenclature. In brackets after each player's name follows some information. If there is a number – for example 500 after Danny Briggs – that indicates that he is Hampshire's 500th players since they entered the Championship at Taunton in 1895 and the side that appeared in that first match has been allocated numbers 1-11, with, as continues to be the case, debuts in the same match determined simply by alphabetical order. Where the number is "Pre '95", that indicates that they played in first-class cricket only between 1864 and the first Championship season of 1895. In a few more modern cases, what appears in brackets is just T20 or List A, which indicates that these men did not play in first-class cricket, but did play in those shorter forms whether 65, 60, 55, 50, 45, 40 or 20 overs per side, played since the introduction of the first knock-out cup competition in 1963. 'List A' is now the common generic term for any single innings, normally one-day match that is longer than Twenty20 (T20) although in the written text I have used the term limited-overs, simply because I believe it is in more common use (still) by most cricket followers. In my use, it means precisely the same as List A. I hope that I have also identified clearly all the Amateurs that played for Hampshire until that term disappeared in 1963, since it indicates something of the nature of cricket all those years ago.

The list is alphabetical, but at times, that is not as simple as it seemed to me in the classroom in 1958, so I offer a couple of explanations, *mostly* derived from other conventions. The alphabetical list here, is close to *Cricket Archive's*, but it differs in a couple of respects for example, from the lists that Hampshire's fine statistician Vic Isaacs published in his statistical records around twenty years ago.

Firstly, there is a modern issue to deal with, about what I shall call essentially Islamic-style names. I make no assumptions here about religious beliefs or practices, merely observe that for example Basil Akram and Wasim Akram are both Hampshire cricketers yet they appear differently in most lists, Basil under A (Akram B) and Wasim under W. At present the normal cricketing convention is to present the names of cricketers born in Pakistan without inverting names, so Wasim Akram will be found here under W, Shahid, Afridi under S, Sohail Tanvir under S again (etc.). By contrast, because Basil Akram, Hamza Riazuddin and others were born in England, they appear respectively under A and R.

This is largely how it is on *Cricket Archive*, although there are at least two inconsistencies. The tragic Hamza Ali, who was born and died in Bristol, is listed under H on *Cricket Archive*, but here he has been moved to A, following the convention above, whereas Owais Shah, born in Pakistan, appears there under S, which is where I have left him – he is perhaps the one anomaly although we should note that *Cricket Archive* lists Imran Tahir under I, yet gives his full name as Mohammad Imran Tahir. We have followed their lead which is why here, Mohammad is in regular type and brackets. The other issue concerns the letter M, where the list here is very different from those published by Vic Isaacs. On advice, and following *Cricket Archive* again, here you will find that Mc is assumed to be an abbreviation of Mac, so after Maartensz, come all the names with Mc or Mac, prior to any Ma names with later letters (Malone, Manners, Mannings etc). The final decision is to treat O'Sullivan as a name beginning with OS which places him last in the short list under the letter O. In some lists, he is first, where the O is deemed to be standing alone. These are not straightforward, particularly when trying to match what appears on a database like the splendid *http://hampshirecricket.net/* created and maintained by Hampshire member and supporter 'Tigger' Miles, where the software requires manipulation to conform!

To a large extent, I inherited this project from my mentor and friend Neil Jenkinson who was my predecessor as Hampshire's Archivist, and the man who brought me into the club in a historical role, almost thirty years ago. More recently, Neil convened a meeting with another fine Hampshire historian, Alan Edwards, statistician Bob Murrell and me to consider whether we could respond to a proposal from the Association of Cricket Historians and Statisticians (ACS) that every county might produce a record of all its cricketers. At the time, our respective workloads and the very thorough criteria meant that we did not proceed, and I am very conscious that this publication is not as complete as

ACS might have wished. But it is at least a start, and where there are some gaps, particularly with full names and place/date of birth and death, that is work that might be picked up and addressed.

I have made significant reference to the excellent *Cricket Archive* a resource which documents the history of cricket around the world, and to 'Tigger' Miles' fine database of Hampshire players, matches, and records which links very nicely with this publication. In addition, for some eight years now I have run a Blog (Hampshirecrickethistory.com) on which I published draft versions of this book, and that helped me enormously in correcting and adding to the records. My acknowledgements to Tigger and my fellow-bloggers are below, and the Blog will continue to add information and amend these entries, with no restrictions on copyright.

In such ways, the work is never finished, and while I am not wholly optimistic for the future of the kind of county cricket I grew to love, I hope that Hampshire Cricket, and most importantly, its cricketers will still be with us when in a few decades, someone decides to correct and update the A-Z.

Dave Allen
Portsmouth
April 2018

ACKNOWLEDGEMENTS

The responsibility for any inaccuracies or errors in the books is all mine, but a number of people have helped considerably in the production of this record. My thanks go in particular to David Cronin, as ever for all his help with bringing this publication to fruition; to my friend and Hampshire's 'Senior Pro' Alan Rayment for his wisdom and his Foreword; to that fine Hampshire Cricket historian Alan Edwards for years of valued contributions to this book and indeed the on-going historical project, and to Tigger Miles for his splendidly accessible and informative database.

In addition, my thanks go to all the 'Bloggers' at hampshirecrickethistory, whose preferred names offered a new alphabetical challenge. They are listed here in order by the first letter of their first name, and with my thanks to them all for comments and kindness: Andy Millard, Blair Kantolinna, Bob Murrell, Colin Price, Dave Pople, Dave Wilson, David Ackland, Ian Laidlaw, Ian White, James, JimTom, Jo, John L, John West, John White, Mike Stimpson, Neil Marshall, Paul Summers, Paul Williams, Ron Griffiths, Sean Child, Stephenfh, Stephen Saunders, & Terry Crump – with apologies, to anyone else I might have missed.

A

Aaqib Javed (415) born Punjab, Pakistan 5.8.1972. Right-arm pace bowler Aaqib Javed who played in 22 Test Matches and 163 ODIs for Pakistan, came to Hampshire for one season in 1991 as an overseas replacement for Malcolm Marshall who was on tour. In 18 first-class matches, he scored just 25 runs, but took 53 wickets at 31.24, three times taking five wickets in an innings, with a best of 6-91 v Nottinghamshire at Trent Bridge. He also played in 22 limited-overs matches, with 27 wickets, including the 1991 Nat West Trophy Final as Hampshire beat Surrey in a tight game. He took no wickets in that game, but returned 2-34 in the semi-final at Edgbaston.

Abbott, Kyle John (525) born Natal, South Africa 18.6.1987. Pace bowler Abbott played in nine first-class matches for Hampshire in 2014, retired from international cricket, and returned in 2017, when in 14 first-class matches, he took 60 wickets at 18.20, and added 418 runs at a fraction under 30 each. He played in all three formats for South Africa from 2012-2017, but was never certain of his place, and signed a four-year Kolpak contract with the county. His best bowling for Hampshire is 7-41 v Yorkshire at Headingley in 2017, and in the same year, his highest score, 97* v Lancashire at Old Trafford. He took a hat-trick v Worcestershire in 2018 during a spell of 24 wickets in three Championship matches, after he had struggled somewhat in earlier matches. He is a very useful lower order batsman, and passed 400 runs in both 2017 and 2018. At the end of the 2018 season, he had 147 first-class wickets for Hampshire at 20.44, plus 981 runs. He plays less frequently in 'white ball' cricket and has seven limited-overs and 27 T20 wickets.

Abdul Razzaq (T20) born Pakistan 2 December 1979. He has played for many teams, including Pakistan in all three formats. He played for Hampshire in 10 matches in the T20 tournament in 2010 and was a member of the side that won the competition. His highest score for Hampshire was 44, and he took seven wickets.

Abdy, Anthony John (Pre '95, Amateur) born Cambridge, 24.4.1856, died Switzerland, 4.7.1924. He was brother-in-law of Hampshire's LG Bonham-Carter. An opening batsman who attended Charterhouse School, Brigadier Abdy was a notable Army cricketer with the Royal Artillery. His brother (RB) played for MCC, while AJ played for Essex v MCC at Brentwood in 1876 (1 & 43*) prior to their first-class status. While living in Gosport, he played in one first-class match for Hampshire, v MCC at Lord's in 1881 scoring 7 and 23. He was awarded a CBE in 1918.

Abercrombie, Cecil Halliday (182, Amateur) born India 12.4.1886, died Battle of Jutland 31.5.1916. He was a middle-order batsman who attended Berkhampstead School. A naval officer, he played first-class matches for the combined Navy & Army side from 1910 and having scored a century for them at Lord's in 1912, he made his Hampshire debut in 1913 and became the first batsman (of six to date) to score a century on first-class debut for the county, making 126 v Oxford University at Southampton. He was not regularly available, but later that season, in his fourth Championship match, at Leyton, he came in to bat after Hampshire had followed-on with the score 186-5 – still a deficit of more than 100. He scored 165, sharing a seventh wicket partnership of 325 with George Brown, still a Hampshire record, which saved the game. In his 14 matches that year, he scored three centuries, nearly 1,000 runs and was capped, but because of naval duties never played for the county again. He was on board *HMS Defence* at the Battle of Jutland, when it was heavily shelled and blown to pieces. He played rugby union for United Services, Portsmouth, and for Scotland, scoring a try v France in Paris in 1911, and is one of their players on the honours list below the Memorial Plaque at the Murrayfield Stadium in Edinburgh. His name is also on the Naval War Memorial on Plymouth Hoe.

Acton, James (Pre '95, Amateur) born Southampton 11.10.1848, died Reading 22.8.1924. He was a batsman who played in two matches for Hampshire, in 1880 and 1882. In 1880, he top-scored (31) in an innings victory v MCC at the Antelope Ground, Southampton, and in August 1882, scored 2 & 8, in a defeat v Somerset at Taunton.

Adams, Andre Ryan (530) born Auckland, New Zealand 17.7.1975. Adams played in New Zealand (one Test Match and 42 ODIs) and for Essex and Nottinghamshire in England, before joining Hampshire in 2015 at the age of 39. A pace bowler, he played in three first-class matches for Hampshire, taking nine wickets (BB 3-69) but had fitness problems, and left before the end of the season. In all first-class cricket, he took 692 wickets.

Adams, Geoffrey Coker Arding (249, Amateur) born London 24.5.1909, died Australia 10.2.1998. He was a hard-hitting middle-order batsman and occasional change bowler, who captained Radley College, before going to Cambridge University in 1928, making his Hampshire debut just before going up. In 1929, he played in twelve county matches in the vacation, and in the following summer, a further five, but with relatively little success. His highest score in 33 innings was 42 v Glamorgan and he did not bowl. He played in college and trial matches, but never for Cambridge University in a first-class game, although he won a rugby 'blue'. In the 1930s he played for Free Foresters, and later for

Boughton Hall in the Liverpool Premier League. Before his death in 1998, he was Hampshire's oldest surviving player.

Adams, James Henry Kenneth (460) born Winchester, 23.9.1980. He was educated at Sherborne School, and as a promising young batsman, played in a strong Hampshire under-19 side, and for England in the same age group. He played for Hampshire 2nd XI from 1999, but did not score the anticipated runs in his first years on the Hampshire staff, and went to Loughborough University to study and play first-class cricket – including a century on first-class debut for them. He had already made his Hampshire first-class debut in the final weeks of 2002 and played regularly from the middle of the next season after term ended, and similarly from late July 2004. After graduating he returned to Hampshire's staff, and in 2005 played a few games. He seemed to establish himself in 2006, when he passed 1,000 runs for the first time with two centuries, including an excellent 262* v Nottinghamshire – the ninth highest innings for the county. Despite this, he was not always a regular player until 2009, when he scored three centuries, averaged over 50 and had his first successful season in limited-overs matches, with Hampshire's top-score (55) in the C&G Final v Sussex at Lord's.

Adams worked with coaches to develop a quicker scoring approach in 'white ball' cricket, which worked superbly in the T20 in 2010, when he scored 668 runs as Hampshire won that trophy for the first time. He was selected for England's Performance and Lions squads in 2010 & 2011, and was appointed Hampshire's captain in 2012 - their first post-war Hampshire-born captain. He led Hampshire to another Lord's trophy, the CB40, while Mascarenhas captained them as they won the T20 again. Adams continued to score runs, and in 2014, led Hampshire to the Division Two title and promotion. He has carried his bat twice for Hampshire, and scored two double centuries in 2013, equalling the record of Mead and Greenidge. He scored 1,000+ runs in five seasons, and is the only man to have played 200 first-class matches for Hampshire in the 21st century. He retired at the end of the 2018 season, having scored 13,298 first-class runs for the county (at 37.88) with 23 centuries, plus 4,032 List A runs (39.52) and 2,393 T20 runs. In 2019, he was appointed to the Hampshire coaching staff.

Aird, Ronald (211, Amateur) born London 4.5.1902, died Sussex 16.8.1986. He was a stylish right-hand batsman, occasional medium-pace bowler, and fine cover fielder. His school was Eton and he won a 'blue' at Cambridge University in 1923, plus another for rackets. Although as an amateur he was not always available, he played for Hampshire in 108 matches between the wars, making his debut in August 1920, and playing his last match in August 1938 (with one first-class match for MCC v Yorkshire in 1939). In 1945 (age 43) he played a non-first-class match for Hampshire v Aldershot Services, when Hampshire lost principally because a man named R Halton scored a century and took seven wickets in the one-day game. It seems nothing more is known of him. Aird's best year was in 1924 when he passed 1,000 runs, including two of his three first-class centuries. He played less frequently in the 1930s but captained the county occasionally, and ended his career with 3,491 runs at 22.81. He was appointed Assistant Secretary of MCC in 1926, took over as Secretary from 1952-1962 and was President in 1968/9. He was also President of Hampshire CCC from 1971-1983. John Arlott (1957) described him as "efficient and … quite remarkably popular". During the Second World War, Major R Aird was awarded the MC.

Airey, Robert Berkeley (161, Amateur) born Southminster, Essex 21.9.1874, died London 23.6.1933. He was a middle-order batsman who went to Tonbridge School. At the age of 36, he played in three matches for Hampshire in August 1911, scoring 52 runs in five innings, including a best of 30 in his first innings v Sussex at Portsmouth. In the 1920s, he played a number of matches for the Royal Army Ordnance Corps.

Akram, Basil Mohammad Ramzan (List A) born Leytonstone, Essex, 23.2.1993. Basil Akram was a right-arm pace bowler and useful batsman who played in one limited-overs match v Yorkshire in 2014, scoring one run and taking 0-24. He played also for Loughborough University, scoring two first-class centuries, with his best bowling 5-54. He played for various county 2nd XIs, and in various leagues across southern England, including for Sarisbury Athletic in the Southern Premier League in 2015.

Ali, Hamza (538) born Bristol 8.8.1995, died Bristol 9.6.2016. A right-arm pace bowler, he played limited-overs matches for Rawalpindi in 2014/16 and made his first-class debut for Hampshire v Cardiff University in April 2016, taking 2-17 and 0-12. He played club cricket in the Bristol area for Stapleton for some years, then in 2016 joined the MCC staff and played for Hampshire 2nd XI. At the age of 20, he was drowned in an accident, two months after his first-class debut.

Ali, Kabir (501) born Birmingham 24.11.1980. He was a right-arm pace bowler who played for Worcestershire from 1999-2009 and for England in one Test Match (2003) and 14 ODIs. He joined Hampshire in 2010 and played for three seasons, before moving to Lancashire. He played in 17 first-class matches with 54 wickets for Hampshire (31.37) and a best return of 5-33 v Essex at Chelmsford in 2010. He struggled with fitness and played relatively rarely in limited-overs matches, but he bowled the vital final over in the Lord's Final of 2012, when Carter's failure to score from his last ball, won the trophy for Hampshire.

Allenby, Marmaduke Cecil (84, Amateur) born York 30.8.1873, died Plymouth 16.4.1932. Cecil Allenby was one of 19 players to make his Hampshire debut in 1900, when Hampshire finished last in the Championship – as they would again in each season from 1902-1905. Only three of those men played in ten or more matches for the county, and only one, James Stone, became a regular player. In Allenby's one match for Hampshire v Sussex at Portsmouth he batted at number nine, was dismissed for a 'duck' in his one innings and did not bowl. The match was drawn. He played for the MCC, and for Devon (HS: 54) and in 1910 for the Royal Navy v Army at Lord's; the Army side won by an innings, with three Hampshire players, Bradford, Poore and W White.

Alsop, Thomas Philip ('Tom') (528) born High Wycombe (Bucks) 26.11.1995. Alsop made his Hampshire debut in 2014 as a left-handed batsman who had elsewhere kept wicket quite regularly. but initially he preferred to focus on batting, and enjoyed a successful season in 2016, with 737 first-class runs at 35.09, including 117 v Surrey at the Oval, and 327 in limited-overs games at 54.50 with a first century. It earned him a place with the England Lions in the winter, although his form was less consistent, and in the following English summer he played less regularly, despite another limited-overs century. When Lewis McManus was injured, he resumed wicketkeeping duties towards the end of the season. In 2018, McManus began the season as first choice wicket keeper before he was injured, after which Alsop took over and retained the gloves, while scoring four Championship half-centuries. Having been omitted from the early games he also enjoyed a successful run in the Royal London Cup and his excellent 72, opening with Rossouw in the Final, created the platform for a winning total. It remains to be seen whether he will now establish himself as a batting-wicketkeeper, or revert to the former role.

Altham, Harry Surtees (192, Amateur) born Camberley 30.11.1888, died Sheffield, 11.3.1965. Harry Altham was a right-handed batsman who bowled occasionally. He attended Repton School and captained the school side of 1908, reputed to be the finest of all school teams. He then attended Oxford University from 1909-1912, winning his 'blue' in the final two seasons. He played for Surrey from 1908-1912 (10 matches, HS: 51) and was capped in 1912. As Major Altham, he served in the First World War and was awarded the DSO and MC. He took up a teaching post at Winchester College, and thereafter played as an amateur for Hampshire in 24 matches from 1919-1923 – all but the first two during the month of August. His first-class playing career, was modest, with a final batting average of 19.70. He made his highest first-class score and only century, 141 v Kent at Canterbury in 1921.

Off the field his contribution to English cricket was considerable. It began with the publication of his *History of Cricket* as a series of magazine articles, then a book in 1926, later revised in two volumes with EW Swanton. He was also one of the three principal authors of Hampshire's first major history in 1957. He served on the MCC Committee from 1941 until his death, was Treasurer from 1949 -1963, and President in 1959. He was Chairman of England's Test Selectors in 1954, one of few without Test Match experience. He served on the Hampshire Committee for more than 40 years, and was President from 1946 until his death. Altham coached at Winchester throughout his time there, was Chairman of

MCC Youth Cricket Association and President of the English Schools Cricket Association. He was the author of the first MCC Cricket Coaching Book in 1952. His son, RJL Altham played for Oxford University. See also, Doggart GHG, 1967, *The Heart of Cricket: A memoir of H.S. Altham*. Altham was awarded the CBE for services to cricket in 1957.

Amla, Hashim Mahomed (552) born Durban, South Africa 31.3.1983. The experienced Test batsman Hashim Amla joined Hampshire as their overseas player for the first part of the 2018 season and impressed, scoring almost 500 Championship runs at 53.71, including centuries at Trent Bridge and Taunton. He played in the first three Royal London Cup matches with one half century, 63 at Hove.

Andrew, Gareth Mark (542) born Yeovil, 27.12.1983. Gareth Andrew was a right-arm pace bowler and lower-order batsman, who played for Somerset and Worcestershire, before joining Hampshire during the 2016 season, to help alleviate an injury crisis. He played in six first-class matches (seven wickets), eight limited-overs A matches (seven wickets and an HS of 70* v Gloucestershire) and nine T20 matches (eight wickets). He played for Canterbury (New Zealand) in 2012/13, and in various leagues in the midlands and north-west of England, most recently for Ombersley (Worcs).

Andrew, Stephen Jon Walter (397) born London 27.1.1966. Andrew was a right fast-medium bowler and lower order batsman who played for England under-19s. He made his debut for Hampshire at the age of 18, in a B&H match at the Oval, taking 3-12 (Man-of-the-Match) and the next day took 3-48 v Essex at Southampton. In the following week, he made his first-class debut at Hove, and took 4-30 in the first innings. In 1987, he played in 14 first-class matches, taking 47 wickets (21.92) and in the following year played in the Hampshire side that won its first Lord's Cup Final, v Derbyshire. During his Hampshire career from 1984-1989, he took 147 first-class wickets (28.91) and became one of their few regular bowlers to take more wickets than runs scored (105). In 36 limited-overs matches, he scored just six runs but was never dismissed. His best bowling in limited-overs was 5-24 v Essex, and in 1990 he joined that county, playing there from 1990-1997, then in Minor Counties cricket for Hertfordshire for three seasons.

Andrew, Walter, but known as **William** (44, Amateur) born Bournemouth, 22.3.1869 died Sligo, Ireland 30.3.1911. Andrew, a right-handed batsman and right arm medium-fast bowler played for Dorset from 1894, and in a non-first-class match for Hampshire v MCC in June 1897. In the following month, he made his first-class debut for the county v the Gentlemen of Philadelphia taking 4-36, and in the next match at Hove he scored 22 & 54* and took 5-157 (in 49 overs) but Hampshire were heavily defeated. That was the only instance of Andrew taking five wickets in an innings, while in his fourth match he scored his only century, 106 v Warwickshire at Southampton, sharing a partnership of 222 with AJL Hill. He played in 12 matches over two seasons, scoring 312 runs and taking 23 wickets and appeared in his final game for Hampshire in 1898. He continued playing for Dorset, and appeared in the Minor Counties Championship from 1902-1906.

Andrews, Arthur John (Pre '95) born Southampton 26.8.1856, died Aldershot 26.2.1943. Andrews was a right-handed batsman who played in seven first-class matches in 1880, 1882 and 1884-1885, scoring two half-centuries with a best of 62* v Sussex at the Antelope Ground, Southampton in 1884 and a county total of 236 runs. After Hampshire lost their first-class status, he played for them in 1886 and 1887.

Andrews, Clifford Jack (289, Amateur) born Swindon 6.8.1912, died Eastleigh 11.12.1973. Jack Andrews was a wicketkeeper and lower-order batsman who played seven matches for Hampshire (five in the Championship – HS 29) from 1938-1948, principally covering the absence of Neil McCorkell. He played for Hampshire 2nd XI and Club & Ground, and during the war for various sides including Southampton Police, the British Empire XI and the Club Cricket Conference. His brother Bill was a player and coach at Somerset for many years.

Arkwright, Francis Godfrey Bertram (227, Amateur) born Bromley, Kent, 30.1.1905, killed in action, Libya, 1.7.1942. He was a hard-hitting batsman, although said to be weak in defence. In 1923, at the age of 18, he scored 175 for Eton v Winchester, an innings that was probably seen by HS Altham, and later in that season he appeared in three matches for Hampshire but scored only 44 runs in five innings (HS 14). Apart from his final innings, batting at number three, he appeared at numbers nine or ten, but did not bowl. He went to Sandhurst at the end of that season, became a career soldier, and two years later played one further first-class match for the Army v Cambridge University (0 & 23 – his highest first-class score). In 1940, he was an officer in the 12th Royal Lancers when they covered the evacuation of the BEF from Dunkirk. For bravery in that action, he was awarded the MC, while in 1942, as a member of the famous 'Desert Rats' in North Africa, he was awarded the DSO. He was killed when his tank was hit by a shell, and laid to rest in the Commonwealth War Cemetery at El Alamein. Further information on his military record is in The Hampshire Handbook 2010 article "Hampshire's World War II Roll of Honour" by Stephen Saunders.

Armitage, Edward Leathley (204, Amateur) born Omagh, Ireland, 26.4.1891, died St Leonard's, Sussex, 24.11.1957. Armitage was a middle-order right-hand batsman. He went to Cheltenham School and then became a professional soldier, playing cricket for the Royal Artillery, before making his Hampshire debut in 1919 (age 28). He played in four matches during August without reaching fifty and in 1920, played just once in early season v Leicestershire. After two more county matches without success in 1921, he disappeared from county cricket until 1925 when he played once v Worcestershire (0 & 3), although he was selected to play in first-class matches for the Army during the 1920s. After eight county matches, an average of 13.07, and a highest score of 42, his county career was over. In a first-class match for MCC v Oxford University at Lord's in 1929, he scored 105 and took 2-29, and he played for the Europeans in Bombay in December 1929.

Armstrong, HH (Pre '95, Amateur) we have no further details of his first names or his dates of birth/death. Armstrong was a right-arm pace bowler who played in 23 first-class matches for Hampshire from 1882-1885, and after the county lost its first-class status he continued playing until 1889. In first-class matches, he scored two half centuries (HS 68) and took 68 wickets at 20.23, with a best of 7-33 v Derbyshire at Derby in 1885.

Arnold, Alban Charles Phidias (169, Amateur) born Chester 19.11.1892, died in action at Ovilliers, La Boiselle, France, 7.7.1916. He was a right-handed batsman and occasional wicketkeeper who went to Twyford then Malvern Schools and Cambridge University (1912-1914), where he won a 'blue' in the final year. He played 16 first-class matches for Hampshire from 1912-1914. He made his first half-century for the county v Derbyshire in August 1914 and followed it with 76 v Somerset in an innings victory in the next match, 51 in the following game v Warwickshire, then 69 v Lancashire. After scoring 20 v Essex he made 54 v Kent in an innings victory at Bournemouth – five half-centuries in six matches. In his 16 first-class matches for Hampshire he scored 542 runs but then went to war and never played county cricket again. His father was vicar of Holy Trinity Fareham, and in 1921 he conducted the service to unveil the town's war memorial, including the names of Arnold and his brother EG, who was killed in 1918.

Arnold, John (254) born Oxford 30.11.1907, died Southampton 4.4.1984. John Arnold was a right-handed opening batsman and very occasional slow-bowler, and one of a number of fine professionals who came to Hampshire from Oxford in the first 60 years of the twentieth century. In 1929, he continued to play for Oxfordshire while qualifying by residence for Hampshire, although he was permitted to play against the South African tourists. Once qualified, he made his Championship debut in June 1930 against Yorkshire and began by taking two wickets, before he was dismissed without scoring – neither performance indicated how his career would develop. In the event, he took just 17 first-class wickets in his career but in that first season passed 1,000 runs with two centuries and in 1931 he reached 1,400 runs, with three centuries. It earned him a Test cap v New Zealand at Lord's but he made a 'duck', and even 34 in the second innings could not secure his place, and he never appeared for England again. It has been suggested that on the first dismissal he was so devastated that he took too long to leave the crease, and the authorities did not approve.

Nonetheless he appeared a number of times for the Players v Gentlemen and in 1934 scored a century for them and another for Hampshire against Bradman's Australians at Southampton. He scored centuries for Hampshire against four different touring sides.

Arnold also played football for Southampton, and for Fulham until 1939, and he won one international cap for England v Scotland at Hampden Park (1932/3), but again there was to be no repeat. Instead he became Hampshire's outstanding batsman of the 1930s and immediate post-war period. In 1932 he passed 1,600 runs, including his highest score of 227 v Glamorgan at Cardiff and after a slight decline, he passed 2,000 runs in 1934 with a best average of 48.10. From the mid-1930s he played only for Hampshire in the Championship or against the universities and tourists. In 1938, his form was poor and he was in danger of not being re-engaged, but in his last six seasons he passed 1,000 runs each year. When first-class cricket resumed after the war he was 38, but in four-and-a-half seasons he scored 11 centuries and in his penultimate match, two fifties against Yorkshire at Bradford. In mid-July 1950, he played at Derby, but serious illness overtook him and he never played for Hampshire again, although he did play for the 2nd XI on the Isle of Wight two years later. Only four men have scored more than his 21,596 runs for Hampshire, at 32.92, with 36 centuries – and that despite missing six seasons to war. In 1961, he joined the list of first-class umpires and remained there until the end of the 1972 season, retiring at the age of 65.

Ayling, Jonathan Richard ('Jon') (405) born Portsmouth 13.6.1967. Jon Ayling was a right-hand batsman and right-arm pace bowler whose early career seemed blessed with good fortune. He played for Portsmouth Grammar School and South Hants Touring Club (now Portsmouth CC) when they won the Southern League, and in 1985 he won the Cricket Society's award as the leading all-rounder in English schools cricket. In May 1988, he made his first-class debut v Oxford University, scoring 41, starting with nine boundaries, and taking a wicket with his first ball (13-8-14-2). He established himself in the Championship side around his 21st birthday, and was selected for the B&H side as they beat Worcestershire to reach a semi-final. Hampshire were then the only side that had never reached a Lord's Final and they had a difficult draw away to Essex in the semi-final, but Jon kept his place and bowled Graham Gooch for 41, although he was not required to bat, as Hampshire won with eight balls to spare. So it was, that in his first full season, he played for Hampshire v Derbyshire at Lord's, returning figures of 9-2-21-1 in a comfortable Hampshire victory. He played in Hampshire's next two Lord's Finals, both won, memorably hitting a six into the Tavern in the twilight as Hampshire beat Surrey in 1991. But by then his luck had turned as the result of a freak accident, colliding mid-pitch with a batsman in a pre-season friendly. As a consequence, he missed the entire 1989 season and often struggled through the next three, although in 1992 he scored his one first-class century, v Oxford University (121) and in Hampshire's last ever match at Bournemouth recorded his best bowling, 5-12, v Middlesex. In 1993, he played in four first-class matches, but just before his 26th birthday he accepted that his knee would never meet the demands of a professional career and retired. Some years later he returned to Hampshire as a coach, and now teaches and coaches at Dauntsey's School (Devizes).

Aymes, Adrian Nigel ('Adi') (403) born Southampton 4.6.1964. Wicketkeeper 'Adi' Aymes was the natural successor to Bobby Parks, although having made his debut in 1987 he had to be patient to establish himself permanently in the first team. Aymes was a local boy who played club cricket for Hursley Park, including in 1984, in the National Village Final at Lord's, scoring a half-century. He played the last few matches for Hampshire in 1990, and thereafter was the first-choice, although having played in the 1991 Nat West Final he missed the B&H Final in 1992 through injury. He was always a very useful batsman, and in 1993 he scored his maiden first-class century v Sussex, and having been promoted, two in successive matches in 1998 including his best of 133 at Leicester. He was then thought to have a good chance of an 'Ashes' tour as a deputy 'keeper but the highest honours never came. He was Hampshire's first choice from 1991-2001 but played just five matches in 2002 losing his place to Nic Pothas. In his first-class career for Hampshire he passed 7,000 runs in 215 matches, at 31.22, with 516 catches and 44 stumpings. There were also 268 limited-overs dismissals and the runs scored in that format (at 23.26) took him close to 10,000 runs for the county in all matches. For some years, he has worked for Havant & Waterlooville FC.

B

Bacon, Francis Hugh (1, Professional/Amateur) Born Sri Lanka 24.6.1869, died at sea off the Kent coast, 31.10.1915. Bacon was principally a right-handed batsman and fine cover fielder and he is number one in the list of Hampshire cricketers by virtue of being *alphabetically* the first of the 11 players who appeared at Taunton in the first Championship match in 1895. His record in 75 first-class matches was modest with just under 2,000 runs at an average 0f 15.77 with one century and five half centuries, but he was one of a number of Hampshire cricketers who also served the county well off-the-field. He enjoyed some success for Basingstoke CC where he was managing a brewery, and was invited to Hampshire for a trial, playing regularly in 1894 when Hampshire's results earned them a return to first-class status, and the properly organised Championship. In his first appearance in that last second-class year, he scored a rapid 114 v Warwickshire, but perhaps his finest match at the higher level was that first Championship game v Somerset, one of just three in the county's history that they have won after following-on. He held two catches as Somerset posted 221, and his 15 runs was third best as Hampshire were dismissed for 94. In 1895, a lead of 127 permitted Somerset to enforce the recent follow-on rule, so when Bacon arrived at 84-4 Hampshire faced defeat, but he and HF Ward shared a partnership of 131, Bacon top-scoring with 92. Somerset's eventual target was 188 and having reached 166-5 they seemed favourites, until Soar bowled Hampshire to a famous victory by just 11 runs.

Bacon did not sustain that form, never averaging better than his 23.69 in 1906, although in 1907 he scored his one first-class century, 110 v Leicestershire at Southampton, while in 1909, he captained Hampshire on a brief trip to Ireland. By the time of his final first-class match at Old Trafford in 1911, he was a tail-ender, but in desperation his captain asked him to bowl and he took 2-23 in a huge total of 676-7 declared. Lancashire won by an innings & 455 runs, just 13 runs short of Hampshire's largest ever defeat. Some years before, in 1903, Bacon had become the first paid secretary of the club, and turned amateur as a cricketer. He played a significant part in improving the fixture list and in recruiting the professionals who formed the nucleus of the fine Hampshire side for decades to come. When war was declared, he was 45, but nonetheless volunteered for the Royal Naval Reserve. In October 1915, his patrol ship *The Aries* was mined, and he drowned.

Badcock, John (128) born Christchurch near Bournemouth 4.10.1883, died, London 24.8.1940. John Badcock was a right-arm fast bowler who had a brief, enigmatic, yet often impressive career. Although he was born in Hampshire he was living in Kent, where he played for their 2nd XI before, in 1906, age 22, he made his first-class debut for Hampshire. Badcock was a big man, bowling at speed for a side recovering from a number of disastrous seasons and in that first year he impressed regularly, taking 96 wickets (24.81). In 1907 his record fell away when despite playing in the same number of matches, he bowled far fewer overs, taking just 49 wickets. He bowled too many no balls and doubts were expressed about his fitness – although he did score over 500 runs with a career best of 74 v Middlesex at Southampton. His form returned to some extent in 1908 with 67 wickets, including a career best 8-44 v Sussex at Portsmouth, after which the county offered him a new contract and engaged a trainer to work on his fitness, but he declined the offer and moved to London where he managed a cinema. Nothing more is known about his cricket career, but in his three first-class seasons, he took 212 wickets at 25.53 – fully fit, bowling alongside Kennedy and Newman, he might have enabled Hampshire to challenge for the Championship.

Bailey, George John (514) born Tasmania, Australia 7.9.1982. George Bailey is a right-handed batsman who played for Australia in all three formats, and for Hampshire as their overseas professional for part of the 2013 season. He returned in 2017 on a two-year contract as captain in first-class matches, but decided not to return in 2018. For Hampshire, he scored 914 first-class runs at 36.56, with two centuries, 358 limited-overs runs at 51.14, and in the T20, 301 runs in ten innings.

Bailey, James ('Jim') (246) born Otterbourne, Hants 6.4.1908, died Southampton 10.2.1988. Jim Bailey was a genuine all-rounder, a left-handed batsman, slow-left-arm bowler and the last man to complete the first-class 'double' for the county. He was part of a generation of talented individuals who replaced the great professionals of Tennyson's side, but despite their individual abilities, only once in Bailey's long career from 1927-1952, did Hampshire finish in the top half of the table - eighth in 1932. His own career was somewhat up-and-down; he made his Hampshire debut in July 1927 just three months after his 19th birthday and played in five matches that season, albeit with little success. In 1931, he established himself as a batsman with almost 1,000 runs, and in the following season he took 76 wickets, including a remarkable analysis of 7-7 v Nottinghamshire at Southampton, which remained his best bowling – yet Hampshire lost. There were centuries in 1931 and 1933, but his bowling fell away, and he took just eight wickets in that latter season. Age 26, he moved to Middlesex to qualify by residence and played for their 2nd XI, plus occasional first-class matches for MCC, but he joined them when the Compton brothers, Bill Edrich and Jack Robertson were coming through, and after two years without a first team appearance, he joined Lancashire League side Accrington as a professional, and became the first English 'pro' to score 1,000 runs in a season. Most of his matches were at weekends, so in 1938, a weak Hampshire side persuaded him to play for them in northern mid-week fixtures. He began with 44 & 69 at Edgbaston and was reasonably successful, although hardly bowling, and in 1939 he re-joined the county. It proved to be his best season as a batsman with 1,329 runs at 32.41, including one century and eight half-centuries, to which he added 44 wickets, including a best of 6-72 v Leicestershire, the bottom side, two places below Hampshire.

When Bailey returned post-war, he was 36. He played regularly for the next four seasons, during which he took 295 wickets, alongside fellow spinners Charlie Knott and Gerry Hill, and also passed 1,000 runs in three of those four seasons, plus 921 in 1947. In 1948, his 1,399 runs (31.79) and 121 wickets (18.13) gave him the 'double', Hampshire's first since Jack Newman in 1928 and never since repeated; only Newman, Bailey, Alec Kennedy and CB Llewellyn have achieved the feat for Hampshire. Bailey was talked of a possible England player, but he played for just one further season, with 1,254 runs and 86 wickets and retired at the age of 41, although he returned as a bowler for one match at Edgbaston in 1952. His career had begun alongside Tennyson's great players, and concluded with Harrison, Gray and Shackleton, who would win county cricket's greatest prize nine years later. He remained in Southampton, was at one time on the Committee, and was always entertaining company. John Arlott (1957) described him as "the unluckiest" of all Hampshire's cricketers, "a solid batsman" who "as a slow bowler was at his greatest, for he had length, flight and spin, and a true cricketing brain".

Bailey, Michael John (384) born Cheltenham 1.8.1954. Michael Bailey was principally an off-spin bowler who played for Hampshire in 20 first-class and three limited-overs matches from 1979-1982, and subsequently for Wiltshire and Herefordshire. He had little success in those matches for Hampshire apart from his best figures of 5-89 v Northamptonshire at Wellingborough in the Hampshire side of 1980 that finished bottom of the table. His innings of 24 in that match was also his highest first-class score, but neither contribution could prevent an eight-wicket defeat.

Bailey, WP (Pre '95, Amateur) we have no further details of name, or dates of birth and death. Bailey played for Hampshire v Middlesex at Islington's Cattle Market in July 1864. He opened the batting but scored just 4 & 10 as Hampshire lost by an innings. That was his only first-class match. He played (with a W Bailey) for the 22 players of Southampton Union v the English XI at the Antelope, Southampton in June 1864 (not first-class).

Bakker, Paul-Jan (402) born Netherlands 19.8.1957. Pace bowler Paul-Jan Bakker, known generally as 'P-J', was a Dutchman, who arrived in Hampshire in 1985 to play for Hampshire 2nd XI and Old Tauntonians in the Southern

League, before making his first-class debut in the following season, during which he reached his 29th birthday. Alongside Cardigan Connor, Stephen Andrew and Kevin Shine, he sought to establish himself as the opening partner for Malcolm Marshall, and over seven seasons with the county played in 69 first-class and 68 limited-overs matches. As a batsman, he averaged under 10, but he took 193 first-class wickets at under 30, and 80 limited-overs wickets at an economy rate around four per over. His best first-class figures were 7-31 v Kent at Bournemouth in August 1987 when he bowled Hampshire to victory, but his finest season came two years later with 77 wickets at 22.49, including four five-wicket (+) returns. 1989 was also his best season in the shorter form with 24 wickets including his best of 5-17 v Derbyshire in a Sunday League victory. His career at Hampshire coincided precisely with the four limited-overs titles won by Mark Nicholas's side, but Bakker never featured in a Lord's Final, or the match that clinched the 1986 Sunday League title. Sadly, he did play in the two frustrating Nat West Trophy semi-final defeats at Northlands Road, by three runs v Middlesex in 1989 and by one run v Northamptonshire in 1990. His one 'cup final' was in 1990 for the Netherlands in an ICC Trophy Final which the Dutch lost to Zimbabwe. After the 1992 season he returned to Holland to play club cricket for Quick Haag, in the mid-1990s he played in a number of ODIs for his native country, and in 1995/6 for Holland in the World Cup in Pakistan, where in their match v England he took the early wicket of Alec Stewart.

Balcombe, David John (489) born London 24.12.1984. David Balcombe was a pace bowler and useful lower-order batsman. He played for Surrey 2nd XI in 2004, for Durham University in first-class matches from 2005-2007, and for Hampshire 2nd XI from 2005. He made his first-class debut for Hampshire in a heavy defeat v Kent in September 2007, taking two wickets and scoring 25 & 29, and in the next match took 3-58 v Yorkshire. After relatively few appearances, he went on loan to Kent in 2011, where he took 33 first-class wickets at 17.81. He returned to Hampshire, and in 2012 enjoyed his best season with 64 wickets at 26.10 including his best figures of 8-71 v Gloucestershire at the Rose Bowl in April – despite which, Hampshire lost. Balcombe, James Vince and Liam Dawson were awarded their county caps early in 2013, but in that year and the following, Balcombe took just 27 more first-class wickets, before returning to his first county, Surrey, for one last year, playing only for their 2nd XI. During his career, he played very occasionally in 'white' ball cricket – 14 limited-overs matches and three T20s. 2012 was his best season with the bat, averaging almost 20 in first-class cricket with a career highest of 73 v Leicestershire, sharing a 10th wicket partnership of 168 in a losing cause, with Chris Wood - it was Hampshire's second highest for that last wicket. In his final first-class match for Hampshire v Gloucestershire in 2014, Balcombe (65*) and James Tomlinson shared a 10th wicket partnership of 115, which was the county's highest ever by their numbers 10 & 11. He took 196 first-class wickets in his career, 141 for Hampshire at 33.27.

Baldock, William Stanford (Pre-'95, Amateur) born Chilworth Common, Hants 20.1.1847, died Somerset 30.8.1923. He was a middle-order batsman and occasional bowler who played in seven first-class matches for Hampshire between 1877-1882. His father played for the Gentlemen of Kent, and his son for Somerset, while he appeared in 1878 as W Stanford. In his seven county matches, he scored 155 runs (HS 40) at an average of 12.91. From 1875-1883 he played regularly for the Royal Artillery side. His last recorded match for Hampshire, not first-class, was v Devon in 1883, age 36.

Baldry, Dennis Oliver (342) born Middlesex 26.12.1931. It is possible to name a complete XI of former Middlesex players who joined Hampshire, and from 1959 Dennis Baldry, an entertaining right-hand batsman and useful occasional bowler was one of those. He played 2nd XI cricket for his native county from 1950; in 1953, he played a solitary first-class match for the county and then appeared more regularly between 1955-1958. In 49 matches he passed 1,000 runs with five half-centuries ((HS 61) and took 11 wickets. On 6 May 1959, he made his Hampshire debut v Glamorgan at Portsmouth and scored 151, becoming the second Hampshire player to pass three figures on first-class debut for the county, and the first in a Championship match (see Abercrombie). There have now been six such players but all played first-class cricket elsewhere previously. Dennis Baldry enjoyed probably the most prolific start of any Hampshire cricketer. After a quiet match v Gloucestershire he returned to Lord's and scored 123 v MCC, in his fourth match v Kent at Southampton he scored 62, took two wickets and was awarded his county cap, next at Old Trafford, coming on second change, he recorded his best bowling figures: 28-7-76-7, followed by 3-28 at Edgbaston (and 75 runs in the match). It seemed that Hampshire had found a new number four, and Baldry finished that season with 1,605 runs at 29.72, including three centuries and 30 wickets (31.13).

He would enjoy further successes over the next three seasons, but less consistently, while newcomer Danny Livingstone seized fourth place for the decade. Baldry's 24 matches in the damp 1960 season brought 678 runs with an average nearer 20 and a best of 93; there would be no more centuries, in 1961 that average dropped again to 19.31, and as that season ran its course to the title, he lost his place to Mike Barnard. Nonetheless his best of that season, 84*, was a key innings in late May at Headingley, when Hampshire, going well, met the reigning Champions Yorkshire, who had won their first three Championship matches. The home side posted 279, Trueman took three quick wickets and Baldry arrived with Hampshire 45-5. He and Sainsbury added 109 and despite another collapse, he remained firm and took Hampshire to a position where they were able to draw the match quite easily. After a run of fairly low scores he played another important innings, described in the *Hampshire Handbook* as "brilliant", v Nottinghamshire at Southampton, when his 61* enabled Ingleby-Mackenzie to declare, after which Hampshire won by 15 runs with just three minutes to spare – the last wicket, a direct throw run out by Baldry. There was a third half-century at Hove and 4-41 at Leyton although both matches were lost, and travelling from Essex to Derby, Mike Barnard returned for a successful late season run. Dennis Baldry had however contributed at key moments to the eventual great triumph of 1 September 1961.

In 1962, he had to wait until early July for his first Championship match, playing in 11 first-class games, although his batting average rose to 25.92 and he took 23 wickets. In the last innings of the year, he arrived with Hampshire 80-5, facing defeat v Surrey, until another century partnership with Sainsbury secured the draw. Baldry was dismissed just ten runs short of 100 and although he would not know it then, also ten runs short of having opened and closed his county career with a century. He took work locally during the winter but as he was preparing to return for pre-season training, he was offered a permanent post, and at 31 he retired from first-class cricket. There would be one further match however, Hampshire's first-ever in the knock-out cup when, with Derek Shackleton injured he was called up to play v Derbyshire and is always delighted to point out that as an amateur for the day, his expenses exceeded his daily wages of the previous season. Hampshire lost that match narrowly but he took 4-70 in his 15 permitted overs. He played club cricket in the Southampton area for many years.

Baldwin, Harry (2) born Wokingham 27.11.1860 died Aldershot 12.1.1935. Harry Baldwin who lived at Winchfield, is generally described as an off-break bowler – "slow medium" by HS Altham (1957) – although he often opened the bowling in Hampshire's early years in the County Championship with fellow professional Tom Soar. In recent years, Harry has been immortalised by the photograph of him hitching up his trousers at Portsmouth, used on the cover of the 'Fatty Batter' book, although he can be seen as a much slimmer cricketer in earlier photographs. He played for Hampshire in a first-class match in May 1877 v Derbyshire, when just 16-and-a-half, but did not return for 10 years, by which time Hampshire were eight years from regaining first-class status. Throughout that period, he enjoyed regular success as they gradually improved. In June 1889, for example they followed-on against MCC at Southampton, managed to set MCC just 64 to win, whereupon Baldwin (six wickets) and Soar bowled them out for 48. His all-round value can be seen when in a poor season for the county in 1891 he was the only batsman to exceed 250 runs in the season.

Baldwin and Soar carried the bowling in Hampshire's first Championship season, taking 191 of the 260 Championship wickets, with Baldwin enjoying his best season with 102 – it would be six years before Llewellyn became the next Hampshire bowler to reach three figures. In that year, Baldwin and Soar bowled unchanged to take Hampshire to an innings victory v Derbyshire and he took 13-76 in the match v Essex at Southampton, as well as eight wickets when Hampshire managed an astonishing victory in two days v Yorkshire at Sheffield. In the next five seasons, he always passed fifty wickets, sometimes significantly more, but after a less successful time in 1901 he did not play over the next two years. This Hampshire side was the weakest in their history however, and he returned in 1904 (age 44) and 1905, taking exactly 100 first-class wickets over those two years. In 1898, he had been the first Hampshire player to be awarded a benefit, which in those days relied principally on a specific match and Harry not unnaturally chose the fixture v Yorkshire at Southampton. Sadly, the first day was abandoned with not a ball bowled, then on the second it became the only match in Hampshire's history to finish in a single day, the visitors winning by an innings. Harry did not help his cause by taking 4-37 and between midday and 6.05 pm, the two sides bowled 115 overs, but the day's takings did not cover the match expenses and the Committee had to help Harry to an eventual benefit of just under £250. Later in that season Baldwin took 15-142 in the match at Hove; still the third best in the county's history, and in that year, he finished eighth in the national averages. From 1907, he spent three years as a first-class umpire, while his son, after playing for Surrey, did the same and stood in Test Matches.

Barber, Thomas Edward ('Tom') (List A) born Poole 8.8.1995. Tom Barber was a promising left-arm pace bowler who came through Hampshire's age group and Academy sides and played his first 2nd XI match in July 2013. During that year, he also played a number of matches for the England U-19 ODI side, and in August 2014 he played in two limited-overs matches for the county, a rain-ruined no result match v Sri Lanka 'A', and a Cup Match v Yorkshire at Southampton where he dismissed Williamson and Gale with consecutive deliveries. Despite that, his 2nd XI performances in the following season were often disappointing and he left Hampshire. In the following two seasons, he played for Somerset and Middlesex 2nd XIs, and his native county in Minor Counties fixtures, before in August 2017, he appeared in two matches for Middlesex in the T20 competition, with a promising debut v Hampshire at Lord's. In the winter of 2017/18 he was selected for an ECB development winter abroad, and played in the series between the South & the North and he played in further Championship and 'white ball' matches for Middlesex in 2018.

Baring, Amyas Evelyn Giles (256, Amateur) born Roehampton 21.1.1910, died Newcastle-upon-Tyne 29.8.1986. Giles Baring was a genuine fast bowler; John Arlott (1957) suggested he had "a yard more of pace than any of the county's other fast men of the period". He made his debut for Cambridge University and Hampshire in 1930, although he played only twice for the University over his first two seasons (five wickets). In 1931, he took 76 wickets for Hampshire, including 9-26 v Essex at Colchester, which was the finest return for any Hampshire bowler until Cottam in 1965, and still stands in second place. Despite Baring's figures, Hampshire lost the match. With Lord Tennyson playing less regularly, the 21-year-old captained Hampshire on occasions in 1931, while at the end of that season he represented the Gentlemen v Players at Folkestone, and he reappeared in the fixture at the Oval in 1934. Baring had come to that match from a meeting with the 1934 Australians at Southampton where he enjoyed one of his finest hours. Replying to Hampshire's 420, Baring reduced them to 10-3, dismissing Woodful, Brown and Bradman – the latter caught by Mead without scoring. The tourists recovered, but Baring finished with five wickets in the innings. Sadly, after his promise of 1931, he sustained dislocated knees in a motor accident, did not play in 1932 and was never quite the same bowler again, although in 1939, his last county season, he took 39 wickets at 22.87. He captained Hampshire in his last match for them v Yorkshire at Bournemouth, dismissing Maurice Leyland, although Hedley Verity bowled Yorkshire to victory. In 1946, he appeared in one last first-class game for MCC v Cambridge University, finishing with 4-43. His batting was unremarkable, with a best of 43 and a career average below 10. He continued to play cricket for the Forty Club and others for at least another 20 years, well into his fifties.

Barker, Keith Hubert Douglas *(2019) born Manchester 21.10.1986. Barker is an allrounder who bats and bowls left-handed (medium pace). He played in 240 matches in all three formats for Warwickshire from 2009-2018, taking 359 first-class wickets. He has signed for Hampshire from the start of the 2019 season. He was a professional footballer playing in the English league with Rochdale, having played once for England under-19s.*

Barnard, Henry Michael ('Mike') (324) born Portsmouth 18.7.1933, died Southampton, 18 December 2018. Mike Barnard was a right-hand batsman, superb slip fielder and early in his career an occasionally effective medium-pace bowler. He played professional football and has one possibly unique claim – that in the top division he played 100+ matches for his home city side, plus 200+ first-class cricket matches for his home county, and in both cases without ever playing for another football league or Championship side. To some extent, this spilt career probably inhibited his progress in both sports, but he was a natural athlete – as a schoolboy he represented Hampshire under-19s at rugby union. He showed promise as a cricketer in 1949, when he averaged over 60 for Hampshire Schools, and in the following seasons he played for England Schools and Hampshire's Club & Ground and 2nd XIs. In 1951, he signed professional forms in both sports, although almost immediately National Service called him away.

He made his Hampshire debut in 1952, on his 19th birthday but with little success and in 1953, there was another unsuccessful game in Portsmouth, while at Christmas he made his football league debut. The 1954 cricket season was his breakthrough, beginning with a last-minute call-up v Middlesex at Southampton, when, batting at number 10, he came in with Hampshire 48-8 and top-scored with 39. Hampshire lost but he followed this with 24* in the second innings. One week later, he came home to Portsmouth v the Pakistanis, scoring just two as Hampshire took a small lead in a low-scoring game. They then lost Rogers and Marshall (his only 'pair') and were effectively 29-2, before Eagar and Horton added 64. Barnard arrived at 71-3 and stood firm as he and

Gerry Hill added 91* for the seventh wicket, Eagar declaring when Barnard reached his first century (101*). The Pakistan target was 261 but after Barnard dismissed both openers, they made no effort, closing on 86-4 in 53 overs, Barnard 10-3-18-2. He would only take another 14 wickets in his first-class career, but to Hanif Mohammad he added victims like Tom Graveney, Don Kenyon and Ted Dexter. There were two further half-centuries that season, but 1955 was a real breakthrough for him as a batsman – and also notable for both his teams. In 1954/5, he played 30 matches for 'Pompey' who finished 3rd in the First Division, then he passed 900 runs with another century (116 v Leicestershire at Bournemouth) as one of the 13 regulars who took Hampshire to third place for the first time. It was a thrilling season, with his unfashionable county led only by the two heavyweights, Yorkshire and Champions Surrey. Over the next few seasons Barnard would compete with Rayment, Pitman, Flood, Baldry and Livingstone for the batting places below the very fine top three of Marshall, Gray and Horton. Whenever there was a doubt, his slip catching could be decisive, and he finished his Hampshire career with 312 catches in 276 matches.

He scored a century v MCC in 1956 and another v the Indians in 1959, while with 123 v Australians in 1964, three of his six first-class centuries were against the tourists, and only two came in the Championship. After a modest 1960 season, and having left football, he began 1961 in the side, but lost his place to Dennis Baldry, as Hampshire sought their first title. Apart from one game deputising for his injured captain v Sussex at Portsmouth, he was not recalled until Derby on 12 August, and then embarked on the finest and most impor-tant few weeks of his county career. Initially his 45 helped Horton add 91 in a victory, after which at Southampton, he made his second Championship century, as Hampshire took full points v Warwickshire. Returning to Portsmouth he had a half-century in an easy victory v Leicestershire, then 77 in defeating Nottinghamshire at Trent Bridge. After an oddly unimportant meeting with the Australians, Hampshire went to Bournemouth knowing that victory would bring the first title. Derbyshire took first innings points and Hampshire needed quick and substantial runs; Roy Marshall obliged of course, but on the third morning it was the stroke-play and swift running of Sainsbury and Barnard, adding 99 in just over an hour, that enabled Ingleby-Mackenzie to declare, and Shackleton to weave his magic. Shortly after 4pm on 1 September 1961 Hampshire had won county cricket's greatest prize – and a rather delightful curiosity was that in the match that clinched the 1961 title, Mike Barnard scored 19 & 61.

His average of 28.73 that season was the best of his career, and in the next few seasons his aggregates were 1,114 runs in 1962 then 980, 814 and 958. By this time, he was often opening with Roy Marshall in the Championship, but in 1966, there were fewer matches, no half-centuries, an average below 15, and Mike retired, taking a testimonial and embarking on a coaching and teaching career. Before that, he had also taken part in the earliest limited-overs, knock-out cup matches, starting with a heroic 98 in Hampshire's first match, a narrow defeat v Derbyshire in 1963. Overall, he scored 315 runs, at an average barely below 40, and in his Hampshire days, he outscored Roy Marshall in the Gillette Cup. As his new career took shape he prepared to take over Hampshire's 2nd XI in 1969, but just before the season began, a serious coach crash robbed him of much mobility. After he recovered somewhat, he coached at the School of Navigation in Warsash, was a regular commentator with BBC Radio Solent, and for the Southampton Hospitals. He also took up bowls, worked on drug testing with the Sports Council, organised the reunions of Pompey's footballers and Hampshire's cricketers, and bore his injuries with incredible fortitude and cheerfulness. His career never reached the heights it promised, but he will be forever one of Hampshire's very few 'Champions', and for his outlook on life, remembered as one of their bravest and best of men.

Barrett, Edward (Pre '95, Amateur) born Farnham 11.6.1846, died, London, 23.12.1923. Barrett was a bowler and tail-end batsman who played in two first-class matches, when approaching his 39th birthday. As a schoolboy at Cheltenham College in 1861, he took six MCC wickets at Lord's and 7-23 against the same opposition at the College. His two county matches, in the weak Hampshire side of 1885, v Surrey and Sussex, both ended in innings defeat, and he took no wickets, with a best score of 13*. His major contribution to Hampshire cricket was as the father of EIM Barrett (below).

Barrett, Edward Ivo Medhurst (34, Amateur) born Surrey 22.6.1879, died Boscombe, near Bournemouth, 10.7.1950. Captain Barrett was a fine, hard-hitting batsman who played in 80 first-class matches for Hampshire in a career from 1896-1925. That he did not play more was because he was a professional soldier, often serving abroad. He was also a fine rugby union player who represented England v Scotland in 1903. He played infrequently in his early years, although there was a century at Hove in 1901 when he averaged 46.70. In 1912, after just 30 first-class matches in 16 seasons he scored 1381 runs at 40.61, including centuries v Derbyshire, Yorkshire and Oxford University, and he was in the Hampshire XI that beat the Australians for the first time. At the end of the season the county rewarded him with a silver cigarette box to mark his fine year. Sadly, he did not play first-class cricket again until 1920, although he appeared in a number of matches for Shanghai while serving there as Commissioner of Police – in 1921 he scored 165 in a match v Hong Kong. In 1920, he returned temporarily to England and scored 92 for MCC v Nottinghamshire, as well as enjoying a full season with Hampshire which included sharing with George Brown their second wicket partnership record of 321 v Gloucestershire at Southampton which included his career best of 215 and was not beaten until 2011. In all matches that year, he passed 1,000 runs and his second Championship century of 148 v Warwickshire at Portsmouth was part of a total of 616-7 declared, at the time Hampshire's fourth highest total. Barrett then returned to Shanghai, but in 1925 he played one last county match, scoring 11 v Worcestershire at Bournemouth at the age of 46. As late as 1931 he was playing major club matches for Incogniti and MCC.

HS Altham described him as "a very strong man ... (and) a splendid driver ... who believed in attacking the ball".

Barrett, Peter (375) born Winchester 3.6.1955, died in a motor accident in the New Forest, 28.10.1983. Peter Barrett was a left-handed opening batsman who was unfortunate to join Hampshire in their strongest-ever period, during the days of Richards and Greenidge, and with Rock and Terry showing considerable potential. He came through the county's colts sides and played regularly for the 2nd XI from 1973, before making his first-class debut at Sheffield in 1975 as Hampshire sought another Championship title. With Greenidge and Richards absent, in the first innings he opened with Andy Murtagh but both were dismissed in single figures. Then Murtagh was taken ill, so he opened with Sainsbury, but managed only five and Hampshire lost by nine wickets. In 1976, Greenidge was on tour and Barrett played at Trent Bridge, scoring 25; then against Greenidge and the tourists at Southampton, where Michael Holding dismissed him twice for an aggregate of 24. He had a run of three Championship matches in July, and in the final innings, his 26 v Somerset at Bournemouth was to be his best score. In July 1976, he played in his one limited-overs match, a victory v Essex at Southampton, in which he opened with Richards and they put on 127 for the first wicket, with Barrett scoring 28 (Richards 101). He remained on the staff until the end of the 1977 season, still only 22 when he was released. He was riding his motor-cycle when he was killed.

Bartley, Edward Leslie Dayrell (259, Amateur) born Stockport 2.3.1896, died Plymouth 7.10.1969. Bartley was a Naval officer, a wicket-keeper and left-handed batsman, who made his first-class debut for the Royal Navy in 1914, and played cricket mainly for them – just three of his 27 matches were for the county. He was selected following the unexpected retirement of Walter Livsey, and before McCorkell appeared, and in 1931 kept wicket along with George Brown and Stephen Fry. For Hampshire, his four innings, included three 'ducks' and a 5*, and he dismissed seven batsmen, although he made four half centuries for the Royal Navy in first-class cricket (HS 84 v the Army at Lord's in 1927). 1931, age 35, marked the end of his first-class career, with the three Hampshire matches and finally one for the Combined Services v New Zealanders at Portsmouth, when he scored 42* & 12*.

Barton, Charles Gerard (3, Amateur) born Romsey 26.4.1860, died Essex 3.11.1919. Charles Barton was a slow-left-arm bowler, whose four-match, first-class Hampshire career is notable mainly because he played in their inaugural Championship match at Taunton in 1895. He played cricket at Sherborne and Tonbridge Schools, for Hampshire in the years before they regained first-class status, and for various Army teams, as he was an Army officer. In his best pre-Championship season, he took 42 wickets at 9.79 in 1891, and in a first-class match for the Europeans v Parsees in Poona in 1893 he took 6-27. For Hampshire, he took three first-class wickets at 50.66.

Barton, Harold George Mitford (155, Amateur) born Mudeford 10 October 1882, died Southampton 3.7.1970. He was a right-handed batsman who played first for Buckinghamshire in 1907, and then from 1910-1912 in eight first-class matches for Hampshire. His highest score was 31 v Derbyshire in 1911 and he scored a total of 146 runs at 11.23. He did not bowl..

Barton, Victor Alexander (4) born Netley 6.10.1867 died Southampton, 23.3.1906. An all-rounder, he was known as 'Bombardier Barton' when he played first as a professional soldier for the Royal Artillery, and then for Kent. He came to their notice when scoring 91 & 102, and taking 6-53 for the former side v Gentlemen of MCC (including WG Grace) at Lord's in 1899. After playing with Kent in 1891 he purchased his release from the Army, and returned to his native Hampshire, while in the winter of 1891/2 he toured South Africa with WW Read's XI. Very few of their matches were regarded as first-class but they played a three-day game v South Africa in March 1892 which was subsequently designated as a Test Match – Barton's only appearance for England. As a consequence, he is often described as Hampshire first Test Match player, but it is not so, as he did not play for Hampshire until 6 June that year. For three seasons with Hampshire, Barton played second-class cricket, but he was in Hampshire's side for their first Championship match at Taunton in 1895, and from then until 1902 he appeared in 143 first-class matches, scoring over 6,000 runs at 25.01 with six centuries and a best of 205 v Sussex at Hove in 1900. It was a remarkable innings in perhaps the poorest of all Hampshire sides; Sussex posted 407 during which Barton took 3-76, then he came in with Hampshire 10-2. He took them to 330-8 overnight, went on to pass 200 and took Hampshire to within 40 of the Sussex score, but it was not enough; Sussex declared and dismissed Hampshire for just 73. Bowling medium pace, he took 130 wickets for the county, with a best of 6-28 (& 3-41) v Surrey at the Oval in May 1901. Barton's eyesight deteriorated and he took a benefit in 1902, retiring to run a bat-making business, and also a pub in his home of Netley. Sadly, he died age just 38, and a fund was established to help his family. Sir Russell Bencraft described him as the most "unassuming, gentlemanly cricketer", in difficult years, he was a significant all-rounder.

Bateman, Richard (pre '95, Amateur) born Farnham 29.4.1849, died, Surrey, 5.11.1913. A batsman, he played club cricket for Guildford and in one first-class match for Hampshire, a two-day defeat v Somerset at Taunton in 1883, in which he scored 4 & 14*.

Bates, Frederick Stanley (209, Amateur) born Berkshire, 25.2.1899, died London 13.8.1969. He was a batsman who played at Marlborough School during the First World War, and in two first-class matches for Hampshire in the Bournemouth week of August 1920, scoring 18 runs.

Bates, Michael David (503) born Frimley, Surrey 10.10.1990. Wicketkeeper Michael Bates was born just across the border in Surrey but was educated at Lord Wandsworth College, played for Hampshire's junior sides and was awarded a development contract in 2010 at which time he played also for the England Under-19 side. He made his first-class debut for Hampshire v Oxford UCCE at Oxford in 2010, and in his first two seasons he played occasionally, before replacing Nic Pothas, and enjoying his finest season in 2012. In first-class matches his 57 first-class dismissals was equal best in Division Two, and along with fellow 'graduates' of the Hampshire Academy, Adams, Briggs, Dawson, Griffiths, Vince and Wood he participated in Hampshire's trophy successes, the only time Hampshire have won two in a season, and Bates appeared in both Finals. On the last day of that season at Lord's, the scores were level with one ball to bowl and Bates, standing up to Kabir Ali, gathered the ball safely as Carter missed it, and Hampshire won the CB40. By the start of the following season, neither he, nor Kabir Ali were in the Hampshire side.

During that winter, Hampshire signed Adam Wheater, who 'kept' for most of the season and was a more effective batsman. There was a view that in the modern game, Bates' batting was not good enough, although in 2012, he scored his maiden first-class century, 103 v Yorkshire at Headingley, and added two half-centuries at an average of 23.04. In 2013 that improved to 25.85, but in just six matches and four innings. Meanwhile Hampshire were developing two promising young wicketkeepers in Alsop and McManus, and after a few matches in 2014, Bates left the staff. Many supporters were disappointed that a wicketkeeper who had been tipped for international honours was allowed to go, but in the following season, he played for Somerset without winning a contract, although he received an enthusiastic and sympathetic reception on his return to the Ageas Bowl. He had played Minor Counties cricket for Berkshire in 2009 and appeared occasionally for Wiltshire in 2015 and early 2016. He played in 119 matches in all formats for Hampshire, but at 23, his Hampshire career was over, having scored 1,124 runs at 21.20, and dismissed 143 batsmen in his 46 first-class matches.

Beadle, Sydney Wilford (162, Amateur) born India, 9.11.1885, died Kent 24.7.1937. He was a middle order batsman and slow bowler who served in the Royal Navy, playing two first-class matches for them, and in 1911 once for Hampshire v Sussex at Portsmouth. Hampshire won the match, thanks mainly to Brown's eight wickets and Mead's 194 - Beadle's contribution was 16 & 6 (he did not bowl). In the same summer, he was one of seven Hampshire cricketers in the match between the Royal Navy and the Army at Lord's.

Bedford Henry (Pre '95, Amateur) born Canterbury 1854, we have no further details of his dates of birth & death. He was a leg-break bowler who played for Hampshire in one match v Somerset at the Antelope Ground in 1882, which Hampshire won by 10 wickets. He bowled only in the second innings (4-2-5-1) – overs then consisting of four balls.

Belcher, Gordon (126 – Amateur) born Brighton 26.9.1885, died in action in France 16.5.1915. Belcher was a right-hand batsman and medium pace bowler who enjoyed success in school cricket at Brighton College, where he was captain in 1903 and 1904. It was a measure of the weakness of the Hampshire side in the early twentieth century that ten men made their debuts for Hampshire in 1904, and another ten in 1905, while 13 of those 20 played only in that one season, with nine appearing only once. Among the latter group was Belcher, whose one match v Warwickshire at Southampton in August 1905 ended with a 'pair' and one over (0-3), and Hampshire lost by 10 wickets. He went to Cambridge University but did not obtain a 'blue' or play in first-class cricket there. He played for Berkshire from 1910-1913. He was awarded the MC; two of his brothers were also killed in the war, while his father Rev. TH Belcher, vicar of Bramley, Hants, who played first-class cricket for Oxford University, died in 1919.

Bencraft, Dr Sir Henry William Russell, (5, Amateur) born Southampton 4.3.1858, died Winchester 25.12.1943. He was known in later years as Sir Henry William Russell-Bencraft. He was a right-handed batsman and pace bowler, who captained Hampshire in their first season in the County Championship, having played for some years previously, after making his first-class debut for the county in 1876 (age 18). In 1889, he had scored 195 v Warwickshire (not first-class), but his first-class career was modest; in 46 matches (all but two for the county) he scored just under 1,000 runs at 15.53 (HS 62* v Derbyshire in 1895) and took five wickets. Nonetheless, when FS Ashley-Cooper published the first history of Hampshire in 1924, he described Russell Bencraft as "the best friend Hampshire cricket ever had – a man who however dark the outlook might appear, kept a stout heart and spread cheerfulness around and whose enthusiasm … is characterised by all the energy which marked his activities of thirty, forty and even more years ago". Bencraft earned that tribute through his various roles in establishing Hampshire as a first-class county, as captain, honorary secretary from a time when the club's future was under threat, chairman for 15 years and eventually president. His father was a medical officer in Southampton, and Bencraft was educated at St George's Hospital, London, before returning to Southampton where he held a number of medical positions, was a director and chairman of Southern Newspapers Ltd, and president of Southampton FC – he had been a football referee. He was also president of Hampshire Rugby Union. In 1937, there was a considerable attendance at a dinner in his city, to honour his sixty years with Hampshire County Cricket Club.

Benham, Christopher Charles ('Chris') (473) born Frimley, Surrey 24.3.1983. Batsman and good fielder Chris Benham was a Hampshire cricketer who emerged through the county's age group and 2nd XI sides, and after appearances for Loughborough University, made his debut in September 2004 v Derbyshire with a promising innings of 74 in a Hampshire victory. His next match in early 2005 was in a defeat at Stratford-upon-Avon, then another defeat – by an innings – in that otherwise successful year, v Surrey at the Rose

Bowl. In Hampshire's first innings Harbhajan Singh took 6-36, with Benham top-scoring with 41, over more than two hours. In 2006, he played in a number of limited-overs matches, and in late September in a televised relegation/promotion play-off v Glamorgan at the Rose Bowl, played a magnificent innings of 158 as Hampshire clinched their place in Division One of the Pro 40 league. His first-class appearances never reached double figures in a season, but in 2009, he averaged 45.11 and scored his only Championship century, 111 v Durham at the Rose Bowl. Earlier that season he was a regular member of the side that reached the Friend's Provident Trophy Final at Lord's, where he joined the injured Nic Pothas at 154-4, with Hampshire pursuing 220 to beat Sussex in 50 overs. The pair were not parted, adding 67* with Benham 37*, as Hampshire won with almost 10 overs to spare. He played in 54 limited-overs matches for Hampshire, scoring three centuries and 1,564 runs average 36.37 – a more impressive return than his first-class record (average 27.05). He played also in 37 T20 matches. Despite the successes of 2009 he lost his Championship place in mid-May of the following year, did not play any limited-overs games (three in the T20) that year, and after one further Championship match at Scarborough, his Hampshire career came to an end at the age of 27. He played for Wiltshire in 2011, and also in the Southern and Surrey leagues.

Benjamin, Winston Keithroy Matthew (422) born Antigua, 31.12.1964. Except when touring with the West Indies, Malcolm Marshall was Hampshire's overseas professional from 1979 until he retired after the 1993 season, and in his place, Hampshire signed fellow West Indian Benjamin, at the age of 29, after eight years with Leicestershire, where he enjoyed some successful days in Championship and limited-overs cricket – particularly with the ball, taking 237 first-class wickets at 26.84. Benjamin's three-year Hampshire career, however, was hampered by fitness problems although he scored a fine century v Essex at Southampton (117) in May 1996, sharing a partnership of 178 for the 7th wicket with centurion 'Adi' Aymes. One week later, with a couple of wickets and a few runs at Edgbaston, he played his final first-class match, and withdrew, injured again, although he did play in some limited-overs games that year and in his last one, as Hampshire lost a Nat West quarter-final, and playing only as a batsman, he top-scored with 41. In his 11 first-class matches for Hampshire, he took 30 wickets overall with a best of 6-46 in the first innings at Worcester in 1994 – this was one of two, five+ wicket hauls for the county, but even then, he batted at number 11 in the second innings and was unfit to bowl again. He played in 21 Test Matches with a best score of 85 and best bowling of 4-46. He played for Cheshire in 1985.

Bennett, Richard Alexander (30, Amateur) born Bournemouth 12.12.1872, died Gloucestershire 16.7.1953. Alexander was a right-handed batsman and wicketkeeper, who played at Eton, and appeared in 23 first-class matches for Hampshire between 1896-99. He played also in first-class matches for MCC, and on tours with his own side (to the West Indies) and Pelham-Warner's XI

(Philadelphia). With Charles Robson wearing the gloves, he had played for Hampshire initially as a batsman, and made his highest first-class score of 47 v Derbyshire at Southampton in 1899, but when Wynyard captained from 1897, Bennett sometimes kept wicket, and on one occasion, was captain. His final first-class match was for the Gentlemen of England v Oxford University in 1903. Overall, in 37 first-class matches, he scored 683 runs and dismissed 73 batsmen.

Bentinck, Bernhard Walter (83, Amateur) born South Warnborough 16.7.1877, died Winchester 27.6.1931. No fewer than 19 men made a first-class debut for Hampshire in 1900, and 16 of them played in fewer than 10 matches, including batsman Bentinck, who played once that year, and once again in 1902, scoring just 26 runs in his four innings, as Hampshire lost both matches. Playing for Alton in 1921 he was dismissed when the ball hit and killed a sparrow and was deflected onto his wicket. He had played at Winchester School, and his brother-in-law CR Seymour played for Hampshire in the 1880s.

Berg, Gareth Kyle (529) born Cape Town, South Africa, 18.1.1981. Berg is an all-rounder who played for Middlesex from 2008- 2014 and joined Hampshire in 2015. In the late 1990s, he played age group cricket in South Africa, then from 2003, club cricket in Northamptonshire and the Home Counties. In 2008, he played for Middlesex in three Championship, and six limited-overs matches, after which he became a regular player. He also played for Italy in T20 matches from 2011-2014. In 2015 he joined Hampshire, and apart from an injury problem in 2016, he has been a regular player in all three formats since. In first-class cricket, he has scored two centuries, but is rather unlucky that his best first-class scores for Hampshire are 99 v Sussex in 2015 and 99* v Yorkshire in 2017. By the end of the 2018 season, he had 113 first-class wickets for Hampshire with a best of 6-56 v Yorkshire in 2016. In limited-overs cricket he has 37 wickets for the county and 26 in T20. He was a member of the side that won the Royal London Cup in 2018, taking 2-43 in the Final, and he had an outstanding match earlier at Hove, taking 3-51 and scoring 65, which rescued Hampshire and took them to what would prove to be an important victory.

Best, Tino La Bertram (541) born Barbados, 26. 8.1981. Hampshire's West Indian fast bowler Fidel Edwards was injured in a warm-up during the second Championship match of the 2016 season, and to replace him they signed another fast bowler from Barbados, Tino Best, who had played in Tests and internationals for the West Indies, and also played for Yorkshire. He made his Championship debut for the county on 1 May, and played in six first-class matches. In his second match, he took 5-90 in an innings defeat at Old Trafford, but overall took just 14 wickets at a fraction under 40 each. In limited-overs matches he took just one wicket, with four more wickets in nine T20 matches. In early July, he had figures of 0-104 at Durham and did not play another Championship game, ending that season playing for Lashings.

Bethune, Henry Beauclerk (37, Amateur) born Worth, Horsham, Sussex, 16.11.1844 died Horsham, Sussex 16.4.1912. HB Bethune was an all-rounder, including slow bowling, sometimes underarm. He played in two first-class matches for the county, twelve years apart in 1885 and 1897, and in the latter, v Lancashire he was 52 years and five months old, the oldest ever Hampshire cricketer in a first-class match. In the period between these two appearances, he played frequently for Hampshire XIs, and in other games in the county, particularly in the Portsmouth area (Combined Services, US Portsmouth, Portsmouth Corinthians, Portsmouth Borough etc.). In September 1888, he played with Arthur Conan Doyle, at the County Ground, Southampton, for the Portsmouth Borough side that lost the Hampshire County Challenge Cup Final to Winchester (including EG Wynyard). His two matches for the county v Somerset at Taunton and v Lancashire at Southampton, were unremarkable; he scored 26 runs (HS 9) and took 1-27 in his 10 overs. At around the same time, two other players with the same surname are recorded as playing non-first-class matches for Hampshire. About one, CC Bethune we know only that he played in 1885 v Devon at Sidmouth but the other, George Maximillion (sic) Bethune, was born in 1854, also in Worth, Horsham, Sussex. It seems too much of a coincidence that GM and HB were not related, although the record books do not suggest this.

Bichel, Andrew John ('Andy') (480) born, Queensland, Australia, 27.8.1970. Pace bowler Andy Bichel played for Australia, and in England for Worcestershire, before he joined Hampshire for a brief period in 2005 approaching his 35th birthday. He played in just four first-class matches and a further seven limited-overs games, despite which he had a considerable impact on Hampshire's history. He made his Hampshire debut at Cheltenham on 3 August and came to the wicket to join Nic Pothas, with Hampshire on 81-7. When they were parted, both had scored centuries (Bichel 138), they had added 257, a new record for Hampshire's 8th wicket which still stands, while Bichel had become the sixth (and to date last) batsman to make three figures on his first-class debut for the county. He took three wickets in the match, which Hampshire won, aiding their challenge for the title – they finished runners-up. A few days later he made his Totesport League debut on the same ground, and within a fortnight was playing in the C&G semi-final v Yorkshire at the Rose Bowl, which Hampshire won to secure their first Lord's Final success in 13 years. In that final, v Warwickshire, he scored 16, helping Hampshire to a total of 290, and when Knight and Bell threatened to win the match, he encouraged the Hampshire supporters from the field, and then dismissed Knight, one of his three victims that day as Hampshire won by 18 runs with four balls to spare. Bichel played just one more Totesport League match for the county, but his brief stay was certainly a memorable one.

Bignell, Guy Newcombe (117, Amateur) born India 3.12.1886, died Switzerland 10.6.1965. Guy Bignell was a right-hand batsman and medium-pace bowler who played for Hampshire across 21 years, but as a professional soldier, never regularly, appearing in just six seasons and a total in 55 matches. He occasionally played under a pseudonym, a practice fashionable among amateurs in the previous century, but in 1919 because he was home from India on sick leave, when he appeared in the Hampshire averages as G Newcombe. He played for notable club sides including MCC, Hampshire Hogs and Free Foresters, and for the county, scored 1,670 runs at an average of 20.61 and took 17 wickets. There was one century v Kent at Portsmouth in 1905, when he was still four months short of his 19th birthday – he remained Hampshire's youngest centurion, until Liam Dawson in 2008. Bignell played most regularly in 1912, but with modest success, although he was a member of the XI that beat the Australians. He also had his best bowling figures that year, 3-67 v Warwickshire at Coventry. In 1908, he was a member of the Hambledon (Hampshire) side that played 'England' in the only first-class match played on Broadhalfpenny Down, Hambledon. The match was held to commemorate the achievements of the team that played there in the 18th century, included the unveiling of the commemorative stone, and was unusual as both sides fielded twelve players. Bignell's older brother HG (below) played briefly for Hampshire at the start of the century.

Bignell, Hugh Glennie (90, Amateur) born India 4.10.1882, died of fever, India 6.5.1907. He played five first-class matches for the county, and while he is described as a fast bowler, he bowled just nine overs without a wicket. As a right-handed batsman he averaged 14.14, although on debut v Somerset at Portsmouth in 1901, he scored 49* and 22* in a Hampshire victory. In the next four Championship appearances he scored 10, 6, 0, 0, 12, 0 & 0. His last recorded match was for North West Frontier v Punjab in Lahore, four years before his premature death.

Bird, Jackson Munro (534) born Sydney, Australia 11.12.1986. Jackson Bird was an Australian pace bowler who signed as Hampshire's overseas player in 2015 but struggled with injuries. In six first-class matches, he took 19 wickets at an average just under 40, there were two wickets in two limited-overs appearances, and four wickets in six T20 matches. He played Test cricket for Australia, and in England also played for Nottinghamshire.

Bird, Percy John (77, Amateur), born Isle of Wight 27.5.1877, died Isle of Wight 11.11.1942. Left-handed batsman Bird went to Cheltenham College, and played just once for Hampshire, scoring 9 & 28 in an innings defeat v Somerset at Southampton in 1900. He also scored 32 & 9 in a non-first-class match v the West Indians at Southampton in the same year, when he kept wicket.

Black, LG (103) born Lambeth 15.9.1881, died Yorkshire 14.8.1959. The *Who's Who of Cricketers* lists him as Lennox Graham Black, *Cricket Archive* as Lawrence Garfield; the latter is more recent, and probably correct. He was a left-handed batsman and left-arm medium-pace bowler, who played for Hampshire v Gentlemen of Philadelphia in 1903, and then in three Championship matches in 1919. In those four first-class matches for the county he scored 36 runs (average 7.20) and took just one wicket. In 1907, 1908, 1910 & 1911 he played for Canada v USA. In 1907, he took 7-46, but Canada lost. They drew in 1911, when he took 7-35.

Blake, David Eustace (319, Amateur) born Havant 27.4.1925, died Portchester, 21.5.2015, When Desmond Eagar arrived as Hampshire's new secretary/captain immediately after the Second World War, he set about assembling a new side, and in the first four seasons, gave debuts to 24 players. One of his tasks was to find a successor to wicketkeeper Neil McCorkell who would retire after the 1951 season, and in the period before Leo Harrison converted to 'keeping', Hampshire selected a number of alternatives, including David Blake, who was also an entertaining left-hand batsman. Blake was the younger brother of JP (below) who had played for Hampshire in the late 1930s. Both boys went to Aldenham School and David represented the Rest v Lord's Schools in 1943 at Lord's, completing three stumpings. He played as an amateur for Hampshire in 50 matches between 1949-1958 – his status being a consequence of his career as a dentist in Southsea. In his Hampshire career, he scored 1,811 runs including one century v Somerset at Bournemouth in 1954, sharing a second wicket century partnership with Neville Rogers; his 30* in the second innings took Hampshire to a ten-wicket victory. He passed fifty on a further 12 occasions, including 56 & 97 v Nottinghamshire at Bournemouth in 1950. In the field, he held 62 catches, adding eight stumpings. He did not play in 1955 when Hampshire finished in third place, but in 1956 appeared in Hampshire's first-ever match at Cowes, when they returned to the Isle of Wight for the first time since the war. Blake also played first-class cricket for a number of non-county sides including MCC, and Free Foresters, and made two tours of the West Indies in the mid-1950s with EW Swanton and the Duke of Norfolk. His last recorded match was for MCC v Sherborne School in 1964.

Blake, John Philip (283, Amateur) born Portsmouth 17.11.1917, died in action in Croatia, Yugoslavia 3.6.1944. Unlike his brother DE, he was a right-handed batsman, who showed promise at Aldenham School and Cambridge University, although his first-class debut at Worthing in June 1937 (age 19) pre-dated his University debut. His main year with the student side was 1939 when he won his 'blue'; scoring 23 in his team's valiant effort to reach 430 to win – they lost by 45 runs. He played in 29 first-class matches, 15 for Cambridge University, averaging nearly 32 (HS 88 v MCC), but in his 14 matches for Hampshire, his average was less than half that, with a best of 48 v Somerset in a victory at Yeovil in 1938. His final Championship match was at Canterbury in August 1939, and while he enjoyed little success at that level, he was still only 21, and clearly promising. A few months later, he enlisted in the Royal Marines and in 1943, joined No. 43 Royal Marines Commando, serving in Sicily, Anzio and then Yugoslavia. His last recorded match, presumably on leave, was for Southampton Touring Club v the

British Empire XI at Northlands Road in June 1943, playing alongside fellow Hampshire cricketers Arthur Holt, Charlie Knott, Lloyd Budd and Jack Andrews. One year later he was awarded the Military Cross for leading dangerous action while serving in Yugoslavia, but in another raid shortly after, he was killed, and is buried in Belgrade War Cemetery.

Blundell, Frederick John (Pre '95, Amateur) born South Stoneham, 19.11.1850, died Botley, 26.4.1929. He was a slow right-arm bowler and lower order batsman who played one match for Hampshire v MCC at the Antelope Ground in 1880. He took 2-22 in 17 four-ball overs, and scored two runs as Hampshire took a lead of 81, which was sufficient to win by an innings – he was not required to bowl again, as MCC were dismissed for 43. He is recorded as playing other matches at that time in the Southampton area for teams such as St Luke's, Gentlemen of Hampshire and Southampton.

Bodington, Cecil Herbert (88, Amateur) born Norfolk 20.1.1880, died in action at Pas-de-Clais, France, 11.4.1917. He was a right-handed batsman and bowler, who played at King's School Canterbury and at Cambridge University, although he did not play for the latter in any first-class matches. He played in ten matches for Hampshire in the weak sides of 1901 (age 21) and 1902, averaging 11, with a best of 36 v Sussex, and taking nine wickets, including 3-19 in the same match at Hove in 1902. Hampshire drew that game, closing on 287-9, and Bodington's innings at number eight made a significant contribution after arriving at 160-6. His final first-class match v the Australians at Southampton in August 1902, ended in a two-day innings defeat. Captain CH Bodington was killed in action in 1917 (age 37). His father was vicar of Upton Grey near Basingstoke, and Captain Bodington is commemorated on the village war memorial.

Bolton, Robert Henry Dundas ('Bertie') (180, Amateur) born India 13.1.1893, died London 30.10.1964. He was a right-handed batsman who first played for Dorset while still at Rossall School, and subsequently for them in the Minor Counties Championship, before making his first-class debut for Hampshire v Cambridge University in 1913 (age 20). He played in Hampshire's next match, a defeat at Edgbaston and then not again until 1921 (two matches) with three more in 1922. In 12 innings, he scored just 121 runs for Hampshire, with a best of 24 (and 22) v Nottinghamshire at Trent Bridge in 1921. He became Chief Constable of Northamptonshire and served on their county cricket club's Committee. He played minor matches for the MCC and regularly for the Forty Club into the 1950s, opening the batting and top-scoring (31) in his last recorded match for them v Ratcliffe College, at the age of 60.

Bond, Shane Edward (491) born Christchurch, New Zealand, 7.6.1975. Shane Bond was a right-arm fast bowler who played for Hampshire as their overseas player for the early part of the 2008 season, having played county cricket for Warwickshire in 2002. He played in 18 Test Matches for New Zealand (87 wickets at 22.09) and also 82 ODIs. On his Hampshire Championship debut v Sussex at the Rose Bowl he took 7-66, the county's best inter-county innings figures on debut, which were equalled by Imran Tahir, later in the same season. He played in only four Championship matches and in his final game v Durham at the Riverside Stadium, he took 5-57 & 4-72, finishing with 19 wickets at 19.21. He took only four limited-overs wickets, but including 3-11 v Gloucestershire in a rain-affected defeat at Bristol. His otherwise impressive career was regularly troubled by injuries, and he retired from all cricket in 2010. In 2017/18, he worked as a bowling coach with England in Australia.

Bonham-Carter, Lothian George (Pre '95, Amateur) born Petersfield 29.9.1858, died Buriton near Petersfield, 13.1.1927. He came from a prominent family in east Hampshire; his son (Admiral Sir SS Bonham-Carter) played first-class cricket for the Royal Navy and his brother-in-law AJ Abdy, for Hampshire. LG went to Clifton College, and played for Hampshire in first-class cricket from 1880 (age 21) until 1885. After they were demoted to second-class, he continued playing until 1888. He was mainly a lively opening batsman, who also bowled slowly in the round-arm style. In his eight first-class matches for the county, he twice passed fifty (HS 67 v Surrey at the Oval in 1884) and took two wickets (2-22 v MCC at Southampton, 1885). He opened the batting in a Minor Counties match v Norfolk at Southampton in May 1887, and his dismissal brought to the crease FE Lacey, whose innings of 323, albeit not first-class, is the highest individual score ever for any Hampshire side. In later years, Bonham-Carter played for Hampshire Rovers and Portsmouth Borough. He became President of Hampshire County Cricket Club 1899-1900, and his portrait in the county's *Guide* of 1899, was that publication's first illustration.

Booth, Clement (pre '95, Amateur) born Boston, Lincolnshire, 11.5. 1842, died Lincolnshire, 14.7.1926. Booth went to Rugby School, playing in the XI from 1859-1861, and then to Cambridge University 1862-1865, captaining the side in 1864, and winning his 'blue'. Subsequently, he played most regularly in first-class cricket (40 matches) for MCC. He is listed on *Cricket Archive* as playing (twice) for King's College, Cambridge at the age of 11, prior to some matches for Rugby School. Having moved close to Alresford, he first played for the Gentlemen of Hampshire in 1872 and made his Hampshire first-class debut at v Kent at Catford in 1875. He played in 20 first-class matches for Hampshire scoring 620 runs at an average of 17.71, with three half-centuries and a best of 77 v Kent at Canterbury in 1877. Although Hampshire lost, his score helped to avoid an innings defeat. He rarely bowled (two wickets for Hampshire). Although his on-field record is modest, he was a key figure for a short period in the revival of Hampshire County Cricket Club. The early 1870s were a bleak period, and after just two first-class matches in 1870, Hampshire played only second-class games from 1871-1874. Off the field there were frequent resignations, changes of officers and poorly attended meetings. In 1874, a meeting considered whether the club "shall be dissolved or not". It was not, of course, and the Club's official history (1957) records how the appointment of Clement Booth as captain and Hon Secretary in 1875, "provided the first element of rescue". In 1875, Booth arranged four first-class matches, home and away against Kent and Sussex. The two home matches were played on separate Winchester grounds – the College's Ridding Field and the St Cross/Greenjackets' Ground. Clement Booth resigned as Hon Secretary in 1879 and returned to Lincolnshire, but in those few years he played a key role in reviving Hampshire cricket. He was replaced by Russell Bencraft from Southampton, who would be an even more important figure in the county's history, on-and-off the field, for many years.

Botham, Liam James (434) born Doncaster, Yorkshire, 26.8.1977. Botham was an all-rounder who bowled medium-fast in a style that looked similar to his famous father. In July 1993, age just 15, he played for Hampshire 2nd XI v Worcestershire 2nd XI at Southampton – an appearance which attracted an extraordinary amount of media attention, and perhaps set in trail the reason for his brief cricket career. The impact was not lessened when he returned Hampshire's best figures of 4-63, as a member of an attack, all five of whom played Championship cricket. There were four further matches that year and more 2nd XI games in the late summers of the following two seasons. Then in 1996, still only 18, he joined the staff and played regularly for the 2nd XI before making his first-class debut v Middlesex at Portsmouth. Almost immediately he dismissed his father's England colleague Mike Gatting and took 5-67. Batting at number eight the next day he scored 30, helping Hampshire to a first innings lead, although Middlesex recovered to win by 188 runs. His bowling performance was among the best by a Hampshire player whose county debut was also their first-class debut, and he retained his place v Glamorgan at Southampton where 'Dimi' Mascarenhas played his first game, and bettered it with 6-88 & 3-62 (Botham 1-59 & 1-33). A fortnight later in his third Championship match he took 0-26 and did not bat in either innings. He had played in the 2nd XI's final match that season and shortly after his 19th birthday that was the end of his professional cricket career, as he chose to concentrate on Rugby Union (West Hartlepool, Cardiff and Newcastle) and Rugby League (Leeds and Wigan).

Bovill, James Noel Bruce ('Jim') (420) born High Wycombe, Buckinghamshire 2.6.1971. Pace bowler Jim Bovill was one of a group of promising youngsters of the early 1990s that the county hoped would replace the players of Mark Nicholas's side. In the event, hardly any did, and in Bovill's case it was injuries that truncated a promising career. His father had played a little for Hampshire 2nd XI 30 years previously, and after a few Minor Counties matches with Buckinghamshire in the early 1990s, Jim Bovill began playing for Hampshire's 2nd XI while studying at Durham University. During his student days, he played for the Combined Universities XI in first-class and limited-overs matches, and at the end of the 1993 season he made his Championship debut v Essex, dismissing both openers with just 13 runs scored, before Hussain and Gooch scored centuries. He played more matches in the second half of the 1994 summer, and then in early 1995 he took 6-39 – his best figures – in the first innings v Durham at Stockton, only to better them with 6-29 in the second innings. He played in a further seven matches, adding just 18 wickets but played regularly in 1995, with 34 wickets and a best of 5-58 v Yorkshire at Harrogate. He took 16 wickets in 18 limited-overs matches for the county, but after playing in nine first-class matches in the first half of 1996, he dropped out through injury and his professional career was over just after his 25th birthday. In his final match, he took 4-62 v Lancashire at Southampton.

Bowell, Horace Alexander William ('Alec') (97) born Oxford 27.4.1880, died Oxford 28.8.1957. Batsman Alec Bowell was a 'double first' at Hampshire – the first of a succession of men who came from Oxford between 1900-1960, and contributed significantly to Hampshire cricket, and with wicketkeeper James Stone, the first of a new group of professionals in the early twentieth century who helped to transform Hampshire from the weakest county side in the early years of the century, to one of the best on either side of the First World War. Since those who followed included Mead, Newman, Kennedy, Brown and Livsey, Bowell's contribution is sometimes overlooked, but he provided a greatly needed stability to the batting when the better amateurs like Poore and Wynyard were rarely available. In a county career that ran from 1902-1927, he played in 473 matches passing 1,000 runs on eight occasions and is one of only 17 men to have scored 25 centuries (or more) for the county. His highest score was 204 v Lancashire at Bournemouth in 1914 – at that time, and for some years, Hampshire's best, as they finished fifth. His 18,466 runs for Hampshire places him 11th in their all-time scorers, his 260 catches places him 13th in the Hampshire all-time list, and while he was not a regular bowler, he took 34 wickets, including 4-20 v Warwickshire at Southampton in 1913 (plus a half-century). 1913 was his best season with 1,627 runs and five centuries, but even in 1926, at the age of 46, he passed four figures and helped Phillip Mead save a match v Worcestershire with a fourth wicket partnership of 248. Also against Worcestershire, his first wicket stand of 204 for the first wicket with George Brown in 1920 was the county's record until broken by Marshall & Gray in 1959. He does retain one partnership record however, having added 192 with Walter Livsey, for the 10th wicket, again v Worcestershire at Bournemouth. Bowell was at number seven as Hampshire batted first, and the pair came together at 118-9. They took Hampshire to 310, after which Kennedy and Newman bowled them to an innings victory. Bowell was also considered a brilliant fielder in the covers. After retiring he took the 'Clump Inn' in Chilworth.

Bowell, Norman Henry (232) born Oxford, 2.2.1904, died Solomon Islands, 5.3.1943, killed by the Japanese when a prisoner of war. Norman Bowell, Alec's son, played two matches for Hampshire in 1924 and was then taken on to an embryonic post-war groundstaff, but stayed only until the end of 1926. For some reason, in this period he played once for Northamptonshire when in 1925, they fielded a weak side in what was designated a first-class match v Dublin

University at Northampton. The county side won by an innings with Norman Bowell scoring 48, but perhaps the greatest interest now is that playwright and author Samuel Beckett was in the visitors' side. Bowell's first county match in 1924 was also against Northamptonshire, in the match which lasted just two overs, during which FJ Hyland made his one appearance for Hampshire. Bowell played in the next match at Trent Bridge scoring 2 & 6 and bowling without success (0-32 & 0-24). His father did not play in those two matches. After leaving Hampshire he returned to play for Oxfordshire in the Minor Counties Championship.

Bowen, Edward Ernest (Pre '95, Amateur) born Co. Wicklow Ireland 30.3.1836, died France 8.4.1901. He was a right-handed batsman and occasional wicket-keeper who went from King's College, London to Cambridge University, but was not selected for the first XI. When he played for Hampshire in 1864, he was a master at Harrow School, and considered to be Harrow's founder of the modern curriculum, beyond the 'Classics'. Prior to 1864, he had played in minor matches for Hampshire, the Gentlemen of Hampshire, the South Hants Club and MCC. Bowen played his one match, in Hampshire's third-ever game, as a non-bowling number 11 (Ubsdell kept wicket); sadly, he recorded a 'pair', and Hampshire lost their third match. Bowen never appeared again, although he is recorded as playing cricket regularly into the 1880s. He was a useful footballer, representing England in their first unofficial match v Scotland in 1870, and appearing in the victorious Wanderers side in the first two FA Cup Finals (1872 & 1873). His brother, CSC played for Hampshire in non-first-class matches.

Bower, Joseph (41) we have no details of his dates of birth or death. He was a pace bowler who played in three matches for the county in 1897 & 1898; he is also recorded as playing for Hampshire 2nd XI (and MCC) in 1899. In 1897, his two first-class matches were not in the Championship; in the first, v Cambridge University at Cambridge, he took 3-55 in an innings defeat, then against the Gentlemen of Philadelphia at Bournemouth he took 4-43 in the second innings of a five-wicket victory. In the following season, he played his one Championship match, a rain ruined draw at Old Trafford in which he took one wicket. He batted at number 11 in each of his three matches, scoring 14 runs.

Boyes, George Stuart (215) born Southampton, 31.3.1899, died Southampton 11.2.1973. Stuart Boyes was Hampshire's 'inter war' cricketer; he made his debut in 1921 and played his final first-class match in 1939. In 1921, he worked for the Ordnance Survey in Southampton and was officially a soldier in the Royal Engineers, but he showed promise, so the club paid half of the sum for him to leave the Army and become a professional cricketer. It was a wise decision, and in his first full season he took more than 90 wickets including on two occasions, match figures of ten wickets. He scored an invaluable 29 as he and Livsey added 70 for the last wicket v Warwickshire at Edgbaston – the celebrated match in which Hampshire won after being dismissed for 15. He was principally a slow-left-arm bowler and fine close field (over 500 catches in all first-class cricket), although in the lower order he also scored 7,515 runs (two centuries) in his 474 matches for the county. He was described as a tall, slim, graceful bowler whose 1,415 wickets for the county places him fourth, behind only the Hampshire 'greats' Shackleton, Kennedy and Newman, and he played alongside, then succeeded the latter two. His career economy rate was 2.41 and he twice performed the hat-trick, while at Trent Bridge in 1934 – its days as a batsman's paradise – he recorded the incredible figures of 80-28-138-3. His figures v Derbyshire at Portsmouth in 1933 were 9.1-6-5-6 (Derbyshire 47 all out). At Yeovil v Somerset, in 1938, he had his best figures of 9-57, and he took seven or more wickets in an innings on five occasions, including 8-37 at Leicester in 1930 – a thrilling match: Leicestershire posted 237 (Boyes 4-84), Hampshire replied with 248 (half centuries for Arnold & Newman), and then came Boyes' fine performance in a Leicestershire innings of just 115. Hampshire, needing 105 to win reached 80-5 (Mead 41), but collapsed and when Boyes was last out (3) they had lost by 3 runs – 101 all out in 72.3 overs. He was awarded his county cap in 1929, the first professional since the war, and reached 100 wickets in a season on three occasions. As the Second World War ended in 1945, he played in friendly matches for Hampshire, but from 1946-1963 he became the coach at Ampleforth College. After retiring, he returned to Southampton and often watched matches on the county ground. He toured India, Burma and Ceylon with MCC in 1926/7 but with more luck he might have bowled for England.

Bradford, Sir Evelyn Ridley (18, Amateur) born India 16.4.1869, killed in action near Bucy-le-Long, France, 14.9.1914. Bradford's mother was the daughter of Edward Knight, who played in major matches for MCC, Hampshire and Kent in the 1820s – prior to the formation of HCCC. His father married twice and through him, Bradford is related to a number of cricketing families, including the Bonham-Carters. Bradford, went to Eton, then Sandhurst and played matches for the Aldershot Division, before he made his first-class debut for Hampshire in 1895, in a heavy defeat v Somerset at Southampton. He batted in the middle order and bowled a few overs. In the following season, he played three more matches and took 6-28 and 5-40 in an innings victory over Essex at Southampton in late August, but he played no more for three years, until he reappeared v the Australians. He took two wickets but was no-balled for throwing, at a time when bowlers' actions were causing concern, and after a return of 4-28 at Derby, this happened again in the match v Leicestershire – although in the latter his 102 was his best first-class score. He then left Hampshire and first-class cricket until 1905, when he appeared once more v Surrey in a rare Championship match at Aldershot, where he scored 60, but did not bowl. In the following years, he represented the Army in a number of non-first-class matches; in May 1913, he scored 251 for Shorncliffe Garrison v Folkestone. He was one of the earliest cricketing casualties of the war.

Brathwaite, Ruel, Marlon, Ricardo (522) born Barbados 6.9.1985. Pace bowler Brathwaite studied at Loughborough and then Cambridge Universities where he played first-class cricket, before joining Durham for whom he played 2010-2012. He joined Hampshire on trial and in September 2013, he made his first-class debut for Hampshire v Northamptonshire, taking 3-112. He took three further wickets in two more matches as that season drew to a close, but after that played no further first-class cricket. He signed a one-year contract in 2014, but played only one first team match, an abandoned limited-overs fixture v Sri Lanka 'A' in which he bowled one over (0-4). He appeared on a few occasions for the Academy side that year, but then left the county.

Bridger, Rev. John Richard (302, Amateur) born Dulwich 8.4.1920, died in a motor accident Burley, Hants 14.7.1986. John Bridger was a stylish opening batsman, one of Hampshire's last regular amateurs, and considered by many to have been good enough to have pursued a full-time career with some success. As a school master, he tended to play only in the summer holidays, appearing in 38 matches for Hampshire. He was educated at Rugby and then Cambridge University, and in 1936, he represented Lord's Schools v the Rest at Lord's, along-side Desmond Eagar who would select and captain him from 1946. During the war, he played for a variety of sides in the Surrey and London area, and appeared frequently in the Cambridge University side, although during that period their matches were not first-class – the 'Varsity Match' of 1942, was at Lord's. but was a single innings, one-day affair; Bridger scoring 75 in a victory. In the following year he opened again, scoring 40 in a drawn match. He made his first-class debut for an Under-33 side v Over-33s, although the latter included Eagar who was not yet 30; Bridger scored 49, and in June 1946, scored 94 for MCC who were defeated by his old University. After those two matches his remaining first-class games were all for Hampshire between 1946-1954; he scored 1,725 runs at 27.82 with two centuries and 10 half centuries. His county career began with two matches in a week at Bournemouth in early July 1946, and after opening with 50 v Sussex in an innings victory, he posted what would be his career best in the next game, 142 v Middlesex at Bournemouth, although a Compton century and 93* from Edrich won the game. After those two matches he played just once more in 1946 and never again began a county match before 30 July. He scored 61 and 102* at Worcester in his last appearance of 1953, and in his final season, he played in eight matches, scoring 365 runs which was his highest season's aggregate. When Desmond Eagar broke his thumb in August – and with Charlie Knott less frequently available – Bridger, as an amateur, captained the side, ending his Hampshire career as he had begun, with a half century v Sussex at Bournemouth. In the club's official history (1957) Eagar wrote "it gave me great pleasure to present John Bridger with his Hampshire cap for all his many services to Hampshire cricket since the war".

Briggs, Rev. Charles Edward (75, Amateur) born Derbyshire 17.9.1873, died Dorset 16.12.1949. He was a middle-order batsman who played in six matches for Hampshire in their poor 1900 season (played 22, lost 16, won 0), scoring 158 runs in 10 innings, with one half-century on his debut – 58 v Sussex at Hove – when he shared a century partnership with Victor Barton; none of his other innings for the county reached 30. In 1909, he played for Buckinghamshire v Surrey 2nd XI. He played in matches for Christ Church and Oxford University Authentics, and in a match for the latter v Leighton in 1894, he scored 160.

Briggs, Danny Richard (500) born Isle of Wight 30.4.1991. Slow-left-arm bowler Danny Briggs was born and raised on the Isle of Wight, one of a number of young cricketers developed there in the 21st century – and almost certainly the best cricketer from the island to have played for Hampshire. He played for the England Under-19 side and when he took his 100th first-class wicket during the 2011 season, he was the youngest English bowler in that style to reach that figure since Derek Underwood. He was capped by Hampshire at 21, and having bowled well in 'white ball' cricket, was selected by England, particularly in T20 Internationals, from September 2012 to early 2014. Despite that impressive start, Briggs was not always a regular choice, especially in the Championship and he left Hampshire at the end of the 2015 season, joining Sussex. He took 158 first-class wickets for Hampshire at an average just under 35, adding 50 limited-overs wickets, and most impressively, 119 x T20 wickets at an average under 20 and an economy rate of 6.86. He was a member of the Hampshire sides that won the T20 in 2010 & 2012, although he was denied a personal double, when England held him back from the 2012 C&G Lord's Final. Briggs often looks a useful batsman, with a first-class career average of 17.53, although that includes 120* for Sussex v South Africa 'A' at Arundel in 2017 and a single half-century for Hampshire – 54 v Gloucestershire at Bristol in 2013, adding 128 for the ninth wicket with Jimmy Adams. His best bowling for Hampshire was 6-65 v Nottinghamshire in 2011 – a thrilling match in which Nottinghamshire finished four runs short of victory with six wickets down. Tony Pigott then convened a gaggle of inspectors, and penalised Hampshire eight points for a so-called "sub-standard pitch". By contrast, Danny Briggs has had to bowl for most of his first-class career on 'standard' pitches, which offer little help to finger spinners.

Brodhurst, Bernard Maynard Lucas (45, Amateur) born India 6.8.1873, killed in action at Ypres 27.4.1915. Brodhurst was educated and played cricket at Clifton College and Sandhurst. He appeared in one match for Hampshire v Leicestershire at Southampton in 1897, batting last and scoring 9. He bowled seven overs in a victory, taking 0-23. Major Brodhurst of the 4th Gurkha Rifles was killed age 41.

Brooks, General Sir Reginald Alexander Dallas (195, Amateur) known also as RA Dallas-Brooks. born Cambridge 2.8.1896, died Australia 22.3.1966. Immediately after the First World War, in his early 20s, Brooks played in nine matches as a batsman for Hampshire, and more extensively for the Royal Navy and Combined Services – often first-class – through the 1920s. For Hampshire, his one century was 107 v Gloucestershire at Southampton, when another Hampshire cricketer and Naval officer, GC Harrison, also reached three figures. For the Royal Navy, Brooks took 38 first-class wickets at 27.63 with a best of 8-90 v the RAF at the Oval in 1927, but he never bowled for Hampshire. He was a fine all-round sportsman who captained the Royal Navy at Golf and Hockey, and represented England in the latter. In his final first-class match, he captained the Combined Services v New Zealanders at Portsmouth in 1931. From 1949-1963 he was Governor of Victoria, Australia.

Brown, George (143) born Oxford 6.10.1887, died Winchester 3.12.1964. John Arlott (1957) wrote of Brown that he was "perhaps the most remarkable all-round player the game has known" describing how he opened the batting and kept wicket for England v Australia, while on other occasions fielded superbly at mid-off, bowled with pace well enough to take 626 first-class wickets, and with 22,962 runs for the county, stands third behind Mead and Marshall in Hampshire's highest scorers. In all first-class cricket, he scored 37 centuries and 111 half-centuries, held 567 catches and added 79 stumpings. In the years since Arlott wrote that about the man who became his friend, the world has seen great all-rounders who bowled, batted and caught superbly, but none could also match Brown's wicketkeeping feats. In fact, he was only briefly Hampshire regular wicketkeeper, when in his forties, he bridged the gap between the retirement of Livsey and the arrival of McCorkell, but that was a decade after his county captain Tennyson brought him into the England side in 1921, to wear the gloves in the third Test against the Ashes-winning Australians. Brown responded with 57 on debut, adding 97 with the previous captain JWHT Douglas. Promoted to open because of Hobbs' illness, Brown scored 46, then 31 in his only innings in the fourth Test, and at the Oval, 32 & 84. Scoring 250 runs in five innings and also keeping wicket was a pretty good start against the strongest Test side of the time, for which he was rewarded with four Tests on tour to South Africa fifteen months later, but that was the end of his Test career, although he was selected in 1926 but withdrew, injured.

Brown had arrived at Hampshire in 1907, having walked from Oxford with his kit bag, and on first-class debut in July 1908, he completed the quartet of great professionals who would transform Hampshire's fortunes – Brown, Kennedy and Newman were certainly all-rounders and while we think of Mead as the greatest Hampshire batsman, even he took 266 wickets. The four were also complementary characters – Kennedy tireless, Mead pragmatic, Newman, somewhat highly strung, Brown of huge build and fearless, whether facing the fastest bowlers (like Gregory & MacDonald) or standing close to take daring catches, notably Jack Hobbs off Kennedy at the Oval. When England turned elsewhere, the explanation might be that Brown's one flaw was inconsistency. In his early pre-war years, he scored 1,327 runs and took 88 wickets in 1911, and two years later 1,263 runs and 85 wickets, but in-between his 1912 figures were only just half those – although he took five wickets for the Hampshire side that beat the Australians. After taking 54 wickets in Hampshire's excellent 1914 season, he never again reached the half-century, although he enjoyed some fine seasons with the bat, including 1,889 runs in 1920, and 2,040 in 1926, while from 1927 (1,866) until his final season in 1933, only once did he fail to reach four figures.

His highest score came in 1920 when he made 232* v Yorkshire at Headingley – he often did particularly well against the best sides, Yorkshire and Australia. His was the major contribution to an astonishing performance by Hampshire against the reigning champions, with Brown and Bowell (95) adding 183 for the first wicket and after the quick dismissal of Barrett, Brown and Mead (122*) took them to 456-2 declared. Kennedy then recorded match figures of 10-135, and Newman 6-110, as Hampshire won by an innings, losing just the two wickets. Hampshire's captain Tennyson sent each member of the XI a signed team photograph that Christmas. Brown also scored 230 v Essex at Bournemouth in the same season, and when Yorkshire came to Portsmouth in 1927 he scored 204 in an innings of 521-8 declared, sharing a third wicket partnership of 344 with Phil Mead which remained a record until the mammoth effort of Carberry & McKenzie against the same county in 2011. He shared a record seventh wicket stand with Abercrombie in 1913 (325 v Essex at Leyton) which still stands, while for 39 years he and Bowell held the first wicket record for the county, and from 1920 until this century, his stand of 321 with Barrett was the county's record for the second wicket.

While his wicket-taking declined after the war, his 602 wickets place him 16th in Hampshire's all-time records, and three times he took at least seven wickets in an innings with a best of 8-55 v Gloucestershire at Cheltenham in 1913. Despite all these fine achievements surely his finest moment came in the historic victory v Warwickshire at Edgbaston in 1922. He was one of the world record eight 'ducks' as Hampshire were bowled out for 15, but in the follow-on, he arrived at 127-4, still 81 behind, and by the time the arrears were cleared two more men had gone. Brown, Shirley and McIntyre then took the Hampshire lead to 66, but with eight wickets down he was joined by wicketkeeper Livsey, defeat looming. The pair added 167, with Livsey (110*) scoring his first century. Brown went for 172 in 285 minutes, by which time Hampshire led by 243, and Livsey and Boyes took Warwickshire's target to 314. Kennedy and Newman then ensured they did not get close. After retiring, approaching his 46th birthday, he was briefly, but not happily, an umpire, then coached at Sandhurst before taking a pub in Winchester. Arlott concluded his profile observing "here was a great cricketer".

Brown, Michael James (469) born Burnley 9.2.1980. Right-handed opening batsman Michael Brown played first-class cricket for Middlesex (1999-2003) and Durham University (2001-2002) before moving to Hampshire in 2004. He played there for five years before a brief, injury-hit spell at Surrey, retiring at 29. In his first Hampshire season, he scored 838 runs with two centuries but was less successful in the next two years before, in 2007, he passed 1,000 runs for the only time (43.12 with three centuries). He was only 60 runs short of four figures in 2008 (40.86) and then moved to Surrey. In his only full season for them he scored 992 runs but hardly played in his last two seasons. Brown scored seven first-class centuries for Hampshire, including his highest in the Championship, 126* v Durham which was very close to a special record. Hampshire hung on for a draw in the match, despite Ottis Gibson taking 10-47, as Brown carried his bat with 56*. He was poised to repeat the feat in the second innings, until last man David Griffiths stayed for twenty minutes, without scoring to deny Durham. Brown played in just 14 limited-overs matches for Hampshire in five seasons but there was an innings of 96* v Worcestershire in 2008, leading Hampshire from 65-6 to a four-wicket victory with 202-6. He played in ten T20 matches, without reaching fifty.

Bruce, James Thomas Anthony (464) born London 17.12.1979. Bruce was a right-arm pace bowler who played age 14 in matches for Hampshire 2nd XI, while still at Eton. He then studied at Durham University, playing in first-class matches for them, before making his Hampshire debut in 2003. Given the rarity of Hampshire-produced pace bowlers down the years, he showed promise and ability in his five seasons and was capped in 2006 but at 27 retired for a career in the City. He had a good record in limited-overs matches with 44 wickets at 22.18 and an economy rate below five, and he played in the 2007 FPT Final v Durham at Lord's – the only Final Hampshire have lost. He took 119 first-class wickets for Hampshire (32.23), three times with five wickets in an innings, including a best of 5-43 in 2006, as Hampshire beat Nottinghamshire at the Rose Bowl. In his last match in 2007 he took 5-73 v Yorkshire at home, but then left first-class cricket. He has played since for Eton Ramblers, Hampshire Hogs and the Arabs.

Brunnschweiler, Iain (450) born Southampton, 10.12.1979. Brunnschweiler had that least enviable of roles, a wicketkeeper deputising for an established 'keeper – or in his case two: 'Adi' Aymes and Nic Pothas. He played in six first-class and four limited-overs matches, although one of the latter was in the days when the county Cricket Boards competed in the C&G Trophy, and the final one was for Hampshire v the Zimbabweans. In the C&G match he held two catches and top-scored (37) in a defeat v Shropshire. Just three of his six first-class matches were in the Championship, but perhaps most notably he was a member of the Hampshire side that defeated the Australians in 2001, holding five catches, and with 10* was at the wicket when the match was won. His Hampshire first team career lasted from 2000-2003 after which he moved into fitness and coaching, and worked for some time at his county. He was a goalkeeper, who played a good standard of non-league football, including for AFC Totton in the FA Vase Final at Wembley.

Brutton, Charles Phipps (213, Amateur). born Portsmouth 20.1.1899, died Sussex 11.4.1964. He was a right-handed batsman who came to Hampshire from Winchester College. His father played one first-class match for Hampshire (below) and his uncle played first-class cricket and international rugby for England. CP made his first-class debut in 1921, and played quite regularly that year, scoring two half-centuries (average 19.10). He played in every year in the 1920s, and one last match in 1930 and occasionally deputised for Tennyson as captain. His best season was 1926 when he played in 19 matches, scoring 679 runs, average 27.16, with three half-centuries. His highest score was 119* v Worcestershire at Worcester in 1923 – one of three centurions in an innings victory. He played without success in an innings defeat at Bradford in 1930, then retired from first-class cricket. Brutton bowled 22 overs for Hampshire with neither a wicket nor a maiden. He played later for Cheshire, Denbighshire and Dorset. He scored 2,052 first-class runs for Hampshire at 17.84.

Brutton, Septimus (111, Amateur). born Newcastle-upon-Tyne 26.7.1869, died London 29.9.1933. He moved to Hampshire and became a partner in a law firm in High Street, Old Portsmouth. He had a lengthy career with Northumberland (1887-1901), but played just once for Hampshire, v Yorkshire at Portsmouth in 1904. Hampshire were a weak side, finishing bottom of the table, and lost to that season's runners-up by an innings, Brutton scoring 15 and seven.

Buck, William Dalton ('Bill') (360) born Southampton, 30.9.1946. Bill Buck was a pace bowler who played in just two first-class matches but with an unusual twist. He played for Hampshire 2nd XI from 1968-1970, but in early June 1969, while a student in Exeter, he appeared for Somerset at Taunton v the first tourists of that year, the West Indians and in the second innings dismissed both openers. He then returned to Hampshire's 2nd XI and two months later played his one match for his native county v the other tourists, the New Zealanders at Southampton. Sadly, after a Richards century, the match was ruined by rain, with Buck's figures in the one innings 14-4-25-0. That was the end of his first-class career.

Buckland, Edward Hastings (22, Amateur) born Middlesex 20.6.1864, died Winchester 10.2.1906. He played just four matches for Hampshire in their first Championship year of 1895. He had previously played at Marlborough School and Oxford University, where he won his 'blue' in all four seasons, 1884-1887; scoring his one first-class century – 148 v Surrey, and taking 7-17 v MCC. From 1885-1888, he appeared in nine matches for his native Middlesex (one half-century, BB 5-15 v Nottinghamshire) and then in his thirties he played for Hampshire. His record shows he was an all-rounder, and his bowling was particularly interesting as he was initially fast underarm, but then became a slow off-break bowler. He had a fine debut for Hampshire, taking 5-30 & 2-31 at Sheffield, as Hampshire beat Yorkshire, one of the strongest sides in the Championship. A few days later the inconsistent Hampshire side lost by an innings to Derbyshire, then Buckland top-scored with 73, as Hampshire lost at Edgbaston and finally, after a Championship career lasting less than three weeks, he took just one wicket in another defeat, v Sussex at Southampton. His brother FM played for Oxford University and Middlesex, while EH was also an all-round sportsman, including rackets (for Oxford University) football and golf.

Budd, William Lloyd (271) born Hawkley, Hampshire 25.10.1913, died Southampton, 23.8.1986. Lloyd Budd was a useful pace bowler and lower-order batsman, with two half centuries in a Hampshire career of 60 matches. It might have been significantly more, but that the Second World War began as he approached his 26th birthday, although he had played not at all in 1939, returning for a few games in mid-summer 1946. He made his first-class debut at Bournemouth in late August 1934, and played more regularly in 1935, although his 17 wickets cost nearly 55 each. In that year, he scored 67* v Glamorgan, batting at number 11, sharing a last wicket partnership of 125 with AL Hosie. After a few matches in 1936, he bowled and took wickets most often in 1937, with 27 at 31.07 and his best figures of 4-22 v Essex at Southend. Essex struggled in pursuit of a target of 142, losing eight wickets, but strangely Budd was not called upon again. After 11 wickets in eight matches in 1938, he did not play from late June. During the war, he served in the Southampton Police and played cricket quite regularly, returning for four county matches in 1946, when his three wickets were all taken in one innings in a victory over Lancashire at Old Trafford. In his fifties, after a couple of decades away from the game, Lloyd Budd came back as a first-class umpire, retiring at the end of the 1982 season, although there were two appearances in the following two seasons. In the mid-1970s he stood in four Test Matches and a number of ODIs, including the World Cups in England in 1975 & 1979.

Budden, Charles (72) born Fareham 18.71879, died Winchester 26.11.1969. Charles Budden was a pace bowler who played two matches in 1900 in the weakest of Hampshire sides and with no significant success. Perhaps his most notable achievement was the innings of 32* on debut, in a last wicket partnership of 54 with Harry Baldwin, as Hampshire drew at Edgbaston. Promoted to number nine for his next match, there were scores of just 3 & 0, although this was v Yorkshire in Hull where his one victim in 1-61 was Yorkshire's opening batsman and captain John Tunnicliffe. Budden played subsequently for Devon.

Budden, James Thomas William Frederick (170, Amateur) born Southampton 25.7.1882, died Southampton 5.9.1965. The only scorecard we have of Budden's cricket is a single first-class match for Hampshire v Oxford University in 1912, which Hampshire won by an innings. Budden, a bowler, was not required as Kennedy and Newman dismissed the students with five wickets each, after which CB Fry and Barrett took Hampshire to 453-2 dec. Budden bowled in the University's second innings but without a wicket (12-3-46-0). He is recorded in Who's Who of Cricketers as playing for Devon in 1906, which suggests he might have been related to Charles (above).

B

Bull, G (73) we have no further details of names, or dates of birth or death. Bull was another of those players called up in the difficult days in 1900. He played in three 2nd XI games and two first-class matches. In the first at Hull, he scored 0 & 2, and was one of ten Hampshire bowlers in an innings defeat (0-25); in the second at Leyton, only he and wicketkeeper (FN Harvey) did not bowl in the match, and he was absent injured in Hampshire's first innings, although his last act for Hampshire was to score ten, before becoming the final victim in another heavy defeat.

Burden, Mervyn Derek (330) born Southampton 4.10.1930, died Whitchurch, Hants 9.11.1987. Off-spinner Mervyn Burden was both one of the nicest and least lucky of Hampshire cricketers. He was a member of the post-war group of Hampshire-born players that Desmond Eagar found and encouraged – leading in 1955, 1958 and 1961 to what were then the three finest years in the county's history. In the war, his Southampton school was evacuated to Poole where he shone rather more at football, and once at work he attended cricket nets to maintain his fitness for the winter game, which was where he was spotted by Eagar and Hampshire's coach Sam Staples. He was invited to join the ground-staff in 1947, but on his first day, consumed by nerves, his first ball flew over the nets, smashing a window, and before he could bowl another, a shot from Johnny Arnold struck him on the ankle. Limping, he was sent to the square to help the groundsman, where he kicked over a bucket of whitewash! They sent him home to rest the ankle, but he returned, had a couple of good years with the Club & Ground and then went on National Service where he played regularly as a pace bowling all-rounder. On return to the county, realising that Hampshire's fine spinners were all reaching their careers' end, he switched to off-breaks. In 1951 & 1952 he played regularly for the 2nd XI during Hampshire's brief spell in the Minor Counties Championship, and at the end of the 1953 season, he made his first-class debut at Worcester, taking one wicket. In the next match v Champions Surrey at Bournemouth he took 6-70, and though Surrey won by nine wickets, took the one to fall in the second innings. In 1954, he had to wait until June to play, but then took 46 wickets at 21.1, including 7-48 at Leicester, while in 1955 he was one of just 14 men (including one match for Ingleby-Mackenzie) who took Hampshire to third place in the table for the first time in their history – he had 70 wickets this time, again at around 21 each, and he formed a spin partnership with another local youngster Peter Sainsbury. He would never reach 70 wickets in a season again, but after falling away somewhat in 1956, he was generally an important member of the side, particularly when the ground and weather suggested the ball would turn, which for Burden it often did considerably. Even in 1956 he had a wonderful day when somewhat unusually selected at the seamers' favourite ground, Portsmouth, he took 6-23, Champions Surrey collapsed to 126 and Hampshire won.

In 1958, Ingleby-Mackenzie's first year in charge, his 56 wickets at 22.42 helped Hampshire to the runners-up spot and he took 7-72 v Yorkshire

43

at Bournemouth, although by then a disappointing August had ended Hampshire's challenge. In 1959, the sun shone all summer and there was a brief experiment with covered pitches, as Burden took 45 more expensive wickets at 33.82; his average was around the same in 1960, with just 36 wickets, as Hampshire briefly tried the amateur spinner, 'Dan' Piachaud. With slow-left-armer Alan Wassell also showing promise, Burden could not be sure of his place as 1961 began, but early on he took 8-38 in an important victory v Somerset at Bournemouth, and over the season he took 50 wickets at under 23 apiece. He nonetheless, lost his place to Wassell mid-season, not playing after mid-July, although he was the regular and faithful twelfth man. He was not selected at Bournemouth for the great game v Derbyshire at the end of the season, but after Hampshire clinched their first title, one of the most famous photographs shows the side on the balcony, with the captain shaking Burden's hand, the latter smiling with the pleasure of it all.

In 1962, he took 65 wickets, but after a few games in 1963 his career was over, at an age when spinners are often at their best, although even then not before 6-84 won his penultimate match v Gloucestershire at Southampton. He took 481 first-class wickets for Hampshire at 26.11 and while his 901 runs at 6.82 tells its own tale, there was a rather special day v Warwickshire at Portsmouth in 1960, when as nightwatchman, he resumed on the final morning 4* (one shot, from an edge) and posted his only first-class half-century (51). Despite that, it is almost typical of his career that Derek Shackleton stole all the headlines, taking 9-30 and leading Hampshire to an improbable victory. John Arlott wrote that no-one "who has ever shared a day's cricket with Mervyn Burden would wish to change him. With a laugh full of teeth, he could reduce the tensest cricket match to its true stature – a game. In his acceptance of ill luck, and the wholeheartedness of his effort he is a model for any cricketer." In 1971, he came back to the County Ground to bowl 23 overs against Rachel Heyhoe-Flint's England Women's side, taking 5-76. The fates were still not finished with him, and he died just after his 57th birthday – the first of the 1961 Champions to go.

Burrows, Thomas George ('Tom') (478) born Wokingham, Berkshire, 5.5.1985. Tom Burrows was one of those Hampshire wicketkeepers who, particularly postwar, were destined to spend a few years as an understudy, with an occasional appearance before their careers ended. In May 2005, he made a promising first-class debut at Canterbury, deputising for Nic Pothas, and scoring 42, after Hampshire's largely international top-order had slumped to 130-7. His captain Warne scored a century and Hampshire reached 328 in just 73.5 overs. Burrows also held five catches in the match, but Kent held on to draw at 447-9. Despite this start it would be another 12 months before his next match v Loughborough University and again three more months before an isolated match v Warwickshire. His career continued in this way, with one or two matches each season, until in 2009, he played in six first-class matches, with 15 victims including his only stumping, and seven limited-overs matches. Despite this, and with Nic Pothas approaching the end of his career, Hampshire chose to promote Michael Bates from 2010, and Burrows' career was over. He played briefly in the Southern League with South Wilts.

Bury, Lindsay (Pre '95, Amateur) born Manchester 9.7.1857, died Bradfield, Berkshire 30.10.1935. Bury, mainly a fast, round-arm bowler, was educated at Eton and Cambridge University, winning his 'blue' in 1877. In the same year, he played his one match for Hampshire at Derby, taking one wicket in an innings defeat. In 1878, he played in just one first-class match for the University v an England XI, dismissing WG Grace. He was a successful footballer at the University, and capped by England at full back. He was also an athlete of some note.

Busk, Richard Dawson (197, Amateur) born London 21.6.1895, died Dorset 24.12.1961. Busk, a right-hand fast bowler, went to Marlborough School and played regularly for Dorset from 1912-1939. He played twice in first-class matches for Hampshire in 1919, v Australian Imperial Forces and Surrey, taking just two wickets and without scoring in his three innings (two not outs). In 1938, he played as a batsman for Dorset v Hampshire 2nd XI at Southampton, age, 43.

Byng, Arthur Maitland (121, Amateur) born Southsea 26.10.1872, killed in action with the Royal Fusiliers, at Vailly, France 14.9.1914. He was predominantly a middle-order batsman who played three matches for Hampshire in 1905, and was also a fine player in Army cricket before the war. In 1896/7, he played in first-class cricket in Jamaica and he served in the Boer War. In the same year that he played for Hampshire, he scored 204 for Hampshire Hogs v Royal Navy at Portsmouth, adding 335 for the first wicket with DA Steele of Hampshire. He was less successful in county cricket, scoring just 40 in five innings, and bowling six overs without a wicket.

C

Cadell, Alexander Richard (223, Amateur) born India 19.8.1900, died Petersfield 14.5.1928. Cadell was a right-arm pace bowler and lower-order batsman, who made his first-class debut for the Royal Navy in 1922, and also played first-class cricket for MCC and Free Foresters. He played in two matches for Hampshire at Portsmouth, in 1923 v Leicestershire and 1927 v Warwickshire. In the former he bowled just four overs (1-7) in a low-scoring defeat, but the second game in late August, was remarkable. Cadell took 1-18 in the Warwickshire innings of 364, to which Hampshire replied with 352; Kennedy then took 7-8 in a Warwickshire total of 36 which ended in the 20th over, Hampshire won by nine wickets, and Cadell was not required in either second innings, having scored six in Hampshire's first. He was killed in the following May in a motor accident.

Cadogan, Edward Henry (266, Amateur) born India 11.9.1908, died Lymington 7.2.1993. Cadogan was a fast bowler and lower order batsman, who went to Winchester College, and played first-class cricket for the Europeans in Bombay in 1929, and also in three games for the Army (1933-1936). His four Championship matches for Hampshire were in 1933 &1934, and in the following year, he played v the South Africans. His county batting average was below eight (HS 27 v South Africans) while he took 17 wickets at 23.82, with a best of 5-52 (& 2-70) in a two-day victory v Middlesex at Southampton in 1934. His last recorded match was for a services side at Canterbury in 1942, alongside Hampshire players GCA Adams and PA MacKenzie.

Calder, Henry (Pre '95, Amateur) born South Stoneham 14.4.1858, died Southampton, 19.5.1938. Calder was a middle-order batsman and useful change bowler, who played in five first-class matches for Hampshire, 1882-1885, and continued playing for three years after the county lost its first-class status. In the 1890s he played first-class cricket in South Africa, and also was a member of WW Read's tour of 1891/2, which included Victor Barton. Their match v the South African XI was later designated a Test, but Calder was not selected. For Hampshire, he averaged 14.22, with a best score of 44 v Kent at Southampton in 1885, and took five wickets at 23.60.

Campbell, Alastair, Keyon (146, Amateur) born South Stoneham 29.5.1890, died Portsmouth 16.6.1943. Campbell was a batsman who went to King Edward VI in Southampton, and in 1908 & 1909 played in seven matches for Hampshire, scoring 91 runs in 10 innings with a best of 21. He was a more notable foot-baller, playing in 199 matches for Southampton FC. While serving with the Royal Artillery in the Second World War, he died of pneumonia in Queen Alexandra Hospital, Cosham.

Cannings, Victor Henry Douglas ('Vic') (321) born Bighton, Hants 3.4.1919, died Buckinghamshire, 27.10.2016. Pace bowler Vic Cannings was a mainstay of the Hampshire attack through the 1950s, but he came by a circuitous route to play for his native county. After playing in his teens for Farnham, he spent the war in the Palestine Police playing cricket regularly. He returned to England at the conclusion of the war, but Hampshire, obliged to re-engage pre-war players, could not afford to offer him a contract, and on recommendation, he joined Warwickshire, made his debut and won his county cap in 1947, making his highest first-class score of 61 v Nottinghamshire, and taking 63 wickets at less than 30 each. He played less regularly in the next two years, with a total of 25 wickets, but with Herman, Heath and Bailey ending their careers, he finally signed for Hampshire in 1950, making his county debut just after his 31st birthday. He took 83 wickets in that first season, and forming an important partnership with Shackleton, reached three figures in each of the next four years, and then 94 wickets at his best average of 17.64, as Hampshire finished third in 1955.

There were 86 wickets in 1956 and then fewer each year until his retirement after his benefit in 1959, but in a career from age 31-40 it is a remarkable that he took 834 wickets for the county at 21.69. He took 7-52 v Oxford University in that first season, and then on three more occasions, seven wickets in an innings in the Championship, including 7-53 v Middlesex at Portsmouth in 1952. He had first opened with 'Shack' at Lord's in 1950, dismissing among others Denis Compton, and he got him again two years later, as Hampshire won by an innings – Compton was considered Vic's 'bunny'. In that same year, the opening pair bowled unchanged through the match to beat Kent at Southampton (Cannings 8-55 in the match). His batting was unremarkable, with a Hampshire career average below 10, but against the same opponents in 1950 he scored 10* as he and Charlie Knott added 21 for the last wicket in a low-scoring match. When Doug Wright dismissed Knott, and the match was tied. Similarly, i 1955 at Eastbourne, he and Peter Sainsbury added 55 for the ninth wicket, before the last two wickets fell on 139 and another match was tied. He liked thrilling finishes – in 1955 he won another match v Kent by dismissing Wright with the final ball, and in 1956, took two wickets with the final two balls, to beat Oxford University by one run. John Arlott (1959) suggested "his primary assets have always been stamina and steadiness", adding, "no man in our cricket thinks about the game more deeply". That must have helped after leaving the county, when he coached for many years at Eton, before handing on to Hampshire's John Rice, and enjoying a long, happy retirement.

Caple, Robert Graham ('Bob') (347) born Chiswick 8.12.1939. Off-spinner Bob Caple was an all-rounder, batting left-handed, who made his first-class debut for MCC v Oxford University in 1958, played two first-class matches for his native Middlesex v the two universities in 1959, age 19, and then joined Hampshire. His first match for them was v Oxford University in 1961 and the next against the same opponents in 1963, so in his sixth season he had played five first-class matches for three sides, all against the two universities. Then in August 1963 he was brought into the Hampshire side v Surrey at Southampton, scoring 31 in the second innings and sharing a century partnership with Roy Marshall. He remained for a run of five Championship games, scoring 45 in an innings victory v Leicestershire at Portsmouth, but bowled just three wicketless overs in the last match. In 1964 and 1965, he played more regularly, scoring five half centuries, with a best of 64* v Surrey in 1964 at the Oval, but he bowled rarely and took no wickets until 1966 when with 3-37 v Derbyshire he recorded his best Championship figures. He took 13 wickets in 1967 but that included 5-54 v Oxford University and with spin bowling competition from Sainsbury, Wheatley and Wassell, his chances were limited; having averaged around 16 with the bat in the last two seasons his first team days were over. He returned to play four 2nd XI matches late in 1968, and his last recorded match was for a Hampshire XI v the Army at Aldershot in 1969, when among the opposition was Larry Worrell, the next off-spinner to join the county.

Carberry, Michael Alexander (482) born Croydon 29.9.1980. Left-handed opening batsman Michael Carberry played initially for his native Surrey – the Cricket Board in 1999, and then the county side in 2001-2002. Seeking regular matches, he moved to Kent from 2003-2005, but after scoring four first-class centuries he had an injury problem, played in just one first-class match in 2005, and moved again to Hampshire, where he established himself immediately, becoming one of their finest players in all formats for the next decade. He passed 1,000 first-class runs for the first time in 2007 and after a less successful 2008, averaged 69.50 with four centuries in 2009 and was a member of Hampshire's FPT cup-winning side at Lord's. There was a period in that season when he scored over 900 runs in 11 first-class innings, averaging 115.75. He repeated his 'white ball' successes in the T20 in 2010 & 2012, and in the latter season, his thrilling 68 from 36 balls at Hove in the C&G semi-final, took Hampshire to Lord's again, and a Final victory over Warwickshire. By then he had made his Test debut for England in a victory v Bangladesh in March 2010, scoring 30 & 34. It would be two-and-a-half years before he was given another opportunity when he opened with Cook on England's disastrous Ashes tour – England lost all five matches, with the closest margin, 150 runs. Despite this, Carberry had a respectable record, batting for long periods, and his 281 runs in 10 innings compared favourably with most of his colleagues, although it was not enough for him to retain his place.

On two occasions, Carberry has struggled with serious illness and on the first he recovered in 2011, and participated in two record partnerships. One of 373 with Jimmy Adams for the second wicket at Taunton, and just before that, with Neil McKenzie, posting a mammoth 523 for the third wicket v Yorkshire. When Hampshire declared in what was then a 'dead' match, Carberry, having just reached 300*, was only 16 runs from Hampshire highest ever innings. The match was as dull as any might be, but Carberry's effort was heroic. In 2016, he was taken ill with cancer and when he returned the following year and began with a century v Cardiff University, it was welcomed throughout the cricket world. Sadly, he never really found form after that, apart from a couple of T20 innings, and in late summer, unable to agree terms with Hampshire, he moved to Leicestershire, signing a two-year contract and was appointed captain for 2018. That appointment however was terminated a few weeks into the season, after which he played no more that year and at the end of the 2018 season he left his fourth county. Through his career, he bowled some of the slowest off-breaks (17 first-class wickets) and was a superb fielder at deep point or the covers. In the reduced 21st century Championship seasons, only Carberry and his frequent partner Adams, scored over 10,000 runs for Hampshire (his average 42.64 with 28 centuries), to which can be added 3,519 limited-overs and 3,066 T20 runs. He proved himself through those years as one of the toughest and also most entertaining of Hampshire batsmen.

Carter, Andrew ('Andy') (543) born Lincoln 27.8.1988. In a 2016 season blighted by illness, injury and tragedy, Hampshire turned in some desperation to emergency signings to boost the side, and one of those was pace bowler Carter, who had only just moved somewhat unhappily from Nottinghamshire to Derbyshire. He made his debut on his former home ground, Trent Bridge, taking 4-52, but played in just one more Championship match taking two more wickets. He did not play for Hampshire in 'white ball' cricket.

Carter, George (Pre '95, Amateur) born Warblington, 4.8.1846. We have no further details of date or place of death. He was a right-hand batsman and occasional bowler who played in 12 first-class matches for Hampshire, scoring 274 runs with an average of 11.91 and a best of 34. He first played for the county in 1866 then in four first-class matches in 1869 & 1870. After Hampshire lost first-class status for a few years he played in a further eight first-class matches in 1876-1878. He also played in various non-first-class matches for the county, up to 1890, and in 1868 he played for the East Hants Club on their Southsea ground v the Australian Aboriginals, taking 4-30 in his round-arm fast style, in an innings defeat.

Cartridge, Donald Colin ('Don') (327) born Southampton 31.12.1933, died Southampton September 2015. Batsman Don Cartridge joined Hampshire's staff in the early 1950s, after attracting their attention while at Itchen Grammar School, where he had also represented Southampton Schools FA. Over the years, he proved himself to be a fine all-round sportsman, not least as an accomplished table tennis player. In 1953 at the age of just 19 he made his first-class debut for the county, playing in three matches, but with the arrival of Roy Marshall and Henry Horton in the same year, his chances were limited, and he had an unhappy time at first-class level, as in six first-class innings he scored just six runs. He decided to study at King Alfred's College in Winchester, after which he became a teacher at Millbrook School, spending 35 years teaching PE and mathematics. In later years, he played cricket around the region with Deanery, Southampton Touring Club, Southampton Wednesday, and Trojans, who he captained in their early days of the Southern League, and for the Forty Club. In June 1963, he appeared once more for Hampshire 2nd XI v Sussex at Hove.

Carty, Richard Arthur ('Dick') (317) born Southampton 28.7.1922, died Bishop's Waltham, 31.3.1984. Pace bowler Dick Carty promised to be one of the new post-war generation of local players sought by captain Desmond Eagar and in a six-year career of 55 county matches, he took 138 wickets - on eight occasions with five or more in the innings. He might have become Derek Shackleton's opening partner, but his early twenties were lost to the war, and injuries plus the 'return' of Vic Cannings meant that his career ended eventually at 32, in 1954. Although he batted in the lower order, he managed two half-centuries, and an average approaching 15. Carty's first season, 1949, was his most successful, with 34 wickets at 25.82, and a best of 6-110 v Middlesex at Bournemouth, including Robertson, Brown and Edrich. He improved on that with 7-50 & 4-67 in a narrow victory v Glamorgan in 1952, probably his finest game, although his first-class best was 7-29 v Oxford University at Basingstoke in 1951. In June 1954, he took 6-61 against the students again, but with just one wicket in two Championship matches in the following month, his Hampshire career came to an end.

Case, Dr George Henry (Pre '95, Amateur) born Fareham 4.4.1839, died Fareham 21.4.1911. Batsman George Case has one slightly odd place in Hampshire's history – apart from being one of half-a-dozen medical doctors to play for the county – since he was first man in the club's history to be listed absent in an innings on the completed scorecard. This occurred in the county's inaugural first-class match as a fully constituted club, v Sussex at the Antelope in July 1864. On *Cricket Archive*, Case is listed as absent ill, but Alan Edwards (2014) has suggested this is unlikely, and he had probably been called away to a medical emergency. In his absence, Hampshire were put out for just 63, and the impact of his absence was emphasised when he opened in the second innings and made 48, the top score in the match, although it was not enough to save Hampshire from an innings defeat. Case played once more v Middlesex in the following month scoring 11 & 26, and bowling a few wicketless overs, after which he was a member of the club's Committee. As a medical man, he had a position on the Isle of Wight which he left in 1862 returning to Fareham to become the town's Medical Officer for Health in 1874. Through the 1860s and early 1870s he played a number of matches for the Gentlemen of the South, the Isle of Wight, the East Hants Club (Southsea), the Gentlemen of Hampshire, and his home town Fareham.

Castell, Alan Terry (348) born Oxford, 6.8.1943. Apart from the impact of Shane Warne on Hampshire cricket in the early 21st century, leg-spinners played little part in the club's history until the recent emergence of Mason Crane. Just before the war, Tom Dean made a promising debut but after six years away at war, he could not recapture the skills required for the first-class game. One of Dean's teammates was Arthur Holt who, in 1959, as Coach, was sufficiently excited on discovering Castell, that he invited him to join the staff without a formal trial, and after one match for Northamptonshire 2nd XI, he began playing for the Club & Ground and 2nd XI. Castell was the last of the fine line of cricketers who had come to the county from Oxford, and at Hampshire he played as a teenager, for almost five years - perhaps the first Hampshire cricketer to reflect the new phenomenon of 'teenage' fashions, having appeared initially with a hairstyle resembling the young Elvis, that evolved through the 'swinging sixties' to resemble rather more 007, then the Beatles – including briefly, the later 60s bearded look, which did not meet with approval among the hierarchy and did not last long. Castell was a 'character' and these matters were not perhaps wholly irrelevant in considering that while his Hampshire career lasted until injury intervened in 1971, he was never capped. He played in 110 first-class matches for the county, plus 30 limited-overs games; the most by any Hampshire cricketer to have ended without a cap, while many who did a good deal less, were so rewarded.

He had played one first-class match in the title-winning year, v Oxford University at Portsmouth, and against the same opponents in 1962 he took 3-45 in the second innings. He was selected at the end of that season to play in the last three Championship matches, and while his bowling showed promise, there was just one wicket, of Brian Close at Bournemouth, and it was his batting that made the impression. In the first game at Bournemouth, Castell (14*) and Burden resisted the best efforts of Yorkshire's bowlers to capture the final wicket on their march to the title, while two games later at Southampton he scored 76 v Surrey, accompanying Danny Livingstone (200) in a record partnership of 230 for the 9th wicket which stands to this day. In 1963, he played a few more matches and took 28 wickets at 18.85, including 5-46 & 5-56 v Somerset at Bournemouth, when Somerset's Australian Bill Alley, suggested he was more promising than Richie Benaud at the same age. Despite that, he took just four wickets in five appearances over the next two years, until reinventing himself as a pace bowler, after which he played more often from 1966. Hampshire's bowling in the 1960s was dominated by the finest pace trio in their history, Shackleton, White and Cottam but it was a difficult decade for the spinners, with Burden departing in 1962, the youngsters Caple, Castell, Wassell, and Wheatley struggling to establish themselves, and even Peter Sainsbury took far fewer first-class wickets than previously.

In 1966, Castell the pace bowler, came into the Championship side in early July and took 36 wickets at 22.55, including 6-69 v Worcestershire at Portsmouth and then 6-49 v Derbyshire at Southampton on Saturday 30 July 1966. Unfortunately, that performance did not hit the headlines, as they were stolen by a hat-trick from another (Essex) county cricketer at Wembley. At the start of his limited-overs career, Hampshire played only in Gillette Cup matches, until the Sunday League arrived; when it did, Castell played regularly in the 1970 season, taking 12 wickets, while overall there were 28 wickets, and a best of 4-52 (and 23) in a quarter-final defeat v Sussex at Hove in 1967. In first-class cricket 1967 and 1968 were quieter, but in 1969 he took 50 wickets for the only time, including 6-22 v Somerset at Bath as Somerset were dismissed for 88, despite which they won a thrilling game by just two runs. He also had three wickets and 61* in a victory v Sussex at Portsmouth – one of four half-centuries. In 1969, his wickets had cost 25.90 each but in 1970, 43 came at nearly 40 and in 1971, 27 around 30 each, after which he was gone – and a rather romantic dream went with him.

Causton, Edward Postle Glynn (202, Amateur) born London 27.11.1876, died Torquay 18.4.1957. He was a batsman who played a single match at the age of 42 for Hampshire v Essex in 1919, scoring 21 in the county's only innings of 408 (Mead 207). He also bowled one over for four runs; the match was drawn. Before the war, he had played for the Royal Navy (not first-class).

Cecil, Aubrey Bruce Cooper (Pre-'95, Amateur) born Bedfordshire, 10.3.1847, died, Queensland, Australia, 26.8.1918. He played in one first-class match, a defeat at Derby in 1876, and batting in the lower order, scored 4 & 2. His younger brother, EDC Cecil (below) played also for the county in the previous year – clearly their parents enjoyed being playful with their initials! ABC played also for his native Bedfordshire, 1876-1878.

Cecil, Egerton Dodge Cooper (Pre-'95, Amateur) born Worthing, 4.7.1853, died Surrey 25.9.1928. He played once for Hampshire v Kent at Catford in 1875. In an innings defeat, he took 0-8, scored four runs in the first innings, and was absent hurt in the second.

Chance, Geoffrey Henry Barrington (178, Amateur) born Berkshire 16.12.1893, died Wiltshire 11.7.1987. He was a left-handed batsman and medium pace bowler, sometimes known as GH Barrington-Chance. After Eton and matches for Eton Ramblers, he played in one first-class match for the county, v MCC at Lord's in 1913, age 19, scoring 0 & 0* and taking 0-42. In 1922, he played a second first-class match, for MCC v Scotland taking 0-5, but not batting in an innings victory. He played for Berkshire in the Minor Counties Championship in 1912 & 1913.

Chandler, G (Pre '95) we have no further details of names of dates of birth or death. In the club's second season, 1865, Chandler played in one match v Middlesex at Islington, keeping wicket in an innings defeat. He had two stumpings and a catch, and scored 0 & 16. In the same season, he played at least two minor matches for Hampshire.

Charters, Frank Henry (175) born Plymouth 17.1.1884, died Boscombe 25.1.1953. He was a right-handed batsman who played once for Hampshire in 1913, scoring 9 & 5 v Derbyshire at Southampton in an eight-wicket defeat. In 1920, he played at least two matches for Surrey 2nd XI, and during that decade he played also for the RAF in various non-first-class matches.

Chignell, Thomas Alexander (92, Amateur) born Havant 31.10.1880, died Portsmouth 25.8.1965. He was a left-handed batsman and medium-slow bowler who played in 19 matches for Hampshire from 1901-1904. He averaged 10 with the bat (HS 29*) and took 33 wickets at 33.57, with a best of 5-68 v Derbyshire at Southampton in 1903, when he also scored 24* in the only Championship match they won that year – and by 261 runs.

Chivers, Ian James (401) born Southampton, 5.11.1964. Ian was an off-spinner on the staff in Mark Nicholas's early years as captain, when Cowley and Maru were generally the selected spinners. He made his first-class debut v Oxford University in 1985, and in the second innings, took one wicket. Two years later he played in his only Championship match, at Swansea, and took another wicket, adding 20* in a drawn match. He played mainly for the county's 2nd XI, but no more after that season. He played in the Southern League for Old Tauntonians, Calmore Sports and Winchester Krakatoa Simmarians. He also played representative matches for the Southern Cricket League, and the Club Cricket Conference.

Christian, Daniel Trevor ('Dan') (506) born, New South Wales, Australia 4.5.1983. Medium-pace all-rounder Dan Christian played in all three formats for Hampshire as an overseas player in 2010, but will always be remembered for one ball – the last one of the 2010 T20 Final v Somerset at the Rose Bowl. Christian, on strike, was injured and had a runner, and Hampshire's score was one behind Somerset's, when a single to bring the scores level would give them the trophy on a 'count-back'. Christian hardly hit the final ball, but the non-striker and the runner took off and completed the winning run. In the excitement, so, incorrectly, did Christian, and had Somerset run him out, they would have won – but they did not realise, and Hampshire took the title! He had been signed that year to appear in the T20, in which he played 12 matches (HS 10* and nine wickets) but he also played in one drawn Championship match for Hampshire at Taunton, and a victory over Durham in the CB40 at the Rose Bowl. He is a 'modern' travelling cricketer who has played in his native Australia for his country in 'white ball' matches, and for three state sides, as well as in the IPL, and for Gloucestershire, Middlesex and Nottinghamshire.

Clapp, Dominic Adrian (465) born Southport 25.5.1980. Batsman Dominic Clapp is one of those strange inclusions in the list of Hampshire's 'first-class' cricketers. He played for Sussex in one first-class match in 2002 scoring six against Leicestershire, although he enjoyed more success in his one limited-overs match for them, top-scoring with 43 v West Indies 'A' at Hove. In 2003 & 2004 he played a number of matches for Hampshire 2nd XI, but appeared also for Somerset 2nd XI in that period, while in May 2003, he and Mark Thorburn, both 'on trial', were taken to the Parks to make up the numbers in a depleted Hampshire side, v Oxford University. Clapp, listed at nine, did not bat in the first innings and promoted, was dismissed for four in his only first-class innings for the county.

Clark, Stuart Rupert (487) born Sydney, Australia 28.9.1975. Stuart Clark was a right-arm pace bowler who represented Australia in 24 Test Matches (94 wickets at 23.86) and played also for New South Wales, Middlesex, and then Hampshire as an overseas player in 2007. He played in six first-class matches, taking 24 wickets, including a best of 7-82 v Lancashire in a rain-affected, drawn match at the Rose Bowl. He was very effective in limited-overs matches, taking 21 wickets in seven games, including 6-27 v Surrey in the FP Trophy, then 3-38 in the semi-final victory v Warwickshire at the Rose Bowl. Sadly, his stint with Hampshire then finished and he missed the Lord's Final – Hampshire's only Cup Final defeat (v Durham). He did not play in any T20 matches for the county. Having played those 13 matches in the one season, he was awarded his county cap.

Clarke, Michael John (470) born New South Wales, Australia, 2.4.1981. For many post-war years, Hampshire generally looked to the West Indies or perhaps South Africa, to sign overseas players, but after the arrival of Hayden in 1997 and Warne in 2000, the Australians became first-choice, with Katich, Watson, Thornely, Clark, Bichel and Michael Clarke arriving in quick succession. The latter came in 2004, by which time he had played for some years for his home state, and from 2003 for Australia in limited-overs matches; he would make his Test debut in the winter after his season with Hampshire. He was principally a right-handed batsman, who scored 709 first-class runs in 12 matches at 35.45 for the county. He made an immediate impression with a debut top-score of 75 from 86 balls in a victory v Durham but this was followed by two 'ducks' and in the next 11 innings just one half-century, until he went to Trent Bridge. As John Crawley posted the first of two undefeated triple centuries, Clarke made a century in both innings, 140 & 103, and in the next match at Cardiff, he scored 109 as Hampshire won. There were just two more matches before he teamed up with the Australian Test squad, and in October made his debut at Bangalore. He would eventually captain his national side, playing in 115 Test Matches and 245 ODIs. In limited-overs cricket for Hampshire, he scored almost 300 runs in 12 matches (27.09) and took six wickets (plus one in first-class) bowling slow-left-arm.

Cole, Canon George Lamont (151, Amateur) born Sussex 5.9.1885, died Kent 14.10.1964. He was a right-handed batsman who was educated at Sherborne School, played in one first-class match for Cambridge University in 1908, one Championship match for Hampshire in 1909 and a further five for the county in the late summer of 1911. He had a highest score of 33 and an average of 12.22, and was a member of the side that beat Yorkshire at Portsmouth in his penultimate match.

Coles, Matthew Thomas ('Matt') (520) born Maidstone 26.5.1990. Matt Coles is a strong pace bowler, and hard-hitting lower-order batsman but also a 'restless' cricketer who has found it hard to settle with any county, and was once, with Ben Stokes, sent home from an England Lions tour for disciplinary reasons. He joined his native Kent as a teenager and played for their first team from 2009 until June 2013, when he played against Hampshire at the Ageas Bowl. He played no more for Kent, and some ten weeks later made his debut on loan for Hampshire at Southport, scoring 68, in an eighth wicket partnership of 191 with Wheater, despite which Hampshire lost heavily. In his third match, he made 50* and generally took a few wickets in each innings, then in his final match of 2013 he took 6-71 and 4-83 as Hampshire beat Essex by an innings. He signed with the county and played regularly through 2014, adding another half-century although scoring fewer runs, but taking 41 wickets at less than 30 each. His limited-overs performances were disappointing for so talented a player, but 54 v Essex remains his highest T20 score, and 18 wickets his best aggregate in a season. His final first-class match for Hampshire was at Cardiff in September 2014, as the county clinched the Second Division title, but then he returned to Kent, welcoming the chance to play again for his home county. He spent three years with them in the second division, before joining the new County Champions Essex at the end of 2017.

Collins Thomas Hugh (273) born Nottingham 4.3.1895, died Nottinghamshire 19.5.1964. Collins, a left-handed batsman and slow-left-arm bowler played two matches for his native Nottinghamshire in 1921, age 26 and then played two more matches for Hampshire, fourteen years later, at Derby and Hull. Both matches ended in an innings defeat. He scored 31 runs in four innings and took 1-22. He is recorded as playing one match for Devon in 1921.

Connor, Cardigan Adolphus (398) born Anguilla 24.3.1961. In 1984, pace bowler Cardigan Connor was living and playing league cricket in the London area and in Minor Counties for Buckinghamshire, when Hampshire's reserve wicketkeeper, Chris Goldie, recommended him to the Cricket Chairman Charlie Knott. Knott, concerned with loss of a number of pace bowlers in recent years, and the absence of Malcolm Marshall on tour, believed Hampshire needed immediate reinforcements. Connor played on trial for the 2nd XI, was signed, and on first-class debut v Somerset at Bournemouth, took three wickets as their opponents were reduced to 25-5. In that first season, he took 62 wickets at just over 30 each, with 7-37 v Kent at Bournemouth, but he was not so successful again until 1989, when he took 59 wickets at 21.27, with 7-31 v Gloucestershire at Portsmouth. In some respects, it was fortunate for Hampshire that he grew more effective as Marshall reached the end of his career; on the other hand, performing at their best together, they must surely have brought Nicholas's side a Championship title.

By 1989, he had played with Hampshire's third Sunday League Champions (1986) and their first Lord's Cup winners, and he was one of a small number who appeared in the first three Lord's Finals of 1988, 1991 & 1992. His batting was generally unremarkable, albeit as cheerful as his general disposition, although he did score two half-centuries with a best of 59 at the Oval in 1993. In 1996, he became one of Hampshire's (then) twelve bowlers to take nine wickets in an innings – 9-38 v Gloucestershire at Southampton – although oddly he failed to add the one wicket required for 10 in the match. It was however, Hampshire's record analysis at their old headquarters. By the end of his career he had played in 300 limited-overs matches for Hampshire as well as 200 in the Championship. He stands 15th in the county's all-time first-class wicket-takers, and only Marshall and Udal of those who played in the past 40 years have more than his 614 wickets. In addition, his 411 limited-overs wickets are more than any other Hampshire cricketer, and it was his final over at the Oval in 1986 that brought that last Sunday League title. Cardigan Connor was a delightfully happy cricketer, and hugely popular with Hampshire's supporters. He is now Parliamentary Secretary for Tourism in Anguilla.

Cork, Dominic Gerald (496) born Newcastle-under-Lyme 7.8.1971. Pace bowler and useful batsman Cork, played for Derbyshire from 1990-2003 and for England in Tests and ODIs for a decade from 1992. In 37 Tests, he scored three half-centuries and took 131 wickets (best 7-43). He joined Lancashire in 2004 and played there for five seasons before joining Hampshire in his late thirties, enjoying a successful end to his county career. On debut for the county v Worcestershire in 2009, he took 4-10 and 2-27, scoring 25 in a seven-wicket victory. He captained the side in 2010 & 2011, and overall took 94 wickets at 27.77, plus 39 limited-overs wickets at under 30, and 43 wickets in the T20. In 2009, he took 4-41 and was Man-of-the-Match in the FP Trophy Final v Sussex at Lord's, and in the following season led Hampshire as they won the T20 for the first time, beating Somerset at the Rose Bowl. His last game was in the T20 semi-final of 2011, when Hampshire lost to the same opponents in a super over, after the scores were level (D/L method).

Cornwallis, Oswald Wykeham (212, Amateur) born Kent 16.3.1894, died Froxfield Green, Hants 28.1.1974. He was a right-handed batsman, who came from a family of cricketers, including his brother, Wykeham, who became the 2nd Baron Cornwallis of Linton and was an effective pace bowler for Kent. OW Cornwallis played first-class and other cricket for the Royal Navy and in mid-May 1921 he was selected by Hampshire against Kent at Southampton – quite possibly because his brother was in the opposition. Hampshire batted first and Brown and CB Fry opened with a century partnership. At lunchtime, the two brothers were informed that a third brother, an army officer, had been killed in an IRA ambush, at which they left the ground and took no further part in the match. Cricket Archive records them as Absent Hurt but Absent is more appropriate. While Kent's Cornwallis continued to play for the county until 1926, OW Cornwallis never appeared for Hampshire again, so he never actually appeared on the field, although he does appear in the team photograph taken at the start of that match.

Cottam, Robert Henry Michael ('Bob') (351) born Cleethorpes 16.10.1944. Bob Cottam was one of the finest fast-medium bowlers in Hampshire's history, and bowling through the 1960s, was a member of a trio with Shackleton and White that was surely the most complete Hampshire pace attack. Cottam played for Hampshire 2nd XI in 1962, age 18, and the next year, made his first-class debut in the annual Whitsun match v Kent at Southampton. He took 73 first-class wickets in his first two seasons, then in successive years from 1965, he took 73, 62, 102, 130 and in 1969, 109 wickets. In 1965, he took part in two remarkable games against the two 'Roses' counties. At Middlesborough in mid-May, he took 6-47 in the match, as Hampshire's pace trio dismissed Yorkshire for 125 & 23 – their lowest ever total – and won by 10 wickets. A month later, they beat Lancashire at Old Trafford by 13 runs after Cottam took 9-25, still the best figures in Hampshire's history. While he was mostly an orthodox right arm fast-medium bowler, he also learned to cut his pace and bowl cutters to great effect - especially in those days when the weather enhanced the effect of uncovered pitches.

In 1968/9, he went to Pakistan, after the tour of South Africa was cancelled following the selection of Basil D'Oliveira. He played in two Tests for England, taking 4-50, 2-35, 2-52 and 1-43 – a decent debut record but not one that secured his place. Four years later he played in two more Tests in India, but by then he seemed to have become disenchanted with a transitional period in Hampshire's history and had moved to Northamptonshire from the start of the 1972 season – age just 27. After five years there he retired, having taken over 1,000 first-class wickets. For Hampshire, he took 693 wickets at 20.71 – only Andy Roberts, Derek Shackleton and Malcolm Marshall can better his average, and he caught well close to the wicket, although he was a true tail-end batsman with an average of 5.44 from 615 runs (HS 35) – one a small group of regular players with fewer runs than wickets. For Hampshire, he also took 91 limited-overs wickets at an average of 21.15 but he is one of the finest Hampshire players of the past 60 years, never to have been in a Trophy-winning side and ultimately, there is a feeling that this very fine bowler did not entirely realise his full potential – perhaps it was not always recognised? After retiring he played for Devon and became a respected coach, working with England, Somerset and

Warwickshire. In 2018, he was appointed to one of the new scouting positions, advising the England selectors.

Court, Richard Charles Lucy ('Dick') (280) known later as RC Lucy-Court. Born India 23.10.1916, died Southampton 10.4.1974. Court was a fast bowler who joined Hampshire's growing ground staff in 1936, age 19, and after matches for the Club & Ground and 2nd XI, he made his first-class debut at Old Trafford in May 1937. He played three matches in that first season with a best of 3-41 in a high-scoring draw v Sussex at Portsmouth. In 1938, he had a run of Championship matches in July, taking 13 wickets at 22.46, although his best figures that year came v Cambridge University. He recorded his career best figures of 4-53 (after 3-70) v Essex at Brentwood in 1939 and then played regularly until late July, but not thereafter – his 15 wickets cost more than 50 each. After the war, he worked alongside Desmond Eagar, firstly as assistant, then as joint secretary of the club until 1950, but he played no more cricket for any of the county's sides.

Cowans, Norman George (423) born Jamaica 17.4.1961. Norman Cowans was a fast bowler whose main career was for England (19 Tests from 1982/85) and Middlesex (1980-1993). He joined Hampshire in 1994, to form a new opening partnership with Winston Benjamin, but it was less effective than Mark Nicholas and the Cricket Committee had hoped. Cowans played in 12 first-class matches, taking 26 wickets at just under 38 each with a best of 4-76 v Durham at Portsmouth in late August, which was sadly his final Championship match; he did not return in 1995. He also took 22 wickets in 21 limited-overs games with a best of 4-36 v Worcestershire at Worcester in a B&H semi-final, despite which Hampshire lost by three wickets. In all first-class cricket, he took 662 wickets at 24.86. He continued to play in notable non-first-class matches, at least until 2014, age 53.

Cowie, Alexander Gordon (156, Amateur) born Lymington 27.2.1889, died of his wounds in Mesopotamia 7.4.1916. Cowie, educated at Charterhouse, was an erratic fast bowler whose most notable moment was probably in the University match of 1910 when he bowled two wides and took two wickets in his first over. He won his Cambridge 'blue' only in that year, although he played in 1911 in other matches. In 1910, he played also in two matches for Hampshire; a victory at Chesterfield (two wickets) and a defeat v Lancashire at Southampton, when he took 5-94 & 2-85 in what would be his last county match. In 1913 & 1914 he played in two first-class matches for the Army. During the war, he was in the Seaforth Highlanders, and had been wounded in 1915, prior to his death a year later.

Cowley, Nigel Geoffrey (373) born Shaftesbury, Dorset, 1.3.1953. Off-spinning all-rounder Cowley played for the 2nd XI when Gilliat's team won the Championship in 1973, but with the departure of O'Sullivan he came into the side in the following season, although he bowled very little for the first three years (17 wickets). For almost the whole of that first season it seemed he would start his first-class career as a County Champion, but when rain wrecked the last two matches at Bournemouth he was one Hampshire's disappointed runners-up. While Cowley became an effective Championship cricketer, it would be in limited-overs cricket that he would enjoy most success – and make most impact – beginning perhaps in the 1977 B&H semi-final when he arrived following a Procter hat-trick at 18-4, and added 111 with David Turner, top-scoring with 59, albeit not quite enough to take Hampshire to Lord's. He played very little when Hampshire won the Sunday League in 1975, but contributed to the next two titles in 1978 (when he was capped) & 1986. His highest first-class score of 109* came at Taunton in 1977, with a second first-class century v Leicestershire at Southampton in 1982, to which he added a career best 6-48. In 1978, he took 56 first-class wickets at around 30 apiece, and matched that total in 1984, while in three other seasons he passed 40 wickets; 1984 was also the season in which he reached 1,000 runs for the only time. In 1986, he was a member of the Hampshire side who won their third and last Sunday League and in 1988 he played in their first Lord's final, making a significant contribution with 1-17 in his 11 overs, and executing the throw from deep to run-out Derbyshire's most threatening batsman, John Morris. After just one first-class match in 1989, he left Hampshire and joined Glamorgan for one season, after which he became a first-class umpire, retiring in 2017. He scored 6,773 runs and took 425 wickets for Hampshire in 257 first-class matches, to which he added almost 3,000 runs and 233 wickets in 288 limited-overs games. For fifteen years, he was a valuable all-rounder in both forms, going about his work in a quiet, efficient and determined manner, alongside some of the biggest stars to play for the county. He was then a first-class umpire before retiring after the 2017 season.

Cox, Rupert Michael Fiennes (414) born Guildford 20.8.1967. Rupert Cox was a promising left-handed batsman who had followed Mark Nicholas from Bradfield School but found it difficult to break into the strong Hampshire batting line-up. This was not made easier because he made his first-class debut in 1990, the same season as another left-hander, David Gower. When Gower and Robin Smith went to the Test Match v India in July, Cox made his first-class debut at Arundel, scoring 35* in the second innings, and two weeks later, with Gower and Robin Smith absent again, he scored 104* at Worcester, sharing an undefeated partnership of 161 with Tony Middleton. Gower and Smith then returned for a match at Taunton, and Cox was dropped. He played a few matches each year for five seasons, and as captain of the 2nd XI was seen as a possible successor to Nicholas, but it was not to be. He was one of a number of promising Hampshire youngsters of his generation whose careers never fulfilled their apparent promise.

Crane, Mason Sidney (535) born Shoreham-by-Sea 18.2.1997. He is a leg-break/googly bowler and right-hand batsman, who played at Lancing College, coached by Raj Maru, and played for England under-19s from 2014-2016. He joined Hampshire, and made his debut in all three formats in 2015. He played in three first-class matches for the county that year, and took 5-35 v Warwickshire at the Ageas Bowl, still his best in the Championship. He played more regularly in the following year, taking 31 Championship wickets, but in 2017, in just seven Championship matches, with a best of 5-40 v Somerset in the first of those games. He has often been most effective in T20 matches for Hampshire, and has 21 wickets from 18 games with a good economy rate of 7.25, and he has 32 limited-overs wickets from 20 matches. In 2016/17, he played first-class cricket for New South Wales, the first overseas player to do so for some decades. In 2017, he played for England Lions, then for the full England side in two T20s v South Africa, and in the winter, went on the 'Ashes' tour to Australia, where he made his Test Match debut in the final Test, taking 1-193. He joined the England Lions in the Caribbean but came home with a back problem, which prevented him from playing any first-class matches that season. He did appear in the Royal London Cup, missing only the semi-final but was clearly unfit in the Final and bowled just seven overs (1-53) and that finished his season - with no T20 matches. At the end of the 2018 season, he had played in 24 first-class matches for Hampshire with 61 wickets, plus 47 wickets in limited-overs games for the county and 21 wickets in the T20, at an economy rate of 7.31.

Crawley, Cosmo Stafford (220, Amateur) born Chelsea 27.5.1904, died Westminster 10.2.1989. Right-handed batsman Crawley, came from a large cricketing family and played cricket at Harrow School, then first-class for Oxford University (no 'Blue'), Free Foresters, Harlequins and Middlesex (1929). Six years previously, he played once for Hampshire v Oxford University, just before his 19th birthday, scoring 14 & 8 in a four-wicket defeat. At University, he won 'blues' for Royal Tennis and Rackets.

Crawley, John Paul (457) born Essex, 21.9.1971. Right-handed batsman John Crawley played for Lancashire from 1990-2001 and after leaving in somewhat difficult circumstances joined Hampshire, and on debut at Canterbury scored 272 – the highest innings ever by a debutant for the county, and Hampshire's highest maiden century, yet in his eight seasons, he would exceed it on two further occasions. Although born in Essex, Crawley was educated at Manchester Grammar School. He played at Cambridge University from 1991-1993, captaining them in the last two years, and played for England's age group sides and then in 37 Tests from 1994-2003, scoring 1800 runs with four centuries (HS 156*) and for a player of his ability, a slightly disappointing average of 34.61. He played also in 13 ODIs (HS 73). Overall, he scored just under 25,000 first-class runs at 46.49, and for Hampshire 7,210 runs at 45.06.

Having joined Hampshire at the age of 30, he was a magnificent batsman for his second county. In that debut season, he passed 1,000 runs at an average of 53.80 but in the following year, pressed into deputising for the banned Shane

Warne as captain, he scored just 878 runs at 33.76. He had left Lancashire after being replaced as captain and there was a feeling that captaincy affected his batting, although he did not agree. But when Warne returned in 2004, his average went back above 50 with almost 1,000 runs, including an innings of 301* at Trent Bridge which was just 15 short of Hampshire's highest innings, when they declared. In 2005 against the same opponents, he reached 311*, when Warne declared again, despite having plenty of time to conclude what would be an innings victory, and although Crawley never made Hampshire's highest score, he is the only man to score two triple centuries for the county. He always seemed happiest playing first-class cricket, but he scored 102 in a limited-overs match v Durham in 2003, and two years later he was a member of the Hampshire side that won the C&G Trophy, beating Warwickshire at Lord's. His highest T20 score was just 23, from 10 appearances. He deputised occasionally as a wicketkeeper, in 2005 equalling Hampshire's then record of six victims in an innings; he was also a good short-leg fielder. He retired after the 2009 season, and teaches at Oundle School.

Creese, William Charles Leonard ('Len') (248) born Transvaal, South Africa 27.12.1907, died Dover 9.3.1974. Len Creese was a valuable all-rounder in the Hampshire side of the 1930s, and one of many cricketers whose career was curtailed by the war, which came when he was just 31; he played in 278 first-class matches for the county, but it might have been many more. Creese came to England as a young man in the hope of establishing himself in the county game, from a family that was involved in the administration of cricket in Transvaal for many decades, although his father WH, was born in Monmouthshire and played Minor Counties cricket there before emigrating and playing a couple of first-class games in South Africa. Len Creese's first recorded match is as a schoolboy against a touring side captained by Lionel Tennyson – Creese ended the tourists' innings with just his third ball (1-0) but sadly recorded a 'pair', despite which he became a member of Tennyson's last Hampshire sides. He was a hard-hitting left-handed batsman who scored six centuries for Hampshire between 1933-1939, including 241 v Northamptonshire in that last year, with 37 boundaries. There is some uncertainty about his bowling which was left-handed, but in accounts varies from medium-slow to fast-medium. He did not generally take the new ball and perhaps bowled at a similar pace to Derek Underwood. He took 401 wickets for Hampshire at 27.87 and a best of 8-37 v Lancashire at Southampton in 1936. That was his finest year as a bowler, taking 95 wickets at just under 23 each – and with 1,331 runs was just five victims short of the 'double'. In each season for four years from 1934, he took over 50 wickets and on 13 occasions in those years, he took at least five in an innings; just once he took 10 in the match, against Warwickshire at Bournemouth in 1937, after Dick Moore's record 316 on the first day, as Hampshire won in two.

His first few years at Hampshire were a struggle but he established himself in 1933 with 1,275 runs at what would be his best season's average of 35.41, and he followed this with 909 runs in 1934, and then, scored over one thousand runs in four of the next five years – the exception was an injury-hit season in 1937. In his last two seasons, he took just 70 wickets, but there is some uncertainty as to whether his form slipped, or he was under-used, in a weak Hampshire side. Creese was a fine fielder, holding 190 catches for the county. During the war, he played a number of matches for the Army and in 1946, represented them in two first-class matches. He played also for Dorset from 1949-1951. Subsequently he was a coach at Sherborne School, and then groundsman at Hastings and Hove. His character often matched the exuberance of his batting, but in later years, following a family tragedy, life was less easy.

Crofton, Edward Hugh (Pre '95, Amateur) born Plymouth 7.9.1854, died Dublin, 15.5.1882. He was a batsman who played in three first-class matches for Hampshire in 1881 when a soldier, living in Winchester. Two of his matches were against MCC, the other v Sussex and his career was unremarkable with 32 runs in five innings, to which he added one wicket. He died in Ireland at the start of the following season, age 27, but we have no details of his death.

Crofts, Edmund Sclater (Pre '95, Amateur) born Winchester 23.1.1859, died Bedford 23.12.1938. Crofts was a batsman who attended Winchester College and then Sandhurst. He played one match for Hampshire v MCC at Southampton in 1885, and batting at number three scored 3 & 2, in an innings defeat.

Crookes, John Edward (208, Amateur) born Lincolnshire 7.3.1890, died Surrey, 8.9.1948. Crookes, a sergeant-major in the Army, was principally a batsman, who played regularly for Lincolnshire in 1909 and once in 1910. In July and August 1920, he played in three first-class matches for Hampshire, scoring 1, 3, 36* (in an innings victory v Worcestershire at Portsmouth), 8 & 2. He bowled one over for six runs.

Crowdy, Rev James Gordon (Pre '95, Amateur) born Wiltshire 2.7.1847, died Winchester 16.12.1918. He attended Rugby School and Oxford University but did not play for the University in first-class matches. His debut at that level was for MCC against the University in 1872 and in 1875, 1877, 1882 & 1884 he appeared in six first-class matches for Hampshire. He played also for Gentlemen's teams in Worcestershire, Devon and Hampshire, and in later years for Winchester. In his county career, he played 12 innings with a highest score of 21 v Sussex in 1875, and bowled once, taking 1-31 in the same year.

Cull, George (Pre '95) born Lymington 3.3.1856, died, Sandown IOW 9.5.1898. Cull was a wicketkeeper and batsman who played in a county colts match in April 1877 and then twice in first-class matches for the county in the following month. He scored 14 runs in four innings and held one catch, although in neither match did he keep wicket.

Currie, Cecil Edmund (Pre '95, Amateur) born Berkshire 4.4.1861, died Staines 2.1.1937. Currie came from a cricketing family, and was a lower-order batsman, slow right-arm bowler and fine field. After attending Marlborough College, he was at Cambridge University where in 1883, he played in just two first-class matches (no 'blue'), but his first-class debut was for Hampshire v Sussex at the Antelope Ground in 1871. He played most regularly for Hampshire in 1884 & 1885 and thereafter until 1893, as they lost their first-class status. For the county, he scored 284 first-class runs at 13.52 (best 32) and took 56 wickets at 21.87, including 8-57 v Somerset on his one appearance in 1882, and 5-53 v Sussex in 1885 – both matches were at Southampton and both won by Hampshire. He was a solicitor, at some point based in London.

Curzon, Christopher Colin (389) born Nottinghamshire 22.12.1958. Through the 1980s, Hampshire's wicketkeeper was Bobby Parks, and Curzon, who had played 17 first-class matches for his native county 1978-1980, joined Hampshire as his deputy, playing in just one first-class match v the Sri Lankans at Bournemouth in 1981. He scored 31* and 22 (one catch) and left Hampshire after that season, although he played once for Derbyshire in the 2nd XI Championship, and also in league cricket in Nottinghamshire.

D

Darby, James Herbert (39, Amateur) born Fareham 26.10.1865, died Fareham 7.11.1943. Darby was a middle order batsman who is number 39 for his three appearances in 1897, but played his first Hampshire first-class match v Sussex at Hove in 1884. In his four appearances, he scored 78 runs with a best of 35, and an average of 13.0. He played also for Fareham, Hampshire Rovers and occasionally for Hampshire in second-class matches in the early 1890s.

Dare, Reginald Arthur ('Reg') (318) born Blandford 26.11.1921, died Bournemouth, 10.1993. Reg Dare was a slow-left-arm bowler and useful lower-order batsman who came into the side in 1949, as Hampshire's older spin bowlers, Bailey, Dean, Hill and Knott were approaching their final years. He played in just two matches, but was fairly regular in 1950, scoring his first half-century and taking 43 wickets at 31.53 including 6-28 v Oxford University, which would remain his best figures. In 1951, he played in 12 matches, but scored fewer than 50 runs and took just eight wickets at 71.62. Hampshire persevered with him and in the next two seasons he took exactly 100 wickets at around 34 each. At the end of the 1952 season at Bournemouth, he followed 4-52 with his only century, 109*, v Worcestershire, including a 10th wicket partnership of 117* with Ralph Prouton. In 1954, he began the season in the side, and in mid-May v Derbyshire at Southampton took 5-49, scored 41* and then promoted to number five in a run chase, added a rapid 74 as Hampshire won. He was capped, but by the end of that season, he, Knott and Hill had all played their last first-class match for the county, as the young spinners Sainsbury and Burden took their places. He played 2nd XI matches in 1955 (and one in 1967) and also played in Devon, and from 1958-1963 for Buckinghamshire. He played football for Southampton and Exeter.

Dashwood, Thomas Henry Knyvett (108, Amateur) born Hitchin, Herts, 31.1.1876, died Fulham 24.1.1929. He was a right-handed batsman and good fielder who was educated at Wellington College and Oxford University, where he played first-class cricket in 1899, although no 'blue'. He played first-class matches for RA Bennett's XI on a tour of the Caribbean in 1901/2 and in one week in 1904, in two county matches for Hampshire. He scored 8 & 7 at Leicester, and 7 & 12 at Leeds, and while unimpressive, the latter innings was top score as Hampshire were dismissed for 36, in a defeat by 370 runs. That was the end of his first-class career, although he played in a number of Minor Counties matches for Hertfordshire.

Davey, Joshua Henry (List A) born Aberdeen 3.8.1990. Davey was an all-rounder from Middlesex who guested for Hampshire in a limited-overs match v Bangladesh 'A' at the Ageas Bowl in 2013. He scored 19 and took 1-62, as Hampshire won by eight runs.

Davies, Henry Gwyn Saunders (Pre-'95, Amateur) born Pembroke, Wales 2.2.1865, died Patching, Sussex 4.12.1934. He was a right-handed batsman, sometimes known as Saunders-Davies or Davies-Scourfield. He played cricket at Winchester College and for the South Wales Cricket Club, and in 1883, a first-class match for Hampshire at Hove, top-scoring with 42 in the first innings, but adding just three as Hampshire lost by an innings.

Dawson, Gilbert Wilkinson (309) born Bradford 9.12.1916, died Glasgow 24.5.1969. When Desmond Eagar arrived as captain and secretary after the war, he set about recruiting players to replace members of his ageing side. He looked north for some, and the great success was Derek Shackleton from Todmorden, but he also found two Yorkshiremen, both called Dawson but not related. Of the two, Gilbert was the more successful, coming into the side age 30 in 1947. He was fairly regular for three seasons, playing 60 first-class matches but then left the club. His first season brought mostly modest rewards with one half century and 254 runs in his first 11 games, until in the last match of the season at Bournemouth, he opened the batting and scored 124 against his native county. This seemed to give him confidence; there was another century v Derbyshire at Portsmouth in 1948, and 1229 runs at 23.63. He added two not out centuries in 1949, 106* v Sussex at Hove and his best of 158* v Nottinghamshire at Trent Bridge, and four half centuries as he passed 1,000 runs again and improved his average to 33.29. Approaching his 33rd birthday, however, that was the end of his county career. His final recorded cricket match came in mid-September 1949 in a one day, single-innings match at Bournemouth for Hampshire against a side led by the Duke of Edinburgh. He died in tragic circumstances age just 52, found in his car after a crash, apparently involving no other vehicle.

Dawson, Harold (308) born Todmorden, Yorkshire 10.8.1914, died Todmorden 14.5.1994. Dawson, a right-hand batsman, played for his home town Lancashire League club regularly from 1932-1964 – a long spell interrupted only intermittently in the war, and during his years in southern England with Hampshire, and briefly in Devon. He played in 10 matches for Hampshire in 1947 & 1948, scoring 236 runs at 13.11 with a best of 37 v Cambridge University, and two other scores in the thirties in Championship matches.

Dawson, Liam Andrew (490) born Swindon 1.3.1990. Although from Wiltshire, where his father and brother both played, all-rounder Liam Dawson played for Hampshire's age group sides from his early teens, and also captained England under-19s. He has played for Hampshire in first-class and limited-overs matches since 2007, and T20 since 2008 – his first match, a limited-overs game, was at Northampton when he was just 17 years and six months old, and in September 2008 he scored 100* at Trent Bridge, the youngest man to score a first-class century for Hampshire. He is an all-rounder who bowls slow-left-arm, and a fine fielder whose seven catches at Northampton in 2012 equalled the Hampshire record. In his earlier years in Championship cricket he sometimes seemed to be a batsman who bowled, and in other years the opposite – for example in 2011 he scored 908 runs at 36.32 but took just three wickets, in 2012 there were fewer runs but 26 wickets, and in 2013, 1,060 runs at 48.18, with 11 wickets. In 2015, however, he scored 922 runs at 40.08 and took 29 wickets at 31.93, while in 2017 he had his best bowling year with 37 wickets, including 8-129 in the match at Taunton. In 2018, he scored just under 400 first-class runs with one half-century, but took only 20 wickets and he enjoyed more success in the two 'white ball' tournaments. For Hampshire, by the end of 2018, he had scored 6,299 first-class runs, and taken 171 wickets, while in limited-overs cricket he has 2,488 runs and 87 wickets, and in T20, 982 runs, and 75 wickets at 23.54, with a good economy rate of 7.37. He has played for England in all three formats since 2016, with Test Match bests of 66* v India and 2-34 v South Africa, while in six T20 matches he has a best of 3-27 v Sri Lanka. He went to Sri Lanka with the England side in the autumn of 2018 but after playing in two rain-affected matches, returned home with a side injury.

Day, Harold Lindsay Vernon (218, Amateur) born India 12.8.1898, died Hertfordshire 15.6.1972. Batsman Harold Day was a very talented all-round sportsman, but because of his army career he played just 78 matches over 10 seasons, despite which he scored four centuries and 17 half-centuries. He played for Bedfordshire from 1920-1922 and also for West of Scotland, MCC and Royal Artillery, and made his Hampshire debut v Kent at Southampton in 1922, scoring 56 & 91 on first-class debut (no Hampshire batsman has ever scored a century on his first-class debut, playing for the county). His second innings included a partnership with Mead of 219 in 150 minutes. A week later v Leicestershire he scored 75 and at the end of that season he had passed 1,000 runs at just under 40 each innings and was invited to tour South Africa – a tour which included a number of Hampshire players. Unfortunately, his duties as an officer prevented that and he played in just three matches in the following season. He returned regularly in 1924 with 1,119 runs including a century v the South Africans and his best score of 142 v Somerset at Bath. From 1925-1928 he played occasionally (28 games in total) with a fourth and last century v Middlesex at Bournemouth in 1926, and then disappeared until 1931 when he played in four matches with little success. John Arlott (1957) described him as "natural games player", adding "there was no halfway stage in his batting, it was either free, forcing play or, based on the same quick footwork, careful – even pawky – defence". He was a rugby wing three-quarter, who played for Leicester and England (four Tests, 1920-1926), scoring two international tries, kicking two conversions, and two penalties, and publishing two books on the game.

Dean, Thomas Arthur ('Tom') (295), born Gosport 21.11.1920, died South Africa 4.6.2004. Tom Dean was born in Hampshire but lived most of his life in South Africa. He was one of those cricketers whose career might have been significantly different were it not for the interruption of the war. Still in his teens, he made a considerable impression as a leg-break bowler and superb close fielder in late August 1939 in three matches at Bournemouth: on debut, v Somerset he took his first wicket and made 20* & 8* in an innings defeat, then v Worcestershire 4-38 including a hat-trick, and when Champions Yorkshire arrived, he took 5-58. Hampshire lost all three matches, but Dean had ten wickets at 22.20 each. His next first-class match came after six years away, and the slim teenager, nicknamed 'Split Pin', was a bigger figure who seemed less able to turn the ball so effectively. He played in 13 matches in 1946, but took just 21 wickets, which included 7-51 v Derbyshire at Ilkeston. That remained his best analysis, although he took 6-73 in a first-class match v Combined Services in 1949, but he took only three wickets in three subsequent Championship matches, and his county career came to an end. In the field, he held 31 catches in 28 first-class games, setting a Hampshire record of seven catches in the match v Essex at Colchester in 1947, since equalled by Raj Maru and Liam Dawson. Overall, he took 51 wickets for Hampshire at 31.11. In 1954, he played in the Minor Counties for Devon, and in 1956/7, having returned to South Africa, he played one first-class match for Eastern Province.

Dean, William (136) born Australia circa 1882, we have no further details of names or dates of birth/death. William Dean was a bowler who played in one first-class county match v the South Africans in 1907. He scored 3* in his only innings and bowling only in the second innings, had figures of 21-7-52-2.

Deane, Marmaduke William (12) born Petersham, Surrey 25.3.1857, died Dorking 7.11.1936. He was a wicketkeeper who played one first-class match for Surrey in 1880, and then four matches for Hampshire in 1895. He took six catches and three stumpings, but scored only 15 runs at an average of 5.00. His final match was in July 1895, after which Charles Robson took over as the regular wicketkeeper.

Debnam, Alexander Frederick, Henry (322) born Belvedere, Kent 12.10.1921, died Newcastle-upon-Tyne 26.1.2003. Leg-break bowler Debnam played for his native Kent's 2nd XI from 1946, then in county matches from 1948 (as an amateur) & 1949 (professional) as understudy to Doug Wright. With few opportunities, he came to Hampshire as a professional, making his debut in 1950 v Yorkshire at Portsmouth, taking a wicket and top-scoring with 21 in an innings defeat. He played in 10 matches in two seasons, but took just four first-class wickets for Hampshire. His top score was 64 v Cambridge University in 1951, his final season in first-class cricket.

Delmé-Radcliffe, Arthur Henry (36, Amateur) born South Tidworth, Hampshire 23.11.1870, died Dorset 30.6.1950. He was a right-handed batsman who played second-class matches for Hampshire in 1889, and then in seven first-class matches for the county, one in 1896, five in 1899 and one final game in 1900. In 1897, he played in the Minor Counties for Berkshire. His best score for Hampshire was 43 v Yorkshire, in a nine-wicket defeat at Southampton in 1899. As with a number of occasional amateurs, he played mostly in home matches, with one journey to Old Trafford for a wet, low-scoring draw. His final match for Hampshire was a non-first-class game v the West Indians at Southampton in 1900.

Denham, Harold Alfred (26) born India 13.10.1872, died Eastbourne 25.2.1946. He was a batsman who played some cricket at Sandhurst in the early 1890s, and in one first-class match, a victory v Sussex at Southampton in 1896, scoring 1 & 7. He played matches in Ireland a few years later, including one match for Ireland v the South Africans at Dublin in 1901.

de Wet, Friedel (509) born Durban, South Africa 26.6.1980. Pace bowler de Wet, who played in two Test Matches for South Africa in 2009/10, signed for Hampshire in 2011. He played in four first-class matches in that season, taking nine wickets at 52.22. He did not play in limited-overs or T20 matches.

Dibden, Richard Rockley (428) born Southampton 29.1.1975. Off spinner Richard Dibden played for Hampshire 2nd XI from 1994-1998, and appeared in four first-class matches for Hampshire in 1995, taking six wickets at 71.33 with a best of 2-36 v Yorkshire. In seven innings (two not out) he failed to score a run. In the following season, he played in one first-class match for the British Universities v the Indians. In 2001 & 2002 he played in three limited-overs matches for the Hampshire Cricket Board in the C&G Trophy. He played for some years for BAT Sports, and then Totton & Eling in the Southern League.

Dible, William Guy (Pre '95) born Sholing 5.11.1861, died Fareham 15.8.1894. He was also known as William Charles Dible, and was a fast bowler who played for Surrey in one first-class match v the Australians in 1882. He made his first-class debut for Hampshire in the following season and played regularly in the next three years (25 matches), after which the county lost its first-class status. He was an effective bowler, taking five or more wickets in an innings on five occasions, and ten in the match v Sussex at the Antelope in 1893 (4-16 & 6-50), having already taken 5-69 earlier that season in an innings defeat at Hove. Two years later, again v Sussex, he recorded his best figures of 7-60. He took 90 first-class wickets for Hampshire at 22.17 and continued to play in second-class matches until 1890, but died four years later, age just 32.

Dickinson, Calvin Miles (549) born South Africa 3.11.1996. Dickinson is a wicketkeeper who was educated on the Isle of Wight and at St Edward's

School Oxford, and played for Worcestershire 2nd XI in 2015, Essex 2nd XI in 2016, before joining Hampshire in 2017. While at Oxford Brooks, he made his first-class debut for Oxford University MCCU v Worcestershire in 2016, and in 2017, made his debut for Hampshire v South Africa 'A' and became the only man to score 99 on first-class debut for the county. He played in one Championship match at Uxbridge as a batsman later in the season, while playing more regularly at the top of the order in T20 matches, scoring 51 at Canterbury. In February 2018 he played for Hampshire in six matches in the Caribbean Regional 50 tournament, but during the following domestic season he spent some time with Warwickshire 2nd XI and after just one more T20 match, scoring one run v Gloucestershire, he left Hampshire at the end of that season.

Dighton, Michael Gray (List A) born Queensland, Australia 24.4.1976. Dighton appeared in two limited-overs matches for Hampshire in 2004, while with Greenock CC in Scotland. The two matches, both at Bristol, were played one week apart in May and he top-scored with 74 in the first, a league victory, adding 12 as Hampshire were knocked out of the C&G Trophy. In Australia, he played for Western Australia and Tasmania, and in England for Derbyshire in 2007.

Dixon, Cecil Egerton (253, Amateur) born Scotland 21.7.1903, died Battle, Sussex 3.3.1973. Dixon was a batsman who played at Wellington College and Sandhurst, and represented the Army v Public Schools at Lord's in 1928. In the following year, he played in two matches for Hampshire in late May, scoring just 10 runs in four innings, and both matches, v Gloucestershire and Derbyshire, ended in innings defeats.

Dodd, William Thomas Francis (260) born Steep, Hampshire 8.3.1908, died New Forest 13.2.1993. Dodd was a slow-left arm bowler who had the difficult task of challenging Stuart Boyes for a permanent place during his first-class career from 1931-1935. In the event, he played in just 10 first-class matches, taking 10 wickets at 32.10, with a best of 5-63 v Middlesex on a rain-affected pitch in his penultimate match. Perhaps his best performance was 3-59 v Yorkshire at Hull in June 1935 in a total of 315-5 declared, including a Sutcliffe century; Hampshire lost by an innings in two days. His final match was v Glamorgan at Cardiff in July 1935, and Boyes replaced him in the following game.

Donald, Aneurin Henry Thomas (2019) *born Swansea, 20.12.1996. Right-hand batsman Donald joined Hampshire on loan from Glamorgan late in the 2018 season but appeared only as a substitute; he has signed a full contract from 2019. He played for England under-19s and then Glamorgan from 2014, with a highest first-class score of 234 v Derbyshire in 2016, his only Championship century. He played in more than 100 matches in the three formats for Glamorgan.*

Dorey, Lewis Hugh John (236, Amateur) born St Alban's 23.10.1901, died Surrey 31.7.1958. He attended Harrow School and played in one first-class match for the county v Leicestershire at Ashby-de-la-Zouch in 1925. He batted at number nine, did not bowl and was dismissed twice without scoring in a low-scoring victory for Hampshire.

Down JH (189) we have no further details of name or dates and places of birth/death. He was a slow-left-arm bowler who was on the MCC groundstaff and was selected to play in two matches for Hampshire in one week in June 1914: v Sussex at Horsham, and Worcestershire at Dudley. In his first innings, he scored 31* at number 11 in a partnership of 61, although he bowled just seven overs in a Hampshire victory. In the second game, he took his first wicket as one of nine bowlers in a Worcestershire score of 493, but he did not bowl in the second innings; the match was drawn. Alan Edwards has endeavoured to discover more about him, and believes he might have been Australian, or at least not English. Despite the mystery, he appears in a familiar team photograph from the match at Dudley.

Downer, Harry Rodney (299, Amateur) born Southampton 19.10.1915, died Canada, March 1980. Downer was a right-handed batsman who played in two matches in 1946, but scored just eight runs in four innings. His first match was at Lord's v Middlesex, and he was somewhat unfortunate that the last of the four innings was a run out v Gloucestershire at Southampton, but that was the end of his first-class career. He was an optician, and in 1952 moved to Canada, where he continued to play cricket and field hockey.

Drake, Edward Joseph ('Ted') (261) born Southampton 16.8.1912, died Raynes Park, Surrey 29.5.1995. Ted Drake was principally a batsman, and one of a number of Hampshire cricketers who also played professional football; indeed, he was probably Hampshire's outstanding footballer, although this made it difficult for him to succeed at the summer game. He played in 16 matches for Hampshire from 1931-1936 but with 219 runs in 27 innings his average was below 10; he also took four first-class wickets. His best score of 45 came on debut v Glamorgan at Portsmouth. He played various non-first-class matches during the war years but he was then fully engaged in football, as a forward who played for Southampton and Arsenal and won five England caps. In 1935, he scored all seven of Arsenal's goals v Aston Villa, and the only goal when Arsenal won the FA Cup in the following year. After the war, he managed and coached at various sides, and as manager led Chelsea to their first league title in 1954/5.

Dumbleton, Horatio Norris (Pre '95, Amateur) born India 23.10.1858, died Winchester 18.12.1935. He was a batsman and round-arm bowler most noted for his performances in military matches. At Portsmouth in 1884 he scored 325 for the Royal Engineers v Royal Marines and in that same year he played his single first-class match for Hampshire v Somerset at Bath, scoring seven and nine (run out) in an innings defeat (also 0-14). His last recorded matches in the 1890s were in Hong Kong, where he designed the course at the Royal Golf Club.

Duncan, Arthur James (Pre '95, Amateur) born Southampton 21.11.1856, died London 26.8.1936. He was a batsman who played twice in first-class matches for Hampshire at the Antelope, with a gap of five years: v Kent in 1878 (0 & 2), and v Sussex in 1883 (0 & 26). He played alongside his brother (DWJ, below) in the former.

Duncan, Dunbar Wilson Johnston (Pre '95, Amateur) born Southampton 8.7.1852, died London 12.12.1919. He was principally a batsman who played for Hampshire more frequently than his younger brother – in 17 matches from 1875-1885 he scored 581 runs at 22.34 with a best of 87* v Somerset in 1884, and also three half-centuries v Kent (best 75) in 1876 & 1877. He had played non-first-class matches in the county, particularly for the Gentlemen of South Hampshire, from 1870 when still in his teens. His last recorded matches were at Lord's in 1905.

Duthie, Arthur Murray (158, Amateur) born India 12.6.1881, died Dorset 3.6.1973. He was an opening bowler who attended Marlborough School, and played in army matches for the Royal Engineers before appearing in one match for Hampshire v Derbyshire at Southampton in 1911. He took 3-85 & 2-56, and scored 1& 5 in a Hampshire victory.

Dutton, Henry John (Pre '95, Amateur) born London 17.1.1847, died Hinton-Ampner House, Hampshire 1.1.1935. After attending Eton, he played in one match for Hampshire in 1875, which Kent won by an innings, after scoring 333 (Dutton 9-7-8-0) while Hampshire were dismissed for 34 & 82, with Dutton undefeated in both innings scoring 0* & 7*. In the same year, he is recorded as playing for the Portsmouth Garrison XI.

E

Eagar, Edward Desmond Russell (297, Amateur) born Cheltenham 8.12.1917, died Devon 13.9.1977. As a Hampshire cricketer Desmond Eagar had a fairly modest record: he was essentially a batsman and in 311 first-class matches he scored just over 10,000 runs at an average of 21.02 with eight centuries in 12 seasons. Including 1939, pre-Hampshire, he passed 1,000 runs in six seasons, but as a player his outstanding contribution was taking catches close to the wicket – mainly short-leg – and he is one of the few regular Hampshire cricketers to average better than one catch per match. At Oxford University Eagar took 16 wickets in 23 games, bowling slow-left-arm, but with Hampshire he took just 15 in total.

Beyond that playing record, however, Eagar was one of the most important figures in Hampshire's history. At the age of 14 he played first at Lord's, against an Elementary Schools XI, for whom a young Denis Compton scored a century, and he played county cricket for his native Gloucestershire in 1935 age just 17 (and in 21 matches from 1935-1939). After Oxford University ('blue' in 1939) and war service, he applied successfully for the twin roles of captain and secretary at Hampshire, and by combining them retained his amateur status on the field. As with many counties, he inherited an ageing side of men returning from war and initially sought to introduce fresh blood recruiting amateurs, but the austere 1940s and early 1950s hardly helped that approach, so he set about assembling a group of good professionals from elsewhere, occasionally overseas, and crucially a core of promising local youngsters. Reflecting his own skills, he insisted on high standards of fielding, and appointed one of his pre-war professionals Arthur Holt as coach.

As captain his great year was 1955. Colin Ingleby-Mackenzie deputised for Leo Harrison in one match, otherwise Eagar led just 13 men to third place in the Championship for the first time. Those 13 included six Hampshire-born, home-grown players, Gray, Burden, Sainsbury, Barnard, Heath, and Harrison plus Vic Cannings, recruited from Warwickshire but Hampshire-born. In the next two years, Eagar gave Ingleby-Mackenzie opportunities to develop his captaincy skills and the young man took over in 1958, at which point Eagar became full-time secretary and saw his efforts come to fruition in 1958 (second place) and 1961 (Champions). That side was ageing, so he set about building another, with men like Jesty, Turner, Greenidge, Lewis and his apparent successor Richard Gilliat in the role of captain and Assistant Secretary. In 1973 Eagar saw that side win a second title and they had begun to win limited-overs titles when he died unexpectedly, while on holiday at the end of the 1977 season. Eagar was a great collector of cricket literature and cricketana and an expert on cricket history, and he played university and county standard hockey, reporting on it for the *Telegraph* newspapers. But he will be remembered very fondly, primarily as the chief architect of the fine Hampshire sides of the first three post-war decades. John Arlott (1958) speculated that even after retiring, Eagar would lead out a side somewhere and "demonstrate that cricket is by no means a restful pursuit, but a fever, a problem, a challenge, and a wholly absorbing task".

Eccles, Charles Vernon (Pre '95, Amateur) born Cheshire 20.8.1843, died India 21.2.1890. He was a right-hand batsman and occasional lob bowler who attended Cheltenham College and in 1870 & 1875 played in two first-class matches for the county, scoring 36 runs in four innings. There is an extensive record of his minor matches for clubs like I Zingari, and teams in the county from 1863-1879; by 1881 he was in India, and played one match for Poona v Bombay. His brother (WH) played for MCC, and was Hon Secretary of Hampshire, 1867-1869, but did not play for Hampshire.

Ede, Edward Lee (Pre-95, Amateur) born Southampton 22.2.1834, died Southampton 7.7.1908. He made his first-class debut for Hampshire v MCC in 1861, two years before the founding of the County Club, and from their first match in 1864 he was a regular, playing in all 14 matches against other counties up to 1870. He was also a member of the founding Committee, sometimes deputising for his twin brother (GM) as acting secretary, and was subsequently the county's scorer, and editor of the Hampshire Cricket Guide. The twin brothers opened the batting in Hampshire County Cricket Club's inaugural first-class match v Sussex in 1864. He was educated at Eton although he did not play for the first XI, but played regularly for the Gentlemen of Hampshire, before and after the founding of the county club. He was an all-rounder who batted, bowled lobs, and kept wicket. He enjoyed considerable success in the many 'minor' matches he played, while in first-class cricket his highest score was 49 v Kent at Southborough in 1867, and his best figures were 4-79 v Sussex at Hove in 1864. His son played for Hampshire in the early years of the twentieth century. For a more complete biography of the brothers see Alan Edwards (2014) *Hampshire's First Eleven*.

Ede, Edward Murray Charles (99, Amateur) born Southampton 24.4.1881, died Sydney, Australia 23.7.1936. The son of EL and like him a pupil at Eton, he was a lower-order batsman who played in 14 first-class matches for Hampshire from 1902-1906, scoring 218 runs at 12.11. He was more effective with the ball, taking 38 wickets at just under 30 each, with a best of 7-72 v Derbyshire in a drawn match at Derby 1905, and 5-49 v Surrey in 1906, despite a heavy defeat. That match was also CP Mead's Championship debut. His final first-class match was the historic game at Broadhalfpenny Down, for Hambledon v England in

1908, although he did not bowl. In 1924, he was convicted of fraud, and after serving his sentence, emigrated to Australia.

Ede, George Matthew (Pre '95, Amateur) born Southampton 22.2.1834, died Liverpool 13.3.1870. He was principally a batsman, bowling less than his brother, although in first-class cricket his 257 runs came at an average below 10 apiece with just one half-century v Sussex at Hove in 1864. He has a particular place in Hampshire's history as the first man to score a century at the Antelope Ground – 122 for the South of the county v the East, and on the same ground he and his brother played v the Australian Aborigines in 1868. In first-class matches, he captained Hampshire between 1864-1869 and was secretary during the same period, but struggled to find the time to devote to his duties. He was also an experienced steeplechase jockey, but this was to prove his downfall. In 1868, he rode to victory in the Grand National, but having raced in it again in 1870, he accepted another ride at Aintree the following day, and the horse fell, crushing him, and causing injuries from which he died three days later.

Edwards, Fidel Henderson (531) born Barbados, 6.2.1982. Edwards is a fast bowler from the Caribbean who made his debut for Hampshire in 2015, having played in all three formats for the West Indies (55 Test Matches). In 2015, his 45 Championship wickets at 20.88 played a major part in ensuring that Hampshire (just) escaped relegation, while in the following season when they were reprieved only by the Durham penalty, he suffered an injury in a pre-match warm-up and took just three wickets, missing all but the first two games. He returned in 2017 and took 33 wickets, then in 2018 was Hampshire's leading Championship wicket-taker with 54 at 26.72. His best for Hampshire remains 6-88 in the vital match at Trent Bridge that ended the 2015 season. At the end of the 2018 season, he had 135 first-class wickets for Hampshire (25.36), plus 31 in limited-overs matches and eight T20 wickets.

Eggar, John Drennan (291, Amateur) born India 1.12.1916, died, Hinton St George, Somerset 3.5.1983. He attended Winchester College and Oxford University, obtaining his 'blue' in 1938 when, in August, he also played in two matches for Hampshire. The first was a drawn match at Worcester in which he batted once for 28, followed by a defeat at Cheltenham (10 & 0). After the war, he played in 31 matches for Derbyshire, and scored 219 v Yorkshire at Bradford in 1949.

Elms, Richard Burtenshaw (379) born Sutton, 5.4.1949. He was a left-arm pace bowler who played for Kent in 55 first-class matches from 1970-1976, before moving to Hampshire, where he played 17 matches in two seasons. Perhaps his biggest impact at Southampton came in the final match of the 1973 season with Hampshire celebrating their Championship title. Kent scored 322 and in reply, Richards & Greenidge took Hampshire to 241, just eight runs short of their (then) record opening partnership, when a ball from Elms fractured Richards' cheek and he retired hurt – Elms recorded a 'pair' in the drawn match and took 1-112. For Hampshire, his highest first-class score was 48 v Derbyshire in 1978 and his best bowling, 4-83 against his former county, at Canterbury in 1977 – overall his 27 wickets cost 37.59 each. He played in eight limited-overs matches for Hampshire, taking seven wickets.

Emery, Kevin St John Dennis (391) born Swindon 28.2.1960. Pace bowler Kevin Emery made a considerable impact in his debut season of 1982, taking 83 first-class wickets at 23.72; three times taking five or more wickets in an innings, with 10 in the match v Glamorgan at Portsmouth, including his best of 6-51 (& 4-50). He was selected for England 'B' (effectively England Lions) and seemed to have a highly promising future, but sadly in the following season, he struggled with injuries and loss of form, and in six first-class matches he took just five wickets at 52.40. He had played regularly in limited-overs matches in 1982, taking 27 wickets at less than 25 each, but in the following two seasons he played just two more such games, with an aggregate analysis of 11-0-48-0. His final match for Hampshire was in the B&H Cup at Bristol in May 1984; in a matter of just two years, he had come and gone. Like his father, he played for Wiltshire, before joining Hampshire, and he continued to do so through the 1980s.

English, Edward Apsey (49, Amateur) born Dorking 1.1.1864, died Tiverton, Devon, 5.9.1966. A batsman, English played in 18 matches for Hampshire from 1898-1901, scoring 565 runs at an average of 18.83 – a modest record, despite which he was 'capped', a not uncommon occurrence with amateurs. Later in life he was notable as the first man to play for Hampshire in the County Championship to reach his personal century, and at the age of 102, was then believed to be the oldest English first-class cricketer. His major contribution on the field came against his native Surrey at the Oval in 1898 in his second first-class match. Hampshire trailed by 56 on first innings, and slumped to 21-4, until English (98) and Webb (67*) put together a stand of 164, ended when Tom Richardson bowled English with the first ball of the final over, just two runs short of his century. There would be one more half-century v Essex in the following season. Returning to the Oval for his only match in 1901, he was dismissed for a 'pair', the conclusion of his first-class career. The *Hampshire Handbook* carried a feature on English to celebrate when he eventually reached his century.

Ervine, Sean Michael (475) born Zimbabwe 6.12.1982. Ervine, is a left-handed batsman who came to Hampshire as a pace-bowling all-rounder in 2005, but following an injury became increasingly a specialist batsman. His first match at the Rose Bowl was the inaugural international there, playing for Zimbabwe v South Africa. In his first season for Hampshire he scored centuries in the semi-final and final of the C&G Trophy which Hampshire won, in 2009, his 167* v Ireland was the highest limited-overs score at the Rose Bowl, while in 2010 he hit his best score of 237* v Somerset at the Rose Bowl, the highest innings by any Hampshire batsman in the lower half of the order. In 2009, 2010 &

2014 he averaged over 40 in first-class cricket, and in 2016, in his benefit season, passed 1,000 runs for the first time at 57.36. With the ball, he took 42 wickets in his first county season but never reached 30 after that, and from 2015-2017, took just 18 wickets. He played in just one Championship match in 2018, went briefly to Derbyshire and then his career ended, not entirely happily. He played in 188 first-class matches for Hampshire, scoring 9,040 runs at 35.17 and taking 214 wickets (43.16). In limited-overs games he added 154 matches, 3,842 runs and 109 wickets plus 2,518 runs and 50 wickets in 144 T20 matches. He played in five trophy-winning sides at Hampshire, in 2005, 2009, 2010 and 2012 (twice) and with the Division Two Champions of 2014.

Evans, Sir Alfred Englefield (196, Amateur) born South Africa 30.1.1884, died 29.12.1944. He was once recorded as having died in Dorset, but subsequently over the north Atlantic after an aeroplane from Canada went missing. He was a right-arm medium-pace bowler who played most of his first-class cricket for the Royal Navy, in which service he rose to the rank of Vice-Admiral. He came from a cricketing family, including two brothers, DM (Hampshire) & WHB (Hampshire & Worcestershire), an uncle AH (Hampshire & Somerset) and two cousins, AJ (Hampshire, Kent & England) and R duB (Hampshire) - their details follow. AE Evans played in five first-class matches for Hampshire in 1919 and 1920 when already in his mid-thirties – four of those were in 1919 when all first-class county games took place over two days. He took 14 wickets at 29.07 including a best of 4-74 v Surrey at the Oval against whom he also made his top score for the county, 47 at Southampton. His final match for Hampshire was v Middlesex at Lord's in 1920 and his final first-class match came five years later on the same ground for the Royal Navy v the Army.

Evans, Alfred Henry (Pre '95, Amateur) born India 14.6.1858, died Devon 26.3.1934. He was a good pace bowler and useful lower-order batsman, who won his Oxford University 'blue' in four years 1878-1881, captaining them in the last year, before playing six first-class matches for Somerset (1882-1884) and then three matches for Hampshire in 1885 before they lost their first-class status. He was at that time, a master at Winchester College. In all first-class cricket, his 44 matches brought 908 runs at 13.75, with three half-centuries, and his pace bowling, 204 wickets at 16.08; 20 times taking five wickets in an innings, including 9-59 for an England XI v Richard Daft's American XI. His best bowling for Hampshire was 4-47 and his highest score 33, both v Sussex at Southampton, a match that Hampshire won. He played briefly for Hampshire in non-first-class matches after 1885, and also for MCC and I Zingari. At Oxford, he also won his rugby 'blue'.

Evans, Alfred John (145, Amateur) born Highclere, Hampshire 1.5.1889, died London 18.9.1960. Another of the Evans family, he was a good all-round cricketer who captained Oxford University, and played in seven matches for Hampshire between 1908-1920. He then played for Kent in 36 matches from 1921-1928 and in his first year with them he appeared in his one Test Match, v Australia, and was dismissed twice by McDonald, scoring 4 & 14. For Hampshire, he scored two half centuries in a total of 307 runs at an average 27.90, and he took five wickets. During the war, he won fame for his escape exploits as a German prisoner of war, and afterwards wrote two books on the subject.

Evans, Bertram Sutton (74, Amateur) born Charterhouse, Surrey 17.12.1872, died Paris 2.3.1919. He is not one of the Evans family described here. He played in just five matches for Hampshire from 1900-1909, his appearances limited by his naval career. He did not bowl and scored just 67 runs at 11.16, with a highest score of 18*.

Evans, Dudley MacNeil (115, Amateur) born South Africa 11.12.1886, died Petersfield 18.12.1972. He was an all-rounder, and another member of the Evans cricketing family. After attending Winchester College where he played in the first XI, he appeared in 15 first-class matches for Hampshire, in 1904, 1905 and mainly, 1911. He scored 382 runs at an average just below 16, with two fifties and a best of 64 v Yorkshire, while bowling medium-pace he took 55 wickets at 26.34, including five or more wickets in an innings on four occasions. His best bowling was 6-81 v Derbyshire at Southampton in a match Hampshire won by just 20 runs, as Derbyshire lost their last two wickets to Evans for just four runs. Both of these best performances came in 1911, when he played 12 of his matches, and he finished with 50 first-class wickets at 24.86.

Evans, James (179) born Shropshire 9.11.1891, died Upham, Hampshire, 26.8.1973. He was principally a batsman and occasional wicketkeeper. His best score of 41 came on debut v MCC at Lord's, his only appearance in 1913, and he appeared in the same fixture in 1914. He then played in 11 matches in 1920 and twice more in 1921, as a batsman, but his overall first-class average was just 10.31. In those post-war years, his best score was 23*, and he managed double figures just four times in 22 innings. He did nonetheless play at Headingley in 1920 when Hampshire recorded a great victory against Yorkshire, losing just two wickets, and winning by an innings. Evans had started that season opening the batting, by then was at number nine or ten, and in that game, was not required.

Evans, Ralph du Boulay (173, Amateur) born Newtown, Hampshire 1.10.1891, died in a road accident in Los Angeles 27.7.1929. Another member of the Evans cricketing family, he attended Winchester College and at the age of 20, played one first-class for Hampshire at Leyton. Batting at number 10, he was 4* at the close of the first day (Hampshire 353-8 dec) but it then rained for two days, there was no further play, and he did not represent the county again. He played in four further first-class matches, three for Cambridge University in 1913 (no 'blue') and once in 1914 for Free Foresters v the University. Unusually, one of the first-class matches in 1913 v LG Robinson's side, was contested between two teams of twelve players, and Evans made his best score of 70.

Evans, William Henry Brereton (95, Amateur) born South Africa 29.1.1883, died in a flying accident at Farnborough 7.8.1913. Another of the cricketing family, he played in 20 first-class matches for Hampshire from 1902-1910. He attended Malvern College and played once for Worcestershire in 1901 age 18, then won his 'blue' at Oxford University in the four seasons, 1902-1905 (captain 1904). His cricket was limited by his career in the Egyptian Civil Service, otherwise he might have been selected by England. For Hampshire, he scored 940 runs at 26.85 with four half-centuries, and 115 v his first county, Worcestershire at Worcester in 1904. He also took 45 wickets at 33.13 including 7-59 v Gloucestershire at Bristol in 1909 while Gilbert Jessop scored 161 (and in the second innings 129) in a total of 295 all out. At Oxford, he also obtained his football 'blue' and was a fine rackets player.

Exton, Rodney Noel (304, Amateur) born Bournemouth 28.12.1927, died London 22.12.1999. He was a batsman who played four matches in the first year after the war as Desmond Eagar sought to bolster an ageing side with amateur players. At the time, he was still at school and playing in the Clifton College XI. Sadly, in his four county matches, he started with a 'duck' and scored just 39 runs at an average below ten, with a best of 24* v Yorkshire at Bournemouth in the last Championship match of the season, when Hampshire inflicted a surprising defeat on the newly-crowned champions. His final first-class match came in the same week v Surrey at Kingston, first-class but not Championship, and held to raise funds for playing fields. In his history of the club, Eagar (1957) recorded how Exton was then "struck down with a dangerous illness" and was never fit to play first-class cricket again, although he played for the Forty Club in the 1970s.

F

Fellowes, James (Pre '95, Amateur) born South Africa 25.8.1841, died Essex 3.5.1916. Fellowes was another of the professional soldiers who played for Hampshire and, as he moved postings, also for other counties. He played most of his cricket for the Royal Engineers and made his first-class debut for MCC in 1870. He had played for Devon the previous season, in 1873-1881 played for Kent and from 1883-1885 played in 11 first-class matches for Hampshire. He continued to play for them after they lost their first-class status, and was also secretary from 1883-1886. He was a founder of two notable club sides, the Devon Dumplings and the Hampshire Hogs. He was principally a fast, round-arm bowler, and took 11 wickets for Hampshire at 35.72 with a best of 3-38. His highest score was 26.

Feltham, Walter George (Pre '95) born Ringwood 23.4.1864, died Ringwood 23.9.1904. He was a left-arm fast bowler who played in three matches for the county in 1884, taking 12 wickets at 21.16. His best figures were 4-54 & 3-41 in an innings victory v Somerset at the Antelope Ground, Southampton, but he never played for Hampshire again, except in a non-first-class match v Uppingham Rovers in the following week.

Fenley, Stanley (272) born Kingston-upon-Thames 4.1.1896, died Bournemouth 2.9.1972. Fenley was a leg-break bowler who played in 116 first-class matches for Surrey from 1924-1929 (345 wickets at 28.70). In 1935, at the age of 39 he appeared in three matches for Hampshire, but took just one wicket, on his county debut at Trent Bridge.

Fielder, Albert Edward (159) born Sarisbury Green 3.4.1889, died Southampton 29.4.1947. He was a fast-medium bowler who played two matches in a week in 1911 and a third in May 1913. On debut at the Oval he took 5-128 in a Surrey innings of 499, in which every Surrey player reached double figures but no one reached a century. In his next match, he scored 35 in a last-wicket partnership of 147 with his captain EM Sprot (125*) and concluded the Gloucestershire innings with his second ball. In his remaining brief time in first-class cricket, he scored one run but took no more wickets.

Fielder, Walter George (225) born Fareham 6.3.1899, died Sarisbury Green 7.1.1968. Although there is a link to AE Fielder with the Fareham/Sarisbury Green area, it appears they were not related. WG Fielder played in one drawn match in 1923 at Leicester scoring 2* and taking 0-26 in the one Leicestershire innings of 466-8 declared.

Fisher, Reginald Wordsworth Cecil (50, Amateur) born Lincolnshire 17.4.1872, died Hemel Hempstead 31.12.1939. He played in one match at Old Trafford in 1898 and batting at number nine scored three runs in a drawn match, with no play on the first day, and one over on the last. He did not bowl in the Lancashire innings of 195.

Flint, Darren Peter John (419) born Basingstoke 14.6.1970. Slow-left-arm bowler Darren Flint was one of a number of promising Hampshire cricketers, in the early 1990s, of whom Aymes, Udal and (briefly) Ayling, established themselves in the county side, while others were unable to build a full career. That was the case with Flint who, in 1993, took 5-32 on debut at Bristol in a thrilling game that resulted in a victory for Hampshire by one wicket (Flint 1*). Those bowling figures are among the best on first-class debut in Hampshire's history, and he played nine further matches in that first season. After this there were just three matches in 1994, two in 1995 and overall in his 15 matches he took 34 wickets at 38.76. He played for Wiltshire in 1996, and for Winchester in the Southern League, and in his native north Hampshire he has become a respected coach, especially of spin bowling.

Flood, Raymond David ('Ray') (336) born Southampton 20.11.1935, died Lyndhurst 13.3.2014. Batsman Ray Flood was born in Southampton, but spent much of his life in the New Forest, a member of a sporting family including his brother John who played football for Southampton FC. Ray Flood first played in the two matches of the Portsmouth week in August 1956, v Essex with Trevor Bailey and Northamptonshire with Frank Tyson, and scored just 26 runs in three innings. In the very wet summer of 1958, he played just once at the end of the season, scoring 7 & 0 but in 1959, with sunshine and experimental covered pitches he seemed to have made his breakthrough. Despite the arrival of Dennis Baldry and Danny Livingstone, he played in 20 matches, scoring 780 runs at 25.16, including 138 v Sussex at Hove – his one first-class century. Sadly, he then struggled with injury, and having top-scored with 72 opening the batting v Oxford University in 1960, his county career came to an end, age just 24. He played club and representative cricket in the New Forest area for some years.

Foley, Jake Matthew (List A) born Colchester 21.9.1994. Jake Foley is a leg-spin bowler who played in one limited-overs match v Sri Lanka 'A' at the Ageas Bowl in 2014. The match was abandoned after 18 overs, and he neither batted nor bowled. He played in the Southern League for South Wilts.

Forster, Harold Thomas (157, Amateur) born Winchester 14.11.1878, killed in action, France 29.5.1918. He was a slow-medium left-arm bowler who made his county debut at Lord's in May 1911, where MCC won a thrilling match against the county by one wicket, despite Forster's match figures of 9-92 (5-38 & 4-54). He played four more times in that season, but took only one more wicket. Col-Sgt Forster was another of Hampshire's Army cricketers; he was awarded the DSO and Bar, the MC and Bar, and was five times Mentioned in Dispatches, making him the most decorated of English county cricketers.

Forster, Henry William (13, Amateur) born London 31.1.1866, died London 15.1.1936. He attended Eton and Oxford University ('blue' 1887-1889) and played first-class cricket for Hampshire in 1885 and then again twice in June when they regained first-class status in 1895. In his five county matches he scored 76 runs and took five wickets, but he had an extensive first-class career playing in 43 matches for nine sides, mainly the University. He was President of MCC in 1919 and Kent in 1921, he represented Sevenoaks as an MP from 1892-1919, was Governor General of Australia from 1919-1925, and in 1919 was created Lord Forster of Lepe.

Foster, Francis George (Pre '95, Amateur) born Havant 6.11.1848, died Canada 10.12.1931. He was a right-handed batsman who played one match for Hampshire v Derbyshire at the Antelope in 1876, scoring 10 & 2. He played minor matches in the county from 1868-1889.

Fowler, Robert St Leger (228, Amateur) born Co. Meath Ireland 7.4.1891, died Co. Meath, Ireland 13.6.1925. He was a right-handed batsman and off-break bowler who pursued a military career while playing first-class cricket for various sides, including three matches for Hampshire in 1924, but is best remembered for a two-day schoolboy match at Lord's in 1910, captaining Eton v Harrow. He made 21 in Eton's first innings of 67 all out and 64 in their second innings of 219 – both times top-scoring. He also took 4-90 in the first Harrow innings of 232, and when they batted again needing just 55 to win, Fowler took 8-23 as they fell ten runs short. For Hampshire, he scored one half-century, 51, on his return to Lord's v Middlesex, and took four wickets, including 3-68 in the return match at Portsmouth. He played most frequently for the Army, including a best of 92* v MCC and 7-22 v Royal Navy. He was appointed to captain MCC to West Indies in 1924/5, but the tour was postponed by one year, and Fowler died age just 34 in the interim.

Fox, Dr Thomas Colcott (Pre '95, Amateur) born Broughton, Hants 13.6.1849, died London 11.4.1916. He played two matches for Hampshire in 1875, scoring 10 runs in four innings and taking 0-26. In the 1870s he played other non-first-class matches for the Gentlemen of Hampshire, and in the following decade for Incogniti CC.

Francis, John David (456) born Bromley 13.11.1980. John Francis and his older brother Simon were promising Hampshire cricketers, both having developed through the county's age group sides. John played for Loughborough University and British Universities but after a short career at Hampshire, he and his brother both moved to Somerset before leaving the first-class game. John was a batsman who played in 17 matches from 2001-2003, scoring five half-centuries with a best of 82 at Leicester in 2002. While his Hampshire career coincided with the difficulties experienced by many young batsman on the new Rose Bowl pitches, he was particularly successful in limited-overs matches, scoring 818 runs at 40.90, including 103* from 87 balls v Northamptonshire in late September 2002, as Hampshire won with three balls to spare. He played at Somerset regularly from 2004-2006 but after just three first-class matches in 2007 and April 2008, his career ended, age just 27. In 2013, back in Hampshire, he played for St Cross.

Francis, Simon Richard George (440) born Bromley 15.8.1978. Simon, older brother of JD, was a pace bowler who came through Hampshire's junior sides, represented England under-19 and played at Durham University. He played first-class cricket for Hampshire from 1997-2000 and in the 2nd XI for one further season, before moving to Somerset where he played from 2002-2006, and then briefly for Nottinghamshire in the following season. In 14 first-class matches for Hampshire he took 24 wickets at 45.79 including a best of 4-95 in a thrilling match v Surrey at the Oval in 2000. Hampshire, chasing 266 to win were 173-9 when Francis joined Mascarenhas; he scored 30* and Hampshire reached 263 before Mascarenhas (59) was caught-and-bowled by Alex Tudor, and Surrey won by two runs. Francis ended his first-class career, not yet 30, with 136 wickets – in limited-overs matches he enjoyed little success until he joined Somerset. He is Director of Cricket at Warwick School.

Frederick, Sir Edward Boscawen (106, Amateur) born Shropshire 29.6.1880, died London 26.10.1956. He was a slow-left-arm bowler who played at Eton and in his early twenties, five matches for the weak Hampshire sides of 1903 & 1904. He took nine wickets at 36.77, including 3-44 in a heavy defeat v Leicestershire in 1904, while his 32 runs for the county came at an average below seven. He played non-first-class cricket for a variety of sides including MCC, Eton Ramblers, Sandhurst College, the Royal Fusiliers and the First Army Corps (at Aldershot).

Frederick, John St John (Pre '95, Amateur) born London 6.1.1846, died Camberley 10.9.1907. He was the uncle of EB Frederick (above) and played for Oxford University 1864-1867 and for Hampshire between 1864-1869, although only once after 1866. He was principally a batsman although he bowled fast, round-arm. In five matches for Hampshire, he averaged 17.10 with a best score of 44 (& 39) v Middlesex in a 10-wicket defeat at the Antelope Ground in 1864. He took wickets in only one first-class match, but his 4-45 v Middlesex was the best analysis for Hampshire in that first season. His last recorded match was for MCC in 1888.

Freemantle, Frederick William (78) born St Mary Bourne, Hampshire 27.6.1871, died Stockbridge 12.9.1943. He was an opening bowler who played two matches for Hampshire in August 1900 without taking a wicket. On debut, he batted at number 10, but promoted to open, scored 26 in the second innings. In the next match, he scored 0 & 2. Hampshire lost both games.

Frere, Henry Tobias (Pre '95, Amateur) born Odiham 27.9.1830, died Westbourne 15.8.1881. He played a first-class match for Hampshire v All England in 1850, and played in Hampshire County Cricket Club's inaugural first-class match v Sussex in 1864. He was described as a fast, round-arm bowler and in six matches for Hampshire, took six wickets and scored 92 runs at 10.22 each, with a best of 23. After playing first-class for Hampshire for three seasons, he appeared once for Sussex, probably due to domestic circumstances, and he also played for various Gentlemen's XIs. Alan Edwards (2014) records that in non-first-class cricket he was particularly successful v the All England XI with 35 wickets in nine games. In 1873, he played at Southsea for the East Hants Club v the United South of England XI, in whose side WG Grace made his first appearance in Hampshire – Grace scored 49 & 11 and took 4-42 and 8-53 against the 22 players of the home side in a drawn match.

Fry, Charles Anthony (345, Amateur) born Henley-in-Arden, Warwickshire 14.1.1940. A batsman, Charles was the third generation of his family to play for Hampshire (see below), appearing in five first-class matches for Hampshire in 1960 at the end of the Oxford University term. He went to Repton, and then won his 'blue' over three years 1959-1961, scoring two first-class centuries, but his brief period with Hampshire was not particularly successful, with 134 runs at 16.75 and a best of just 38 on county debut at Trent Bridge. In 1962, he played in one championship match for Northamptonshire. His last first-class match was for Free Foresters v Oxford University in 1968. He was President of MCC in 2003.

Fry, Charles Burgess (147, Amateur) born Croydon 25.4.1872, died London 7.9.1956. As a county cricketer, Fry's finest achievements were with Sussex for whom he played 236 first-class matches from 1894-1908 (captain 1904-1908), but even in his relatively short time with Hampshire, playing 44 matches from 1909-1921, he was an outstanding performer. He moved counties after taking up a post in the Hamble River on the training ship HMS Mercury; beyond cricket, he is one of the most remarkable figures in British sporting and social history, sufficiently talented to have been a triple 'blue' at Oxford University in cricket, football and athletics, and only missing a rugby 'blue' through injury. In football, he went on to represent England and Southampton FC (in a Cup Final) and once held the world long-jump record.

He played in 26 Test Matches for England with two centuries, captaining them in the 1912 Triangular series v South Africa and Australia – by this time he was also a selector, and is perhaps the only undefeated official England captain.

For Hampshire, his first-class average of 58.90 exceeds all their other major batsmen, and included 14 centuries (two doubles) and 15 half-centuries in 72 innings. His highest score in first-class cricket for any side was 258* for Hampshire v Gloucestershire at Southampton in 1911, having scored 123 & 112 v Kent at Canterbury in his previous two innings. He played most frequently for Hampshire in 1911 & 1912 (37 matches). After the war, there were two matches in 1920 and seven in 1921. In November 1921, his magnificent first-class career ended with two matches for the Europeans in India. In later life, he was India's representative at the League of Nations, he became a cricket correspondent, and was once invited to become King of Albania – he declined.

Fry, Stephen (217, Amateur) born Portsmouth 23.5.1900, died London 18.5.1979. He was the son of CB and father of CA (above); a batsman, occasional wicketkeeper and occasional captain. He played in 29 first-class matches for Hampshire in 1922 and then 1929-1931, scoring 508 runs at 10.58, with one half-century, 78 v Warwickshire at Edgbaston in 1929, when he opened with George Brown in the second innings. His last recorded non-first-class match, was for MCC v India Gymkhana at Lord's in 1934.

Fuller, James Kerr (2019) born Cape Town, South Africa, 24 January 1990. Fuller is a right-handed all rounder who bowls fast-medium. He has played in New Zealand for Otago and Auckland and in England for Gloucestershire (2011-2015) and Middlesex (2016-2018). Through his career he has played most often in T20 matches scoring 547 runs at 21.03 and taking 94 wickets at 23.91 and an economy rate of 8.90. He has joined Hampshire for the 2019 season.

Fynn, Charles Garnet (258, Amateur) born London 24.4.1897, died Bournemouth 26.8.1976. He was a leg-break & googly bowler who played in nine matches for Hampshire in 1930 & 1931. Before the war, he had been a young fast bowler but injured in conflict, he was told he would not bowl again. Instead he converted to spin, and at the age of 33, had a remarkable first-class debut, taking two wickets in his first over v Lancashire, the eventual Champions. His best figures of 3-92, came at Canterbury in 1930, a season when he took 10 wickets, but there was only one more in the following year. He enjoyed subsequently a full career in Bournemouth club cricket, being one of the founders of Bournemouth Amateurs, and in recent years his son Lionel, also a good local cricketer, produced his father's county cap, showing he was so rewarded.

G

Gale, Henry (Pre '95, Amateur) born Winchester 11.7.1836, died Bournemouth 3.3.1898. Gale was a right-handed batsman who played at Marlborough School, and then in five matches for Hampshire in 1865 & 1866, scoring 144 runs at an average of 18.00. His best score of 44 was on debut v Middlesex at Islington when Hampshire were dismissed for 89, and in the next match he scored 42 v Surrey at the Oval. He played for Norfolk from 1864-1866.

Galpin, John George (Pre '95) born Gosport 13.1.1843, died Luton 5.3.1917. Galpin was a right-handed batsman and fast, round-arm bowler who played in six matches from 1875-1877 and one further in 1880 – Hampshire were not first-class in 1879. From 1870, he played in a number of matches in the midlands and north of England, including non-first-class matches for Buckinghamshire and Northamptonshire. For Hampshire, he took 28 wickets at 16.50 with a best of 6-68 v Kent at the Riding Field, Winchester, despite which Hampshire lost by an innings, and 5-42 v Derbyshire at the Antelope in 1876. In the latter, he came to the wicket at number 11, to join RG Hargreaves (35*) and scored 1* as they added the ten runs Hampshire needed to win by one wicket. Derbyshire's Mycroft had match figures of 17-103, one of two occasions when an opposition bowler has taken 17 Hampshire wickets – and Hampshire won both.

Gandy, Christopher Henry (68) born London 24.6.1867, died Brentwood 18.6.1907. Gandy a left-arm opening bowler was one of 19 debutants for Hampshire's weak side of 1900. He took 2-84 at the Oval in an innings defeat (recording a 'pair'), and 1-33 in a seven wicket defeat v Somerset at Bath, where after a third 'duck' he reached 6* in his final innings for the county. In that same season, he played in a few 2nd XI matches.

Garaway, Mark (431) born Swindon 20.7.1973. Wicketkeeper Garaway was understudy to 'Adi' Aymes., appearing in four first-class matches between 1996-1999, although none were in the Championship, and in two limited-overs games. He was born in Swindon, but learned his cricket on the Isle of Wight, playing for Ventnor, and he subsequently played in the Southern League for Waterlooville and Winchester. For Hampshire, his best score was 55 v New Zealanders at Southampton in 1999, an innings that helped them to draw the game with one wicket standing. Since leaving Hampshire he has enjoyed a very successful career as an analyst (at one time with England) and as a coach, including the first team at Somerset, and in Ireland where he was Director of

Cricket. He was also an assistant to the goalkeeping coach at Newcastle United FC, and is currently in charge of cricket at Millfield School.

Garnier, Rev. Thomas Parry (Pre '95, Amateur) born Longford, Derbyshire 22.2.1841, died Switzerland 18.3.1898. He was a right-handed batsman who attended Winchester College and then Oxford University, winning his 'blue' in all three years, 1861-1863. In the following year, he played once for Hampshire v Middlesex at the Antelope, scoring 6 & 23 in a ten-wicket defeat. In 1863, he played for Lincolnshire and in 1864 for Norfolk. His father, uncle and brother all played first-class cricket.

Gatting, Joe Stephen (523) born Brighton 25.11.1987. Batsman Gatting, a member of a cricketing family, played for his native Sussex from 2009-2013, before joining Hampshire, where he played for two seasons. In first-class matches, he made little impact in the first year, averaging 17.36, but in 2015 he made two first-class half centuries with a best of 64* in a defeat at Lord's, and averaged 46.66. He nonetheless lost his place, and left Hampshire at the end of the season. Despite his reasonable limited-overs record at Sussex, his four innings for Hampshire brought just 55 runs, while in T20 his best score was 22. Since leaving Hampshire, he has been the Cricket Professional at Norwich School, and has played for Swardeston CC. He played football with Brighton & Hove Albion FC.

Gay, Leslie Hewitt (69, Amateur) born Brighton 24.3.1871, died Sidmouth 1.11.1949. He was a wicketkeeper who after attending Marlborough, won his 'blue' at Cambridge University in 1892 & 1893, played briefly for Somerset in 1894, and in the winter of 1894/5 toured Australia, playing in his only Test Match, in which he scored 33 & 4 and dismissed four batsmen. In 1900, he played in nine matches for Hampshire, with 14 dismissals and a batting average of 10.25. He then played in one final first-class match in 1904 for MCC v London County. He was a good footballer, keeping goal at University, and for England.

Gentry, Jack Sydney Bates (205, Amateur) born Essex 4.10.1899, died Sussex 16.4.1978. Gentry bowled slow-left-arm and after leaving Christ's Hospital he played in one match for Hampshire, age just 18, in 1919, v his native Essex at Bournemouth. He bowled eight overs without a wicket, and scored three runs in his one innings. He played first-class cricket subsequently for Surrey (1922/23) and Essex (1925), taking 36 wickets at 22.05 in 12 matches. In 1936, he played a number of games in Argentina.

Gibbons, Herbert Gladstone Coe (238) born Berkshire 12.3.1905, died Southampton 13.1.1963. He was a lower-order batsman and leg-break bowler who played in seven matches for Hampshire from 1925-1928 scoring 70 runs at an average of 10.00, but taking no wickets in his 16 overs. During the Second

World War, he was one of a number of Hampshire cricketers who played for the Southampton Police side.

Giddins, Edward Simon Hunter (461) born Eastbourne 20.7.1971. Pace-bowler Giddins played for Sussex 1991-1996, when he was sacked and banned, after testing positive for using cocaine. He moved to Warwickshire, 1998-2000, and during the latter period he played in four Test Matches, taking 5-15 v Zimbabwe in the second game. He then moved to Surrey for two seasons, before joining Hampshire at the start of the 2003 season, but struggled with fitness, played in just three first-class matches and left at the end of June with 13 wickets at 25.84. He played also in five limited-overs matches (six wickets) and at the start of the inaugural T20 competition. He plays poker professionally and works as an analyst for Sky TV.

Gilliat, Richard Michael Charles (353) born Ware, Herts, 20.5.1944. Left-handed batsman Gilliat was an outstanding schoolboy cricketer at Charterhouse and at Oxford University won his 'blue' in four seasons, 1964-1967. By the last of those he had made his debut for the county (1966) and on graduating he became Hampshire's Assistant Secretary, then vice-captain, and from 1971, captain. He was a very good county batsman; in 220 first-class matches for Hampshire he scored 9,358 runs at just over 30 per innings, with 16 centuries and 49 half-centuries, plus nearly 3,000 limited-overs runs. His best season was 1969, including his highest score of 223* v Warwickshire at Southampton, and he was considered an England prospect, but after missing most of 1970 with an injury, he took on the captaincy, and it is in that respect that he is best remembered. With the exception of Peter Sainsbury, he was building a side to replace the Champions of 1961 and in the first two years in charge he lost Marshall, Livingstone, White as well as Cottam, Castell and others. Despite that challenge, in his third season as captain, Hampshire won the title for the second time against all expectations, and in 1974, with the addition of Roberts, an arguably stronger side deserved a second title, denied them when the last two matches were wrecked by the weather.

In 1975, they challenged again, although third place was rather more the result of injuries and a lack of consistency. This was and remains nonetheless, the finest three years in Hampshire's history, and there was compensation in 1975 when the Sunday League brought their first limited-overs trophy. With Greenidge and Roberts touring, 1976 was a relatively fallow year and while there were a number of semi-finals in his period in charge, the one disappointment was that his side with Richards, Greenidge, Jesty, Roberts and others, never reached a Lord's final, although they won the Sunday League again in 1978 after a difficult year in which Richards and Roberts walked out mid-season. In addition, the secretary Desmond Eagar had died unexpectedly and rather than take on that position, Gilliat retired from cricket, moving first to a position in the city, and then for a long teaching career back at Charterhouse. A modest, quiet man, his record might be considered the finest of all Hampshire's captains. He was a good footballer, who captained Oxford University in both sports.

Gladdon, Frederick (127) born 9.6.1881. We have no further details of his place of birth or date and place of death. He played in one match for Hampshire v Warwickshire in late August 1905, scoring 1 & 0, and opening the bowling in the first innings returned figures of 28-11-44-0, in a 10-wicket defeat.

Godfrey, John Frederick (294) born Headington Oxfordshire, 18.8.1917, died Newton Abbott, 10.1995. Godfrey was a fast-medium bowler and tail end batsman who played in one match for Hampshire v West Indians at Bournemouth in 1939 when he was presumably not yet qualified by residence to play in the Championship. In the first two seasons after the war, he played in 11 further matches. He took 15 first-class wickets at 50.20, with 61 runs at an average below five per innings, and his best figures were 4-116, in a seven-wicket victory v Derbyshire at Portsmouth in 1947.

Goldie, Christopher Frederick Evelyn ('Chris') (393) born South Africa 2.11.1960. Chris Goldie was a wicketkeeper who played club cricket in the London area and for Middlesex 2nd XI, then won his 'blue' at Cambridge University in 1981 & 1982. In the following year, he joined Hampshire as understudy to Bobby Parks and over three seasons, played in three first-class matches – none in the Championship. He was elected to the MCC Committee in 1983, was also a member of the Middlesex Committee, and played at Richmond CC for 37 seasons. In 2015, he was captain of the County Cricketers' Golf Society.

Goodwin, Jake (T20) born Swindon 19.1.1998. Jake Goodwin was a batsman who played age group cricket for Wiltshire, then for the Hampshire Academy and 2nd XI sides. In 2016, he opened the batting and scored 32 in a T20 victory v Somerset at the Ageas Bowl but that was his only first team appearance. He was released, and in 2017 he returned to Wiltshire in the Minor Counties competitions. He also appeared for Sussex 2nd XI, including a match at Horsham v Hampshire 2nd XI, scoring 40 in his one innings.

Gornall, James Parrington, known as **Peter** (222, Amateur) born Farnborough 22.9.1899, died Lower Froyle, Hants, 13.11.1983. After attending Christ's Hospital, he went to Cambridge University and appeared in the Freshman's match but not in first-class matches. He joined the Royal Navy, playing in matches for them through the 1920s, including three first-class matches. In 1923, he played for Hampshire in a victory v Warwickshire at Portsmouth, scoring 11 & 7. He was awarded the DSO in June 1945.

Gower, David Ivon (413) born Tunbridge Wells 1.4.1957. Left-handed batsmen Gower was one of the finest post-war English batsmen, playing in 117 Test

Matches for England, with 8231 runs at 44.25 including 18 centuries. He also played in more than one hundred ODIs. He captained England in the mid-1980s, including a successful Ashes campaign, but his leadership was not always without controversy; while on one tour of Australia he literally flew into trouble. His final Test Match was v Pakistan at the Oval in August 1992. He captained his first county Leicestershire from 1984 through most of the 1980s, and for that county scored over 10,000 runs in 196 first-class matches. He moved to Hampshire in 1990 and played in 73 first-class matches, scoring 4,325 runs at 40.80 with seven centuries, including a best of 155 v Yorkshire at Basingstoke in 1992. He played in 75 limited-overs matches although often appeared tired of that form of the game, and averaged under 30 for Hampshire. One of his great days for the county nonetheless, was captaining them at Lord's in 1991 when, with Nicholas injured in the previous match, they won the Nat West Trophy v Surrey. In all first-class cricket, he passed 1,000 runs in each of his four seasons with Hampshire, but pursuing a career in the media, at the start of the 1994 season he asked to be allowed to cover a tour of the West Indies. Hampshire refused the request, Gower retired around his 37th birthday, and became one of the main television presenters of cricket on Sky Sports.

Graf, Shaun Francis (385) born Melbourne, Australia 19.5.1957. Graf was a useful batsman and fast-medium bowler who played for Victoria and Western Australia and in 11 limited-overs internationals for his country. In the English season of 1979 he played for Wiltshire, and in the following year joined Hampshire with the impossible task of being the overseas replacement for their two tourists, Greenidge and Marshall. Hampshire had a new and inexperienced captain, Nick Pocock, had seen the recent break-up of their Champions of 1973, and 1980 was the one season since the dreadful run from 1900-1905, when they finished at the foot of the Championship table, winning only one game when Marshall returned towards the end of the season. Graf played in 15 first-class matches with a batting average of around 20 and one half-century, plus 20 wickets at 44.45 – and never more than two wickets in an innings. His best performances were with the ball in limited-overs matches, taking 17 wickets at 18.23 and an economy rate below 3.5 runs per over. He pursued a coaching career after his retirement in 1985, and in the 1990s, returned briefly to Hampshire in that capacity.

Gravett, Mark (58) born Milford, Surrey 11.2.1865, died Godalming 8.2.1938. He was a slow-left-arm bowler who played in four matches for Hampshire in 1899 & 1900, taking 15 wickets at 29.66. His best figures were 5-50 (& 3-49) v Lancashire at Old Trafford in 1900, despite which Hampshire fell to a heavy defeat. He dropped out of major cricket after his action was queried. He had played a full season with Burnley in the Lancashire League in 1895, and in 1901 played for Staffordshire v MCC. In 1929 & 1930 he stood as an umpire in four first-class festival matches at Eastbourne.

Gray, James Roy (314) born Southampton 19.5.1926, died Southampton 31.10.2016. Opening batsman Gray scored 22,450 first-class runs for Hampshire, with 30 centuries and a best of 213* (& 84*) v Derbyshire at Portsmouth in 1962. His career total places him fourth in Hampshire's batting records, behind three Test cricketers, Mead, Marshall and Brown – and he is the highest Hampshire-born run scorer. In addition, he took 451 first-class wickets with a best of 7-52 v Glamorgan at Swansea in 1955. Fielding often in the slips, he held 350 catches, and, wicketkeepers apart, he stands alongside Newman, Sainsbury, Jesty and Udal as one of Hampshire's finest native cricketers.

He was 20 when first-class cricket resumed after the war, and after making his debut at Aldershot in 1948 he generally batted in the middle order until, with the retirement of McCorkell, he gradually established himself as an opener. In 1951, he passed 1,000 runs for the first of 13 consecutive seasons, and in the following year scored his first Championship century, v Essex on his home ground. In 1955, as Hampshire finished third, he spent his first season opening with the dashing Roy Marshall and his run-scoring and average declined some-what, but it was a temporary set-back, they established a famous partnership, and with the sunshine of 1959 and a brief experiment with covered wickets, he passed 2,000 runs three times in four years, including 1961, when the addition of 34 wickets at 31.00 played a significant part in Hampshire's first title success. In the previous season, he and Marshall had set the then record for Hampshire's first wicket of 249 v Middlesex at Portsmouth. 1962 was statistically his most successful season, but there was a decline with the bat in the following year, and as he took up his new teaching career he played less frequently, finally retiring after the 1966 season. He was the consummate professional and a good enough all-round sportsman to have been briefly on Arsenal's books; he played football in the Southern League for Bedford Town. He spent his whole life in Southampton, and succeeded Charlie Knott as Chairman of the Cricket Committee from 1988-1997, when Mark Nicholas's side enjoyed success in limited-overs competitions.

Greenfield, George Price (Pre '95, Amateur) born Winchester 24.1.1843, died Ealing 3.9.1917. He was a fast, round-arm bowler, who played in five first-class matches; three for Surrey, one for the Gentlemen of the South, and in 1875, one for Hampshire in an innings defeat v Kent at Winchester, scoring 0 and with figures of 0-32. He played at other times for various sides including MCC, Huntingdonshire and clubs including Tooting and Wimbledon.

Greenhill, Hubert Maclean (89, Amateur) born Christchurch 18.9.1881, died Dorset 22.1.1926. He was a slow-left-arm bowler who attended Sherborne School, and in May 1901 played twice for Hampshire at Southampton, v the South Africans and Derbyshire. He took 3-39 in the first match as Hampshire won by an innings, but there were no further successes. He played most of his cricket for Dorset from 1903-1925 and also in minor military matches.

Greenidge, Cuthbert Gordon (363) born Barbados 1.5.1951. Opening batsman Gordon Greenidge stands alongside Hampshire greatest batsmen, but unlike Mead, Marshall, Richards and Smith he came to the county from his home in Reading as a junior, playing in Holt's Colts and the 2nd XI from 1966 until his first-class debut in 1970. Indeed, by today's criteria he might have played for England, not least when the West Indies went for the 'safe' option of Ron Headley in 1973, after their first choice, Camachao, had his tour ended with an injury sustained at Southampton. That Greenidge was not chosen was fortunate for Hampshire, as he and Richards formed an opening partnership that was a key element in their second Championship title. In that year, Greenidge eclipsed Richards with five centuries and 1,656 runs at 48.70 and the pace at which he and his partner scored, eased the task for their bowlers.

In 1974, his county record was less impressive, but he made his Test Match debut in India, scoring 93 & 107 in his first Test. There would be 108 Tests by the end, with 19 centuries, 7,558 runs at 44.72, and another great opening partnership with Desmond Haynes. He played also in 128 ODIs with 11 more centuries, and an average of 45. For Hampshire, he scored 19,840 first-class runs at 45.40 including a best of 259 v Sussex at Southampton in 1975 when he reached every fifty and hundred with one of 13 sixes. In that same year, he scored 177 v Glamorgan in the second round of the Gillette Cup, sharing a double century partnership with Richards in the county's record limited-overs total of 371-4, which still stands. The only surprise is that he never appeared in a Lord's final for the county over the 18 seasons of his career, although he won two World Cup medals there and played in all three Hampshire sides that won the Sunday League – most significantly in 1978, when, after Richards and Roberts quit Hampshire mid-season, he scored three consecutive Championship centuries, equalling the records of Mead, Fry and Poore, before adding 122 v Middlesex at Bournemouth in the decisive final Sunday League match which Hampshire won by 26 runs. Then in 1986 he became the first man to score centuries in four consecutive innings for the county, including a double hundred at Northampton. In 1978 he was one of *Wisden's* Cricketers of the Year, for his performances for the West Indies in 1977.

When he left, he held Hampshire's record scores in all three limited-overs competitions, adding 173* in the B&H Cup in 1973 and 172 v Surrey in the Sunday League (1987) – only Vince (178) has yet bettered those three innings. Greenidge was the last Hampshire batsman to pass 2,000 runs in a first-class season. In 1988, he came to the County Ground with the tourists, and scored 103, with eight sixes, despite which Hampshire released him. His departure was not altogether a happy affair, but the pleasure he gave to Hampshire's supporters over many seasons was considerable. He was simply one of the greatest Hampshire cricketers.

Greenwood, Sir Granville George (Pre '95, Amateur) born London 3.1.1850, died London 27.10.1928. His father played two first-class matches for Cambridge University in 1821, and his brother first-class for MCC in one match in 1875. The brothers had attended Eton College, and in that same season, batsman GG played in one match for Hampshire v Kent at Winchester, but was dismissed for just one run in each innings, as an inexperienced Hampshire side lost heavily – Hampshire used nine bowlers but not Greenwood. He played in two matches for the Gentlemen of Hampshire v Yorkshire United at Lyndhurst in 1874. He was MP for Peterborough 1906-1918.

Gregory, John Thomas (183) born Chesterfield 22.4.1887, killed in action near Zonnebeke, Belgium 27.11.1914. He was on the Trent Bridge groundstaff from 1905-1907, but did not play for Nottinghamshire, and enlisted in the King's Royal Rifle Corps. In military matches, his bowling was successful, perhaps he impressed Hampshire's selectors in a match at Aldershot in May 1913, when taking 10-15 for his regiment v 2nd Worcestershire Regiment. Two months later, he played once for Hampshire v Oxford University but batting at number 11, was dismissed without scoring, as the Hampshire innings closed on 532. The University side replied with 554, and while he is described in the record books as a slow-left-arm bowler, he and Jaques took the new ball, with Kennedy as first change. He took 0-72, and after Hampshire declared, 0-15, again opening the bowling. The match was drawn.

Greig, Canon John Glennie (85, Amateur) born India 24.101871, died Milford-on-Sea, Hants 24.5.1958. During the first-half of the twentieth century Hampshire often called on church men and service personnel to appear as amateurs, and all-rounder Greig was both, in a rich and varied life which included 125 first-class matches. He was educated at Downside School, but returned to his birthplace, India, as an army officer, and played a number of first-class matches there in the 1890s for the Europeans, as well as two games in England for MCC and AJ Webbe's XI. Fellow officer Major RM Poore, recommended him to Hampshire, and in May 1901 he made his Championship and county debut v Lancashire at Portsmouth. After scoring just 28 runs in his first four innings he recorded his first century for the county (119) v South Africans at Southampton, but in the next three matches there were just 43 runs in his six innings, with three 'ducks', at which point his Championship average was 7.10. Then came a match at Liverpool where, batting at number four, his 47* was one of just two innings to reach double figures in a total of 106. Hampshire batted again 307 behind, and Greig asked to open, and scored 249, batting for more than five hours. In that season, he scored 1,277 runs at 41.19 as Hampshire, for the only time from 1900-1905 finished away from last place. He also took 27 wickets including 6-38 v Derbyshire at Southampton, although he bowled relatively little in future years. He went overseas with his regiment again and did not return until 1905; in that year and 1906 he appeared in 27 first-class matches, but his appearances were always intermittent with 13 matches in 1910, 10 in 1914, and 11 after the war from 1920-1921. In that sense, he exemplified the problems Hampshire faced, assembling sides that relied on amateurs – for them he appeared in 77 first-class matches in a period covering 21 years, scoring 4,375 runs at 34.17 with 10 centuries and taking 64 wickets at 32.03. In his final playing season of 1922 he took over as Hampshire's secretary, before training as a Roman Catholic priest. He was Hampshire's President in 1945/6.

Griffiths, David Andrew (484) born Isle of Wight 10.9.1985. He was a right-arm pace bowler and left-handed batsman who learned his cricket on the Isle of Wight during a period when the island produced a number of very capable cricketers. In 2004 & 2005, he played for England under-19s, by which time he was playing for Hampshire's Academy and 2nd XI sides. He made his first-class debut v Loughborough University in 2006, and his Championship debut in the following season v Durham, taking 4-46 and supporting Michael Brown to save the match, with Hampshire nine wickets down. In 2009, he played in 10 first-class matches with 32 wickets at 32.46, and in 2010 he took 5-85 v Essex. He played in 36 first-class matches for Hampshire from 2006-2013, taking 105 wickets with a best of 6-85 v Nottinghamshire in 2011, but was often troubled by injuries and in 2014 he moved to Kent, playing mostly in limited-overs matches, until he left after the 2016 season. He played in 22 limited-overs matches for Hampshire, taking 27 wickets and enjoyed his happiest day as a member of the 2012 side that won the CB 40 v Warwickshire at Lord's, dismissing Ian Bell on 81. He is now coaching at Basingstoke & North Hants CC.

Griffiths, Gavin Timothy (T20) born Lancashire 19.11.1993. Pace bowler Griffiths played for his native Lancashire from 2014. In 2016, he joined Hampshire on loan, appearing in four T20 matches, taking five wickets at 20.20 with an economy rate of 8.41. He joined Leicestershire in 2017.

Gross, Frederick Albert (230, Amateur) born South Stoneham 17.9.1902, died Birmingham, 11.3.1975. Gross was a leg-break and googly bowler who attended King Edward VI School in Southampton and played in 34 first-class matches for Hampshire, 1924-1927 and 1929, taking 50 wickets at 37.00 each. His best figures were 5-53 in a drawn match v Yorkshire at Sheffield in 1927. In 1934, he appeared once as a professional for Warwickshire, also v Yorkshire, and his final first-class wicket was Len Hutton. Through the 1930s he played club cricket in the midlands for Mitchell & Butler's.

Guard, David Radclyffe (303, Amateur) born Romsey 19.5.1928, died Sussex 12.12.1978. Batsman David Guard attended Winchester College and was one of a succession of young amateurs who played under the new captain Desmond Eagar in the years immediately following the war: Downer, Parker, Shirreff, Bridger, Guard, Exton, Kimish and Rimmell made their debuts in that order in 1946, after the one professional Neville Rogers. Apart from Bridger (38 matches), Guard with 15 games over four seasons played the most, and in a short time, amateurs were a rarity. Guard was still a schoolboy in 1946 and represented the Southern Schools v The Rest at Lord's. In his four first-class years, he scored 405 runs at 15.57, with two half centuries and a best of 89 v Glamorgan at Cardiff in 1949, rescuing Hampshire from 96-5, following Glamorgan's 337. Otherwise his only notable score was 58, helping a victory v Combined Services at Portsmouth in his final first-class match. During that last season, he played a number of matches for the county's 2nd XI in the Minor Counties Championship.

Gunner, Charles Richards (Pre '95, Amateur) born Bishops Waltham 7.1.1853, died Bishops Waltham 4.2.1924. He played just once for Hampshire, v Derbyshire at Derby in 1878, but in a match truncated by rain, held one catch but neither batted nor bowled – the first of three men to have such a record for the county (see also Cornwallis & Hyland). Some years later he played for Swanmore Park (v Hambledon), the Gentlemen of Hampshire, and in non-first-class games for Hampshire – from which it appears he was a lower-order batsman who did not bowl. CR represented England at Rugby Union, while his son (below) later played for the county.

Gunner, John Hugh (132, Amateur) born Bishops Waltham 17.5.1884, died of wounds in Belgium 9.8.1918. Like his father, he attended Marlborough College and was a middle-order batsman who played in six matches for the county scoring just 65 runs at 8.12 with a best of 32 v West Indians on debut. He attended Oxford University winning a 'blue' for hockey, but did not play cricket for the university side. He played for Oxford University Authentics, MCC and Hampshire Hogs. As Captain John Gunner, he was the third and last brother to die on active service in the war.

Gutteres, Rev. George Gilbert (Pre '95, Amateur) born London 11.10.1859, died Algiers 2.3.1898. He was a brilliant cover fielder and opening batsman who attended Winchester College, then Oxford University, playing two first-class matches there in 1881 (no 'blue'). In 1882, he played for Hampshire in one match v Somerset at Taunton, scoring 24 & 28 in a five-wicket defeat. He had played for Devon in 1878. He was ordained as a priest in 1885.

H

Hake, Herbert Denys (207, Amateur) born Christchurch 8.11.1894 died Sydney, Australia 12.4.1975. His uncle SM Toyne played one match for Hampshire, while batsman Hake played in five first-class matches at Cambridge University without obtaining his 'blue' – he did win them for hockey and rackets. Between 1920-1925 he played 21 matches for Hampshire, scoring 478 runs at 17.70, with three half-centuries including a best of 94, opening the batting v Leicestershire at Hinckley in 1921. He was a member of the Hampshire side that won a memorable innings victory v Yorkshire at Headingley in 1920, but Hampshire lost just two wickets and Hake neither batted nor bowled. He did not play in 1924 and after three matches in late August 1925, his first-class career ended. His last recorded matches were in Holland and Portugal.

Hall, Clifford Geoffrey (267, Amateur) born Breamore, Hants 19.1.1902, died Breamore 9.7.1982. Batsman Hall played in five matches for Hampshire 1933 & 1935, scoring 77 runs at 11.00, with a best of 37 v Somerset at Taunton in 1935. He played for the Club & Ground, and for Wiltshire between 1935-1938.

Hall, Ernest (Pre '95, Amateur) born Newmarket 29.4.1851, died Botley 6.3.1936. He was a batsman and wicketkeeper who played 11 matches for Hampshire from 1880-1885, after which they lost their first-class status. He scored 198 runs at 10.42 with a best of 22 and dismissed 14 batsmen. His son, PM Hall (below) played for Hampshire after the First World War.

Hall, Patrick Martin (201, Amateur) born Portsmouth 14.3.1894, died Fareham 5.8.1941. Batsman Hall went to Winchester College and then Oxford University, for whom he played three first-class matches in 1919 (no 'blue'), including 101 v Free Foresters. Like his father, he played in 11 first-class matches for the county between 1919-1926 (not 1922 or 1924). His record was modest with just 164 runs at 10.25 but there was one innings of 94* v Lancashire at Southampton in 1920 (Hampshire 325 all out).

Hamblin, James Rupert Christopher (453) born Kent 16.8.1978. His father played first-class cricket for Oxford University, and James, a pace bowler and useful lower-order batsman, played first-class and limited-overs cricket for Hampshire from 2001. He played 2nd XI cricket for Sussex in 1997, and for Hampshire from the following year. After making his debut in 2001, he played in a further five first-class matches in both of the next two seasons, with three half-centuries and 14 wickets including his best bowling of 6-93 v Derbyshire – the only Championship match in which he took more than one wicket in an innings. His most consistent performances were in limited-overs, playing 48 games in four seasons, with two half centuries and 28 wickets. In 2003, the first season of the T20 he played in all five of Hampshire's matches, averaging 24.80 and taking seven wickets. He left Hampshire at the end of the following season but has continued to play regularly for MCC and Charterhouse Friars.

Hansen, Thomas Munkholt, (441) born Denmark, 25.3.1976. He was a left-arm pace bowler who played for Denmark under-19s and then the full national side, before joining Hampshire's staff. From 1997-1999 he played regularly for their 2nd XI and in September 1997, he made his first-class debut v Worcestershire at Southampton in a match when Hick & Moody added 438* for the third wicket. In that context, his figures of 24-10-61-0 were quite respectable, but it was two years before he played again. In three matches at the end of the 1999 season, he took five wickets, including a best of 3-59 v Sussex, but none in his final game v Somerset. He left Hampshire, in 2000 playing one match each for the 2nd XIs of Leicestershire and Northamptonshire.

Hardy, Jonathan James Ean (394) born Kenya 2.10.1960. He was a left-handed batsman who had the misfortune to be on Hampshire's staff in a period when their batting was perhaps the strongest in their history. After school at Canford he joined the staff and played quite regularly in 1984 & 1985 – 29 first-class matches with 1,255 runs at 35.85, including seven half-centuries and one century, 107* in an innings victory v Essex at Southampton in 1985. He was less successful in his 21 limited-overs matches, averaging 17.45, with just one half century in a victory v Northamptonshire in 1984. In 1986, he joined Somerset and played in 87 first-class matches, followed by 10 for Gloucestershire in 1991. He played also for Western Province from 1987-1991; overall, he scored 6,120 first-class runs at just under 30, plus 2,798 limited-overs runs at 24.76. He played for many years for Dorset and also ran a bat manufacturing business.

Harfield, Lewis ('Lew') (239) born Cheriton, Hants 6.8.1905, died Winchester 19.11.1985. He was a batsman who bowled occasionally, and played in 80 first-class matches for the county, from 1925-1931, scoring 2,460 runs at 20.00 with 13 half-centuries and a best of 89 v Sussex in 1929 – one of four dismissals in the 80s in his last two seasons of 1929 & 1931. He missed the whole of the 1930 season with illness and John Arlott (1957) recorded how ill health "prevented (him) from developing into the consistent, long-serving county player he promised to be". In May 1932, he was reported to be seriously ill, so the county paid his summer wages of 20 weeks at £2 per week, and he left the staff. He bowled occasionally, taking 14 first-class wickets with a best of 3-35 v Derbyshire in 1931.

Hargreaves, James Henry (Pre '95) born New York, USA, 1859, died Portsmouth 11.4.1922. He played under the alias J. Smith in two matches for Hampshire in 1884 & 1885, scoring just 15 runs at 3.75. He did not bowl. In 1896 & 1897, he is recorded playing a few games for Hampshire Rovers, when he also kept wicket.

Hargreaves, Reginald Gervis (Pre '95, Amateur). born Accrington 13.10.1852, died Lyndhurst 13.2.1926. He was a middle order batsman and lob bowler who played in 12 first-class matches for Hampshire between 1875-1885. After school at Eton, he attended Oxford University but played no first-class cricket there, although he won a 'blue' for Royal Tennis. For Hampshire, he scored 307 runs at 15.35, with a best of 38*, and took 14 wickets, including 4-55 v Derbyshire in 1878. He is perhaps best remembered as the man who married 'Alice in Wonderland', Alice Liddell, the girl on whom Lewis Carroll based his story; the couple who lost two sons in the First World War, are buried together in the parish church at Lyndhurst. RG played other first-class matches for MCC, an England XI, I Zingari, and Gentlemen of England.

Harold, Frederick Vere (149) born Eling, Hants 5.9.1888, died Southall 17.12.1964. He played two matches for Hampshire, in 1909 & 1912. On debut v Derbyshire at Blackwell he batted at number 11, scoring 0, and bowling one over for seven runs. Three years later, v Sussex at Eastbourne, he bowled three overs (0-8) and promoted to number eight, scored 16. He neither batted nor bowled in the second innings.

Harris, George Woodrouffe (65, Amateur) born Chelsea 6.8.1880, died Chorley Wood 10.7.1954. He was a batsman and good field who attended Uppingham School and played in trials at Cambridge University, but his sole first-class match was for Hampshire v Surrey at the Oval in 1899. He scored 10 in Hampshire's 74 all out, in reply to Surrey's 459, and in the second innings failed to score, as Hampshire lost by an innings. His last recorded match was for MCC at Hereford in 1912.

Harris, Henry Edward (Pre '95) born Brighton 6.8.1854 died Littlehampton 8.11.1923. He was a batsman who played in three matches for Hampshire in 1880 scoring 53 runs at an average of 10.60. He is also recorded as playing for St George's Rifles (for whom he bowled) v MCC, for Brighton and for 18 of St Luke's v the Australians at the Antelope in non-first-class matches. His son ELJ, played for Sussex in the 1920s.

Harrison, Bernard Reginald Stanhope ('Bernie') (337) born Worcester 28.9.1934, died Basingstoke 18.3.2006. Although born in Worcester, 'Bernie' Harrison was a Basingstoke man who played for the local club for many years, and with Phil Bichard, wrote a club history. As a top-order batsman, he was unfortunate that his time at Hampshire coincided with the finest achievements of Marshall, Gray and Horton and his 14 first-class appearances were spread over six seasons, 1957-1962. He played for the county 2nd XI in 1956 and made his first-class debut v Oxford University in 1957. He waited a year for the next game and his Championship debut v his native county at Portsmouth, but scored just a single in his one innings. In every season, one of his matches was v Oxford University, and at Portsmouth in 1961 it brought his one first-class century, 110; his two half-centuries were also against the University. He played a few Championship games when Marshall was injured in that title-winning season, and in 1962 played in five matches, but with little success. That was the end of his first-class career, and his time on the county staff, but he played for Hampshire 2nd XI over 10 seasons from the start of the 2nd XI Championship in 1959. He took up a teaching career which he combined successfully with coaching, and for many years he compiled the county's 2nd XI statistics. He was good footballer, playing for Crystal Palace, Southampton and Exeter City.

Harrison, Gerald Cartmell (188, Amateur) born Congleton, Cheshire 8.10.1883, died Nottinghamshire 10.8.1943. He was a batsman who played for Devon and then made his first-class debut for the Royal Navy in 1912. He played in 20 Championship matches and two other first-class for Hampshire either side of the First World War, and first-class for Combined Services in 1920. Nine of his Championship matches came in 1914, there were seven in 1919 and a further four in 1920. In all 22 first-class matches for Hampshire he scored 991 runs at 28.31 with one century (111 v Gloucestershire in 1919) and four half-centuries, including 82 v Warwickshire in 1920 in a Hampshire total of 616-7 declared. In 1914, he scored 91* for Hampshire v MCC, coming in at 55-5 and taking Hampshire to 198 all out.

Harrison, Leo (296) born Mudeford, 5.6.1922, died Mudeford 12.10.2016. Leo Harrison lived his whole life in Mudeford – Hampshire when he was born, Dorset when he died, but he was a Hampshire man through-and-through, making his county debut as a teenager and returning in 1946 to become eventually the last pre-war Hampshire player, when, in emergency, he made his final first-class appearance in 1966. By then, he had succeeded Arthur Holt as Hampshire's coach, helping to bring through new players, some of whom would follow his 1961 side, as the second and, to date, last title-winning side.

He came to Hampshire having impressed as a young batsman, oddly, having switched from left to right-hand, and his promise was spotted by the former Essex cricketer Charles Bray who suggested in a newspaper article he might be the new Bradman. But during the war with the RAF, his eyesight deteriorated and he spent much of his career playing in glasses. He was demobbed later than some of his colleagues, so that in 1946 he played a mixture of first-class games for the county, the Combined Services and the RAF. There followed a number of seasons when he struggled to establish himself as a batsman; only in 1947 when he scored 567 runs did he average (just) over 20, and in 1950, age 28, 10 matches brought just 152 runs. Then in 1951 came his first century v Worcestershire at Southampton, 1,189 runs and an average over 30. He earned a reputation as a superb outfielder but as Hampshire sought a permanent replacement for Neil McCorkell, he competed with Ralph Prouton and the occasional amateur David Blake, for the gloves. In 1952, there were three more centuries and another 1,000+ runs, then from 1954 he became the regular wicketkeeper, a position he held for nine seasons, retiring from full-time play after his 40th birthday. His batting became less significant and he moved down the order, with his last century in 1954, but he became a fine wicket-keeper to the varied Hampshire attack in their best seasons to that date from 1955, to the title in 1961. In that wonderful season, his average went beyond 20 for the first time in more than a decade, and with Mike Barnard, he shared an important eighth-wicket century partnership v Warwickshire that rescued Hampshire, setting up a vital victory. In 1959, he set a Hampshire record with 83 victims, and over his career there were 567 catches and 99 stumpings. John Arlott wrote "he is wise in cricket and shrewd about people" and in later years Harrison became Colin Ingleby-Mackenzie's regular if unlikely companion, on the younger man's lively social jaunts. Arlott also paid Harrison the compliment of taking his famous saying "It ain't half a blooming game", as the title of his one fictional short story.

Harrison, William Henry (101, Amateur) born Nursling, Southampton, 1866, died Salisbury 23.12.1936. In 1893, he played in two non-first-class matches for Hampshire during their demotion to second-class. Then, in late August 1902, he played in one first-class match v Warwickshire at Bournemouth, scoring 0 & 12*. But those modest figures hide an intriguing match in which Llewellyn put out the visitors for 99 after which Harrison's 'duck' was one of a number of failures, as Hampshire fell from 95-1 to 131 all out. Warwickshire struggled to 152, leaving a target of 121. Hampshire reached 39-1 and 57-2 but wickets continued to fall, and Harrison, demoted to number 10, arrived at 86-8, so his 12* was a brave effort to win the game, which Hampshire eventually lost by eight runs.

Hart, Asher Hale-Bopp, Joseph Arthur (545) born Carlisle 30.3.1997. All-rounder Asher Hart joined Hampshire from Durham at the start of the 2017 season and played in two first-class matches – v Cardiff University, taking 3-17, and v South Africa 'A' scoring 36. In the winter of 2017/18 he played in five limited-overs matches for the county in the Regional Super 50 tournament in Barbados, taking three wickets. He left Hampshire at the end of the 2018 season. He played Minor Counties cricket for Northumberland in 2016.

Hartley, Peter John (442) born Keighley, Yorkshire 18.4.1960. Pace bowler Hartley played briefly for Warwickshire in 1982, then joined his native Yorkshire, from 1985-1997. At 38, he came to Hampshire and played for three years in 34 first-class matches, taking 102 wickets at just under 30 each, and 73 limited-overs wickets at 21.56 and an economy rate just over four runs per over. His outstanding Championship performance of 8-65 for Hampshire came in a defeat v Yorkshire at Basingstoke in 1999, a season in which he took 54 wickets. There were fewer successes in 2000, and his career ended against his native county in the last match ever at Northlands Road; he was 0* as fellow Yorkshireman Alex Morris was dismissed from the last ball to give Yorkshire victory. In that final season however, his 5-20 v Sussex at Hove was the best performance in his limited-overs career. In his whole career in first-class and limited-overs matches he took more 1,000 wickets, and he scored two first-class centuries for Yorkshire – for Hampshire there was one half-century. He retired after the 2000 season, and became a first-class and international umpire.

Harvey, Rev. Frank Northam (61, Amateur) born Southampton 19.12.1864, died Southampton 10.11.1939. He was a wicketkeeper and lower-order batsman who played in three first-class matches in 1899 & 1900, scoring 20 runs at 5.00 and dismissing three batsmen. He played also for the South Hants Club and the Hampshire Hogs.

Harvey, Ian Joseph (T20) born Victoria, Australia, 10.4.1972. He had an extensive career, playing in ODIs for Australia and among others, for five counties. In 2008, he played as an overseas professional for Hampshire in the T20 competition, scoring 197 runs at 21.88 (best 34) and taking seven wickets at 27.00 (best 2-20).

Haslop, Peter (350) born Midhurst 17.10.1941. pace bowler Peter Haslop was born and raised across the border in West Sussex, where he first played for Woolbeding age 10, and after taking 100+ wickets in a season, moved to Midhurst CC age just 16. He played there against touring sides and was recommended to Hampshire who signed him after a trial, and he began playing for their 2nd XI in mid-1961. Twelve months later he made his first-class debut in a televised match at Bournemouth v the Pakistanis, and in their one innings, his figures were 34-5-84-2. In that match, he was deputising for the rested first-choice seamers Shackleton, White and Heath, and with Shackleton now 38 and Heath about to retire through injury, Haslop had the chance to win a first-team place. Shackleton however continued playing regularly for six more years and in 1963 the highly promising Bob Cottam appeared. Haslop continued to play for the 2nd XI to the conclusion of the 1965 season, by which time leg-spinner Alan Castell had converted to pace, and it appeared that his chance had gone. He followed his mentor and friend Arthur Holt as a coach, playing for many years for the Deanery club in Southampton (eight years as captain) and in representative matches for the Southern League, until, in 1971, he was suddenly selected to deputise for the injured White in a Sunday League match v Leicestershire at Portsmouth. He dismissed opener Duddleston but Leicestershire chased down their target of just 114 without difficulty. He bowled a tight but wicketless spell in the following week at Worcester, then White returned. At the end of that season, White and Cottam both left Hampshire, along with Castell, and the county set about rebuilding their attack. Haslop, now 30, played two matches in a west country weekend in May, dismissing Somerset's Burgess and Kitchen, while his final wicket, at Bristol, was the crucial one of Mike Proctor as Hampshire forced a tie v Gloucestershire, with a last ball run out.

Hayden, Matthew Lawrence (436) born Queensland, Australia, 29.10.1971. Powerful left-handed opening batsman Hayden played 103 Test Matches and 160 ODIs for his country in an outstanding career, which included 30 Test Match centuries. In 1997, he had one very fine season as overseas professional in a weak Hampshire side – the first of a run of players from his country to play for Hampshire over the next decade. In that year he scored almost 1,500 runs at an average of 53.55, including 235* & 119 v Warwickshire at Southampton – the second Hampshire player (after Mead) to score a double and single century in the same game, and the highest aggregate in one match for Hampshire. It was at the time also Hampshire's highest maiden century. Hayden scored a century in the next match v Derbyshire, and shortly after 150 v Northamptonshire at Basingstoke. In limited-overs matches that year he scored 980 runs at 46.66, with three more centuries, and he even had time to take 2-16 v Sussex at Southampton, in his penultimate Championship match. Meanwhile the Australians had chosen other openers ahead of Hayden for their tour of England, for which Hampshire could feel very grateful. It would not occur again, although he did play for Northamptonshire for two seasons.

Haygarth, Edward Brownlow (Pre '95, Amateur) born Cirencester 26.4.1864, died Gloucestershire 18.4.1915. He was a wicketkeeper and lob bowler from a family of first-class cricketers who represented various counties. EB went to Lancing College and played two matches for his native Gloucestershire in 1883, but prior to that he had appeared once for Hampshire v Sussex at Winchester's Green Jackets Ground in 1875. Sussex won by an innings, and playing as a batsman, Haygarth scored 6 & 4. He also played for the Gentlemen of Hampshire in non-first-class matches.

Hayter, Ernest ('Ernie') (274) born Bournemouth 31.7.1913, died Southampton, 12. 2005. He was a batsman who played mainly for the 2nd XI and Club & Ground, but he also played one Championship match at Chesterfield in 1935 and then two more in 1937, v Cambridge University at Basingstoke and v Northamptonshire at Rushden. Sadly, on debut he recorded a 'pair', there was another nought v the University and just 17 & 10* in his last match.

Hayter, Montague William (109) born Ringwood 16.11.1871, died Christchurch 6.5.1948. Hayter was a batsman who played seven matches for the Hampshire side that finished last in the Championship of 1904. He was one of seven consecutive debutants for the county, who played only in that season, in a total 14 matches. Hayter scored 166 runs at a modest 13.83 but there was one fine innings of 82 v Derbyshire at Derby, as the county won one of just two victories that year.

Hayward, Arthur John (237) born Christchurch 12.9.1905, we have no details of his death. He is described as a batsman and leg-break bowler, but in his four matches for Hampshire in 1925 & 1926 he did not bowl – even when, on his debut, Middlesex scored 456. Meanwhile, batting mostly in the lower order, he scored just 17 runs in four innings.

Hayward, Mornantau ('Nante') (493) born South Africa 6.3.1977. Fast bowler 'Nante' Hayward played in 16 Test Matches and 21 ODIs for South Africa, and in England he played for four counties, including Hampshire in 2008. He was signed principally to play in the T20 competition and in ten matches he took 13 wickets at 21.38, but after Hampshire's involvement in that competition ended, he also appeared once in a Championship match v Nottinghamshire at the Rose Bowl. He took 2-87 in the first innings but after one ball of his fourth over in the second, he left the field injured.

Hayward, Richard Edward (390) born Ickenham, Middlesex, 15.2.1954. He was a left-handed batsman who played for Middlesex 2nd XI in the early 1970s, for Buckinghamshire from 1978, and he played in one first-class match for the Minor Counties v the Indians in 1979. Shortly after, he began playing for Hampshire 2nd XI, and in July 1981 he made his first-class debut for the county v the Sri Lankans and became the third of six men to score a century on Hampshire debut (101*), but like the other five, this was his county, not first-class, debut. In 1981 & 1982 he played in 13 first-class matches for Hampshire, adding two half-centuries to his debut innings, with an average of 25.22. In 1985, he played for Somerset and scored 100* v Cambridge University, by which time he had emigrated to New Zealand, where he played for Central Districts, captaining them in 1984/5. He returned to Hampshire to coach in the early 1990s.

Hazleton, Brigadier General Edwin Hills (Pre '95, Amateur) born Southampton 16.12.1861, died Simla, India 25.7.1916. He was a batsman who played in three first-class matches for Hampshire in 1883, scoring one half century on debut v Sussex at the Antelope Ground, and averaging 16.60. He played one match in India in 1888.

Heath, Allan Borman (Pre '95, Amateur) born East Woodhay, Hants 19.1.1865, died Devon 21.6.1913. He was a right-hand batsman, fast-medium bowler and good cover point, who made his first-class debut for Hampshire in 1883 while still at Cheltenham College. He played a total of seven matches for the county from 1883-1885, when they lost first-class status, although he returned to play a number of matches in 1892. In his first-class career, he averaged 9.42 with the bat, including 42 v Somerset in 1884, and took 2-28 v Surrey in 1885, his only bowling for the county.

Heath, George Edward Mansell (282) born Hong Kong 20.2.1913, died Fareham 6.3.1994. Heath a right-arm pace bowler, first played in the Bournemouth area, joined the groundstaff in 1934, and played for Hampshire Club & Ground v the United Services at Portsmouth in May 1935 where his first victim, bowled, was Hampshire's amateur batsman, JE Manners. Heath spent two years playing for the Club & Ground, then in May 1937 he made his first-class debut, again at Portsmouth, v Essex and in the second innings he took 4-76, although Essex won. In that first season, he took 79 wickets at 22.92, three times taking five or more wickets in an innings, then in 1938, 97 wickets at 23.77 including 7-89 v Kent at Southampton. John Arlott (1957) said "he bowled a late outswinger, which troubled the best batsmen in the country … (and) as a shock opening bowler he was of very high quality indeed", also suggesting that in that second season "he was seriously considered for Test selection against Australia". That did not happen, and his third season brought 57 more expensive wickets, followed by the six-year break, and when he returned he was already 33. In the first three post-war seasons, he took 155 wickets at around 30 each, including his best of 7-49 v Derbyshire in 1947, but with Derek Shackleton playing regularly, there were just four games in 1949 after which he retired. He played all of his 132 first-class matches for Hampshire, taking 404 wickets at 28.11. He was no batsman scoring 586 runs at 5.58 with a best of 34*.

Heath, Malcolm Brewster (334) born Ferndown, Dorset 9.3.1934. In late August 1949, 15-year-old pace bowler Malcolm Heath played his first Minor Counties Championship match for Hampshire 2nd XI v Wiltshire. His team were so dominant that he did not bowl, but in the following season he played more frequently, and his first wicket was the future Gloucestershire captain, Derrick Bailey. Hampshire have produced very few of 'their own' genuine fast bowlers through their history, and while they had a highly effective opening partnership in the 1950s in Shackleton and Cannings, the arrival of Malcolm Heath gave them the edge of pace and lift that other counties enjoyed – although Heath was always the nicest of men; a 'gentle giant'. He continued to play for the 2nd XI until making his first-class debut age 20, at Leicester in August 1954 and he finished that first season with 17 wickets at 15.41. 1955 was, the marvellous year in which just 13 men, plus Ingleby-Mackenzie in one match, took Hampshire to third place for the first time, and Heath was one of the six local 'graduates', all of whom would be there when they went one better in 1958, and then won the title in 1961. Heath contributed 33 wickets at 20.45, and his record was similar in 1956, after which came his best years. In 1957, he took 76 wickets (67 in the Championship) and won his cap. Then came the wet summer of 1958; Hampshire's and Heath's finest. He was replacing Vic Cannings as Shackleton's opening partner by now, and took 126 wickets at 16.42

In that year, he took 6-53 v Gloucestershire at Bristol, 13-86 v Sussex at Portsmouth in the match, including his career best 8-43, and then in the extraordinary game at Burton-on Trent, he and Shackleton bowled unchanged, with Heath's match figures 13-87. Improbable as it sounds, Hampshire lost by 103 runs, and that probably consigned them to second place rather than the title. 1959 was the season of endless sun, covered wickets and the arrival of the fast, and more aggressive 'Butch'White, and Heath's return of 71 wickets cost more than double his average of 1958. From this point, he was generally selected as first-change, and often came in on the hard Portsmouth wickets, while the spinners played at Bournemouth and elsewhere. Still for the next two seasons he averaged in the mid-20s and his 54 Championship wickets certainly contributed to the first title in 1961. On 22 August, he took 3-42 in an important victory v Leicestershire at Portsmouth, but the left-arm spinner Wassell played in the final three matches, including the historic meeting v Derbyshire at Bournemouth. Heath was less successful in 1962 and struggling with a hip injury, his career ended at the age of just 28. He took 527 first-class wickets for Hampshire at an average of 25.11 – he is 18th in their list of all-time wicket-takers and will probably remain there in today's reduced programme. His batting was rather more modest – he was a genuine number 11, scoring 569 runs at 5.86 and a best of 33 v Sussex in 1955, although towards the end of the 1961 season, he enjoyed hitting 28 against the Australians at Southampton. In later years, he coached at Lord's, and played for MCC, and in club cricket in northern England.

Hebden, Geoffrey George Lockwood (285, Amateur) born Chiswick 14.7.1918, died Surrey 27.3.2000. His father GL played in 28 matches for Middlesex, either side of the First World War, and Geoffrey Hebden made his Hampshire debut in the Bournemouth week of late August 1937, taking two Northamptonshire wickets as Hampshire won by an innings, before finding Yorkshire more formidable. 11 years later he played again in the same Bournemouth week, and again Yorkshire came down, but there was to be little success post-war, with no more wickets, and just 49 runs in his four matches. From 1952-1960, he played for Dorset, and he also appeared in matches for MCC and the Club Cricket Conference.

Hedley, Sir Walter Coote (119, Amateur) born Taunton 12.12.1865, died Berkshire 27.12.1937. He was an all-rounder who played for various first-class sides, initially Kent, most frequently his native Somerset (84 first-class matches, 1892-1904) and in 1905 in three matches for Hampshire, for whom he scored 69 runs at 11.50, and took two wickets. It is interesting that he was still bowling in 1905; in his career, he took 343 wickets at under 20 apiece, but in 1900, when there were several controversies around throwing, the captains of the first-class counties condemned his action. The majority of his wickets were taken before that point, and he did not play or bowl again until 1903, although he played for Dorset in 1902. After his county career ended, he played principally for the Royal Engineers.

Hemsted, Edward (Pre '95, Amateur) born Whitchurch 10.10.1846, died Weymouth 12.3.1884. He went to Lancing College and in 1863 (age 17), 1866, 1867, and 1869, he played in seven matches for Hampshire, scoring 204 runs at 17.00, and taking eight wickets at 12.25, including 5-14 v Surrey in 1866, as

Hampshire won by 10 wickets, only their second first-class victory. Over a period of at least 14 months in 1872-1873, he played matches in Canada.

Henley, Dr Anthony Alfred (Pre '95, Amateur) born Sherborne 7.11.1846 died Suffolk 14.12.1916. He was a wicketkeeper whose father played for Middlesex, and like his brother Robert (below), he played one match for Hampshire, in his case in 1866 v Surrey at the Oval, scoring 7 & 9, as Surrey, despite following on, won by 59 runs. He did not keep wicket in this match. He played for some years for the Gentlemen of Dorset.

Henley, Robert (Pre '95, Amateur) born Sherborne 10.6.1851, died Ovington, Hampshire 21.3.1889. Like his brother, his school was Sherborne and he played once for the county, in 1875, scoring 14 in his one innings v Kent at Ridding Field, Winchester. Kent won by an innings, but in the first, for whatever reason, and prior to Hampshire fielding, he was recorded as absent injured. He batted at number three in the second innings. He played also for Winchester Garrison and Dorset.

Herath, Herath Mudiyanselage Rangana Keerthi Bandara (505) born Sri Lanka, 19.3.1978. Slow-left-arm bowler Herath has become one of the finest spin bowlers in the world with over 400 Test Match wickets, but his brief spell with Hampshire early in the 2010 season was not particularly successful. He played for Surrey in 2009, and then for Hampshire in four first-class matches, taking 10 wickets at 46.43, including 4-98 in a Somerset innings of 524 at the Rose Bowl. He played also in five limited-overs matches, taking five wickets.

Herman, Oswald William ('Lofty') (252) born Oxford 18.9.1907, died Southampton 24.6.1987. Pace bowler 'Lofty' Herman was one of a number of good county cricketers who came from Oxford to Hampshire in the first half of the twentieth century, and in a career from 1929-1948 he played in 321 first-class matches and with 1,041 wickets, was one of only seven men to take more than a thousand for the county. He played briefly in Minor Counties cricket for his native county before making his Hampshire debut at Swansea in May 1929. He did not play regularly in that first month, then twice took six wickets in an innings, v Glamorgan and Surrey, and he ended his first season with 60 wickets for Hampshire at 25.01. There were just 38 wickets in 1930, although he recorded his best of 8-49 v Yorkshire at Bournemouth, and through that decade he was consistent, taking over 100 wickets in 1932, and 1936-1938. His 101 wickets in 1938 included a hat-trick v Glamorgan at Portsmouth, but surprisingly he left the county and in 1939 played in the Lancashire League for Rochdale.

After the war, he returned to Hampshire, taking 115 wickets at 20.51 in 1946; in the following two seasons, there were a further 112 wickets, but in 1949 he played only for the 2nd XI, as Derek Shackleton emerged and he retired, playing for Wiltshire, and coaching at Oxford University, Harrow, and in South Africa, before eventually becoming a first-class umpire (1963-1974). Although he will always be remembered as a pace bowler, he enjoyed his batting, scoring over 4,000 runs – often at a rapid rate – with a best at Leicester of 92 in 1948, scored from 125 while he was batting. John Arlott (1957) suggested his "great quality lay … in his pace from the pitch" although necessity and a shortage of regular supporting bowlers in the 1930s, "made him a defensive bowler".

Herman, Robert Stephen ('Bob') (366) born Southampton 30.11.1946. Pace bowler 'Bob' Herman, the son of 'Lofty', was born in the county but raised mainly in London and joined Middlesex, playing 92 first-class matches from 1965-1971 and while there he had a hand in Hampshire's history, when at Portsmouth in 1967, he bowled Bob Cottam with the last ball of the match – the fourth and last tie in Hampshire's history. At the end of the 1971 season, pace bowlers Cottam, White and Castell all left Hampshire, and they began the construction of a new pace attack by signing Herman. In his first season with Hampshire he took 81 wickets, his best total, at 21.66, and including match figures of 9-127 against his former county at Lord's, and his career best of 8-42 v Warwickshire. In 1973, Herman had a regular new partner in Tom Mottram, supported by new signing Mike Taylor from Nottinghamshire. Along with Jesty and spinners Sainsbury and O'Sullivan they exceeded all expectations and bowled Hampshire to their second title, Herman bowling the most overs and taking 64 wickets. In 1974 when the addition of Andy Roberts made them stronger but less lucky, Herman rose to the challenge, playing in every match with 74 wickets at less than 20 each. He had bowled superbly for those three seasons, taking 217 wickets, but he struggled with control in the next two seasons, taking just 52 wickets at an average of 36.88. In early May 1977 he played at Edgbaston, returning figures of 14-1-48-0 and his first-class career came to an end. He played fairly regularly in limited-overs matches for Hampshire, although when they won their first trophy, the Sunday League, in 1975 he did not play from late July – in total, he took 137 limited-overs wickets for Hampshire at 21.03, and an economy rate below four. In 1978 and 1979 he played for Dorset, and in the Southern League for Trojans, and in the early 1980s was a first-class umpire.

Hervey-Bathurst, Sir Frederick Thomas Arthur (Pre '95, Amateur) born London 13.3.1833, died London 20.5.1900. His father (also Sir Frederick) was one of the key figures in the creation of Hampshire County Cricket Club and the purchase of the Antelope Ground, and had played first-class cricket for Hampshire, but prior to the club's formation, so is not included here. His sons, FTA and Lionel (below) both played for the county. FTA Hervey-Bathurst was a pupil at Eton, made his first-class debut for MCC in 1852 and also played for Devon and Wiltshire. He played in three matches for Hampshire in 1861 v MCC (4-104), in 1865 v Surrey when he top-scored with 30 in an innings of 64 but did not bowl, and 1866 v MCC – his final first-class match. In the early 1860s he was MP for South Wiltshire, and he fought in the Crimean War.

Hervey-Bathurst, Lionel (Pre '95, Amateur) born Wiltshire, 7.7.1849, died Hertfordshire 4.5.1908. He was a batsman and wicketkeeper, half-brother to FTA, and after Rugby School played two matches for Hampshire v Kent in 1875, scoring 30 runs at 7.50. In the second match, he is recorded as wicketkeeper, yet bowled four overs (0-8). Hampshire lost both matches by an innings. In 1905, he changed his name to Lionel Paston-Cooper.

Heseltine, Christopher (6, Amateur) born London, 26.11.1869, died Lymington 13.6.1944. Fast bowler Heseltine attended Eton but did not make the XI, and then Cambridge University where he did not play first-class cricket. He played for the MCC from 1890 – including a non-first-class match against Hampshire at Southampton, although he did not bowl. He made his first-class debut for MCC in 1892, and made his Hampshire debut in a non-first-class match v South Africans in 1894. After three first-class matches for MCC early in 1895, he played in Hampshire's inaugural match in the County Championship when they returned to first-class cricket at Taunton in late May, although he bowled just one maiden over, and did not play another match that summer. Despite this, he played in two Test Matches in the following winter, although not quite the 'Test Matches' with which we are familiar. Lord Hawke took a touring party to South Africa, playing mostly second-class matches, but they also met South Africa in three first-class matches which were retrospectively deemed Test Matches. Hampshire's AJL Hill played in all three, and Heseltine in the second and third, while RM Poore, serving in South Africa, played for the home country. It is a measure of the status of that England side that when they next played a Test in the following summer, only one man remained – Heseltine never played any further 'Tests', but he does have a best bowling of 5-38 (his only wickets in the two matches). He played in 52 matches for Hampshire until 1904, taking 114 wickets at 27.45, with a best of 7-106 at Derby in 1899, when he took 45 wickets; his best in one season. He played very little after that, serving in the South African 'Boer' War, and subsequently in the First World War in his mid-40s. He was President of Hampshire in the 1920s, and again from 1936-1944, and his son CCP, played once in a non-first-class match for Hampshire in 1943 v the Empire XI.

Hesketh-Prichard, Hesketh Vernon ('Hex') (70, Amateur) born India 17.11.1876, died Hertfordshire 14.6.1922. He was a fast bowler who played in 60 first-class matches, taking 233 wickets at 23.45 each – 15 times taking five wickets in an innings, and four times 10 wickets in the match. But such bare facts go no way towards accounting for the extraordinary life of this man, who died at 45 as a result of his experiences in the war, yet packed into those years more than most people who live many years longer. There are two biographies of the man known as 'Hex', one by Eric Parker, published two years after his death, which focuses mostly on other aspects of his life, and more recently, Simon Sweetman's, for the 'Lives in Cricket' series published by ACS (2012). Sweetman tells us how 'Hex' went on many voyages of exploration, publishing accounts of them, wrote popular pulp fiction with his mother, was "rated the best game shot in Britain … and went out to the Western Front and taught the British Army and some of their allies how to snipe and how to avoid being sniped at". Sweetman adds "he was destroyed by the war, even though it made him famous".

His father an army officer in India, died of Typhoid in the month before he was born as Hesketh Vernon Prichard – he added the second, hyphenated Hesketh himself in later years. As a cricketer, he bowled impressively at Fettes, but left before his final year, and living in Sussex, played club cricket at Horsham along with some county players. He played also for JM Barrie's authors' XI, the Allahakbarries, as he had already begun writing, and in 1897 met Arthur Conan Dolyle. Their friendship provided a link with cricket in Hampshire, although it seems he was never actually qualified by residence. In 1900 however, Hampshire were in a desperate state, with an already weak side losing amateur soldiers to the Boer War, and 'Hex' made his debut v Somerset at Bath, taking 3-34, although there were just nine wickets in the four matches in his debut season.

He did not play in 1901, travelling instead to Patagonia to report for the *Daily Express* on a search for the Giant Sloth, but back in 1902, 13 matches brought 40 wickets for the county and he appeared in the first of four games for WG Grace's London County XI – at various times he would also appear for MCC and the Gentlemen v Players, including perhaps his most famous match in 1904 at Lord's. The Gentlemen trailed by 156 on first innings, and when the Players were dismissed – 'Hex' 5-80 – the victory target was an improbable 412. They were 108-3, then lost the fourth wicket at 302, subsiding to 320-6. When 'Hex' arrived, they were 400-8 and he had a justified reputation as a 'real' number 11, except that on this occasion that place was taken by the injured HC McDonell, who would later play for Hampshire. In his first-class career 'Hex' scored 724 runs at 7.46, never once reaching 40, and his style was likened to a child on the beach, digging a sandpit, but this time he stayed with Arthur Jones (56*) as they scored the twelve runs for a famous victory. This was also the year that he took 104 wickets in the season, although it was the following season when he recorded his best figures of 8-32 v Derbyshire – in another four Championship innings he took seven wickets. He played regularly in 1905, but thereafter very little until 1912, and there were just five Championship appearances in his last first-class season of 1913. In 1914, he played matches for I Zingari in Egypt but then came the war, fame, a DSO and MC, but also gas, and the horrors which left him a changed man. He continued to write but there was little if any cricket, and when he died he was as surely a casualty of that terrible conflict as the men who died in battle. He was nonetheless – and despite his amateur approach – one of the finest of Hampshire's fast bowlers, and perhaps the most extraordinary character in their entire history. (There is some debate as to whether his 'new' surname was hyphenated. He is included here under H, rather than P, his original surname).

Hill, Anthony Ewart Ledger (206, Amateur) born Sparsholt House, Hants 14.7.1901, died Winchester 25.10.1986. He had the burden of being the son of AJL, a leading Hampshire cricketer in their early years in the Championship, who played for England (below) although without that connection he might have played little if any first-class cricket. AEL Hill made his first-class debut in 1920, shortly after leaving Marlborough, and through the decade appeared in 18 matches, but with little success, scoring 193 runs at 7.42 and a best of 24. He played in one first-class match for MCC v Wales in 1928. He played for Hampshire Hogs, and toured Canada with the Free Foresters.

Hill, Arthur James Ledger (7, Amateur) born Bassett 26.7.1871, died Sparsholt House 6.9.1950. AJL Hill, known as Ledger, was predominantly a batting all-rounder, who enjoyed a successful first-class career for Hampshire from 1895-1920. He played at Marlborough and Cambridge University, winning his 'blue' in all four years 1890-1893, and by then was playing in Minor Counties matches for Hampshire. In 1895, he played in Hampshire's first match in the County Championship, opening the batting, but being run out in both innings. He toured variously with Lord Hawke to India in 1892/3, USA in 1894 and South Africa in 1895/6 when the three matches against South Africa were subsequently designated Test Matches. In the last of them, Hill scored 124 and took 4-8 but never played for England again, mainly because many strong players were not on that tour, but also because as an amateur he remained in South Africa on business through that year. As a consequence, he missed the 1896 county season but returned in 1897, although he never played in more than the 16 first-class games in that year and only in 1898 (14) did he play more than 11 times – post-war, he played seven matches in three seasons, including 90 v Middlesex in his second match of 1919. His final game v Gloucestershire at Southampton began on the day following his 50th birthday. Despite not playing regularly – he never made 1,000 runs in a season – his career record was none-theless indicative of his ability; for Hampshire, he scored 8,381 runs at 30.58 with 17 centuries including a best of 199 v Surrey at the Oval in 1898, and he took 199 wickets at 31.22, with 7-36 v Leicestershire at Southampton in 1897. In 1905, he scored a century in both innings v Somerset at Taunton and averaged 46.53, and his century v Surrey at Aldershot was the only three figure innings by a Hampshire player on that ground. He and his son both played in 1920, although not in the same first-class match, and in later years he was a member of the club's committee, chairman from 1935-1939 and President in 1929.

Hill, Gerald ('Gerry') (264) born Totton 15.4.1913, died Lyndhurst 31.1.2006. Off-spinning all-rounder Gerry Hill was a cheerful cricketer who played for Hampshire in 371 matches from 1932-1954, a period when the first group of great professionals were retiring, and during which Hampshire rarely rose from the bottom reaches of the Championship. In those 17 years, he played under six 'official' captains (all amateurs) and a number of deputies, five in the 1930s alone, although the arrival of Eagar in 1946 brought greater stability. He was discovered by Arthur Conan Doyle who recommended him to Hampshire, and a trial was followed by a contract, making his first-class debut in 1932. There would be 371 first-class matches by the end of his career, but unlike many amateurs, or major players, he was a one-team man – every game for his county. His all-round status is confirmed by 9,085 runs and 617 wickets but it was not the case that in every year the return was a balanced one. For example, he batted at various times in all eleven positions for Hampshire and while there were 28 half-centuries, his conversion rate was low, on just four occasions he reached three figures. In 1936, he struggled with the bat scoring just 276 runs at 8.36, but two years later he scored 935 runs at his best average of 28.33, and in both 1946 and 1947 he reached four figures in the season.

With the ball, he broke through in 1935 with 93 wickets at just below 25. There were just 43 wickets in the difficult 1936 season, but then 83, although in the last two seasons before the war his tally fell again. He took 51 wickets on return, and 48 in 1947 but thereafter never more than 35 – he was part of a strong spin attack in those later years with Charlie Knott, Jim Bailey and Reg Dare, who were succeeded by the youngsters, Sainsbury and Burden. He finished in 1954, then played for some years with JS White's at Cowes, and lived out his long life in the New Forest. He remains in the Hampshire records for his 5th wicket partnership of 235 with 'Hooky' Walker v Sussex at Portsmouth in 1937, which has never been broken. By strange coincidence JH & HW Parks set the Sussex record for that wicket in the same match, and it too still stands.

Hill, Michael John ('Mick') (370) born Berkshire 1.7.1951. Hill was one of the wicketkeeping understudies; in his case to Bob Stephenson, who rarely missed a match during the 1970s. Hill played for Hampshire 2nd XI from 1970 and made his debut v West Indies in 1973 – indeed three of his six matches were against touring XIs. In 1976 covering injury, he had a run of four first-class and three limited-overs games in May, but that was the end of his first-class career, although he remained on the staff until the end of the following season, and the arrival of Bobby Parks. He would often take charge of the 2nd XI, especially after the death of Geoff Keith.

Hindley, Richard James Edward (467) born Portsmouth 25.4.1975. Off-spinning all-rounder Hindley has been a leading Southern League cricketer with Havant for many years, winning a number of titles. He became one of the most interesting of Hampshire's many 'one match wonders', when in 2003, he was one of six men, who made their first-class debut for the county and played only in that season. The most notable were Test cricketers Wasim Akram and Ed Giddins who, after playing eight games between them, departed mid-season. Hampshire had started the season replacing their suspended captain Shane Warne and struggled, but Hindley's one match in mid-July v Glamorgan at the Rose Bowl proved to be one of the most remarkable in their history as one of just three games that Hampshire won after following-on. Hindley was selected because Shaun Udal was injured, but on the first day Glamorgan scored at better than four runs per over, and when they were all out the next morning they had reached 437, with Hindley's figures 9-0-46-0. They then dismissed Hampshire for 185 and by the close of day two, Hampshire, 114-4, still trailed by 138. On day three however, Nic Pothas scored a century, and Mascarenhas 75, so when Hindley arrived at 343-6, the lead was approaching three figures. Hindley had his hand broken by the Australian Kasprowicz, but added 51 with Mascarenhas, and with the tail took Hampshire to a lead of 197, carrying his bat for 68*. He departed for hospital to learn that his season was over, but by the close Glamorgan were 33-3, and with wickets falling regularly on the fourth morning (Tremlett 6-51) Hampshire won before lunchtime by 93 runs. Hindley never played first-class cricket again, but without his contribution, it is unlikely that would have been the final result. He became a coach in the county, and 15 years later, he still plays for Havant in the Southern League.

Hitchcock, Lt Gen. Sir Basil Ferguson Burnett (31, Amateur) born Chatham 3.3.1877, died London 23.11.1938. He was also known as Burnett-Hitchcock. He attended schools at Harrow and Brighton, and played in two matches for Hampshire in the season before his twentieth birthday. He did not bowl, and batted at number 10 v Derbyshire, making his highest score of 21. In his next match v Yorkshire he was the last man in, was dismissed for a single, and was absent injured in the second innings.

Holder, John Wakefield (358) born Barbados 19.3.1945. Pace bowler Holder played for Hampshire 2nd XI from 1965, showing considerable promise, at a time when Hampshire were looking to find successors to their Championship-winning bowlers – especially Shackleton who retired from full-time cricket after the 1968 season. In June 1968, Holder made his debut v Somerset at Portsmouth, taking 5-96 (including Greg Chappell) and 2-29. In that first season, he generally replaced the injured White and took 18 wickets at 26.72. After few matches in 1969, he took 55 wickets in 1970, then 19 in 1971 and 40 in 1972, including his best innings return of 7-79 at Gloucester, and a hat-trick v Kent at Southampton. In those five seasons his average never exceeded 28, but his team-mate Andy Murtagh has written a recent biography revealing, with photographic evidence, how his open-chested action, anticipating fellow Bajan Malcolm Marshall, was altered to the 'classic' side-on, after which he experienced problems with no balls and wides. Despite a career record of 139 first-class wickets at 24.80 and 46 limited-overs wickets at 26.36, his Hampshire career ended at Derby in August 1972 with five wicketless overs in the first innings, and when Derbyshire followed-on and drew the game, he did not bowl. He moved to Lancashire, playing as the professional for Rawtenstall through the 1974 season, and he played briefly in South Africa, but in the 1980s he became a first-class umpire in the English game, then officiated in international matches and became well known in the media as an authority on 'difficult' decisions. He umpired in first-class cricket from 1982-2009, and in Test Matches from 1988-2001.

Holland, Ian Gabriel (547) born Wisconsin, USA, 3.10.1990. He is a medium -pace bowling all-rounder who was born in the USA, but grew up in Australia and played in one first-class match for Victoria. He played for Fleetwood in the Northern Premier League from 2013-early 2016, but also for Hampshire 2nd XI from 2015. He joined the county staff in 2017, made his first-class debut and scored 234 runs in 13 matches at 26.00, including 58* v Surrey, taking 19 wickets with 4-16 v Somerset, which remains his best. He missed the winter tournament in Barbados with an injury, but came back into Hampshire's Championship side from the middle of the 2018 season, although he plays rarely in 'white ball' cricket. He has scored two first-class half centuries for the county (average 19.42) and taken 34 wickets at 23.67. In 2017, he played for South Wilts in the Southern League and in 2018 for St Cross.

Hollingworth, Thomas Vernon (250, Amateur) born New York, USA, 27.7.1907, died Topsham, Devon 2.10.1973. He attended Bromsgrove School in the midlands, and played in two matches for Hampshire in 1929, scoring 14 runs in three innings, and bowling three overs (0-17). He also played in two first-class matches for the Europeans in India in 1933 & 1934. From 1933-1948 he played for Devon.

Holmes, Henry (Pre '95) born Romsey 11.11.1833, died Southampton 6.1.1913. Holmes was a medium pace round-arm bowler, useful batsman and occasional wicketkeeper, who played for Hampshire before the formation of the County Cricket Club, and then in 27 of their first 28 first-class matches from 1864-1878 (there were also five matches for five other first-class sides). His appearances included Hampshire County Cricket Club's inaugural first-class match in July 1864 v Sussex at the Antelope Ground and in his publication about that game Alan Edwards (2014) described Holmes as "one of the unsung heroes of Hampshire cricket", despite a relatively modest career record. For the county club, he scored 692 runs at 15.04 and took 22 wickets at 22.90, but Edwards describes him as a "cricketer of considerable ability", including being an accomplished and versatile fielder. He had played for Wiltshire, and was professional at the Southampton Union Club, the East Hants Club in Southsea, then the South Hants Club in the mid-1860s, but circumstances determined that he was in his thirties when the match v Sussex took place – he took two wickets in a 10-wicket defeat. In the return later that season, he made his highest score for the county, 71, and took part in Hampshire's first century partnership, while in 1876 he took 5-57, his best bowling, at Derby. In 1877, Holmes began another phase of his cricketing life as a first-class umpire; this continued until he was 65 in 1899 – he stood in the match when Yorkshire's openers set the first wicket world record of 554 at Chesterfield in 1898, by which time he had also been Hampshire's groundsman. In later years, he played cricket at the Totton Club, but he was also involved in some rather odd 'incidents', described in detail by Edwards, who suggests he was "independent (and) … sometimes pig-headed".

Holt, Arthur George (275) born Southampton 8.4.1911, died Southampton 28.7.1994. Arthur Holt was entirely a Hampshire man, perhaps even more, one of Southampton's finest. For his home town club, he played with some success at football, through the 1930s, scoring 46 goals in 206 league matches, and captaining the side. As a cricketer, he played for Hampshire's youth side and Deanery before joining Hampshire's staff in 1934 and making his debut at 24 in 1935. He took some time to make an impression; centuries at Leicester (117) and Edgbaston in 1938 & 1939 helped, but then like many others he lost six seasons to the war – in his case from the age of 29.

There would be no more centuries, but his return in 1946 brought his most consistent season with 891 runs at 24.75. Gradually however, younger batsmen like Rogers, Dawson, Gray and Harrison began to establish themselves, and Holt's last first-class match came at Worthing in 1948 – a season of just 218 runs and one half century. He left first-class cricket with a record of 2,853 runs in 79 matches at 22.46, and one wicket – of the Warwickshire captain Peter Cranmer in the same 1939 match that he scored 115. If that was his tale, he would be another unlucky cricketer, deprived of six seasons and with a modest record, but when the Hampshire coach Sam Staples was taken ill, Desmond Eagar saw Arthur Holt as the obvious replacement. It was a fortuitous appointment and over the next two decades, 'Holt's Colts' included Sainsbury, Heath, Barnard, Wassell, White, Timms, Castell, Cottam, Jesty, Lewis, Turner and Greenidge, as he, Eagar and others built the two sides that brought the Championship to Hampshire. More than that, he gave opportunities to many young cricketers to test themselves in his Colts, Club & Ground and 2nd XI teams, and he took sides around the county, as ambassadors for the county club, playing against the local clubs. He did all this with a smile and great good humour and is still remembered with great affection. With good reason, the pavilion on the Nursery/2nd XI ground at the Ageas Bowl is named in his honour.

Hopkins, Frank Jesse (129) born Birmingham 30.6.1875, died Southampton 15.1.1930. Jesse Hopkins was a left-arm medium pace bowler who took 25 wickets in 11 first-class matches for his native Warwickshire (1898-1903) and then moved to Southampton and became the groundsman at Northlands Road. He played in two first-class matches for Hampshire in 1906 and one more in 1911, but his record was modest, with 12 runs at 4.00 and four wickets at 43.75, but was nonetheless a loyal member of the Hampshire staff; before the war he declined an invitation to move to Lord's as groundsman, and as late as 1925, age 50, he was supervising the boys on the groundstaff.

Horton, Henry (326) born Herefordshire 18.4.1923, died, recorded as either Birmingham or Colwall, 3.11.1998. Henry Horton was the archetypal professional sportsman of the mid-twentieth century. He played football for Blackburn Rovers from 1946-1950 before moving to Southampton for whom he played 75 matches from 1951-1953. By then he had played cricket as an amateur, then professionally for Worcestershire, where his older brother Joe played before the war. Henry's career with his first county was not a success; he averaged under 10, with a best of 21, and in 1949, he turned his back on the summer game.

When he arrived in Southampton, however, he met Arthur Holt who was linked to both clubs, and he persuaded Henry to return to cricket. In May 1953, he scored 99 in a non-first-class match for Hampshire v the Army, and a couple of weeks later made his Championship debut, scoring 49 v Leicestershire at Portsmouth, already a month past his 30th birthday. He would play for Hampshire into his mid-40s but it is extraordinary to consider that despite this very late start, he scored 21,536 runs, placing him sixth in the list of all-time run scorers for the county (average 32.83 with 32 centuries). More than that, from 1955, Horton, Jimmy Gray and Roy Marshall formed as good a top three as was to be found anywhere in the Championship, and their contributions to third place that year, second in 1958 and the title in 1961 were considerable. Horton passed 1,000 runs for 12 consecutive seasons starting in 1955, and from 1959-1961, over 2,000 runs each year. In the 'batsman's summer' of 1959, his total of 2,428 runs has been bettered only by Mead and Marshall and he led Hampshire's averages with 47.60. While he had a reputation of being somewhat dour, with a rather odd stance, Jimmy Gray would suggest that in second innings run-chases, he was as likely to win the game as the more illustrious Roy Marshall. Perhaps surprisingly he never reached 150 in a Championship match. He played in the early years of knock-out cricket, with two half-centuries in 13 matches. Henry Horton was the bravest of cricketers in the days with minimal protection, no helmets, and some lively pitches, especially on outgrounds. He played less often in 1967, and then retired to become a coach with Worcestershire, and a first-class umpire from 1973-1976.

Hosie, Alexander Lindsay ('Alec') (187, Amateur) born Wenchow, China 6.8.1890, died Southampton 11.6.57. He was a right-handed batsman and occasional bowler, who played five first-class matches for Oxford University (no 'blue') in 1913, the last of which was against Hampshire at Southampton, and having made a half-century, one month later he made his Championship debut at Harrogate. After three matches, he did not reappear in 1914 but played some matches while serving in India towards the end of the war. He remained a serving officer in India and thereafter only played in English first-class cricket when home on leave. In 1921, he played a full season (21 matches, including one for Free Foresters) scoring almost 1,000 runs for Hampshire, with 122 v Gloucestershire, but he did not play in England again until 1925 (12 matches), then 1928 scoring 1,213 runs for Hampshire with three centuries, including 155 v Yorkshire at Southampton, his highest for the county, sharing a partnership of 240 with Phil Mead. Hosie played for a variety of first-class sides in India and England, including MCC, the Gentlemen and the Free Foresters and appeared in 11 more first-class matches in 1930, and 12 in 1935 – mainly for Hampshire. His final first-class record for Hampshire was 3,542 runs in 80 matches at 26.83. He also made a number of overseas tours, and in emergency, played a match for Tennyson's side in India in 1937/8. In the following year, he played his last first-class game for MCC v Cambridge University. While at Oxford University he won 'blues' for lawn tennis, hockey and football.

Hotham, Admiral Sir Alan Geoffrey (86, Amateur) born Edinburgh 3.10.1876, died London 10.7.1965. He was a batsman and Naval officer, who played in one match in 1903 v Lancashire at Portsmouth, while stationed in the city, scoring 5 & 11 in an eight-wicket defeat. Two years later, he played for Devon in the Minor Counties Championship, and he played non-first-class matches for the Royal Navy and MCC.

Howell, Benjamin Alexander Cameron ('Benny') (511) born Bordeaux, France 5.10.1988. All-rounder Howell played for Hampshire 2nd XI in 2005, age 16, and developed through the Academy to make his first team debut in 2011 v Lancashire at the Rose Bowl. He began with a 'duck' but when Hampshire followed on, his 71 was top score in a ten-wicket defeat. Despite that promising start, he did not play first-class cricket again that year, but having played in two limited-overs matches in 2010, he was more regular in 2011, and scored a superb century (122) v Surrey at Whitgift School. He played in thirteen T20 matches for Hampshire, averaging 30.75 with the bat, although he bowled little. Since he was just 22, he seemed to have a promising future but following what was suggested to be misbehaviour, he found his career with Hampshire at an end. He joined Gloucestershire in 2012, and has enjoyed a good career there, particularly in T20 cricket where he has been spoken of as a possible international, notably for his bowling, with 82 wickets at less than 20 each and an economy rate below seven per over.

Hughes, Philip Joel (507) born New South Wales, Australia 30.11.1988, died Sydney, Australia 27.11.2014. Australian Test batsman Hughes played three first-class matches for Hampshire towards the end of the 2010 season, scoring 85 runs at 14.16, and in two limited-overs matches (32 & 1). It was not a record that reflected his ability, but sadly Hughes is now remembered for the tragedy of his death; struck by a short ball under the helmet in a match for South Australia v New South Wales when 63*, he did not recover and died in hospital two days later.

Humphrey, William (Pre '95) born Mitcham Surrey 15.9.1843, died Norwich 24.2.1918. Humphrey was one of four brothers who played first-class cricket – most notably 'Tom' Humphrey (born 1839). William was a right-handed, round-arm fast bowler who played in eight first-class matches in 1864, four each for Surrey and then Hampshire – an indication of the somewhat 'liberal' approach to qualification in those days. During this period, he was a profes-sional with the South Hants Club, and also played for his home club Mitcham.

His matches for Hampshire began with the county club's inaugural first-class match v Sussex at the Antelope and he was one of only four men to play in all four of Hampshire's matches that season, yet he never appeared in first-class cricket again. Instead he moved to Norfolk as professional for East Dereham. He played also for Norfolk at least until 1880, and umpired some matches for them – a more complete biography can be found by Alan Edwards (2014). In his four matches for Hampshire, he scored 50 runs at 7.14 and took four wickets at 25.00.

Humphreys, Walter Alexander senior (82) born Southsea 28.10.1849, died Brighton 23.3.1924. He was a useful lower order batsman, but mainly one of the last regular underarm lob bowlers, who took 718 first-class wickets in a career that began with 248 matches for Sussex from 1871-1896. In 1894/5, he toured Australia with AE Stoddard's side. When he umpired in first-class matches in 1896, his career seemed to have ended until, in 1900, age 50, he appeared in two matches for his native county, Hampshire, v Kent and Leicestershire, taking nine wickets at 27.33, with a best of 5-71, in the first match at Tonbridge. His son (same name) played for Sussex from 1898-1900.

Hyland, Frederick James ('Fred') (233) born Battle, Sussex 16.12.1893, died Cheshire 27.2.1964. Hyland is one of Hampshire's 'one match wonders', and in recent years has become a certain kind of historical 'celebrity'. He was selected for one match, at Northampton in 1924 in a match that lasted just two overs, and since Hampshire were in the field, with Kennedy and Newman bowling the two overs, it is entirely possible that Hyland never touched the ball. The first day ended with Northamptonshire 1-0, there was no further play, and Hyland never played again in first-class cricket. For many years, little was known about him, but Keith Walmsley's research for his publication Brief Candles (2012) revealed more, noting that he had outstanding seasons for Ringwood CC in 1923 & 1924. He added that after the one match, Hyland travelled with the team to Trent Bridge, but was not selected, before playing for Hampshire Hogs at Northlands Road, and then to the Isle of Wight to play for a full Hampshire side against the Islanders. He moved to Norfolk and also played for Broughty Ferry CC in Scotland, before settling in Cheshire and working as a groundsman and in horticulture. His 12-ball career is not the shortest for Hampshire (see Cornwallis) but Walmsley says it is the shortest in all first-class cricket.

Hyslop, Hector Henry (Pre '95) born Southampton 13.12.1840, died Cosham, Portsmouth 11.9.1920. In 1876 & 1877 he appeared in seven matches for Hampshire, during which time he also played for the Players of the South v the Gentlemen of the South. He was a batsman and wicketkeeper, although he also bowled a little in first-class matches. His final first-class match was at Harrogate in 1886, for the touring Australians v an England XI and he had also played for the tourists (non-first-class) in 1878 in an emergency, because it was believed he was born in Australia. For Hampshire, he scored 106 runs at 8.83, dismissed 17 batsmen with the gloves (11 stumped), and also took two wickets, with a best of 2-12 v MCC at Lord's – one of nine Hampshire bowlers. MCC won by nine wickets. It is said that he died by his own hand.

I

(Mohammad) **Imran Tahir** (495) born Punjab Pakistan 27.3.1979. He was a leg-break bowler who played in Pakistan, and briefly for Middlesex and Yorkshire before joining a struggling Hampshire side in late July 2008, and was immediately successful, taking 7-66 in the second innings v Lancashire at Old Trafford, completing the best debut match figures for the county of 12-189. He followed this with 5-96 v Kent, 4-37 v Yorkshire, 7-58 in the match v Durham, 4-29 v Surrey and 8-113 in the match v Nottinghamshire. Hampshire, threatened with relegation when he arrived, ended in third place. He returned in 2009 with 52 wickets, played for Warwickshire in 2010, then back to Hampshire in the second half of 2011. At the end of the 2014 season he suddenly re-appeared in the last two Championship matches, displacing Danny Briggs as Hampshire (successfully) pursued promotion, with his contributions 3-140, 2-11 and 1-29 – the wicket which brought the title, and elevation. In 2015 & 2016, he played for Nottinghamshire, and in 2017, in the T20 for Derbyshire – some years earlier, he had moved to South Africa and he played in all three formats for his adopted country, with most success in the 'white ball' games. For Hampshire, his 130 wickets cost 25.46, there were 35 limited-overs wickets and in T20 games another 25. He is in many respects the modern 'wandering' cricketer, but for a few seasons, he made a valuable contribution to Hampshire's fortunes.

Ingleby-Mackenzie, Alexander Colin David (323, Amateur) born Dartmouth 15.9.1933, died London 9.3.2006. Colin Ingleby-Mackenzie will occupy for ever a central place in the history of Hampshire County Cricket Club, as the first captain to lead them as runners-up in 1958 *and* the Championship title three years later. This achievement by such a flamboyant man has often been attributed to his gambler's instincts in encouraging the opposition to make generous declarations, but it is a myth; only three of Hampshire's 19 victories in 1961 were won against opponent's declaration and they equalled Yorkshire in capturing all twenty wickets in 15 of their victories. Where Ingleby-Mackenzie's approach was perhaps key, was in encouraging his team to "entertain or perish", and by-and-large the experienced professional group he inherited were happy to follow his lead. Had they not suffered a disastrous August in 1958, they might have won the title then, but he was able to strengthen that first group of players with the addition of White, Wassell, Livingstone and Baldry, and even years later, his team of tough, experienced professional cricketers would happily acknowledge the natural brilliance of his man-management.

He was a left-handed batsman who learned his cricket at Eton, and was spotted in Southampton's Easter nets in 1946 – his father, a naval officer, was stationed at Portsmouth at one time. In 1951, he appeared in representative schools matches at Lord's, top-scoring with 67 v a strong Combined Services side, followed by a Championship debut at the end of the season v Sussex. Sadly, the match was ruined by the rain, but not before the debutant had begun with a 'duck'. By the following season, he had followed his father into the Royal Navy, albeit only on National Service, and played a number of non-first-class matches for them as well as seven first-class matches for Hampshire; coming in at 38-3, he scored 91 v the Indians at Bournemouth. In 1953, he played in just two first-class matches for the Combined Services, while 1954 was his first full county season with four half-centuries in 29 matches. By contrast, as Hampshire finished third in 1955 he played only once, deputising for Leo Harrison, in his capacity as an occasional wicketkeeper. There were more matches in 1956 including his first centuries, then in 1957 he began to deputise as captain and passed 1,000 runs, repeated in the next two seasons. Apart from a shortfall of just two runs in 1960, he would complete four figures each year from 1957-1962, by which time he had led his team to the title, again keeping wicket in a few games, while in 1958, he scored the fastest first-class century of the season. He celebrated the years of success with a somewhat premature, but amusing autobiography *Many a Slip* and a number of 'pleasure' cricket tours abroad, principally to the Caribbean.

What followed was something of an anti-climax as his team of Champions aged, and his form declined. At the end of the 1965 season he retired with 11,140 runs and ten centuries for the county at 24.59, although he returned in 1966 as a wicketkeeper in the Gillette Cup, including Hampshire's first semi-final appearance which ended in a defeat at Worcester, and the conclusion of his Hampshire career. He toured Singapore as a player with MCC as late as 1981/2, and was subsequently their President, playing a key role in admitting women to membership. In 2005, he was awarded an OBE for services to cricket, by which time he was Hampshire's President, remaining in post until his death. His importance to the county was recognised in the naming of the new East Stand a few years later.

Isherwood, Lionel Charlie Ramsbottom (203, Amateur) born Southsea 13.4.1891, died Guildford 30.9.1970. Isherwood was a right-handed batsman who attended Eton College but was 28 when he played for Hampshire in the first year after the war. Over five seasons he played in 26 county matches, the majority in 1921, scoring 453 runs in 15 matches at 20.59, including three half-centuries, and a best for Hampshire of 61* v Somerset at Southampton in an eight-wicket victory – he also scored 61 v Surrey later that season. From 1925-1927 he switched to Sussex, playing 28 matches, and had a very similar record to that at Hampshire, where overall he had scored 627 runs at 16.50. He played also in a number of matches for MCC. John Arlott (1957) described him as "a conscientious, careful batsman with limited strokes, but much patience".

J

Jackman, Frederick (Pre '95) born Fareham 15.51841, died Horndean, Hants 5.9.1891. Jackman played two first-class matches for Hampshire in 1875 and 1877, scoring 26 runs and taking one wicket with his fast, round-arm bowling. At various times, he played other matches for Hampshire Colts, Players of Hampshire, Fareham and Chichester Priory Park.

James, Kevan David (400) born Lambeth 18.3.1961. All-rounder Kevan James was a left-handed batsman and left-arm medium-fast bowler who played club cricket in the Middlesex area and for England Young Cricketers, before joining the Middlesex staff. He made his debut for their 2nd XI in August 1978, age 17, playing regularly from 1980, when he made his first-class debut v Oxford University in the Parks. In 1981, there was a Championship debut in a rain-affected match, and one game v the Pakistanis in 1982 before he appeared more regularly in 1983 – but there were just two matches in 1984. He spent some winters in New Zealand playing for Wellington, but with a Middlesex batting average of 21.44 and 20 wickets at under 20 each, he chose to move to Hampshire to seek more opportunities. In that first season, there were two particularly notable days; his first century (124) v Somerset at Taunton, when he and Tim Tremlett set a county record for the eighth wicket, and 6-22 v the Australians, who were 'skittled' for 76 in a drawn match. Thereafter he became a valuable all-rounder in a strong Hampshire side, in both forms of the game. In 1986, he played a vital innings of 54* at the Oval, rescuing Hampshire from 95-7, and enabling them to post a total which just won the match, and crucially clinched their third Sunday League title – there was also a fine catch in the last over. Despite this he could not always be sure of his place, or his role, and when Hampshire reached their first Cup Final two years later, he was omitted.

In 1987, he batted effectively in the middle order, including a second Championship century; 142* v Nottinghamshire at Bournemouth. In 1989, he approached 1,000 runs at 28.88 including 162 at Cardiff, which remained his best, but then missed almost the whole of the following season after a back operation. With the departure of Greenidge and Chris Smith, he moved up the batting order, and there were 1,000+ runs in 1991 and 1992, as well as appearances in Hampshire's next two cup-winning sides at Lord's. Meanwhile as a bowler he generally took between 35 and 40 wickets each first-class season, and despite a couple of fallow years, he ended his Hampshire career with 359 wickets at 32.47 and a best of 8-49 v Somerset at Basingstoke in 1997. With 8,189 runs (31.01), and a good limited-overs career of 2,340 runs and 223 wickets, James was a fine adaptable all-rounder who played an important role in two Hampshire sides – the trophy-winning one under Nicholas and then a team that struggled in transition. For many years, he has been a sports reporter on BBC Radio Solent and the ball-by-ball commentator on Hampshire's matches. But above all that of course, Kevan James will be remembered as the first man ever in first-class cricket to score a century and take four wickets in four balls (including Tendulkar and Dravid) in the same match – for Hampshire v the Indians at Southampton in 1996. A modest man, and a good cricketer, he deserved his moments in the spotlight.

Jameson, Thomas George Cairnes (257, Amateur) born India 6.4.1908, died Henley-on-Thames 18.1.1987. He was principally a batsman who made his first-class debut for the Royal Navy v Army at Lord's in 1929. In 1930, he played in two matches for Hampshire at Hove and Coventry, with a third at Hastings the following year. For the county, he scored 44 runs at an average of 14.66 with a best of 23*, and bowled four overs (0-11). His last recorded match (not first-class) was in a rain-ruined match for the Royal Navy v the Army at Lord's in 1939.

Jameson, Tom Ormsby (198, Amateur) born Co. Dublin, Ireland 4.4.1892, died Co. Dublin Ireland 6.2.1965. Army officer Tom Jameson was an all-rounder on the cricket field, and further was an accomplished rackets and squash player. He was a pupil at Harrow, and made his first-class debut for MCC v Oxford University with Lord Tennyson in July 1919, followed quickly by his Hampshire debut v Yorkshire at Dewsbury (age 27). He bowled what John Arlott (1957) called "slow 'rolled' leg breaks" and on his debut Hampshire used 10 bowlers with Jameson's 3-82 being the best figures, but they lost by an innings. Because of his duties, he never played a full English season, although he found time for a number of private tours; his busiest county season was in 1925 when he made the first of his two Championship centuries, 103 v Warwickshire at Southampton in an innings victory, and in the next match recorded his best bowling figures of 7-92 at Old Trafford, despite which Hampshire lost. Thereafter he continued to appear in first-class cricket for various sides, playing his last match for Hampshire in 1932, but his last first-class game for Tennyson's side in India in January 1938. For Hampshire, 53 matches brought 2013 runs at 24.85 and 77 wickets at 33.20.

Jaques, Arthur (176, Amateur) born China 7.3.1888, killed in action, Loos, France 27.9.1915. Jaques was a tall pace bowler who played at Aldenham School until 1907, but at Cambridge University only a little college cricket. He played club cricket for Hampshire Hogs and in the winter of 1912/13, he made his first-class debut on a tour of the West Indies, then in the following season he made his debut for Hampshire, taking just over 50 wickets. He played extensively in the following year, using his in-swing to develop an early version of what came to be called 'leg theory', and the result was 117 first-class wickets at 18.69, although his selection for the Gentlemen v Players was not a success. But for the county, in their best-ever season to that date, he was superb, and three times took seven or more wickets in an innings, including his best of 8-21 v Somerset at Bath in June, when he and Kennedy bowled unchanged, dismissing Somerset for 83 & 38. Jaques' match figures of 14-54 are the fifth best in Hampshire's history and by the time they came to 1914's final match v Kent in September he was captaining the side regularly in Sprot's absence. In that innings victory he had match figures of 9-86, but there would be no more cricket. Little more than a year later, he was killed in action at the age of 27, on the same day as his brother, and we are left to wonder, how much he – and Hampshire – might have achieved in those lost years.

Jean-Jacques, Martin (418) born Dominica 2.7.1960. He was principally a pace bowler who played for Buckinghamshire, then Derbyshire from 1986-1992, before moving to Hampshire for two seasons. On first-class debut for Derbyshire he scored 73 batting at number 11, setting a 10th wicket partnership record for the county, and then dismissed Geoff Boycott as his first victim. For Hampshire, played in seven first-class matches, scoring 94 runs and taking nine wickets with a best of 3-44 v Kent at Canterbury in his penultimate match. He played in nine limited-overs matches, scoring just 16 runs and taking nine wickets, and again, coincidentally, best bowling of 3-44, v Surrey at Southampton in his final limited-overs match.

Jefferies, Stephen Thomas (404) born Cape Town South Africa 8.12.1959. He was a left-arm swing bowler and useful batsman who played for Western Province, Lancashire, and Derbyshire before deputising for the touring Malcolm Marshall in 1988, and then remaining with Hampshire as an 'understudy' for one further season. He played in 22 first-class matches for the county scoring 707 runs with two half-centuries, and taking 46 wickets at 41.69. In limited-overs matches he averaged just over 20 with the bat and took 58 wickets at 21.60. Among those figures were two fine performances; in the Championship, he took 8-97 at Gloucester, but topping that was his 5-13 v Derbyshire in the B&H Cup Final at Lord's in 1988. Derbyshire batting first, reached 27-0 before Jefferies took four wickets while they added just five runs. They never recovered, there was a fifth wicket towards the end, and Hampshire – the last of the counties to reach a Lord's Final after 25 years of trying – won the match easily. Jefferies was the Man-of-the-Match and secured his place in Hampshire's history.

Jefferys, Arthur Frederick (Pre '95, Amateur). Born Sydney Australia 7.4.1848, died London 14.2.1906. Although born in Australia and playing one first-class match for New South Wales, he was educated at Eton and Oxford University (no first-class matches), and was a barrister in London. A batsman, he played 26 first-class matches in total, 15 for MCC and 10 for Hampshire for whom he scored 203 runs at 11.94 with one half-century, 51 v MCC at Lord's, as Hampshire followed on – and lost. He was MP for the Northern Division in Hampshire from 1887 until his death.

Jellicoe, Rev. Frederick Gilbert Gardiner (Pre '95, Amateur) born Southampton 24.2.1858, died London 29.7.1927. He was principally a left-handed, round-arm bowler who was educated at Haileybury School, and Oxford University, which is where he played most of his first-class matches, winning his 'blue' in 1877 & 1879. He played four times for Hampshire, once in 1877 and three times in 1880, including figures of 7-23 & 4-48 (11-71) v MCC at Lord's as Hampshire won by nine wickets. He took 23 wickets for Hampshire at 10.56 – a remarkable average, even though he bowled just 712 balls (four-ball overs). In his first-class career of 18 matches, he took 78 wickets at 14.92, with a best of 8-36 for the University v Gentlemen of England. His brother, an Admiral, commanded the British fleet at Jutland, in which CH Abercrombie was killed.

Jephson, Rev. William Vincent (102, Amateur) born Hertfordshire 6.10.1873, died Bath, Somerset 12.11.1956. He was educated at Haileybury and Keble College Oxford, but did not play for the university. He made his first-class debut age 29, v Derbyshire at Southampton in1903, but despite that late start and his amateur status, he played 57 first-class matches, mostly up to 1913, with one further game in 1919. He scored 1,571 runs for the county at 16.89, with six half-centuries and a best of 90 v Worcestershire at Southampton in his debut season. His one century came in the only first-class match ever played at Broadhalfpenny Down – 114* for Hambledon v an England XI. Hambledon won the 12-a-side three-day match by five wickets. He played also in the Hampshire side of 1912, the first to beat the Australians, scoring 55 in his one innings. From 1920-1925, he played Minor Counties cricket for Dorset.

Jesson, Robert Wilfred Fairey (138, Amateur) born Southampton 17.6.1886, killed in action, Mesopotamia 22.2.1917. He was educated at Sherborne, playing in the XI, and then at Oxford University playing in various matches, but only one first-class (no 'blue'). He was a Southampton solicitor who played in 14 matches for Hampshire, mostly in 1907, plus two in 1908 and one in 1910. He was a leg-break bowler and hard-hitting batsman who scored 191 runs with a best of 38, and took 21 wickets (24.42). He made his Hampshire debut v Warwickshire at Southampton in 1907, and after scoring 23* batting at number seven, took 5-42, despite which, Hampshire lost. He could not sustain that, but did once take the wicket of Jack Hobbs – albeit after Hobbs scored 135. In the same match, Jesson made his highest score of 38. He fought in the Great War and rose to become a Major in the 5th Wiltshire Regiment. He was wounded at Gallipoli, recuperated from shell-shock at the old Netley Hospital, returned and was killed near Kut, Mesopotamia in 1917. He was also a rugby half-back for Trojans, and Rosslyn Park, one of 85 members of that club to die in the War. Their story is told in *The Final Whistle: The Great War in Fifteen Players*, by Stephen Cooper.

Jessop, Rev. Gilbert Laird Osborne (265 – Amateur) born London 6.9.1906, died London 16.1.1990. His father, Gilbert Laird Jessop, was one of the great fast-scoring batsmen, who played in 18 Test Matches (one century). GLO Jessop played cricket at Cambridge University but not first-class, made his first-class debut for MCC in 1929, and played in three matches for Hampshire in 1933, captaining them in the absence of Tennyson. He scored 47 runs at 9.40, and took one wicket. In 1936, he played for Cambridgeshire and from 1939-1954 for Dorset.

Jesty, Trevor Edward (355) born Gosport 2.6.1948. All-rounder Trevor Jesty was one of the finest of all Hampshire-born cricketers, and while he represented England in limited-overs internationals in Australia, it is extraordinary that a man of his ability and achievements never played Test cricket. He came through Hampshire's junior sides, played for the 2nd XI in 1965, and in August 1966 made his first-class debut v Essex at Portsmouth. There were a few matches in 1968 and from 1969 he became a regular member of the side in both formats and both disciplines, in addition to being a good fielder. He was a member of the side that won the Championship in 1973 and the Sunday League in 1975 and in 1978; it was in the mid-1970s that he took 50 wickets in a season for the first time (1974) and in 1976 he passed 1,000 runs for the first-time and somewhat belatedly scored his first Championship century. Having achieved that, he scored 11 centuries in three seasons, and after a couple of less successful years with the bat, in 1982 he scored 1,645 runs at 58.75, with eight centuries – a record only Phil Mead has surpassed for the county. For his performances in 1982, he was nominated as one of *Wisden's* Cricketers of the Year. In 1981, he took 52 wickets at 19.86, although after this there would be just over 100 more in his final decade, as he became more a specialist batsman. In 1984 v Northamptonshire, he hit 32 runs from one six-ball over by Robin Boyd-Moss, which is a Hampshire record.

In 1984, he scored centuries in both innings at Worcester and through his career he played some fine limited-overs innings including 96 in 40 minutes v Somerset in 1980, and 166* v Surrey at Portsmouth, easily outscoring Gordon Greenidge in a stand of 269*. In that match, he became the first player to score 4,000 runs and take 200 wickets in the Sunday League. As vice-captain, he would deputise for Nick Pocock in the early 1980s, but when Pocock announced his retirement near the end of the 1984 season, Jesty was overlooked in favour of Mark Nicholas, and disappointed, departed for Surrey, Lancashire and then a full career as a first-class umpire and coach. It was a sad end to the fine Hampshire career of a local man. He scored 14,753 runs with 26 first-class centuries for Hampshire, took 475 wickets, and in limited-overs cricket there were 6,859 runs with six centuries and 334 wickets – an outstanding record.

Jewell, Guy Alonzo Frederick William (325, Amateur) born Axford, Hampshire 6.10.1916, died Basingstoke 23.12.1965. Guy Jewell was a slow-left-arm bowler, who played for Berkshire before the war, and for Hampshire 2nd XI from 1950, although he was a leading club cricketer in north Hampshire for many years, captaining the Basingstoke & North Hants Club. In a 12-a-side match for them v PI Bedford's XI in August 1956, he took all 11 wickets for 52 runs including a hat-trick, and he passed 100 wickets for the club in eight seasons. In 1952, he and Mike Barnard made their Hampshire debuts v Glamorgan at Swansea but while Barnard was embarking on a long career, it was Jewell's only first-class match, in which he scored 0 & 1 (run out) and for his one wicket, dismissed Willie Jones. Hampshire won by 21 runs, but Jewell never appeared again; he became Deputy Head at Queen Mary's School, Basingstoke. In his honour, the Basingstoke Club created a T-20 style knock-out 'Jewell' cup competition in the 1950s. He was awarded the MC in March 1945.

Johnson, Neil Clarkson (454) born Zimbabwe 24.1.1970. Johnson was a left-handed batsman and useful bowler who concluded his international career in 2000, and was therefore available full-time, when he played for Hampshire in 2001 & 2002. In the first year, he scored 1,000 first-class runs with two centuries, but while his best score of 117 came the following year, there were fewer runs and his average dropped from mid-40s to just above 30. He took 45 first-class wickets in the two seasons and in both years, he exceeded 600 limited-overs runs, with two centuries, adding 27 wickets. Although his performances declined a little in the second season, he was a reliable performer who was not retained with the expected return of Shane Warne. In the event, Warne was suspended and did not arrive in 2003. Johnson now coaches in England.

Johnston, Alexander Colin (96, Amateur) born Derby 26.1.1884, died Woking 27.12.1952. He was principally a batsman whose father played for Derbyshire but was later Director General of Ordnance Survey in Southampton. Johnston came to Winchester College and played for Hampshire in 1902, when just 18. He was a professional soldier, reaching the rank of Colonel and playing football, hockey and polo in the Army. Despite those duties, he played fairly regularly for the county, although missing the seasons of 1907 & 1909, and he played first-class cricket also for MCC, Gentlemen v Players and the Army. When he returned in 1910 he achieved his best aggregate of 1,158 runs at 36.18, and was invited to tour West Indies with MCC but withdrew. He reached four figures again in 1912 with an average of 54.94 and his highest score of 175, followed by 100* in the second innings, v Warwickshire at Coventry. There was a third century that season v Worcestershire at Portsmouth and a suggestion that he might have played for England in the triangular tournament, but the captain CB Fry was apparently unable to contact him. Fry, Johnston and Mead headed the English averages that season. He fought at the front from 1914, until badly wounded and sent home in the autumn of 1917. He was awarded the DSO and MC, but the injury left him with a permanent limp; he tried to return to the first-class game with a runner, but the authorities were not sympathetic, so post-war he played just one Championship match (73 for once out) and two other first-class games, although he continued to play, touring Egypt as late as 1930. His last recorded match was for Aldershot Division v RAF in 1941. For Hampshire, he played in

108 first-class matches, scoring 5,442 runs at 30.74 with ten centuries, and bowling occasional leg-breaks, took 18 wickets. John Arlott (1957) recorded CB Fry's view that with his timing and technique he was "the best of all our soldier batsmen".

Joliffe, John Henry (93, Amateur) born Isle of Wight 28.9.1865, died Isle of Wight 5.7.1936. He played in one match v Derbyshire at Southampton in 1902, scoring one run in his two innings, and holding one catch.

Jones, George Leonard (284, Amateur) born Lockerbie, Scotland 11.2.1909, died Shropshire 17.6.1954. At one time his death was reported in Normandy, France on D-Day, 6.6.1944, but recently corrected. He played for Dorset from 1925-1934 and in 1937, appeared in nine matches as a batsman, scoring 169 runs at 14.08, with a best of 37* v the New Zealanders. His best day with Hampshire was a friendly match v Isle of Wight at Newport, when he opened the batting and scored 80.

Jones, Simon Philip (508) born Swansea, 25.12.1978. Right-arm fast bowler Jones is best known for his England Test career when playing for his native county Glamorgan, and particularly for his part in the famous 'Ashes' series of 2005, and three years before that, the terrible injury he suffered in the field in a Test Match in Brisbane. In 2005, he took 23 Test wickets at 21.13, but missed the final Test and never played for England again, as the injury continued to cause him difficulties. In 2008, he played for Worcestershire, missed the whole 2009 season, and joined Hampshire in 2010, seeking to regain his fitness. He stayed for two seasons but played in just two first-class matches, taking five wickets. There were also six limited-overs matches and a further nine wickets, and he played most regularly in T20 games – 14 with 23 wickets, including 4-10 on tour in Barbados. In the middle of that second season, he returned to Glamorgan where he played in just one further first-class match, although he continued until 2013 in limited-overs games, and in his last match he took 2-36 in the YB 40 overs Final at Lord's. In 2006, he was one of the 'Ashes'-winning team awarded an MBE.

Joseph, Linden Anthony (412) born Georgetown Guyana 8.1.1969. Linden Joseph came to Hampshire for the season of 1990, playing regularly for the 2nd XI but also in six first-class matches. Although he was selected as a pace bowler he has an 'interesting' first-class batting record for the county, having scored 152 runs in five innings, but only dismissed once, leaving him with an average of 152.00. His best innings and highest career score was 69* v Oxford University. His bowling was less effective however, with just seven wickets at 66.00. He left Hampshire and in the next two seasons played in England for Enfield in the Lancashire League but he played the majority of his 39 first-class matches for Guyana, while also appearing for West Indies 'A' and under-23s; from 1986-1995, he took 98 first-class wickets at 29.75.

Judd, Arthur Kenneth (234, Amateur) born Sunbury-on-Thames 1.1.1904, died Newton Abbot, Devon 15.2.1988. He was principally a batsman, although bowling leg-breaks, he took 30 first-class wickets for a variety of first-class sides. After school at St Paul's he won his 'blue' at Cambridge University in 1927, by which time he had also made his Hampshire debut. From 1925-1935 he appeared in 64 matches for the county although in the 1930s his appearances were restricted after a posting in Nigeria. He played most regularly in 1927 and 1930, and although he appeared only occasionally in 1931, 1933 and 1935, he sometimes deputised as (amateur) captain, when Tennyson was not available. He scored 1,625 runs for Hampshire at an average of 17.47 with one century, 119 out of 465 v Warwickshire at Portsmouth in 1926, plus five half-centuries. He continued to play in Nigeria until 1938.

Judd, William George (Pre '95, Amateur) born Bramshaw, New Forest 23.10.1845, died Boscombe 12.3.1925. He played in just one first-class match for Hampshire, v Kent at the Antelope Ground in 1878. In a defeat by 98 runs, he batted last, scoring 7 & 1, with bowling figures of 0-28 and 1-22. In the previous year, he stood as an umpire in Hampshire's first-class match v Derbyshire, also at the Antelope.

K

Katich, Simon Mathew (463) born Western Australia. 21.8.1975, Left-handed batsman and occasional unorthodox slow-left-arm bowler, Katich was one of a succession of Australian Test players who came to Hampshire in an overseas capacity following Hayden in 1997. He had previously played for Durham, and would also have spells with Derbyshire and Lancashire, while his time with Hampshire was split, starting in 2003-2005. In the first year, in a struggling side, his 1,143 runs at 60.15 included four centuries; he also took 17 wickets at 34.76, scored over 700 runs at nearly 50 each in limited-overs games, and added 179 in the new T20 at 59.66. All his statistically best performances for Hampshire came in 2003. He then played some county matches in 2004 & 2005, but both county seasons were interrupted by Test Match duties; v Sri Lanka in 2004 and v England in England in 2005, and he did not play in the 2005 C&G Final. In 2012, he returned to Hampshire, scoring 738 first-class runs at 35.14, and playing in the CB40 winning team at Lord's, and the successful T20 Final at Cardiff. For Australia, he played in 56 Test Matches and 45 LOIs.

Katinakis, George Demetrius (116, Amateur) born London 25.7.1873, died in an air raid, Suffolk 15.5.1943. In 1904 & 1905, batsman Katinakis played four matches for Hampshire, and scored 46 runs at 9.20. Although he was born in England, he played for Bulawayo in South Africa in 1899, and his brother, MD, played for Buckinghamshire.

Kay, Henry George (Pre '95, Amateur) born Bedhampton, nr. Portsmouth 3.10.1851, died London 8.9.1922. Kay was an occasional wicketkeeper and batsman, who had two innings in two matches for Hampshire in 1882 but failed to score in either; he bowled six overs (0-20). He was the father of Anton Dolin, born in Austria, who became a notable ballet dancer and director, and appeared in many films, including Powell and Pressburger's *The Red Shoes* (1948). *Wikipedia* suggests Dolin's father (Kay) was a circus clown.

Kaye, James Levett (Pre '95, Amateur) born Hertfordshire 27.12.1861, died London 17.11.1917. He was a right-handed opening batsman and wicket-keeper who played for Hampshire v MCC at Lord's in 1881, scoring 3 & 11 in a seven-wicket defeat. He had played cricket at Winchester College and attended Sandhurst, after which he was a professional soldier, serving in the Sudan and India for many years. His brother, HW Kaye, played three matches for Middlesex.

Keech, Matthew (421) born Hampstead 21.10.1970. Batsman and occasional medium-pace bowler, Keech was one of a number of Middlesex cricketers who moved to Hampshire, particularly post-war. He played for England under-19s, and in 20 first-class matches for his first county, before making his Hampshire debut in 1994. He played most regularly for Hampshire from 1996-1998, in 1996 scoring 793 runs with one century at 44.05, while in the following year there were two further centuries, including his best of 127 v Oxford University. He played frequently in limited-overs matches (74) scoring 1,440 runs at 22.85, and his best of 98 came v Worcestershire at Southampton in 1995 in an exciting tied match – he shared a partnership of 158 with Paul Whitaker. He left the staff after the 1999 season, having scored 2,240 runs for Hampshire in 49 first-class matches at 32.46, and subsequently played for Dorset in limited-overs cricket, and in the Southern Premier League, before pursuing a coaching career.

Keith, Geoffrey Leyden ('Geoff') (349) born Winchester 19.11.1937, died Southampton 26.12.1975. Geoff Keith was a batsman and occasional off-break bowler who was born in Hampshire, but from mid-1950s played for Somerset 2nd XI and from 1959-1961, in 15 first-class matches. In 1962, he returned to his native county, as Hampshire looked to replace their ageing Championship-winning side, and he played in 60 first-class matches until 1967, without establishing himself. There was one century, 101* v the touring South Africans in 1965, otherwise just eight half-centuries and an average of 21.38. In the winter of 1968/9 he played in South Africa for Western Province, and in 1971, after Leo Harrison retired as coach, and his intended successor Mike Barnard was badly injured in a coach crash, Keith returned to Hampshire in the coaching role which in those days consisted principally of running and playing for the 2nd XI. He was a very popular man with his players, who included at various times Greenidge, Turner, Jesty, O'Sullivan, Mottram, Lewis and Murtagh, all of whom played in the Championship-winning side of 1973 – and on one occasion, his team included the pace bowling statistician Bill Frindall. Sadly, he was diagnosed with a form of Leukaemia, and although he remained in post in the 1975 season, he died that winter, age just 38.

Kendall, William Salwey ('Will') (433) born Wimbledon 18.12.1973. Batsman Will Kendall attended Bradfield College and played representative schools cricket, before his Hampshire 2nd XI debut in 1992, age 18. At Oxford University, he played from 1994-1996, winning his 'blue' in the last two years. He played for the Combined Universities side, and in 1996 scored 145* v Cambridge University at Lord's. In the following month, he made his Championship debut for Hampshire, in an innings defeat at Taunton, and in the next match at Southampton, scored 42 & 63 against a Gloucestershire attack led by Courtney Walsh. In all cricket that year, he passed 1,000 runs and after two seasons in-and-out of the Hampshire side, seemed to establish himself in 1999 with 1,186 runs at 39.53 including 201 v Sussex which brought his county cap. He was appointed vice-captain and seemed a likely successor to the senior role, as his average improved slightly in 2000 with four figures again and three more centuries.

In 2001, however, Hampshire moved to the Rose Bowl, where the pitches were difficult for batsman in the early years. In his four seasons there, his average dropped to the mid-twenties with 705 runs in 2002 the best aggregate, and his only century was back at his old university ground. As an example, he was the first player to 'carry his bat' at the Rose Bowl, with an innings of just 53*, in an innings defeat v Leicestershire, reminiscent of the days of uncovered pitches and 'outgrounds'. He was just 30 when his promising career came to an end. He seemed best suited to first-class cricket, but played in 127 limited-overs matches for the county, passing 2,000 runs at 21.90. His one limited-overs century came v Middlesex, ironically at the Rose Bowl, when, captaining the side he arrived at the wicket with the Hampshire score 6-3, guided them to 241-7 and led them to victory by 24 runs. He has played for some years for Bradfield Waifs, particularly in the Cricketer Cup. He was a fine all-round sportsman, once offered terms to play professional football by Reading FC.

Kendle, Charles Edward Compton (62, Amateur) born Amesbury, Wiltshire 10.2.1875, died Sussex 3.1.1954. He was a lower-order batsman and wicket-keeper who played in two matches for Hampshire in 1899 at Leicester and Bradford, scoring 27 runs (9.00) and dismissing three batsmen, one stumped. He played for Wiltshire in the Minor Counties Championship from 1911-1914, and some years later in club cricket in the London area.

Kendle, Rev. William James (Pre '95, Amateur) born Romsey 9.4.1847, died Dorset, 30.1.1920. He was a batsman and the uncle of CEC Kendle (above). He studied at Cambridge University without winning his 'blue', and played in five matches for Hampshire, one each in 1869 and 1875, and three in 1878. In that period, he played also for the Gentlemen of Hampshire; in first-class matches, he scored 66 runs at 7.33.

Kennard, John Adam Gaskell (193, Amateur) born Chelsea 8.11.1884, died Hove 6.4.1949. He was a middle-order batsman who had been at Harrow and was one of 14 Hampshire debutants when first-class cricket resumed after the war, and one of four who played only in that season. He was dismissed twice in scoring 46 runs in his two matches and bowled two overs (0-17). In the early 1920s he played Minor Counties cricket for Oxfordshire and he played quite often in non-first-class matches for MCC.

Kennedy, Alexander Stuart ('Alec') (139) born Edinburgh, Scotland 24.1.1891, died Southampton 15.11.1959. Pace-bowling all-rounder Alec Kennedy was born in Scotland, but was otherwise solidly a Hampshire man since his family moved then when Alec was a young boy. From an early age, he would spend hours at the county ground and bowl at anyone in the nets. On leaving school at 14, he joined the groundstaff and along with Alec Bowell, Phil Mead, Jack Newman, George Brown and Walter Livsey, formed Hampshire's first significant group of major professionals. From 1900-1905 Hampshire were only once free from last place in the Championship, but when this fine group of players came together, they were never again in danger of that ignominy.

Kennedy was just quicker than medium pace, with swing and cut, and until Derek Shackleton arrived was Hampshire's leading wicket-taker; his 2,549 wickets at 21.16 will keep him in second place for ever more. He made his county debut not yet 17 at Leicester in July 1907, taking 4-33, although Hampshire lost by an innings, but he retained his place and took three wickets in a victory at Edgbaston. There were 80 wickets in the first four seasons, then, just into his twenties, in 1912 he took 139 wickets at 17.60, including 11 in the match, as Hampshire beat the Australians. He was taken ill and recovered from an operation at the start of 1913, but still had time to take 82 wickets – this was one of only two seasons until 1933 when he did not reach three figures (the other, 87 in 1926) and his total of 190 wickets in 1922 is the highest figure for Hampshire. While he was principally Hampshire's leading opening bowler, he was a capable batsman, appearing in a variety of positions. In his Hampshire career of 596 matches – second only to Phil Mead – he scored 14,925 runs at 18.51, with ten centuries and 59 half-centuries – the total places him 18th in the Hampshire list. In 1921 he carried his bat with 152* at Trent Bridge. He was also a capable fielder with 484 catches, third behind Mead and Sainsbury.

There are too many fine performances to list them all, especially with the ball; he completed 1,000 runs in four seasons, 1921-1923 & 1928, and in each of them completed the 'double' in all matches; on 40 occasions, he took seven or more wickets in an innings, with a best of 9-33 v Lancashire at Liverpool, a match which Hampshire lost by one run, and while no Hampshire bowler has ever taken 10 wickets in an innings for the county, Kennedy did so (10-37) for the Players v Gentlemen at the Oval in 1927, dismissing his opponents, captained by Tennyson, for just 80. Perhaps as remarkable was his analysis of 13-7-11-8 (all before lunch) v Glamorgan at Cardiff in 1921, or 10-7-8-7 v Warwickshire at Portsmouth in 1927, while in 1922, he had match figures of 15-116 v Somerset at Bath. On three occasions, he and his partner bowled unchanged through two completed innings – once with Jaques and twice with his great partner Jack Newman; he also took three hat-tricks. In 1933, he was nominated as one of *Wisden's* Cricketers of the Year. While Derek Shackleton took more wickets for Hampshire, only four men have exceeded his career total of 2,874, yet he played in just five Test Matches for England, all on the tour to South Africa in 1922/3, where he had 31 wickets at 19.32, with a best of 5-76, yet he was never selected again. After the 1935 season he became coach at Cheltenham College, returning for a few matches in the holidays of 1936. While there, he coached the young Desmond Eagar, who asked (1960) "has there been a better or more conscientious coach? I doubt it. He gave to his work all that he had to give, and in giving it, gave happiness and pleasure to many hundreds of boys". Later he moved to a similar coaching role in a South African school, before returning to Southampton to run a local shop, when he enjoyed visiting the county ground.

Kenway, Derek Anthony (437) born Fareham 12.6.1978. Derek Kenway was a top-order batsman and occasional wicketkeeper, especially in limited-overs matches. After progressing through the county's age group and 2nd XI sides, he made his county debut in late 1997 v Warwickshire at Southampton, an extraordinary match which, with 1706 runs, set the record aggregate involving Hampshire. Only 23 wickets fell, but Kenway, was still not out when Hampshire's ninth went, and they faced defeat, until he faced 49 balls, Bovill 20, and they saved the game. He did not appear again for more than a year, and there were just three games in 1998, but he established himself in 1999, scoring 1,055 runs at 42.20. There were fewer runs in 2000, but in 2001 with Hampshire at the Rose Bowl, he was just short of four figures and added two centuries. He seemed to have a promising future, but was not the only young batsman to struggle on the pitches at the new ground in the early years; from 2002-2005, he scored about 1,500 runs and averaged in the lower twenties, and after just one first-class match in 2005 he left the staff. In limited-overs, he was at his best from 1999-2003 – in the latter there were two centuries, but after this, again his performances declined. On occasions in these matches, he was selected as the Hampshire wicketkeeper, and there were five stumpings in 2000. He played in ten T20 matches in the first two seasons, but in 2004 could barely score a run. This was all very sad, for was only 27 when he left the staff, having shown such promise in the earlier years. In first-class cricket, he ended with 4,382 runs at 29.60. Since then he has played in the Southern League for a number of sides including Portsmouth, Totton & Eling and Burridge.

Kimish, Arthur Edwards (305, Amateur) born Southampton 5.7.1917, died Warwickshire 5.2002 (precise date not known). Arthur Kimish was a batsman and wicketkeeper, who played in two Championship matches for Hampshire in 1946, and also in one first-class fund-raising friendly v Surrey at Kingston. He scored just 18 runs at 6.00 and dismissed six batsmen (three stumped). He played for Old Tauntonians from 1939 through to the late-1950s.

King, James (pre '95) born Southampton, 1855. We have no further details of his birth or death. He was a left-arm fast bowler who took 10 first-class wickets at 22.30 for Kent (two matches in 1881), and played for Hampshire, and on his only first-class appearance, took 4-64 & 1-29 v Somerset at Taunton in 1882. Don Ambrose (*Cricket Archive*) has reported that a man of this name was living in Tonbridge as a carpenter in the 1881 census – if it is the same man, this would explain why he appeared for Kent.

King, Matthew John (List A) born Basingstoke 25.2.1994. He played for Hampshire 2nd XI from 2012-2015 and in two friendly limited-overs matches for Hampshire, v Bangladesh 'A' in 2013 and v Sri Lanka 'A' in 2014. He opened the bowling in the second match which was abandoned after just 18 overs. In 2016, after leaving Hampshire, he was a member of the MCC groundstaff.

Kitchener, Frederick George (27) born Hartley Row, Hants 2.7.1871, died Co. Durham 25.5.1948. He was principally a fast-medium bowler, who played in 10 matches for Hampshire in 1896 & 1897, and three more in 1902 & 1903, taking overall 28 wickets at 22.50. From 1902-1906 he played regularly for Sefton in the Liverpool League, and also represented the Liverpool & District side. His best performances for Hampshire were 6-59 v Derbyshire at Derby and 5-21 v Sussex at Southampton, both in the first year, when his 18 wickets came at 18.27. The game v Sussex was his first-class debut, and he bowled Hampshire to victory, having not bowled in the first innings. He was a tail-end batsman whose 80 career runs came at an average of 5.00.

Kleinveldt, Rory Keith (494) born Cape Town, South Africa, 15.3.1983. All-rounder Rory Kleinveldt has represented his country in four Test Matches and 10 ODIs, and in addition to playing domestic cricket in his native country, he played effectively for Northamptonshire for some years, leaving at the end of the 2018 season. In 2008, when struggling to retain their place in Division One, Hampshire selected him for one match v Lancashire at the Rose Bowl, when it seemed he was not match fit. He scored 20 runs in his two innings, took 1-42 in nine overs, and never played for the county again, other than one 2nd XI friendly v the Army at Aldershot when he batted at number 10, and did not bowl.

Kneller, Arthur Harry (231, Amateur) born Kingsclere, Hants 28.4.1894, died Chichester 19.7.1969. He spent many years in East Africa playing cricket there from 1928-1947, but in 1924-1926 he played in eight matches for Hampshire, scoring 76 runs at 8.44.

Knight, Arthur Egerton (184, Amateur) born Godalming 7.9.1887, died Southsea 10.3.1956. AE Knight played one match for Hampshire v Oxford University in 1913, when he took his only first-class wicket, coming on as the tenth bowler, and dismissing AL Hosie who also played for Hampshire. He then played in three Championship matches in 1920, 1921 and 1923, scoring 41 runs at 5.85; he captained Hampshire in the last two matches in the absence of Tennyson. He was a very good footballer, playing for Surrey at 17, then moving to Portsmouth signing for them as a defender. He played in 31 Amateur Internationals, including the 1912 Olympic Games, where he won a Gold Medal. In 1919, he won two full England caps, and after playing in 219 matches for Portsmouth he joined Corinthians. He was a regular club cricketer in Portsmouth.

Knott, Charles James (290, Amateur) born Southampton 26.11.1914, died Southampton 27.2.2003. John Arlott once described Charlie Knott as the finest amateur bowler in the county's history and suggested (1957) "he was on his day as deadly an off-spinner as you might find". but he was more than that, for in addition to nearly 650 wickets for the county he played a crucial role in developing the Hampshire sides that won a number of trophies in the 1970s and 1980s. He was not a typical amateur, since most came through the public schools and universities, while he was the son of a successful Southampton businessman and remained involved in the family's business interests. These included the fish trade, the skating rink and stadium adjacent to Southampton's County Ground, and Poole Speedway. In his early twenties, Knott played club cricket in Southampton's parks, often in front of huge crowds. He bowled medium pace and was sufficiently successful to win selection for Hampshire at Canterbury towards the end of the 1938 season. He stayed in the side at Worcester, but after two matches had taken just one wicket for 191 runs, while three men had made centuries. Then he cut his pace, began spinning the ball, and in his third game took 5-51 against Gloucestershire including a young student, EDR Eagar. Even as an off-spinner he had a fairly long run, and perhaps anticipated a right-handed Derek Underwood.

Knott and Eagar played a little more, until war prevented further county cricket and when it resumed in 1946, Eagar was captain and secretary at Hampshire, with Knott as one of his key men. He was a leading bowler for Hampshire from 1946-1953 and in that first post-war season took 121 wickets. He played in the Test Trial but while he was measured for a touring blazer a few years later, greater honours never came. He did nonetheless pass 100 wickets in 1948 and 1949, and as vice-captain he led the side on a number of occasions in 1950 when Eagar was injured. At Eastbourne, with Sussex needing just 98 to win, he took 5-5 and Hampshire won by 60 runs. He also took a hat-trick for the Gentlemen v Players that year. In 1953, he recorded his best figures of 8-36 v Notts at Bournemouth but business pressures forced him to retire after a few appearances in the following season. His career ended with 647 wickets for the county at 23.53, and five or more wickets in an innings on 44 occasions, with a Championship best of 8-36 v Nottinghamshire at Bournemouth in 1953. He was no batsman, but in his 166 matches for Hampshire he just passed 1,000 runs at an average of 7.11 and a best of 27. By the late-1950s, he was captaining the 2nd XI occasionally and he joined the Committee, taking the Chair of the Cricket Committee. Through the 1970s and 1980s he played a central role in building the sides that won a second Championship, three Sunday Leagues and finally reached a Lord's Final. In addition, his links with West Indian cricket brought some fine overseas players to Hampshire – not least Malcolm Marshall. He 'retired' in his seventies, but continued to support the club as a Life Vice-President and member of the (then) Museum Sub Committee, although as a life-long Southampton man, he was never quite reconciled to the county leaving his beloved Northlands Road.

L

Lacey, Francis Eden (20, Amateur) born Wareham, Dorset 19.10.1859, died Warminster 26.5.1946. Francis Lacey was a fine batsman and occasional slow bowler who played first-class cricket for Hampshire in 1880, and was still playing in the three seasons after they were admitted to the County Championship in 1895. In 1887, during the period when Hampshire were relegated to second class, he scored 323* v Norfolk, which remains Hampshire's highest score in any form of cricket, and was at the time the highest individual score in any inter-county match. From the following season until 1893, he captained the still second-class county.

He was educated at Sherborne School and Cambridge University where he won 'blues', for football and cricket (1882). His first-class debut in 1880 was for Hampshire at Hove, when he scored 70 and took two wickets. In addition to 33 first-class matches for Hampshire and three for the University, he played for MCC, the Gentlemen and other first-class sides in a total of 50 matches over 18 seasons, while pursuing a career as a Barrister, and then from 1898-1926, he was Secretary of the MCC. He was knighted in that final year – the first to be so honoured, specifically for services to cricket. He is credited with many significant improvements to the organisation of the MCC, and since it then controlled both English and most world cricket, to the game more broadly. For Hampshire, his 33 matches produced 2,028 runs at 39.76, with four centuries, spanning 16 seasons. There were two hundreds, both at the Antelope, in 1884, including 211 (& 92*) v Kent – his highest, and Hampshire's first double century, while in 1885 he carried his bat v Derbyshire at Southampton. In addition, he took 45 wickets at just 20.93 each, with 7-149 (& 4-32) at Hove in 1882. Hampshire won that game by seven wickets, with Lacey 50*. After retiring from MCC, he was President of Hampshire, in 1927/8.

Lamb, Bruce (48, Amateur) born Andover, 25.8.1878, died Andover 21.3.1932. A batsman, he was educated at Marlborough and played in four first-class matches for Hampshire, three in 1898 and one in 1901. He scored just 29 runs at an average of 4.14 and did not bowl. In 1900, he played for Hampshire 2nd XI and in a non-first-class match v West Indians at Southampton scoring 21 & 10.

Lamb, Gregory Arthur ('Greg') (474) born Salisbury (Harare) Zimbabwe 4.3.1980. Lamb was an off-break bowling all-rounder, who played first-class cricket for Mashonaland in his native Zimbabwe, before coming to England, still in his teens, hoping to establish a career with Hampshire. He played in the Surrey League in 1982, then with Hampshire's Academy and 2nd XI sides, before making his county debut in all three forms in 2004. He played for Hampshire for five seasons; in 22 first-class matches, he scored 684 runs at 21.37 with four half-centuries and in 38 T20 matches, 462 runs at 17.11, but perhaps his best days were in limited-overs matches. Overall, he scored 796 runs for Hampshire at 23.41, including four half-centuries and 100*, his one century for Hampshire, v Northamptonshire at the Rose Bowl in 2005. In that same season, he was a member of the Hampshire side that won the C&G Trophy at Lord's. He took 13 first-class wickets for Hampshire, 25 limited-overs wickets and 19 in the T20. After leaving the county in 2008, he played for Wiltshire for one season, before returning home, where he represented Zimbabwe in one Test Match, 15 ODIs and five IT20s, between 2009-2011, including two World Cups.

Lancashire, Walter (276, Amateur) born Hemsworth, Yorkshire 28.10.1903, died Dorchester 7.6.1981. Lancashire was a right-handed batsman and right-arm medium pace bowler who played for Hampshire Club & Ground in the early 1930s, and from 1935-1937 played in 18 first-class matches for Hampshire scoring 471 runs at 16.82 and taking seven wickets at 51.00. There were two half-centuries, both in 1936, at Southampton, 66 (& 32) v Essex and at Lord's, 54 v Middlesex, when he and Len Creese added 78 in a vain hope to stave off defeat. During the war, he played for Essex Services, and when the war ended he played for Dorset in the Minor Counties Championship.

Laney, Jason Scott (429) born Winchester, 27.4.1973. As a teenager, opening batsman Jason Laney played representative schools cricket, and then with Hampshire 2nd XI from 1991. He made his limited-overs debut for Hampshire at Chelmsford at the end of the 1993 season but had to wait until 1995 to return to the first team in Championship and limited-overs cricket. After a good season in 1995, and a winter in Zimbabwe, he seemed to establish himself in the following year, scoring 1,163 runs including four centuries at 38.76, including his best score of 112 v Oxford University. In addition, he scored 662 limited-overs runs at 34.84, with 153 v Norfolk. In 1998, his performances slipped but they revived in 1999, with another limited-overs century v Essex, and a first-class average back in the high 30s. Richie Benaud noted his promise during a BBC commentary on a limited-overs match, but there would be no more centuries and a gradual decline, with just 11 first-class matches and 426 runs in 2001 & 2002, the first two years at the new Rose Bowl. Like a number of his promising batting peers, he found the conditions at the new ground testing, and disappointingly his career ended after the 2002 season, while still in his twenties.

Langford, William Thomas (100) born Southampton 5.10.1875, died Faversham, Kent 20.2.1957. Langford was a pace bowler, capable of occasional useful innings. He made his first-class debut for Hampshire in 1902, in a defeat at Leicester in which he bowled just two overs. He did not re-appear until the following season, when he played through most of August (seven matches), and then with increasingly regularity from 1904-1907. As a bowler, his best season was 1906, when he took 66 wickets at 26.46, including 8-82 against the West Indian tourists, while his best return in the Championship was 7-84 v Sussex at Portsmouth in 1903, in just his third match, which Hampshire lost by an innings. His figures declined in 1908, which was his final season, and he ended with 215 wickets at 26.88, and 1,663 runs at 12.99 with two half-centuries and a best of 62* v Somerset at Taunton in 1904.

Latouf, Kevin John (485) born Transvaal, South Africa 7.9.1985. Batsman Latouf was born in South Africa but played for Hampshire at least from under-19, for England at under-19, and for the county's Academy and 2nd XI sides from 2003. In mid-July 2005, he scored 25 on his limited-overs debut, a C&G quarter-final at the Oval which Hampshire won by reaching their target of 359 in the 48th over. He then played in some league games, and retained his place but did not bat in the winning semi-final v Yorkshire. In the Lord's Final v Warwickshire, he reached the crease but remained 0*, without facing a ball, nonetheless collecting his winners medal. At the end of that season in which he had played nine limited-overs matches, he was awarded the Olive Ford Trophy as the most promising uncapped Hampshire player, and in May 2006 he made his first-class debut v Loughborough University, scoring 29 in a match ruined by rain. In that year, he also played in one limited-overs match, a friendly v West Indies 'A', but he did not play for the first team at all in 2007, and then appeared in his final game, at Worcester, in May 2008. His limited-overs career concluded with 90 runs in 11 matches at an average of 11.25.

Lawrie, Percy Edward (216, Amateur) born London 12.12.1902, died Teignmouth, Devon 7.2.1988. Batsman Lawrie was educated at Eton and Oxford University, and made his Hampshire debut at 18 v Glamorgan in August 1921, the Welsh county's first season in the Championship, scoring 49 in an innings victory. At the start of the following season, he played for Hampshire again, v Oxford University, and then in two matches for the university but he played in only five first-class matches while a student, and did not win his 'blue'. For Hampshire, he played in 28 matches with 959 runs at 22.30 including one century, 107 at Leicester in 1923, and four half-centuries. That was his most regular and successful season, but after four games in 1924 he appeared again only in 1928, playing in five further games.

Lawson, Howard Maurice (278, Amateur/Professional) born Bournemouth 22.5.1914, died Worthing 21.10.2006. Although pace-bowler Lawson was born in Bournemouth, he was like his father (below) mostly a cricketer in the north of the county, and followed him into the Hampshire side. He made his debut as an amateur in 1935, playing in eight first-class matches including one appearance under Tennyson for the Gentlemen v Players. In the following season, he played in 31 matches and John Arlott (1957) said of him that he had "a lively action", bowled "mainly inswing" and was "at his best with the new ball". In 1936, he took 54 wickets at 31.22, recording his best figures of 5-91 v Gloucestershire at Portsmouth and 5-105 v Kent at Southampton. In 1937, he played in just seven matches and took only five wickets, and it seems that by then he was playing professionally, but that marked the end of his first-class career, with 71 wickets. John Arlott (1957) added that "occasionally he hit hard and was keen in the field" – his highest Championship score of 53 came v Essex at Bournemouth in 1936, sharing a last-wicket partnership of 78 with Gerry Hill. After the war, he was captain of Basingstoke.

Lawson, Maurice Bertie (140, Amateur) born Christchurch 28.2.1885, died Alton 8.8.1961. He was an all-rounder who played in seven matches for Hampshire, before and after the First World War. Five of his seven county matches came in his first season of 1907, when he made his highest score of 36, and took three wickets. He played one further match in 1909, and then again, one match in 1919, the season of two-day games. In his final innings for the county, at Tunbridge Wells, batting at number 10, he scored 30. He played for many years for Basingstoke, captaining them in the 1930s, and taking 9-17 v Alton.

Leat, Charles William (pre '95) born Ringwood 6.12.1855, died Christchurch 18.12.1937. Leat bowled a little right-arm fast, but was also a wicketkeeper who played 16 matches for Hampshire, two in 1878 & 1882, five in 1884 and seven in 1885, after which they lost their first-class status, although he played further matches for the county in the next two years. He scored 323 runs at 11.53 with one half-century, 63 v Kent at Gravesend, in 1884, and on the one occasion he took wickets, 2-10 v Derbyshire at Derby in 1878. In his 16 matches, he dismissed 22 batsmen in the field.

Lee, Arthur Michael (268, Amateur) born Liphook, Hants 22.8.1913, died Midhurst 14.1.1983. His father EC Lee (below) played for Hampshire, and AM Lee was a right-handed batsman who was educated at Winchester and Oxford University. He played in one Championship match for Hampshire v Somerset at Bath in mid-July 1933, but the match was spoiled by rain, and on day three he was bowled by Arthur Wellard without scoring. In the next two seasons, he played in three first-class matches for Oxford University, but did not win his 'blue'. He was awarded the DSO.

Lee, Edward Cornwall (33, Amateur) born Torquay 18.6.1877, died Petersfield 16.6.1942. EC Lee was educated at Winchester and Oxford University, winning his 'blue' in 1898; he also won 'blues' for ice hockey and golf. In 1896, he played one first-class match for Hampshire v Yorkshire at Harrogate, opening the bowling in a 10-wicket defeat. From the following season until 1909, his first-class career mixed matches for the county, the MCC, the University and others. He toured the Caribbean in early 1902, but after a match at Derby later that year, he played just once more for Hampshire, v the Australians in 1909. He played in

46 matches for Hampshire, scoring 994 runs at 14.61 with two half-centuries, and took nine wickets at 74.77 with a best of 2-0 v Somerset at Portsmouth in 1897.

Leveson-Gower, Rev. Frederick Archibald Gresham (64, Amateur) born Titsey Place, Surrey 8.5.1873, died Kent 3.10.1946. He was from a famous cricketing family, his brother HDG ('Shrimp') who played for England, being best known. He was educated at Winchester and Oxford University and played in 16 first-class matches for various sides, including two games for Hampshire, v Sussex at Portsmouth in 1899, and Lancashire at Southampton in 1900. He scored 45 runs in his four innings with a best of 20, and bowled five overs, (0-20). His final first-class match was for his brother's XI in 1909.

Lewis, Arthur Hamilton (251, Amateur) born Basutoland 16.9.1901, died Devon 23.8.1980. He was said to be a hard-hitting batsman and brilliant cover fielder who played some matches while at Cambridge University that were not first-class. In 1929, he opened the batting for Hampshire at the Oval after centuries by Hobbs and Ducat helped Surrey to 490-6 declared. There was no play on the second day, and on the third, Lewis scored 20 as Hampshire made 147-8. He did not play for the county again, but through the 1930s played for Berkshire and the Hampshire Hogs.

Lewis, Richard Victor (356) born Winchester 6.8.1947. Batsman Richard Lewis was one of a group of young cricketers who made their county debuts in the mid-1960s, as Hampshire sought to replace their 1961 Championship-winning side. Lewis played for Hampshire 2nd XI in 1965 & 1966, then in 1967 he made his first-class debut v Oxford University at Bournemouth, opening the batting and scoring 24 in an innings victory. He returned to the 2nd XI, and having scored his first century against the same opponents in 1968, he kept his place through June and July, but he never managed to be sure of a permanent place in the side. In ten seasons, from 1967-1976, he played in 103 matches for Hampshire – one of the few to pass 100 without the award of a county cap, and scored 3,282 runs at 18.97, with one further century v Gloucestershire in 1974. In addition, he played in 82 limited-overs games, scoring five half-centuries at 18.04 with a best of 79 v Surrey at Southampton in 1975, as Hampshire moved towards their first limited-overs title. We might consider that for a man of such potential, his career was disappointing, but the fact is that fewer than 30 men have represented Hampshire in a Championship-winning side, and Lewis is one of them, having played in 13 of the 20 matches in 1973. After leaving Hampshire, he played with Dorset from 1977-1989 and coached at Charterhouse. His final two first-class matches were for the Minor Counties v the Indians in 1979 (scoring 88) and Sri Lankans in 1981 (47 & 53*).

Light, Elisha Edward (46) born Winchester 1.9.1873, died Llanelly, Wales 12.3.1952. He was a left-handed batsman and slow-left-arm bowler who played for Hampshire in 1894 before they regained first-class status, then in 13 first-class matches from 1898-1900, scoring 168 runs at 10.50 with a best of 35, and taking five wickets at 52.60. He moved to Wales and played for Carmarthenshire in the Minor Counties.

Light, William Frederick ('Billy') (46) born Winchester 1.3.1878, died Exeter, 10.11.1930. WF Light was the brother of EE (above) and predominantly a left-arm pace bowler, who played 12 first-class matches for Hampshire in 1897 & 1898, and then for Devon from 1901-1928. In 12 matches for Hampshire, he took 10 wickets at 34.30, and scored 101 runs at 5.94 with a best of 41 v Warwickshire in 1898, sharing a last wicket partnership of 82 with Edward Tate. His best bowling was 3-32 v Lancashire at Southampton in 1898, taking five of his ten first-class wickets in that one match.

Lineham, Edwin (51, Amateur) born Portsmouth 28.4.1879, died Portsmouth 12.8.1949. He was a batsman who played in just one match for Hampshire, at Old Trafford in 1898. In a match ruined by the weather, he was bowled by Johnny Briggs without scoring in the first innings, and having opened the batting in the second innings, did not face a ball in the single over bowled by Mold. He played subsequently for Hampshire 2nd XI, but to add to the disappointment of his only first-class match, he was initially named in reports as Lynam.

Lintott, Jacob Benedict ('Jake') (T20) born Taunton 22.4.1993. Jacob Lintott is an unorthodox slow left-arm bowler who has played for Dorset, Wiltshire, and the 2nd XIs at Somerset, Warwickshire and, in 2017, Hampshire. He played for them in the 2nd XI T20 Finals Day at Arundel, and subsequently for the first XI in one T20 match v his native Somerset at the Ageas Bowl. Hampshire lost, with Lintott's figures 3-0-24-1, and at number 11 he scored eight runs.

Lipscomb, Francis Wallis (Pre '95, Amateur) born Alresford, 20.7.1834, died Southsea, 3.10.1906. His first-class debut was at Canterbury for the Gentlemen of England in 1857. Five years later, he played for the Gentlemen of the South and then in 1881 (age 47) & 1882, he played three matches for Hampshire, all v Sussex. He averaged 18.40 with a best of 53 and best bowling of 2-46. In 1870, he captained Scotland v Cheltenham College Wanderers, in Edinburgh, top-scoring with 44 in the second innings, despite which, Scotland lost by an innings. He was a regular Army officer with the 18th (Royal Irish) Regiment of Foot, promoted to Lieutenant in 1859, and then to Captain, before he retired to become a hop merchant.

Lipscomb, William Henry (Pre '95, Amateur) born Winchester 20.11.1846, died Clapham 9.4.1918. He studied at Marlborough and Oxford University, obtaining his 'blue' in 1868. For Hampshire, he played in four matches in 1866 & 1867, with a batting average of 14.14; he bowled briefly but took no wickets. He played first-class cricket also for the Gentlemen of the South, with another

Lipscomb (Robert) but it seems that none of these three Lipscombs (see above) were related.

Livingstone, Daintes Abbias ('Danny') (344) born Antigua 21.9.1933, died Antigua 8.9.1988. Left-handed batsman Danny Livingstone will always have a special place in the history of Hampshire County Cricket Club, as the man who held the catch which completed their victory over Derbyshire on 1 September 1961, clinching their first Championship title. By that time, he was an important member of the side, having secured the number four batting place which had troubled Hampshire for some time; in that fine season, he passed 1,000 runs for the first time (1,643), and scored his maiden Championship century. He came to England on National Service with the RAF, and played for Warwickshire 2nd XI from 1955, and throughout the 1957 season. When Warwickshire did not offer a contract, he played in London club cricket in 1958, and came to Hampshire in 1959 as a stroke-player, appearing in one match v Oxford University. Having qualified in 1960, he tightened his defence, and after the excitement of 1961, he enjoyed his most successful season in 1962, passing 1,800 runs at an average of 37.08 with 12 half-centuries and two centuries, including a remarkable innings v Surrey at Southampton in the last match of the season. He was dropped first-ball, denying Tony Lock a hat-trick, and when joined by Alan Castell, Hampshire were 128-8. The pair set a ninth wicket record partnership of 230, which still stands, and Livingstone posted his highest score, 200. The next two seasons were good ones for Danny Livingstone, passing 1,000 runs again, with seven centuries, after which he was not always so consistent, but there were four figures again in the 1967 and 1970 seasons. In 1964, he headed the Hampshire averages and scored centuries in both innings v Kent at Canterbury. In 1970, Livingstone and fellow West Indian Roy Marshall set the county's (then) fourth wicket record with 263 v Middlesex at Lord's, and in total there were 16 centuries in his career, including 151 v the West Indians in 1963, which must have brought considerable satisfaction. He played in the early years of limited-overs cricket, including regular appearances in the first two seasons of the Sunday League, and he scored five half-centuries, with a best of 92 v Lincolnshire in 1966, adding 124 with Henry Horton. He played less regularly in 1971 & 1972, after which he retired and went home to Antigua, where he continued to play local cricket and became Chairman of Antigua's Sports Council. He died of a stroke age just fifty-five. He played in 299 first-class matches for Hampshire, scoring 12,660 runs at 27.94. He took one wicket, and was very occasionally a substitute wicketkeeper.

Livsey, Walter Herbert (185) born Todmorden 23.9.1893, died Merton Park, Surrey, 12.9.1978. Wicketkeeper Livsey was one of a number Hampshire cricketers from Todmorden, but when very young, his family moved to Surrey, where he grew up, playing some junior cricket at the Oval. He joined Hampshire in 1912, taking two years to qualify for the Championship, while in 1913, he played one match v Oxford University. The long-serving Hampshire wicketkeeper was

James Stone, but in 1914, Livsey took over, and Stone played some matches as a batsman. Livsey played in 309 first-class matches for Hampshire and his career record as a wicketkeeper makes fascinating reading in the context of the modern game, for of his 628 wicketkeeping victims, 255 (40%) were from stumpings. By comparison, the figure for Hampshire's current wicketkeeper McManus is just under 15%. After that one full season, Livsey spent the war with some of his team-mates in India, and did not return until 1920 when he became Hampshire's wicketkeeper under Tennyson – and also his Lordship's butler! In 1922, he was selected for the prestigious Players v Gentlemen match and then by MCC to tour South Africa, but broke his finger and returned home before the Test Matches started. He did not get another chance at international honours, although he appeared in Test Trials.

Unlike most modern wicketkeepers, he was a tail-end batsman, and aver-aged 15.44 from his 4,818 runs but there were notable performances. In 1921, he shared with Alec Bowell Hampshire's record 10th wicket partnership of 192 v Worcestershire at Bournemouth. Then in the following season he scored his first century in one of the most famous of county matches, v Warwickshire at Edgbaston. Hampshire all out for 15, followed-on and were 274-8, just 66 ahead, when Livsey (110*) joined Brown (172). They added 177, then Livsey and Boyes a further 70, and Hampshire won a famous victory. In 1928, he scored over 800 Championship runs, with a second century v Kent at Dover, but after one more season, and suffering ill-health, he retired.

Llewellyn, Charles Bennett (60) born South Africa 26.9.1876, died Surrey 7.6.1964. Lllewellyn was an all-rounder, bowling slow-left-arm and was effec-tively Hampshire's first significant overseas professional, decades before those men could play with immediate effect. As a consequence, although his eight wickets on debut for the county (8-132) v the Australians in 1899, remains the best debut total of wickets for the county, he would not play first-class for them again for two years, when he made his Championship debut v Lancashire at Portsmouth. In his native South Africa, he played for Natal from 1894/5 and he appeared in Test matches, which brought him to the attention of RM Poore, who recommended him to the county.

He was a very fine all-rounder, for Hampshire, scoring 8,772 runs at 27.58 with 15 centuries and taking 711 wickets at 24.66 – and much of his county cricket was played in the weakest of Hampshire sides. In that first full season, he scored 153 and took 10-183 v Somerset at Taunton, the match 'double', and in his third match for Hampshire he played against his fellow countrymen at Southampton and after scoring 216 he took 2-99 and 4-6, as Hampshire won by an innings. He went straight from there to play *for* them against London County, scoring 88 and taking 6-140 and 7-101 – including WG Grace in both innings. He then played the rest of that season with Hampshire, but started 1902 playing for London County, before also playing regularly for Hampshire. In the winter, he played in three Test Matches v Australia; in total, he played in 15 Tests scoring 544 runs at 20.14 and taking 48 wickets at 29.60. In 1911, he was one of *Wisden's* Cricketers of the Year for his performances in 1910 when he scored 1,232 runs at 29.33 and took 152 wickets at 19.27, and became the first Hampshire cricketer to complete the season's 'double' for the county. That winter he went to Australia, but seeking greater financial security, he turned his back on Hampshire, preferring to play with Accrington in the Lancashire League; he was the first overseas Test cricketer to join a Lancashire League club. He returned to England with the South Africans for the triangular tournament of 1912, which was the end of his first-class career. He played with Accrington to 1915 and returned in 1921, finishing in September 1925, approaching his 49th birthday. See also Jenkinson N (2012) *CB Llewellyn: A Study in Equivocation* ACS

Lodge, Lewis Vaughan (79, Amateur) born Co Durham 21.12.1872, died, Derbyshire, in a drowning accident, 21.10.1916. He was a middle-order batsman who attended Cambridge University but did not play first-class cricket. He played in three matches for Hampshire in 1900, but in four innings scored just six runs, and in two overs took 0-6. From the age of 20 he had played for Durham, and in 1902 appeared for them in Minor Counties matches, but he is perhaps best remembered for his football; he won his 'blue', played once for Birmingham City, and five times for England at full back. His last recorded cricket match was for Free Foresters in 1913.

Logan, Richard James (476) born Stone, Staffordshire 28.1.1980. Pace bowler Logan played for England under-19s and at various times for Northamptonshire, Nottinghamshire, Surrey and Hampshire – the latter in 2005 & 2006 after he had moved from Nottinghamshire with Kevin Pietersen. He played Minor Counties cricket for Berkshire and Cumberland. For Hampshire, he played in nine first-class matches, taking 10 wickets, in seven limited-overs matches, with four wickets, and in seven T20 matches, taking five wickets – four of them in one innings (for 37 runs) in a victory v Surrey at the Oval in 2005.

London, Adam Brian (List A) born Middlesex 12.10.1988. London was a Middlesex player who appeared in one limited-overs friendly match for Hampshire v Bangladesh 'A' at the Ageas Bowl in 2013. He was run out for six, held three catches and did not bowl.

Longcroft, Okeover Butler (Pre '95, Amateur) born Havant 6.3.1850, died Havant 7.9.1871. The *Who's Who of Cricketers* records him as a batsman and wicketkeeper, yet it is his bowling which statistically appears most impressive. He attended Bradfield School, before playing twice for Hampshire in 1869 & 1870, scoring 28 runs at 7.00 and taking eight wickets at 9.37, including 3-15 and 2-29 v Lancashire at the Antelope, *despite* being recorded on the scorecard as keeping wicket. Hampshire played no first-class matches in 1871, but Longcroft played regularly for the Gentlemen of Hampshire in non-first-class matches for some years. His death, age 21, was announced in the *Portsmouth Times,* which noted that as a mark of respect, local shops were closed, and "some thirty townspeople and county cricketers" followed the funeral procession.

Longman, George Henry (Pre '95, Amateur) born Farnborough Hill, Hants 3.8.1852, died Wimbledon Common 9.8.1938. Old-Etonian Longman has been described as a stylish opening bat and brilliant deep field, although he also kept wicket for Hampshire. He played in 27 matches for the county, between 1875-1885, having played first-class cricket for Cambridge University from 1872-1875, winning his 'blue' in all four years and captaining them in 1874 & 1875. For Hampshire, he scored 856 runs at 17.46, with four half-centuries, and he also dismissed 23 batsmen in the field, three of them stumped. His best score in a county match was 78 v Surrey at the Antelope in 1884. He was in many respects the epitome of the Gentleman cricketer of an era long since passed. He was a good footballer, representing Middlesex, while Don Ambrose (*Cricket Archive*) has described how he was also Master of the Surrey Union Foxhounds, was President of Surrey CCC from 1926-1928, and then became their Hon. Treasurer from 1929-1938. He was a member of the publishing firm that bore his family name (and published books by John Arlott) while his son Henry played for Cambridge University, Surrey and Middlesex.

Lord, John Carr (Pre '95, Amateur) born Tasmania, Australia 17.8.1844, died Tasmania 25.5.1911. John Lord played in only one match for Hampshire, but it was their inaugural match v Sussex at the Antelope in 1864 – and given his place of birth, he was in effect, Hampshire's first 'overseas' player. In that one match, which Hampshire lost, he scored 11 and 4*. In March 1873, he played in one match for Tasmania, and that was the sum total of his first-class career. Alan Edwards (2014) has written about him in some detail. His father the Hon. James Lord had been born in England but the family had moved to Australia where his grandfather became a successful businessman. John came to England for schooling, and lived in the Portsea area of Portsmouth, when in his one appearance for Hampshire, he was just 19 years old. He played around the same time for the Gentlemen of Hampshire but then he returned to Australia. Rather delightfully, in a match in 1872 he was dismissed from the bowling of George Herbert Bailey, the great grandfather of Hampshire's Tasmanian Championship captain in 2017. Edwards tells us that "Lord's life in Tasmania was one of wealth and privilege", and in addition to cricket, he was particularly fond of "hunting and horse racing".

Love, Raymond Henry Arnold Davison (226, Amateur) born Chatham 11.5.1888, died Woking 12.10.1962. He was educated at Marlborough and in the early 1920s played for the Royal Artillery; then in July 1923, he played two matches for Hampshire in one week. He scored 2 & 0 (plus 0-6) v Sussex, and 13* v Nottinghamshire.

Lowe, HF (Pre '95, Amateur) we have no further information about names, or dates of birth and death. We know only that he played v Sussex at Hove in May 1882. The match was drawn and in his only innings he was dismissed without scoring.

Lowndes, William Geoffrey Lowndes Frith (229, Amateur) born Wandsworth 24.1.1898, died Newbury 23.5.1982. His father captained Buckinghamshire, and added the surname Lowndes – they had previously been the Frith family. Hampshire's Lowndes was in the Eton XI in 1915 & 1916, then saw war service in Afghanistan before going to Oxford University He made his first-class debut for the Free Foresters v his University in 1921, one week later scored 88 for the University in a first-class match v the Army, and then 216 v Leveson-Gower's XI which earned him his 'blue' in the following month. One first-class match followed in 1923, then he played in two county matches for Hampshire in 1924, scoring just 31 runs in four innings. For the rest of that decade he played occasionally in non-county first-class matches for a variety of sides, returning to the Hampshire XI in 1930, but after one match v the New Zealanders in 1931 he was not seen again for the county until 1934 when Tennyson informed Hampshire that he would be reporting on the Australian tour that summer, playing only occasionally for the county. Hampshire invited Lowndes to take over the captaincy having played just 10 county matches in 10 seasons and he held the position for two seasons, while the younger future captains, Moore and Paris gained experience.

The 1930s were not particularly successful, and in his two seasons as captain, Hampshire finished 14th and 16th (of 17). In all first-class matches, Lowndes came close to 1,000 runs in 1934, scoring two Championship centuries and a famous innings v the Australians when he reached three figures in 75 minutes, and with Phil Mead added 247 in under three hours for the fourth wicket. In that season, he also took over 30 wickets and early in 1935 scored 118 before lunch v Kent at Portsmouth, but there were very few runs after that and a season's average of just 15.53. He then handed on the captaincy to RH Moore, and in 1935 played one last first-class match for the Free Foresters, although he returned to Hampshire in 1949 to play for the Duke of Edinburgh's XI v the county at Bournemouth. For Hampshire, he scored just over 1,500 runs at 21.94 and took 40 wickets at 37.57. John Arlott (1957) suggested that while "he was not robust ... he had the gifts of a considerable all-round player".

Luard, Arthur John Hamilton (38, Amateur) born India 3.9.1861, died Guildford 22.5.1944. He was a batsman who from 1892-1907, played mainly for Gloucestershire (45 first-class matches), but in 1897, also played in five games for Hampshire, scoring 60 runs at 7.50. In the following season, he played some matches for United Services, Portsmouth.

Lucas, Charles Frank (Pre '95, Amateur) born Stowe, Staffordshire 25.11.1843, died Carshalton 27.9.1919. Lucas was a batsman who played for Hampshire between 1864-1880, including Hampshire County Cricket Club's first match, v Sussex at the Antelope in 1864. Edwards (2014) has written about him in relation to that match, revealing how he came to it, in fine form, having scored 106 and 86 in recent games for the Gentlemen of Hampshire. In this first game however, he scored just 1 & 16, although in the following season his innings of 43 & 58* were significant in Hampshire winning a first-class match for the first time, v Surrey at the Antelope. In 1866, he scored Hampshire's first century, again v Surrey and again Hampshire won. He was clearly a player of some ability but was not always available; in his 14 matches for the county he scored 502 runs at 20.08. His cousin, AP Lucas played in the England side beaten by Australia in 1882, which led to the creation of the 'Ashes' and The Times obituary.

Luckin, Verner Valentine (153) born Woking 14.2.1892, died Froxfield, Hants 28.11.1931. He batted left-handed and bowled leg break and googly, playing 10 matches for Hampshire in 1910-1912. For Hampshire, his ten matches brought just 17 runs at 2.42, and he took 13 wickets at 39.46 with a best of 3-39 v Somerset, in his debut match at Aldershot. By 1913 he was playing club cricket in the midlands and after the war, appeared in nine matches for Warwickshire in 1919, then through the 1920s he played for Ormskirk in the Liverpool league. His death was a tragedy, reported in the *Hants & Sussex News* (2.12.1931). He was living in Froxfield with his wife, having come there after playing as a professional that summer for the Huntley Club in Aberdeen, but his attempts to secure employment as a cricketer or groundsman for the following year came to nothing, and he took his own life. His wife who found him, believed it could only be because of worries about employment and money.

Lugsden, Steven (Steve) (446) born Gateshead 10.7.1976. He was a right-arm pace bowler who, after playing for England under-19s, began his county career in his native Durham. At the end of July 1998, he played against Hampshire, taking 3-67 in an innings when captain Robin Smith scored 134. Smith was said to be impressed by Lugsden, and he moved to Hampshire in 1999 but played only in two matches, v Oxford University and the New Zealanders, taking four wickets at just over 40 each. He left after one season, although he returned to the county to play for Kent 2nd XI in 2001.

Lumb, Michael John (486) born Johannesburg South Africa, 12.2.1980. Left-handed batsman Lumb was the son of Richard who opened for Yorkshire 1970-1984. He played for the South Africans under-19 sides and when he came to England to pursue a career in county cricket, he too joined Yorkshire, playing there from 2000-2006 before joining Hampshire, where he played from 2007-2011. He moved then to Nottinghamshire, retiring through injury in 2017. He has also played T20 cricket for various sides around the world. He played in three ODIs for England, including a century v West Indies, and 27 x IT20s, appearing in the England side that won the Caribbean World Cup in 2010. For Hampshire, his best first-class season was 2009 when he passed 1,000 runs at 43.75 and scored 219 v Nottinghamshire, but for the next two seasons he struggled with injury before departing. He had been a very effective batsman in the shorter forms, scoring 1,958 limited-overs runs at 39.16 with two centuries and 19 half-centuries, while in T20 he passed 1,000 runs at 24.46 with a best of 124*.

Lushington, Algernon Hay (Pre '95, Amateur) born Lyndhurst 29.9.1847, died Isle of Wight 13.9.1930. He was educated at Rugby School and played in three matches for Hampshire, one in 1870, and two in 1877, scoring 48 runs at 8.00 and taking three wickets at 32.66. He played for the Gentlemen of Hampshire and other club sides, and by 1880 was playing on the Isle of Wight.

Lynn, Joseph (Pre '95) born London 15.2.1856, died Southampton 2.2.1927. He played in one match for Hampshire v Sussex at Hove in 1875 scoring 4* & 0 and taking 0-9 & 2-25; Hampshire won by 28 runs. Four years later he played for Surrey Colts.

Lyon, Admiral Sir George Hamilton D'Oyly (137, Amateur) born India 3.10.1883, died Midhurst 19.8.1947. In first-class cricket, he played for the Army and Navy in 1911 (scoring 90) and the Royal Navy in 1922. In 1907, he played twice for Hampshire v Sussex and Worcestershire, both at Portsmouth, presumably while serving there. He scored 41 runs at 10.25 and took two wickets. He was good rugby union full-back, representing Surrey and England.

M

Maartensz Sydney Gratien Adair (194, Amateur) born Colombo (Sri Lanka) 14.4.1882, died Woking 10.9.1967. He was a right-handed batsman and wicketkeeper, and while not always available, played in 12 first-class matches for Hampshire in 1919, when Walter Livsey was still stationed in India, and George Brown was often used as a bowler. He scored 283 runs at 18.86, with a best of 60 v Middlesex at Lord's, and dismissed 25 batsmen (four stumped). Otherwise he played cricket in many interesting locations – before the war, he played cricket in Singapore, Penang, Kuala Lumpur, and Hong Kong, and after his season with Hampshire, returned to the east to play until 1929, when for a few years back in England, he played in non-first-class matches for MCC and Incogniti, as well as MF North's XI in the Netherlands. John Arlott (1957) wrote that he was "far above the usual standard of amateur wicketkeepers … and a useful straightforward bat".

McBride, Walter Nelson (241, Amateur) born Croydon 27.11.1904, died Ealing 30.1.1974. He was a medium-pace bowler who was educated at Westminster School and Oxford University where he played first-class cricket from 1925-1927, but won his 'blue' only in 1926 – in the following year he won a football 'blue' as a goalkeeper. For Hampshire, he played 31 matches mainly from 1925-1928, with two final matches in May 1929. He scored 405 runs at 13.96, and took 24 wickets at 37.54 with a best of 3-36 v Lancashire at Old Trafford in 1928 – despite which, Lancashire won by an innings. He played subsequently for Dorset.

McCorkell, Neil Thomas (263) born Portsmouth 23.3.1912, died South Africa, 28.2.2013. During the 1920s Hampshire's regular wicketkeeper was Walter Livsey, while they could also call on the extraordinary all-rounder George Brown, who would stand in for Livsey, and 'kept' for England. Livsey retired after the 1929 season, by which time Brown was in his forties, so they needed a new wicketkeeper. McCorkell learned to play in school and church teams in Portsmouth and was spotted in a match against Hampshire's Club & Ground side in the city. He played in the second match of the 1932 season and thereafter was pretty much a permanent fixture, broken by the war, for twenty years. During his first season, he dismissed 68 batsmen and was awarded his county cap. In 1933, he made his first half-century (v Yorkshire) and two years later he was promoted to open the batting; there was a gradual improvement in that aspect of his game, and later that season he made his maiden century v Lancashire at Southampton (154*) followed by a second v Northamptonshire at Bournemouth. When his career ended after the 1951 season, there had been 17 centuries, all in the Championship, and including in those days, a rare double century, 203 at Gloucester in that last year. Towards the end of his career, he sometimes played as a batsman.

In his 14 playing seasons, he scored 15,833 runs for the county at 25.87 and dismissed nearly 700 batsmen, with a higher percentage of stumpings than any of his successors in the Hampshire side. Only Bobby Parks has more dismissals for the county and John Arlott (1957) said of McCorkell that "he kept equally well to fast bowling and slow and, season in, season out, missed very few chances". He passed 1,000 runs in nine seasons with a best of 1,871 in 1949 and was perhaps an early example of the current fashion for 'keepers' who can bat. It was sometimes felt that he was unlucky never to win a Test cap, although he was in the Players XI v the Gentlemen at Lord's in 1936, and toured India with Tennyson's side in the winter of 1937/8. At the end of the 1951 season he retired and moved to South Africa to pursue a coaching career, after which he enjoyed a very long retirement, becoming just the second Hampshire cricketer from their Championship days, to reach his personal three figures. It is a salutary thought that since McCorkell, very few Hampshire cricketers have come from Portsmouth to pursue a career of any length with the county – and any that have, were privately educated.

McDonell, Harold Clark (144, Amateur) born Wimbledon 19.9.1882, died Inverness, Scotland 23.7.1965. McDonell was a leg break & googly bowler and lower-order batsman, who went to Winchester College and Cambridge University where he played from 1902-1905, winning his 'blue' in the last three years – there was also a 'blue' for golf. From 1901-1904 he played in 13 matches for Surrey, then in 1905 toured North America with MCC, before he played his first match for Hampshire in 1908. He was a school-teacher so never available until mid-July, but he played in some first-class matches in each season to 1921, with 10 in 1909 & 1920 the most regular – for Hampshire he scored 1,747 runs at 16.17, with six half-centuries and took 263 wickets at 22.43, with a best of 7-47 v Somerset at Southampton in 1914 (11-104 in the match). John Arlott (1957) described him as "the keenest of cricketers".

McGibbon, Charles Edward (199, Amateur) born Portsmouth 21.4.1880, died Hamble 2.4.1954. He played in just one match for Hampshire in 1919, v Yorkshire at Dewsbury – the only match Hampshire ever played there – scoring 0 & 1* and taking 0-10 as one of ten Hampshire bowlers in a Yorkshire score of 401-8 declared. Hampshire lost by an innings.

McIlwaine, Richard Johnston (362) born Portsmouth 16.3.1950. McIlwaine was a pace bowler, who while at Portsmouth Grammar School was highly promising, appearing in representative matches for the Public Schools and Southern Schools. He left school and joined Hampshire's staff in 1968, while from 1969-1972 he also trained as a teacher, alongside his summer contract. He made his debut v Northamptonshire at Bournemouth in 1969, sharing a last wicket partnership with Barry Richards (127*) to save Hampshire from following-on. He played in four Championship matches in two seasons, 1969 & 1970, and his victims included Tony Greig, Mushtaq Mohammad and Graham Roope, but after that he played in the 2nd XI until 1972, and for Hampshire v England Women in 1971, before pursuing a teaching career.

McIntyre, Arthur Seymour (210, Amateur) born Hartley Wintney 29.5.1889, died Nottingham 14.3.1945. He played in 28 matches for Hampshire from 1920-1923, with a highest score of 55 batting at number nine, v Yorkshire at Sheffield in 1921, and an average of 11.46.

McKenzie, Neil Douglas (502) born Johannesburg, South Africa 24.11.1975. Right-handed batsman Neil McKenzie played for Transvaal, and South Africa in all three international formats, and in England for Somerset and Durham, before joining Hampshire in 2010 and playing until 2013. He was a fine performer in all formats, scoring 2,898 first-class runs at 47.50 with eight centuries, 912 limited-overs runs at 36.48, and 1,289 T20 runs at 41.58. He scored 52 when Hampshire won the T20 Final in 2010, and was also a member of the 2012 T20 Champions, having got them to Finals day with an innings of 79* in the Quarter-Final at Trent Bridge. He was a member of the Hampshire side that completed the CB40 'double' in that season, and in a 2011 Championship match, he shared with Michael Carberry a partnership of 523 for the third wicket v Yorkshire at the Rose Bowl – a record total for any Hampshire wicket. His share was his highest score for the county, 237 in 475 minutes.

Mackenzie, Percy Alec (287) born Canterbury 5.10.1918, died Rye, Sussex 1.1.1989. He was a right-handed batsman and leg-break & googly bowler who played in three Championship matches for Hampshire in 1938 and a further 19 in 1939. In the latter season, he scored four half-centuries, with a best of 76 v Lancashire at Southampton, and took 17 wickets over the two seasons, with a best of 4-34 v Warwickshire at Edgbaston, also in 1939. Since he was just 27 when cricket resumed in 1946, he might have returned, but after serving in the RAF – and playing for their cricket sides – he pursued a flying career, and played in the Minor Counties with Berkshire. In 1952, he appeared briefly for his native Kent 2nd XI. He was awarded the DFC in May 1942.

McLaren, Frederick Albert (142, Amateur) born Farnham 19.8.1874, died Dartford 23.9.1952. He was principally a bowler who played in two matches for Hampshire in 1908, scoring just four runs in three innings and taking four wickets at 28.50. Neither match was in the County Championship; one was v MCC the other v the Gentlemen of Philadelphia. In 1919, he played one more first-class match in Madras, for the Europeans v the Indians, taking two more wickets.

McLaren, Ryan (536) born Cape Province, South Africa 9.2.1983. McLaren was an all-rounder, who represented South Africa in all three formats in international cricket. He played for sides in various countries; in England for Kent, Lancashire and in 2015 & 2016, for Hampshire. He played in 20 first-class matches for the county and with the bat, averaged 47.23 with one century v Surrey at the Oval in 2016, and seven half-centuries. He took 43 first-class wickets at 38.79 with a best of 5-104, to which he added 10 limited-overs, and five T20 wickets.

McLean, Jonathan James (Jono) (481) born Johannesburg, South Africa 11.7.1980. McLean was a right-handed batsman who played for the South African Academy and Western Province, before joining Hampshire for whom he played in 2005 & 2006. He played subsequently for Berkshire in the Minor Counties Championship. For Hampshire, he scored four half-centuries in seven first-class matches at an average of 33.55 and while his limited-overs record of 60 runs at 15.00 in nine matches is modest, it included an appearance in the winning C&G semi-final side v Yorkshire at the Rose Bowl in 2005.

McLean, Nixon Alexei McNamara (443) born St Vincent, West Indies, 20.7.1973. Nixon McLean was one of last of the West Indian fast bowlers who featured regularly in Hampshire sides across three decades. He represented his country in 19 Test Matches (44 wickets) and 45 ODIs and played for the Windward Islands through the 1990s, joining Hampshire for two seasons, 1998 & 1999. In 30 matches for Hampshire he took 108 first-class wickets at 28.37, adding 51 wickets in 42 limited-overs matches. He played subsequently for Somerset, Kwa-Zulu Natal and Canterbury (NZ).

MacLeod, Alister (191, Amateur) born London 12.11.1894, died Essex 24.4.1982. He was a batsman, who was educated at Felsted School and first played for Hampshire in five matches in 1914. After returning from war, with the Hampshire Regiment, he played two more matches in 1920 and one in 1935. He became secretary of the county from 1936-1939 and last appeared for them in 1938 in four matches. Overall, he scored 271 runs at 15.05 with a best of 87, his only half-century, v Essex at Bournemouth in 1914, when he top-scored in an innings victory.

McManus, Lewis David (532) born Poole, Dorset 9.10.1994. For more than 100 years from the time that James Stone took Hampshire's wicketkeeping position, until the retirement of Nic Pothas, Hampshire had a succession of regular 'keepers', but in the past decade no one player has managed to hold the position; Lewis McManus is one of the current claimants. He played for England under-19s, for his native Dorset, for Hampshire's Academy and after one game in 2011, played regularly for Hampshire 2nd XI from 2013. He made his first-class debut at Headingley in 2015 and was second highest scorer as Hampshire fell to a heavy defeat, while in his next match v Durham at the Ageas Bowl he scored 53*, batting for almost three hours to save the game. Initially, he covered for Adam Wheater when the latter was injured, but from mid-season 2016 established himself as the first-choice wicketkeeper and Wheater returned to Essex. To the end of the 2018 season, McManus has played in 32 first-class matches for Hampshire scoring one century, 132* (and 35) v Surrey at the Ageas Bowl in 2016, despite which, Hampshire lost by an innings, plus five half-centuries, with an average just above 30. He has occasionally opened the batting in Championship matches. He has also dismissed 72 batsmen (nine stumped). In limited-overs matches he averages 21.50, with a best of 47, and in T20 has one half-century. In all 'white ball' cricket, 13 of his 45 victims have been stumped, a far higher proportion than in first-class cricket, and typical of the modern game. He lost his place through injury to Tom Alsop in mid-2018 but returned for the final Championship game and ended the season scoring 44* in a losing cause. He will hope no doubt that Alsop resumes his batting ambitions and that he returns behind the stumps in 2019.

McMillan, Craig Douglas (479) born Christchurch, New Zealand 13.9.1976. All-rounder Craig McMillan played in all three forms of the game for New Zealand, including 55 Test Matches. In domestic cricket, he played mainly for Canterbury, but also in England, for Gloucestershire and for part of the 2005 season for Hampshire. He played in four first-class matches with one half-century, on debut, five limited-overs matches with a best of 49*, and seven T20 matches, including a score of 65* in a victory v Middlesex at Richmond. He took three first-class wickets, adding six in the T20. He played in the Lancashire League for Nelson in 2007 & 2008.

Malone, Steven John (387) born Chelmsford, 19.10.1953. He was a pace bowler, who played for his native Essex from 1975 and in 1980, joined Hampshire, where he played for five seasons, most regularly in 1983, when in 22 matches, he took 48 wickets. His best bowling for Hampshire, and in all first-class cricket, was 7-55 v Oxford University in 1982 but in the County Championship it came at Southampton against Hampshire, after he moved to Glamorgan for one year in 1985. He took 5-38, as Hampshire were dismissed for 115, although they beat Glamorgan by three wickets. He played subsequently for Durham and Wiltshire in the Minor Counties Championship and for Old Tauntonians and Lymington in the Southern League, and was at one time an umpire on the reserve list for first-class matches.

Manners, John Errol (279, Amateur) born Exeter, 25.9.1914. John Manners was an officer in the Royal Navy who, as a batsman, played in the final four matches for Hampshire in 1936 and then three more in 1947 & 1948. On debut in 1936 v Gloucestershire at Portsmouth he scored 81, and in that season batted with Phil Mead as the great batsman's career ended. At Canterbury in August 1947, Manners scored 121, but Hampshire failed to avoid the follow-on and lost by an innings – Manners run out for five in the second. In the same year, he made his first-class debut for the Combined Services v Gloucestershire at Bristol, and in the following year played for them *against* Hampshire at Aldershot. He played no more for Hampshire, but regularly for the Combined Services, in those days enhanced by the inclusion of county cricketers on National Service – at various times his team-mates included PBH May, ASM Oakman, JM Parks, DB Close, FJ Titmus, AE Moss, JG Dewes, R Illingworth, KV Andrew, JB Mortimore, DEV Padgett and R Swetman, all of whom went on to play Test cricket for England. His final first-class match was for the Free Foresters v Oxford University in 1953, and his last recorded match for Wiltshire Queries in 1979, age 64. In 2014 he became Hampshire's third County Championship cricketer (after EA English and NT McCorkell) to reach his personal three figures, and by September 2018 was the first man ever to have played first-class cricket and reach the age of 104. He is also the only surviving pre-war first-class cricketer. He featured earlier in 2018 on a BBC TV programme about older drivers. He was awarded the DSC in July 1945.

Mannings, Dr George (pre '95, Amateur) born Downton, Wiltshire 13.10.1843, died Downton, Wiltshire 28.11.1876. He was a batsman who attended Marlborough College, played for the Gentlemen of Wiltshire in 1863, and once for Hampshire in 1864 v Middlesex at Islington in their first season in first-class cricket as a County Club. He was run out for two in the first innings and dismissed for five in the second as Hampshire lost by an innings. He was just 33 when he died.

Manser, Robert Marsack (110, Amateur) born Tunbridge Wells 10.10.1880, died Parkstone, Dorset 15.2.1955. He was one of 11 players to make their debut for Hampshire in the weak side of 1904, and one of seven who played only in that season – in his case, in one match, v the South Africans at Alton, in which he scored 0 & 1. He was educated at Tonbridge School and played for Dorset from 1909-1929.

Mariner, Edward Charles (35, Amateur) born Winchester 31.1.1877, died Portsmouth 10.5.1949. He played in one match, a ten-wicket defeat v Warwickshire at Southampton in 1896, recording a 'pair' and taking 0-20.

Marshall, Malcolm Denzil (383) born Barbados 18.4.1958, died Barbados 4.11.1999. He was one of the world's greatest fast bowlers, a very capable batsman, and probably the finest overseas cricketer to play for the county, not merely on ability but on attitude and commitment. He was relatively unknown when he signed for Hampshire in 1979, to replace Andy Roberts, but before arriving at Southampton, and after just one first-class match in Barbados, he was chosen to tour India with a West Indies side shorn of major players through the World Series Cricket controversy. In his first Championship match, which Hampshire won, Marshall took 3-45 and 4-23 v Glamorgan at Southampton and he ended the season with 46 Championship wickets at 20.80. In 1980, he took

15 Test wickets on West Indies' tour of England but played only in Hampshire's last five matches in a season when they finished last – he took 4-53 and 5-39 in their only victory. After this he performed for the county with great consistency. In 1981, there were 68 Championship wickets (19.42) and 425 runs (HS 75*) and in 1982, 134 Championship wickets at 15.73 and 633 runs (22.60). In 1983, he played in a Test series in the Caribbean until mid-May, re-joined Hampshire, then missed the middle of the season while playing in the World Cup. Nonetheless in just 16 Championship matches he took 80 wickets at 16.58.

In 1984, he toured England, taking 28 Test wickets at 19.78. In ten seasons from 1981-1990, Hampshire finished in the bottom four in the Championship in 1984 and 1988 when Marshall and Greenidge toured. In the other seasons they were seventh once, never lower than that, and in the top three in 1982, 1983 and 1985 – the impact of those two players was huge. In 1985, Marshall took 95 Championship wickets at 17.68 and scored 768 runs at 24.77, and in 1986 Hampshire won the Sunday League while he took 100 Championship wickets at 15.08.

There were 72 Championship wickets in the following season plus 610 runs at 35.88, including a Championship best of 99 v Middlesex at Lord's (bowled by Fraser). He missed Hampshire's first Lord's Final in 1988, while on tour and in 1989 and 1990 he played in two narrow semi-final defeats. Hampshire won a second Final at Lord's in 1991 but again, Marshall was touring, so when he played in the B&H Final v Kent and won his medal in 1992, it was a special moment, even for a man who had achieved so much. 1993 was his last season in County Cricket; he took 826 first-class wickets for Hampshire and only he (18.64), Andy Roberts (16.70), and Derek Shackleton (18.23) of their major bowlers ended their county careers with an average below 20 – in Marshall's case having bowled mainly on covered pitches. He finished with 150 wickets in the Sunday League and also passed 10,000 first-class career runs. For his performances in 1982, he was nominated as one of *Wisden's* Cricketers of the Year.

He played a little after this for Natal in South Africa and was appointed Hampshire's coach, but in the late 1990s he became ill, and cancer was diagnosed. In September 1999, he came to the County Ground with his son Mali to watch Hampshire playing v Somerset, but he was not seen there again. He died two months later, mourned across the cricket world as a great player and a much-loved man.

Marshall, Roy Edwin (328) born Barbados 25.4.1930, died Taunton, Somerset 27.10.1992. Roy Marshall first came to Hampshire's notice at the county ground in Southampton in 1950, when he arrived with the West Indian tourists straight from their historic Test Match victory at Lord's. Marshall was unable to break into that Test side, but at Southampton he scored 135, and shared a century partnership with Everton Weekes, an innings that made a considerable impression on Hampshire's captain/secretary Desmond Eagar. He was looking to strengthen the county's often weak batting, and persuaded Marshall to turn his back on Test hopes; Marshall spent two years in the Lancashire leagues with Lowerhouse, and two further years qualifying for Hampshire with the occasional non-Championship match, until, in 1955 he could play in all the county's matches.

Hampshire began 1955 with a record of having finished in the top half of the Championship table just once in the previous 22 seasons – and that was just eighth in 1932, but they surprised everyone, including their own supporters, by winning more matches than ever before and reached third place for the first time in their history. At the close they were behind the 'Big Two', Surrey (Champions) and Yorkshire, but they had beaten both, and while there were significant contributions from the 13 regular players, when the captain Desmond Eagar (1957) identified the reasons for this advance he began by acknowledging that "undoubtedly Roy Marshall had much to do with it", through the number of his runs, the way he scored them "so attractively" and the "confidence" that he brought to the rest of the side.

This approach would continue throughout his career. In 18 seasons, he scored 60 centuries for Hampshire with a best of 228* v the Pakistanis at Bournemouth in 1962, and in exceeding 30,000 first-class runs, is second only to the great Phil Mead in the list of Hampshire's highest scorers. In four consecutive seasons from 1958-1961, he exceeded 2,000 runs, and it is no coincidence that Hampshire were runners-up in 1958 and Champions in 1961. In only one season, 1969, did he fail to reach 1,000 runs, having dropped down the order, to allow Barry Richards to open, but his form returned in the final three years with over 4,000 runs. By this time county cricketers were playing in the Sunday League and Gillette Cup, in which Marshall scored 2,190 runs at 32.20, while captaining the county to the runners-up spot in the first season of the Sunday League. In addition, although he was often a reluctant bowler of off-breaks he took 99 wickets for Hampshire at 24.27, with a best of 6-36 v Surrey in 1956, following 6-44 v Yorkshire in a remarkable victory at Bradford in 1955. For his performances in 1958, he was nominated as one of *Wisden's* Cricketers of the Year.

English cricket abolished the distinction between amateurs and professionals from the 1963 season, but when Marshall became captain he was effectively the county's first professional captain, and while he was always a thrilling batsman, he brought a certain pragmatism to the leadership role, and a somewhat cautious approach that seemed at odds with his batting. It was a difficult time for county cricket as the authorities introduced various strategies to 'brighten' what was on offer, and arrest declining attendances. Limited-overs cricket undoubtedly worked in that respect but some – for example limiting Championship first innings to 65 overs – did not, and Marshall's autobiography

Test Outcast was typically intelligent and forthright about the game's future. It also revealed a couple of occasions when he *might* have returned to the international scene with West Indies or England, but that was not to be.

As captain, he was able to enjoy briefly what was probably the best pace attack in the county's history, Shackleton, White and Cottam, but until Richards arrived the batting was less reliable. Hampshire nonetheless finished fifth in 1968 and 1969, and never lower than twelfth, before with obvious reluctance, Marshall handed control to Gilliat in 1971, playing on for two more years. He enjoyed a benefit in 1961, one of the first professionals to be so honoured after fewer than ten years with his 'cap', and a testimonial in 1971. He played in Southampton for Deanery CC, then moved to Somerset and was for a time the Chairman of their Cricket Committee, but for a certain generation of supporters, he will be remembered always, as one of the most entertaining of Hampshire's batsman – and the first such in the post-war era. John Arlott (1961) said of him that he was "one of those batsmen, rare in any period who can consistently please even the confirmed grumblers by the brilliant aggression of their stroke play. Indeed, his very entry into the Hampshire side brought about a complete change in the character of the county's batting".

Martin, Charles (Pre '95) born Breamore, Hants 6.8.1836 died Portsmouth 28.3.1878. He was a fast, left-handed, round-arm bowler who played in four matches for Hampshire in 1869 & 1870, taking nine wickets at 18.66, with a best of 3-38 v MCC at Lord's in 1869, when MCC were dismissed for 190, yet won by an innings. His other first-class match was for the Left-Handed v Right-Handed at Lord's in 1870 – again his side lost by an innings.

Martin, George (55) born Swindon 21.11.1873, died Swindon 25.2.1963. Martin was a bowler who played in four matches for Hampshire, three in 1898, and one more the following year v Warwickshire at Bournemouth, when he took three early wickets in his best performance. In the two following seasons, he played for Wiltshire.

Martin, J? (112) we have no information about his birth or death, but know that a man called (J?) Martin, played once for Hampshire in July 1904 v Somerset at Taunton and had a fairly successful match but was never selected again. He took five wickets for 166 runs, and batting last, shared final wicket partnerships of 76 (the best of the innings) & 48, with his contribution 66 for twice out. Beyond that we knew very little, until cricket historian Keith Walmsley (May 2013) investigated and produced a comprehensive paper, entitled "Not So Mysterious Martin". Walmsley offered evidence that he was a Southampton club cricketer – although in reports of those matches, he seemed to be G Martin, rather than J Martin. Walmsley searched for local men who might have been this cricketer, partly linked to playing with Southampton's Ordnance Survey side. Through the census and other sources, Walmsley seemed to narrow down the possibilities to two men, both named G Martin, although almost certainly, neither were the same as George Martin (above) who played for Hampshire a few years earlier.

Martin, William (Pre '95) born Southampton 19.2.1844, died Southampton 27.5.1871. He played in one match for Hampshire v Kent at the Antelope in 1867, scoring a single in each innings. He appeared in other non-first-class matches for the Players of Hampshire, Southampton Union (etc.) but died, age just 27.

Maru, Rajesh Jamandass ('Raj') (395) born Nairobi, Kenya 28.10.1962. Slow-left-arm bowler Raj Maru played for Middlesex 2nd XI from 1979 and for England under-19s the following year. He made his first-class and limited-overs debut for the county in 1980, but with England spinners Edmonds and Emburey at the club, found it hard to secure a regular place, and after 16 first-class matches with 23 wickets, he joined Hampshire, making his debut in 1984. He took first-class wickets regularly through the next eight seasons, with 73 in 1985, and 71 two years later. From 1992, he played less regularly in the Championship as Shaun Udal established himself as the main spinner, but from 1990-1992, Maru was a fairly regular member of Hampshire's limited-overs sides, taking 40 wickets in that period; he played in the Hampshire side that won the Nat West Trophy in 1991, and having played in the early rounds was unfortunate not to play in the 1992 B&H Cup winning team. Maru was a useful batsman who scored seven first-class half centuries for Hampshire, and he was a fine close-to-the-wicket fielder, holding 240 catches, in 213 matches – one of the few Hampshire catchers to average better than one per game. In 1988, he held seven catches in the match v Northamptonshire at Bournemouth, equalling the county record set by Tom Dean (and since matched by Liam Dawson). With the ball, he took 504 first-class wickets at 33.62, to which he added 82 limited-overs wickets; he is in 19th place in Hampshire's all-time first-class wicket-takers. He played in just one Championship and one tourist match in 1998, his benefit season, after which he retired and took up a coaching position at the club. From 1999-2001, he captained the Hampshire Cricket Board side in the knock-out competitions, including a thrilling, one run, last ball victory against Shropshire. More recently he has been the coach at Lancing College where he was instrumental in the development of Mason Crane.

Mascarenhas, Adrian Dimitri ('Dimi') (435) born London, 30.11.1977. Although born in London, 'Dimi' Mascarenhas was raised in Australia by Sri Lankan parents, and returned to England in 1996, on the recommendation of Paul Terry, initially playing 2nd XI and Southern League cricket in Hampshire. Having impressed, he made his first-class debut v Glamorgan in September and broke an opening partnership of 177, taking 6-88 – one of the best debut returns in Hampshire's history. In the next match, he took seven Kent wickets and won a contract which would lead to a highly successful career in all forms of the game, not least representing England in limited-overs and T20 internationals. He began his Hampshire career as a bowler who batted, and through his career became an increasingly skilful medium-pacer; in 195 first-class matches for Hampshire, he took 450 wickets, with 285 more in limited-overs and another 94 in the T20 – placing him third in Hampshire's all-time list. His batting developed over the years, scoring his first centuries in 2000 & 2001 – the latter, Hampshire's first on their new ground. In 2005 he averaged almost 50, and in 2008 scored 673 runs, his highest aggregate; in first-class cricket, he scored 6,495 runs at 25.07. One of his more notable batting feats was hitting India's Yuvraj Singh for five consecutive sixes in an ODI at the Oval, and he played for England 20 times in limited-overs internationals and 14 x T20s, in which he was the first Hampshire player to complete the career 'double' of 1,000 runs and 100 wickets.

He became Hampshire's captain in 2008 when in the early spring, Warne informed the county he would not be returning, although that May, Mascarenhas became the first English cricketer to appear in the new IPL. Hampshire started the season poorly and seemed threatened with relegation, but they recovered well, and finished in third place, while they were also runners-up in the Pro-40. He continued in charge in 2009, although Pothas deputised while he appeared again in the IPL. On return he captained Hampshire to the Friends Provident Trophy at Lord's, beating Sussex. They were less successful in the Championship but finished clear of relegation. In 2010, he was appointed captain again, but was injured in the IPL, and played just once in a T20 match, so Pothas and Cork deputised, and Cork replaced him in 2010. Mascarenhas was injured when Cork's Hampshire won their first T20 in 2010, but in 2012 he captained Hampshire in the shortest form, and lifted the Trophy at Cardiff after taking 2-20 in his four overs. In 2013, he played in just one first-class match but as his Hampshire career drew to a close he was a regular in the 40-over competition and played in the semi-final v Glamorgan at the Ageas Bowl, taking his leave with eight not out, as Hampshire fell to a defeat. Despite that disappointing end, he will be remembered as a very good, cheerful cricketer; one of the supporters' favourites. He moved into coaching, for a time with New Zealand, and from 2018 with Essex.

Maturin, Dr Henry (Pre '95, Amateur) born Co. Donegal Northern Island 5.4.1842, died Hartley Wintney, Hants 24.2.1920. He was a batsman and round-arm fast bowler, who after attending Marlborough College, played once for Middlesex in 1863, for the Gentlemen of the South in 1864, and subsequently in nine matches for Hampshire, seven from 1864-1867, and one each in 1876 & 1882. In those nine matches he scored 136 runs at 9.71 and took six wickets at 30.00. His best bowling of 4-68 was against Kent in a drawn match at the Antelope in 1867. He played also for Southgate and MCC.

Maundrell, Rev. William Herbert (80, Amateur) born Nagasaki, Japan 5.11.1876, died Deal, Kent 17.6.1958. He was educated at King's School Canterbury and Cambridge University, winning a 'blue' for Athletics but not cricket. He played one innings in his one match for Hampshire, a rain-ruined draw at Derby in 1900, but was dismissed without scoring. In November 1909, he is recorded playing two matches in Hong Kong.

Maxwell, Glenn James (526) born Melbourne, Australia 14.10.1988. Maxwell is a dynamic batsman and off-spin bowler who has played for Australia in all three forms of the game. In 2012, he came to play in the Southern League for South Wilts, 'guested' for Hampshire 2nd XI and was selected to play in that year's T20 competition, although he was unavailable for the Finals Day. He returned to play in the T20 for Hampshire in the overseas Champions League in the winter of 2012/13, played for Surrey in 2013, then in 2014, returned to Hampshire for two limited-overs matches and one Championship match at Worcester, where his 85 in two hours helped Hampshire to save a vital game, after they had followed-on. At the season's end Hampshire finished top of Division Two, with Worcestershire runners-up. For Hampshire, he scored two T20 half-centuries with a best of 66* v Kent. In 2015, he played for Yorkshire.

May, John (Pre '95) born Southampton 26.9.1845, we have no information about his date/place of death. He played in four matches from 1867-1870 scoring 71 runs at 11.83 and taking six wickets, with his best bowling, 4-80 v Lancashire at Old Trafford in 1870. He appeared in a number of non-first-class matches for the Players of Hampshire, Hampshire Colts, Thomas Walker's Team, Grimsby and others.

Mead, Charles Phillip ('Phil') (122) born Battersea 9.3.1887, died Boscombe, 26.3.1958. Left-handed batsman Phil Mead holds a statistical record which will never be matched: in 700 first-class matches for Hampshire he scored 48,892 runs (at 48.84) and that is more runs than any other batsman has ever scored for any single first-class side, anywhere in the world. There is however, a sad 'twist' to that tale, since it came about partly because, in a career that ran from a single match in 1905, to the end of the 1936 season, he played in just 17 Test Matches, and only two of them were in England. They were against the Australians in the final two Test Matches of the 1921 series, which were drawn, despite which Australia won the series 3-0, and Mead, only batting twice, scored 47 and 182*. So, his Test batting average in England was 229.00, yet in a further 15 seasons he was never selected again in England, leaving many county summers in which to score those many runs for Hampshire. In all Tests, he scored 1,185 runs at a fraction under 50 per innings, with four centuries and three half-centuries.

He had moved to Hampshire from the Oval after his contract was not renewed and while qualifying for his new county in 1905, he played only one first-class game, scoring 41* on debut v the Australians. In the next 27 seasons, he went past 1,000 runs every season, in eleven of those he passed 2,000 and while he never reached 3,000 runs in a season for Hampshire, in all first-class cricket, he did so in 1921 – that Test year, when he also recorded his best score of 280* in a defeat v Nottinghamshire – and in 1928. In the single months of June 1921 and July 1923, he scored 1,000 runs, in the latter averaging over 150. In all first-class cricket his 153 centuries places him fourth in the all-time records, again unlikely to be matched, and his total of 138 centuries for Hampshire is more than twice the number by the next in the list, 60 by Roy Marshall. In three seasons, he scored 10 centuries and in 1928, there were 13, while for Hampshire he scored 11 double centuries. Other records included being the first of just two Hampshire batsmen to score a double and single century in the same match; on four occasions, he scored three consecutive centuries, and on three occasions when opening, he carried his bat. At various times in his career, he held Hampshire's partnership records for the second, third, fourth, eighth and ninth wickets and he shared a three-figure partnership for every Hampshire wicket, and with a century v Derbyshire in 1932, he completed centuries against all the other county sides. In addition, he held 633 catches, more than anyone for Hampshire, and having started his career, as a slow-left-arm bowler, took 266 wickets for the county. In 1912, he was nominated as one of *Wisden's* Cricketers of the Year.

He retired after the 1936 season but played for Suffolk in 1938 & 1939 and was their leading batsman in both seasons. After the war, he retired to Hampshire and would visit the cricket but his eyesight had deteriorated rapidly and he was blind for the last ten years of his life. He was made an honorary life member of MCC and in later years at Northlands Road, Hampshire created a new stand in his honour. John Arlott (1957) said of him that "he had a defence which must challenge comparison with that of any player" and that among the cricketers of his time, Mead might be seen as "more nearly approaching the impossible batting standards of infallibility than any other player except Jack Hobbs".

Meaden, Henry JB (Pre '95, Amateur) born Point de Galle, Sri Lanka 1862, we have no information about his death. Don Ambrose (*Cricket Archive*) has found a medical student at Southampton College in the 1881 census, who is probably Meaden – in that same year he played three matches for Hampshire, scoring 20 runs at 4.00; he did not bowl. In 1882 and 1884 he is recorded as playing matches in Colombo.

Melle, Dr Basil George von Brandis (190, Amateur) born Cape Province, South Africa 31.3.1891, died Johannesburg, South Africa 8.1.1966. Melle was an all-rounder who played for Western Province, before coming to England to study and play at Oxford University in 1913 & 1914, winning his 'blue' in both seasons. In 1914, he made his Hampshire debut after the 'Varsity' match, but war was declared on 4 August, and although he began a match at Trent Bridge two days later, when rain stopped play after six overs he left the game to join his Army Regiment; James Stone was allowed to take his place and batted. Melle returned to Hampshire in 1919, playing also for MCC and Free Foresters, and played for Hampshire over the first three post-war seasons, before returning to

South Africa. He played in 27 first-class matches for the county, mostly in 1919, scoring overall 1,207 runs at 29.43 with one century, 110 v Gloucestershire at Bristol in 1919, and taking 25 wickets at 42.96, with a best of 5-70 v Kent at Tunbridge Wells in 1919. His son, MG Melle, toured England with the South Africans in 1951.

Michell, Edward John (Pre '95, Amateur) born Steyning, Sussex 15.6.1853, died New Zealand 5.5.1900. He was a right-handed batsman who attended Harrow School and played in one match for Hampshire v MCC in 1880, scoring seven runs in a match which Hampshire won by an innings.

Middleton, Tony Charles (399) born Winchester 1.2.1964. If timing is the key to a long and successful career as a county batsman then Tony Middleton was particularly unfortunate, for during his time with the county they had the strongest batting line-up in their history. He played first for the 2nd XI in 1982 and between then and his final season, 1995, Hampshire could select at various times from Test batsmen, Greenidge, Terry, Gower and the Smith brothers, plus Jesty, Turner, James, and the captain Nicholas. Middleton made his debut in 1984, at a damp Bournemouth v Kent in a match in which Underwood took 12-121 and 40 wickets fell without any side reaching 200. Hampshire lost and Middleton had to wait two years for his next chance, and a run in the side in the late summer which brought 316 runs at 28.72, and a first half-century. Despite this he played just two more matches in the next two seasons, and seven more in 1989, by which time he had made his limited-overs debut. 1990, was a good season for batting, and was Middleton's breakthrough season, with 1,238 runs at 47.61 and five centuries, and while his record declined somewhat in 1991, he was even more successful in 1992, with 1,780 runs at 49.44, and six more centuries, including 221 v Surrey at Southampton. Meanwhile late in 1991, Chris Smith, having helped Hampshire to their first Nat West Final, departed and Middleton made his 60-over debut in a Lord's Final, and was equal top scorer with 78 as Hampshire won. In a short period, Middleton had gone from a loyal reserve to a leading player and was rewarded with a tour of Australia with the England 'A' side. By his own admission, he tried to adapt his patient game, to a more enterprising one, and it did not work. He scored few runs on tour and in the next two first-class seasons scored just over 500 runs. There were just two games in 1995 and he retired to take up a coaching role with the county which he still holds today. He scored 5,665 runs for Hampshire at 34.75, one of the highest averages by any Hampshire-born batsman, and including 13 centuries. Bowling slow-left-arm, he took five wickets.

Milburn, Stuart Mark (430) born Harrogate, 29.9.1972. Pace bowler Stuart Milburn played for his native Yorkshire from 1992-1995, before joining Hampshire for two seasons. He played in 21 first-class matches, taking 39 wickets at 52.97 with a best of 4-38 v Sussex in his final game for the county in mid-September 1997, and scoring one half-century v the Indians in 1996. He played in 15 limited-overs matches, taking 13 wickets.

Mildmay, Sir Henry Paulet St John (Pre '95, Amateur) born London 28.4.1853, died Dogmersfield Park, Hants 24.4.1916. He was educated at Eton but did not play in the XI. He was an Army officer until 1894 and played in military matches and for MCC and I Zingari, as well as in seven matches for Hampshire from 1881-1884, scoring 137 runs at 11.41 and taking one wicket.

Misselbrook, Henry (Pre '95) born Otterbourne 16.12.1832, died Winchester 11.7.1895. In the 1850s and 1860s he played in many of the more prominent non-first-class matches in Hampshire, and in 1869 he played in one first-class game for the county v MCC at the Antelope. In a thrilling match, he took 4-18 & 2-21, but opening the batting scored just 3 & 0, as Hampshire failed by three runs to score the 71 needed to win the game.

Moberly, John Cornelius (Pre '95, Amateur) born Winchester 22.4.1848, died Bassett, Hants 29.1.1928. He was educated at Winchester College and Oxford University but did not win his 'blue'. He played in one first-class match for Hampshire at Derby in 1877, scoring 27 & 4 in an innings defeat. He was the President of the club in the two years prior to the First World War.

Moorcroft, William (163, Amateur) we have no certain details of birth or death, but the identification of a man of the same name born in Burton-on-Trent in 1878. Otherwise, we know of him only that he played in one match, v Gloucestershire at Southampton in 1911, did not bat and took 0-17 & 0-51 in a drawn game.

Moore, John William Spearink (152) born Winchfield, Hants 29.4.1891, died Basingstoke 23.6.1980. He played in 15 first-class matches for Hampshire in 1910, 1911 & 1913. He scored 256 runs at 13.47 and in 12 overs took 0-72.

Moore, Richard Henry ('Dick') (262, Amateur) born Charminster, Dorset 14.11.1913, died Denbighshire, Wales 1.3.2002. Batsman Dick Moore holds the record for the highest individual first-class score for Hampshire, 316 v Warwickshire at Bournemouth in 1937, scored in one day and including a century before lunch. He was given out lbw in the final over. On three occasions in the 21st century, John Crawley (twice) and Michael Carberry have reached 300, in sight of that record, and each time their captain declared – perhaps the record will never be broken. Having impressed at Bournemouth School, Moore played occasionally for Hampshire between 1931-1933, with a fine century v Essex (159) age just 19, but otherwise a fairly modest record; then in 1934 he passed 1,500 runs at an average of 30.17, and after another relatively fallow year caused by a serious illness, he was appointed captain in 1936, a position he held for two years, scoring four centuries and passing 1,000 runs in each season. When Cecil

Paris replaced him in 1938, Moore was still only 24 and his average of 42.00 from 11 matches was his best, but business made growing demands on him, as it did increasingly on amateurs through the last 25 years of their participation in first-class cricket. There were just four first-class matches in 1939; during the war, he played in a number of services and other matches, and when non-first-class county cricket returned to Southampton in 1945 he played a match v Sussex. After that he moved to Wales and continued to play some cricket there, before becoming Chairman of Colwyn Bay CC, although in 1952, he was reunited with former colleagues for a match at Bournemouth v the current Hampshire side, in aid of George Heath's testimonial.

Mordaunt, Sir Henry John (Pre '95, Amateur) born London 12.7.1867, died London 15.1.1939. He came from a large cricketing family and while at Eton where he captained the XI in 1886, he played one match for Hampshire the previous season, after which the county lost its first-class status, although he played for them again in 1887. He played also at Cambridge University where he won his 'blue' in 1888 & 1889, and in seven matches for Middlesex from 1889-1893. In his first-class match for Hampshire, v Somerset he was dismissed without scoring in his one innings and did not bowl. His career was in education, and he succeeded to the family title in 1934.

Mornement, Dr Robert Harry (130, Amateur) born Norfolk 15.8.1873, died Chatham 16.4.1948. He was a medium-pace bowler, who played in three first-class matches for Hampshire in 1906 and two more for the Combined Army & Navy XI v the Combined Universities in 1910 & 1911. For Hampshire, he scored 41 runs at 8.20 and took six wickets at 28.50, including 3-62 v Yorkshire on debut. He played also for Norfolk, MCC and in other Army matches.

Morris, Alexander Corfield ('Alex') (444) born Barnsley 4.10.1976. Alex Morris was a pace-bowling all-rounder who played for England under-19s and his native Yorkshire, before moving to Hampshire in 1998. He was a good enough cricketer to win his county cap in 2001, but he struggled with injuries – only in that debut season and in 2001 did his first-class appearances reach double figures, and in the latter, he scored 423 runs at 24.88 with three half-centuries, and took 51 wickets at 28.00, as Hampshire won promotion. He was only 24 and highly promising, but there were just four first-class matches in the next two seasons, before he retired. In 15 limited-overs matches he took 18 wickets.

Morris, Robert Sean Millner (417) born Buckinghamshire 10.9.1968. He was a right-handed batsman and one of a group of young players who it was hoped would eventually replace Mark Nicholas's side. He played at Durham University, and for various county 2nd XIs before settling with Hampshire in 1989, while playing also for Lymington in the Southern League. In May 1992, he made his first-class debut for Hampshire v Oxford University and played a few more Championship matches that year plus, in August, his limited-overs debut v Kent. In 1994, he scored his maiden century and added a second in compiling 686 runs at 49.00 – his best was 174 v Nottinghamshire at Basingstoke, but a month later at Portsmouth his hand was badly damaged by a ball from Gloucestershire's Courtney Walsh. He played no more that year, and in a further 15 matches in the next two seasons, passed 50 only once, an innings of 112 v Cambridge University. In both competitions for Hampshire, he averaged just a fraction under 30 with a limited-overs best of 87 v Gloucestershire in 1995, but it seemed perhaps that the injury damaged his confidence, and he retired at 26. Initially, he pursued a career with the PCA, while playing occasionally for Free Foresters, MCC and others, then became CEO of Rajasthan Royals and Masters Cricket League. He was appointed CEO of one of the sides in the South African T20 Franchise, which failed to launch in 2017.

Morris, Zachary Clegg ('Zach') (445) born Barnsley 4.9.1978. He was a slow-left-arm bowler who came to Hampshire from Yorkshire in 1998, with his older brother 'Alex' having, like him, played for England under-19s. He played in just two first-class matches for Hampshire scoring 11 runs but failing to take a wicket. In four limited-overs matches his best bowling was 3-31 v Worcestershire at the Rose Bowl in 2001 – the one occasion on which he took wickets for the county. He left at the end of that season and returned to Yorkshire where he played league cricket for Hoylandswaine.

Mottram, Thomas James ('Tom') (367) born Liverpool 7.9.1945. Tom Mottram was a tall, pace-bowler, not strictly fast but accurate, who played a surprising, but key role in Hampshire's second Championship in 1973. In 1968 & 1969 he played club cricket for Liverpool, and in 1970 played for Lancashire 2nd XI but also for Hampshire 2nd XI. He was an architect and in a sense, a reminder of the old category of amateur players which had been abolished from 1963. He made his first-class debut for Hampshire v the Australians in 1972, taking 3-45, and after a few more games that year played regularly in 1973, forming a remarkably effective opening partnership with Bob Herman. He played in 17 of the 20 Championship matches, taking 57 wickets at 22.00, including a remarkable caught-and-bowled from Northamptonshire's Roy Virgin in the vital match, which precipitated their collapse to 108 all out.

At the end of that season Hampshire chose to sign Andy Roberts in place of spinner David O'Sullivan as their second overseas player, and while O'Sullivan was justified in feeling somewhat hard done by, Mottram too found himself excluded in 1974, although he played some matches in the next two seasons. He continued to play in limited-overs matches until the end of 1977, including as Hampshire won the Sunday League in 1975 – he took 5-21 in the decisive match v Derbyshire at Darley Dale. He played in 35 first-class matches for Hampshire, taking 111 wickets at 24.11 and in 83 limited-overs games, taking 135 wickets at 18.69 – in both cases very fine figures, although he was no batsman, reaching double figures in only three first-class innings, and none in limited-overs games. He has a clear place in the county's history however, as one of the 13 men who took them to their second, and currently last, Championship.

Mujeeb Zadran (T20) born 28.3.2001, Host, Afghanistan. Spin bowler Mujeeb was Hampshire's first overseas player from Afghanistan (they have still never signed an Indian overseas player) and also their first player to be born in the 21st century. He played in 12 matches in the T20 competition of 2018, taking nine wickets at 35.33 and an economy rate of 7.09. He usually batted at number 11 and scored ten runs with a best of 8*.

Mullally, Alan David (406) born Southend, Essex 12.7.1969. Left-arm pace bowler Mullally was born in England, but raised in Australia. After matches for Western Australia, he came to England to play with Hampshire in 1988 but after one first-class match v Oxford University, moved to Leicestershire, with whom he won the County Championship. In 2000, he left Leicestershire and returned to Hampshire, playing there for six more years, with just three limited-overs matches in 2005, his final season. He played in 19 Test Matches for England from 1996, with one final (Ashes') game in 2001 after returning to Hampshire, taking 58 Test wickets at 31.24. Hampshire were relegated in his first season on return, but he took 49 wickets very cheaply, including 9-93 v Derbyshire at Derby, Hampshire's best figures in the *four-day* Championship. In the following year as Hampshire won promotion, his 64 wickets with a best of 8-90 were only slightly more expensive at 18.50; overall, he took 192 wickets for the county at 23.43, 13 times taking five or more in the innings. He played occasional matches subsequently for Lashings, and worked as a county commentator with Kevan James for BBC Radio Solent, but then returned to Australia and is pursuing a coaching career.

Munro, Colin (T20) born Natal, South Africa 11.3.1987. Munro is a left-handed batsman and right-arm medium pace bowler. He was born in South Africa but has played most of his cricket in and for New Zealand, including one Test Match and 43 ODIs. In 2018 he joined Hampshire as one of their overseas players in their disappointing T20 campaign, scoring 211 runs at 26.37 and taking four wickets.

Murgatroyd, Henry (Pre '95) born Swindon 19.9.1853, died Portsmouth 15.3.1905. He played in one match in 1883 v Sussex at Hove, scoring 1 & 1* and taking 0-7, in an innings defeat.

Murtagh, Andrew Joseph (369) born Dublin 6.5.1949. Although born in Ireland, batting all-rounder Murtagh played cricket in the London area and then at Southampton University, where he was spotted by Hampshire and invited to play for their 2nd XI in 1968. He made his Championship and limited-overs debut for the county in 1973, and while always a 'reserve' covering injuries, played in five Championship matches in that first season, one of just 13 men who played their part in Hampshire winning their second title. He did not play in the 1974 Championship but appeared in a few matches from 1975-1977, with a best score of 65 v Gloucestershire at Bournemouth in 1975. Overall, he took six first-class wickets, and played in 48 limited-overs matches with 481 runs at 16.58 and 23 wickets at 19.73, with a best of 5-33 v Yorkshire at Huddersfield in 1977 – including their top-scorer G Boycott. He appeared in eight (of 16) matches when Hampshire won the 1975 Sunday League. After leaving Hampshire, he was a teacher at Malvern College until retiring in 2000, since when he has written a number of admired cricket biographies, including his former team-mates Barry Richards and John Holder, plus George Chesterton, Tom Graveney and Colin Cowdrey.

Myburgh, Johannes Gerhardus (510) born Transvaal, South Africa 22.10.1980. He played in South Africa before coming to Hampshire in 2011, playing in all three formats. In six first-class matches for the county he scored 287 runs at 26.09, adding 81 limited-overs runs in three matches, and most successfully, 223 T20 runs at 44.60 with two half-centuries and a career best of 88 v Windward Islands in the semi-final of the Caribbean T20 tournament. He has played subsequently for Durham and Somerset.

N

Newman, John Alfred ('Jack') (131) born Southsea, Portsmouth 12.11.1884, died Cape Town, South Africa 21.12.1973. When he was quite young, Jack Newman's family moved from Portsmouth to Bitterne and from there he went to watch cricket at the county ground, asked if he might bowl in the nets and was offered a contract. He was a bowling all-rounder, sometimes, particularly in later years, opening the bowling at medium-pace, before cutting his speed and spinning the ball; he was one of a group of professionals who revived Hampshire's fortunes on either side of the First World War, and he formed a formidable bowling partnership with Alec Kennedy.

Newman made his debut with two matches in 1906 and played regularly from 1907-1930, with the exception of 1919, when he was still in India, waiting to be 'demobbed'. During the war, he played five first-class matches in India, two for an 'England XI'. In all first-class cricket, he took 2,054 wickets at 25.02 and is one of only three men in the history of the game to have passed 2,000 first-class wickets, without playing Test cricket. Of the three, Newman, Dennett of Gloucestershire and, post-war, Shepherd of Glamorgan, Newman was the more accomplished batsman with 15,364 runs at 21.57 including 10 centuries and 69 half-centuries. His highest score was 166* v Glamorgan at Southampton in 1921 and in six seasons he passed 1,000 runs; in five of them adding 100+ wickets to complete the season's 'double', while in 1926 there was a match 'double' v Gloucestershire, with scores of 66 & 42* plus 8-61 & 6-87. Even those 14 wickets in the match was not his best, for he holds Hampshire's match record of 16-88 v Somerset at Weston in 1927, and he took seven or more wickets in an innings on 30 occasions, including 9-131 v Essex at Southampton in 1921. In 1908, he took 13-120 for Hambledon v an England XI in a first-class match at Hambledon, in 1909, he took a hat-trick (8-43) v the Australians at Southampton, and he had an analysis of 5-3-3-4 v Glamorgan at Swansea in 1922. On two occasions at Portsmouth, in 1921 & 1923, he and Kennedy bowled unchanged through both innings in which all 20 wickets fell, and his 177 wickets in 1921 is the second highest total in Hampshire's history. He was said to be somewhat highly strung and in 1922 was sent from the field for kicking down the stumps, while he often worried considerably over technical problems – nonetheless John Arlott (1957) described him as an "easy-going ... cricketer with many friends". He moved to South Africa where he coached in Western Province for many years, and was awarded a benefit, and a trip home to visit Hampshire at Northlands Road in 1966.

Newton, Edward (66) born Blackmoor, Hants 31.10.1871 died Edinburgh 9.5.1906. Professional batsman Edward Newton played for the county in non-first-class matches from 1890-1894 and then in 17 first-class matches for Hampshire, in 1900, but nothing further. In that season, when Hampshire finished last, he scored 568 runs at 18.32, with three half-centuries, and a best of 69 v Derbyshire at Derby.

Nicholas, Mark Charles Jefford (381) born London 29.9.1957. Mark Nicholas came from a cricketing family; his grandfather FWH Nicholas played in 76 first-class games for various sides, including Essex for whom he scored a century v Surrey in 1926. Mark Nicholas played at Bradfield and first appeared for Hampshire in the 2nd XI in 1977, scoring two centuries. He added another in the following year when he made his first-class debut v Oxford University, scoring 40*. There were two Championship matches and then four games in 1979, including 105* against the same University side. He played more regularly in the next two seasons and then in 1982 went past 1,000 runs at just under 40 runs per innings, with three centuries. He would reach four figures in nine further seasons and score 34 centuries for the county; only Greenidge, Robin Smith and Turner of those who played with him or since, have exceeded his Hampshire career total of 17,401 runs (33.98). For Hampshire, he added 6,983 runs in limited-overs cricket, and if totals in the two formats are added, he is seventh in Hampshire's all-time list. In the shorter format, he will be remembered principally as the man who at last took Hampshire to a Lord's Final; the last county to do that, after a wait of 25 years. The first occasion was in 1988, when he began by winning the toss, invited Derbyshire to bat, and after a somewhat loose opening, and a first wicket, he posted himself at short leg, and almost immediately held two catches from the swing of Jefferies. In no time, Derbyshire slipped from 27-0 to 32-4, never recovered, and Hampshire chased down the target of 118, with the captain at the wicket, before opening time in London's neighbouring pubs.

One month later they had another chance, with a semi-final at Worcester but it was not to be, and there were other semi-final disappointments; in 1989, Chris Smith's 114 v Middlesex led the pursuit of 268, but injured by a high ball from Fraser he could not take Hampshire home – they lost by three runs, and twelve months later Northamptonshire came to Northlands Road and Nicholas contributed to a fifty partnership, but when Bakker was run out from the final ball, Hampshire lost by one run. Then in 1991, there was a second semi-final triumph in an emphatic nine-wicket victory at Edgbaston which took them to their first 60-over Lord's Final. The scores in that match on a beautiful September day look modest today, but Surrey's 240-5 was a tough task at times and Hampshire got home by four wickets with just two balls to spare. Nicholas was photographed on the Lord's balcony with the trophy but it was all somewhat bitter-sweet, as Hampshire had met the same opponents in a Championship match over the previous three days, where Waqar Younis broke his arm, and Nicholas, in plaster, had to watch the whole day from the dressing room. In 1992, they were back at Lord's again for a damp two-day victory v Kent, notable for it being Malcolm Marshall's first Lord's Final triumph, so, for a few weeks, Hampshire held both limited-overs trophies, while Nicholas's side had reached one or two semi-finals in five consecutive seasons. There would be just one more, another defeat at Worcester in 1994, and to that record must be added Nicholas's first success, the Sunday League trophy, clinched with a tight victory over Surrey at the Oval in 1986. In the shorter form in particular, there was also a period when he bowled medium-pace quite frequently, taking 101 wickets in his career (93 for Hampshire).

Nicholas's successes as an enterprising, astute captain earned him representative honours with MCC and England A & B sides, although ultimately it is perhaps surprising that his side never managed to emulate those of 1961 & 1973, by winning the Championship. The batting was always strong enough, even in what was possibly the most competitive decade in the history of the Championship, but Hampshire's positions in those days are revealing. After his West Indies tour in 1980, whenever Marshall played a full season, they finished 7th, 3rd (twice), 2nd, 6th, 5th, 6th and 3rd (1990). When he was away, they finished 17th, 15th, 15th and 9th and for most of those seasons, Greenidge was with him. Marshall returned in 1992 but from then until Nicholas retired at the end of 1995, they were always in the bottom third as key players retired. In fact, the closest they came to the Championship title was his first season as captain – their hopes were effectively extinguished when Roger Harper hit the final ball of the penultimate game for six, Northamptonshire winning by one wicket. When he retired, he had led Hampshire for eleven seasons – only Tennyson and Eagar have been in that role for longer periods; a length of time almost unimaginable today. Occasionally in his career he marched onto the field, or remonstrated with umpires when he felt justice was not being served – he had a somewhat 'old-fashioned' sense of fairness – yet has become an exemplary modern media man, presenting and commentating on cricket for domestic and international television channels, to which he has added some of the more intelligent and articulate analyses of the current game.

Norbury, Duncan Victor (120) born Bartley, Hants 3.8.1887, died Sutton, Surrey 23.10.1972. He was a right-handed batsman and right-arm fast bowler who played for Hampshire in 1905 & 1906, for Lancashire from 1919-1922 and in between in the Lancashire League and for Northumberland in the Minor Counties. He played one last first-class match in 1935. For Hampshire, his 11 matches brought 179 runs at 10.52 and seven wickets at 75.71.

North, Marcus James (497) born Melbourne, Australia 28.7.1979. Australian Test batsman Marcus North had one of the shortest Hampshire careers. In 2009, he joined them as an overseas player, and on 22 April made his Hampshire debut at Edgbaston, scoring 15 (37 balls, 42 minutes) on the first day of Hampshire's match v Warwickshire. By the second day he had been called at short notice into the Australian squad, Michael Lumb replaced him in that match, and he never played for Hampshire again.

Northeast, Sam Alexander (551) born Ashford, Kent 16 October 1989. He is a right-hand batsman who played for Kent from 2007-2017 before joining Hampshire at the start of the 2018 season. He played for England Lions and the South in the preceding winter. He scored a century at the Oval in his second Championship match but then broke a finger in practice, missing a number of matches. He returned in the Royal London Cup semi-final scoring 58, and followed that with 75* in the Final while being loudly booed by the Kent supporters, after which there was just one half-century in 13 T20 matches and a similar return from his final 14 Championship innings. Over his career to the end of the 2018 season, he has scored 9,060 first class runs at 38.22, with 2,706 runs in limited-overs matches and 2,538 in the T20. He was captain of Kent for a number of years.

Nugent, Brigadier-General Frank Henry (114, Amateur) born Sherborne St John, Hants 5.9.1880, died Kingsclere, Hants 12.3.1942. In July 1904, he played his only match for Hampshire, at Worcester, keeping wicket but recording a 'pair', batting at number 11. He held one catch; Worcestershire won by nine wickets. In 1905, he changed his name to Frank Henry Burnell-Nugent.

Nugent, Thomas Michael (List A) born Bath 11.7.1994. He was an all-rounder who played for Loughborough University and Berkshire. He played for Hampshire 2nd XI 2012-2014 and in 2014, he played in one limited-overs match for Hampshire v Sri Lanka 'A' at the Ageas Bowl. The match was abandoned after 18 overs of the Sri Lanka innings at 84-1 and Nugent took the one wicket (1-15).

O

Olivier, Eric (160, Amateur) born South Africa 24.11.1888, died South Africa 1.6.1928. He went to school at Repton, then to Cambridge University where he won his 'blue' in 1908 & 1909. For Hampshire, he played in seven matches in 1911, taking seven wickets at 51.28, with a best of 4-30, and scoring 87 runs at 10.87. In his first-class career of 22 matches he took 90 wickets at 22.62. He returned to South Africa and played in non-first-class matches v MCC in 1913/14.

Olivier, Sidney Richard (23, Amateur) born Wilton, Wiltshire 1.3.1870, died Horton, Dorset 21.1.1932. In 1891, he played for Wiltshire and in one match for Hampshire in 1895, but was dismissed without scoring. He caught three batsmen. His nephew was the actor, Sir Laurence Olivier.

Organ, Felix Spencer (550) born Sydney Australia, 2.6.1999. Although he was born in Australia, batsman and off-spinner Felix Organ went to school at Canford, Dorset and played for Hampshire's age group sides throughout his teens. He made his 2nd XI debut in 2015 and towards the end of the 2017 season, made his first-class debut, scoring 16 v Middlesex in a low-scoring 'relegation' match at Uxbridge. In the winter of 2017/18, he played for Hampshire in four limited-overs matches in the Regional Super50 Tournament in the Caribbean and signed a new contract at the end of 2018.

Orr, Hugh James (98, Amateur) born New South Wales, Australia 21.1.1878, died London 19.4.1946. He played for the Royal Navy and his final first-class match was for them in 1912. Between 1902-1907, he played in six matches for Hampshire, taking 11 wickets at 32.72 with a best of 3-34, and scoring 59 runs at 5.90.

O'Sullivan, David Robert (365) born Palmerston North, New Zealand 16.11.1944. He was a slow-left-arm bowler who from 1971-1973, played in 26 first-class matches for Hampshire, taking 84 wickets at 23.82, and five times taking five or more wickets in an innings, with a best of 6-26 v Nottinghamshire at Bournemouth in the match before Hampshire clinched the 1973 Championship. He also scored 347 runs at 15.77 with a best of 45. In 1973, he only came into the Hampshire side on a regular basis for the final few weeks, but then his contribution was as important as any players' in securing their second title; in their last six matches, he took 33 wickets at 13.75. Despite that, at the end of that season, Hampshire had to make a choice of their second overseas player between him and Andy Roberts, and O'Sullivan was released. From 1974-1977 he played for Durham when they were still a Minor County. Between 1972/3-1976/7 he played in 11 Test Matches for New Zealand, taking 18 wickets.

P

Page, Thomas Howard (76, Amateur) born Dover 28.5.1872, died Swanage 7.12.1953. He played in two matches in 1900, v Essex at Southampton and v Surrey at Bournemouth. In the first, he took 4-115 in a total of 458, and scored 61* in his first innings, but was unable to repeat those performances.

Palmer, Lt-Col Cecil Howard (59, Amateur) born Eastbourne 14.7.1873, killed in action Gallipoli 26.7.1915. He went to Radley College, and played for Hampshire in two matches in both 1899 & 1901. He served in the South African 'Boer' War, then on 7 July 1904, he played in one match for Worcestershire v Oxford University, scoring 41 & 75*. One week later he played again for Hampshire v Somerset, and in the next two matches for the county. He played one final match for Hampshire at Edgbaston in 1907. In his eight matches for Hampshire he scored 264 runs at 17.60 with a best of 64 v Yorkshire at Bradford in 1899. He was awarded the MC in June 1943.

Palmer, Rodney Howell (255, Amateur) born Sherfield-on-Loddon, Hants 24.11.1907, died Newbury 24.4.1987. In 1929, he played his one match for Cambridge University v Essex and in the following season he made his debut for Hampshire v Kent at Southampton. In 1933, he played two more Championship matches, v Yorkshire at Sheffield and Kent at Canterbury. In his two innings for Hampshire, he failed to score; he took six wickets overall at 31.16, including 5-93 at Sheffield in a drawn match.

Paris, Cecil Gerard, Alexander (269, Amateur) born Bombay 20.8.1911, died Winchester 4.4.1998. He went to King's School, Canterbury and made his Hampshire debut in 1933, playing in just one match. In the following five seasons, he played more regularly for the county and also for MCC (v Surrey) and the Gentlemen v Players. In 1936, he scored 964 runs at 28.35 with his highest innings of 134* v Northamptonshire at Bournemouth, and two years later, as Hampshire's captain for one season, he passed 1,000 runs but he played in only two county matches in 1939. After the war, he returned briefly to the Hampshire side in 1948, playing in four games. He was a solicitor in Southampton, and President of the club from 1948-1989, as well as being the first Chairman of the TCCB, and President of MCC 1975/6.

Paris, William (Pre '95) born Old Alresford, Hants 29.4.1838, died Winchester 12.1.1915. He played as a professional for a variety of club sides including

Winchester and Arlesford and was 37 when he first played for the county. In his six matches he scored just 81 runs at 8.10, but that included an innings of 51* v Kent on debut in 1875, and he took five wickets at 10.40, including 3-28 also in that debut match. He played for Hampshire again in 1876, and then once in 1881.

Parker, Frederick Anthony Vivian (300, Amateur) born London 11.2.1913, died Plymouth 26.5.1988. He went to Winchester College, and in the 1930s played for the United Services, Portsmouth. In 1946, he made his Hampshire debut, age 33, v the Indians and shortly after, played in first-class matches for the Combined Services v Northamptonshire, Surrey and Worcestershire – in the first scoring 116. He then played in one further match for Hampshire v Kent at Canterbury, but for the county he scored just 22 runs in four innings. A few years later, he played for Devon.

Parker, John Palmer (242, Amateur) born Portsmouth 29.12.1902, died Warblington, Hants, 9.8.1984. He was a prominent club cricketer in the Havant area, who played first-class cricket for Hampshire regularly in 1926 & 1927 less frequently in 1928, 1929, & 1932 and then once in 1933. He went on tour to Jamaica with Tennyson's side in the winter of 1926/7 and also played for the Gentlemen v Players at the Oval in 1927. For Hampshire, he scored 1,094 runs in 44 matches at 18.54, with one century, 156 v Kent at Canterbury, sharing a seventh wicket partnership of 270 with Phil Mead in 170 minutes, despite which Kent won by nine wickets.

Parks, Robert James (Bobby) (388) born Cuckfield, Sussex 15.6.1959. Wicketkeeper Bobby Parks was the son and grandson of JM and JH Parks, who both played for Sussex and England, and the great-nephew of HW Parks who played with JH at Sussex. Late in his career, his father moved to Somerset, and Bobby played there briefly for the 2nd XI, before his first games for Hampshire's 2nd XI in 1976. He had to be patient while Bob Stephenson held his place, but Bobby made his first-class debut in in June 1980 v Sussex, was selected regularly through the final weeks of the season and remained in the sides of Pocock and Nicholas, until mid-August 1990. 'Adi' Aymes then came into the side, but an injury meant that Parks was a regular again through 1992, when he played in Hampshire's B&H Cup winning side.

He had played in their first Cup Final in 1988 and in the side that finished Championship runners-up in 1985, and then won the Sunday League in the following season, and in 1986 he appeared behind the wicket for England, substituting for the injured Bruce French. In his first-class career for the county, he dismissed exactly 700 victims, with 630 catches – both Hampshire records, and he set another record v Derbyshire in 1981, with 10 victims in a match; since equalled by Aymes and Pothas. In limited-overs cricket, his 303 victims also set a Hampshire record, as was his five victims in an innings. He was a dependable batsman in the late middle order, scoring 3,936 first-class runs at 19.68 with 14 half-centuries, and a Championship best of 80 v Derbyshire at Portsmouth in 1986. In that season, he shared an unbroken ninth wicket partnership of 35 with Kevan James in the low-scoring Sunday League match v Surrey at the Oval, when Hampshire won the title. In July 1993, he played one match for Kent v Essex, since when he had a varied coaching career with Hampshire, Portsmouth Grammar School and the Vipers women's team at the Ageas Bowl. He retired in 2018.

Parsons, Thomas William (498) born Melbourne, Australia 2.5.1987. He played at Loughborough University and in limited-overs cricket for Kent in 2007. He moved to Hampshire, in 2008, and in the following season, played in one first-class match v his old University side, taking 3-39 in the second innings. In 2010, he played for Essex and Middlesex 2nd XI, and in 2011, for Berkshire and in one first-class match for Middlesex v Sri Lankans, but took no wickets. He returned to Kent, and played league cricket for Sevenoaks Vine.

Parsons, Walter Dyett (Pre '95) born Southampton 26.6.1861, died East Wellow, Hants 24.12.1939. He played two matches in 1882 v Sussex and Somerset, scoring 31 runs at 15.50 and taking one wicket. In 1904, he played a single match in Hong Kong.

Parvin, Alfred William (Pre '95, Amateur) born Southampton 31.12.1859, died Brighton 12.7.1916. In 1885, he played in one match v Kent at Tonbridge scoring 0 & 11, and also for the Gentlemen of Hampshire v Dorset (31 & 2-30).

Passmore, George (29) born Yealmpton, Devon 5.8.1852, died Plymstock, Devon 8.2.1935. He was a wicketkeeper who played in one match in 1896, but, batting once, failed to score – he dismissed three batsmen (one stumped). In 1893, he had played four non-first-class matches for the county.

Patel, Chetan Morar (438) born Islington 12.4.1972. Through the 1990s he played for various county 2nd XIs. He went to Oxford University, played in 11 matches (27 wickets) and won his 'blue' in 1997, after which he played once for Hampshire, v Yorkshire at Portsmouth, but took 0-65 in the one Yorkshire innings of 501-8 declared. The match was drawn. He played also in one Sunday League match v Middlesex at Lord's, but again took no wickets. He played subsequently for the Middlesex Cricket Board in the Nat West Trophy, and in 2001 toured Argentina with MCC.

Paver, Kenneth Edwin (235, Amateur) born Dover 4.10.1903, died Ringwood 20.11.1975. He played in two matches at Portsmouth, v Northamptonshire in 1925 and Somerset in 1926. He batted at number nine in his first innings, scoring 26, was promoted to open and scored four, reverted to number nine and scored 15, was promoted to three and scored seven. He did not bowl. He played subsequently for Chichester Priory Park.

Pearce, Stanley Herbert Hicks (Pre '95, Amateur) born Totton, Hants 21.9.1863, died Oswestry 5.4.1929. He was educated at Winchester College, and played in one first-class match v Somerset at Taunton in 1885; opening the batting, he scored 18 & 0. From 1885-1887 he played in non-first-class matches for the county.

Pearce, Walter Kennedy (221, Amateur) born Bassett, Hants 2.4.1893, died Romsey 31.7.1960. He was educated at Malvern College and played in nine matches for the county, five in 1923, and four in 1926, scoring 127 runs at 18.14, with one half-century, 63 v Glamorgan at Southampton in 1923, sharing a partnership of 162 with Phil Mead for the eighth wicket. In the 1930s, he played a number of matches for the county's 2nd XI and Club & Ground sides. He was Chairman of the club during the late 1930s and crucially the Second World War, when he played a major role in ensuring the club continued to function. In 1953, he was the first man to be elected as a Life Vice President of the club.

Pember, Francis William (Pre '95, Amateur) born Hatfield 16.8.1862, died Cambridge 19.1.1954. He played at Harrow School and in the Freshman's match at Oxford University but not in first-class cricket there. He made his first-class debut for MCC v Hampshire in 1882, scoring 1 & 0, despite which he played in two county matches, v Surrey and Derbyshire. He scored 49 runs at 12.25 with a best of 30.

Persse, Henry Wilfred (118, Amateur) born Southampton 19.9.1885, killed in action, St Omer, France, 28.6.1918. He played in 51 matches for Hampshire from 1905-1909, scoring 889 runs at 11.69 (best, 71) and taking 127 wickets at 30.02 with a best of 6-64 v Leicestershire in 1907. In the war, he was a Major in the Royal Fusiliers and received the MC in 1916 and later a Bar. Renshaw reported from *The Times*, "his fearless example and great skill". His brother EA, was killed in action a few months later.

Phillips, Howard William (63) born Isle of Wight 20.4.1872, died Cape Province, South Africa 17.3.1960. From 1899-1902 he played in five first-class, and other non-first-class matches for Hampshire. In first-class matches, he scored 53 runs at 11.15 with a best of 40 v Leicestershire on debut. He moved to South Africa, where he played in first-class cricket for Border.

Piachaud, James Daniel ('Dan') (346, Amateur) born Colombo, Sri Lanka 1.3.1937. He was an off-break bowler who played for Oxford University from 1958-1961 winning his 'blue' in all four years, and for Hampshire in 12 matches in

1960, taking 29 wickets at 29.31 with a best of 4-62 v Essex at Bournemouth. He played other first-class matches for MCC, Free Foresters, the Gentlemen v Players and Ceylon v a strong MCC side at Colombo in January 1969. Piachaud and his University team-mate CA Fry were the last of the amateurs to be called into the Hampshire XI.

Pietersen, Kevin Peter (477) born Natal, South Africa, 27.6.1980. He played for KwaZulu-Natal in South Africa then came to England, playing for Nottinghamshire 2001-2004. He joined Hampshire and played between 2005-2010, before moving to Surrey. He played in all three formats of cricket for England, including a total of 104 Test Matches, and more Tests for England while with Hampshire, than any other player. He played in six Championship matches for the county, before making his Test debut in the famous 'Ashes' series of 2005. He did not play first-class cricket for Hampshire again until May 2008, when he scored a century at Taunton, his final first-class game for the county. In those seven matches he scored three centuries, and averaged 43.66. He played in 17 limited-overs matches, scoring 651 runs at 43.40, and in two Lord's Finals in 2005 & 2007, scoring 5 & 12. He played in two T20 matches for Hampshire, during which he took 3-33 v Middlesex at the Rose Bowl. In 2006, he was one of Wisden's Five Cricketers of the Year.

Pillans, Albert Alexander (32, Amateur) born Sri Lanka 25.2.1869, died Sri Lanka 28.11.1901. He played in three matches for Hampshire in 1896, scoring 82 runs at 20.50, and taking six wickets at 25.16. He played in matches in Ceylon (Sri Lanka) in the 1890s, and for Hampshire Rovers.

Pink, Alfred (Pre '95) born Portsmouth 1.6.1853, died Portsmouth 12.1.1931. He played in one first-class match for Hampshire v Somerset at Taunton in 1885, scoring 15 & top-score of 39, and taking 1-15. He is recorded as playing one further match in 1886 v Norfolk, after Hampshire lost their first-class status.

Pitman, Raymond Walter Charles ('Ray') (331) born Bartley, Hants 21.2.1933, died Debighshire, Wales 5.6.1998. Batsman Pitman played in 50 first-class matches for Hampshire from 1954-1959, scoring 926 runs at 13.61 with one half-century, 77 v Derbyshire at Bournemouth in 1958. He took one wicket. In the 1960s he played in Scotland.

Plowden, Sir Henry Meredyth (Pre '95, Amateur) born Sylhet (now Bangladesh) India 26.9.1840, died Sunninghill, Berks, 8.1.1920. He played at Harrow School and Cambridge University from 1860-1863, winning his 'blue' in all four years, and captaining in 1862 & 1863. He played for Hampshire in one match in 1865, v Surrey, scoring 34 & 3, and taking 2-46, in an innings defeat. He played in one further first-class match, for MCC against Hampshire in 1866, when he was recorded as 'absent' in the first innings. From 1877-1894 he was in India as a judge at the Chief Court of the Punjab.

Pocock, Nicholas Edward Julian (378) born Venezuela 15.12.1951. During Hampshire's title-winning season of 1973, the 21-year-old right-handed batsman Pocock played four games for their 2nd XI in the two competitions. He returned in 1975, after which he played regularly through that decade. In late August 1976, he made his first-class debut against the reigning Champions Leicestershire at Bournemouth, scoring 68 and taking a wicket as first change, following the openers Jesty and Rice. There would be just three more first-class wickets to follow, but in 127 matches he scored 3,790 runs at 23.10 with two centuries. He played in five limited-overs matches in 1977 and then after the sudden, unhappy departure of Barry Richards the following season, in the last five John Player League matches, including the game v Middlesex at Bournemouth which clinched the title. At the end of that season, Gilliat retired, and in 1979, his deputy Bob Stephenson took over, while Pocock scored his first century v Middlesex at Portsmouth. He played then with some regularity, although never certain of selection, so it was a surprise when he was handed the captaincy, and Stephenson continued as a player for most of one last season. It was a tough baptism for the new captain, with the promising David Rock walking away from his contract at the start of the season, and Hampshire's stars Greenidge and Marshall touring with the West Indies. There were two replacements, Australian all-rounder Shaun Graf who struggled to make an impact, and the astute signing of South African Chris Smith who was the only man to pass 1,000 first-class runs, would become a very reliable batsman for the next ten years, and for good measure, brought with him a talented younger brother.

But while Smith impressed, Jesty and Turner struggled somewhat and while Pocock, playing as a specialist batsman hit 874 runs at 23.62, it was a difficult year. With the ball, Stevenson with 53 wickets at 29.96, was the only regular bowler to average under 30, so it was little surprise that Hampshire finished bottom for the only time since 1905. But there were good signs in addition to Chris Smith, with youngsters Tremlett and Nicholas playing frequently and Parks and Terry appearing along with Malcolm Marshall who came back at the end of the season and helped Hampshire to their one victory. These developments and Pocock's positive disposition would pay significant dividends in the following seasons, as Hampshire advanced to seventh in 1981 and third in 1982 & 1983. They also reached quarter-finals in 1982 & 1983, and then a semi-final at Canterbury in that latter season. Having never reached a Lord's Final they would have hoped for success when Marshall and Tremlett each took four wickets, and dismissed Kent for 173 in their 60th over; sadly, it was not to be, as Hampshire were bowled out in the 40th over for 102. Nonetheless, Pocock had done a fine job of bringing through those younger cricketers, as well as Raj Maru and Cardigan Connor. In 1984 when, with Greenidge and Marshall touring again, Hampshire were less successful, Pocock played regularly to the end of June, and then once more in mid-July, scoring 40, while Mark Nicholas with a superb 158 took Hampshire to victory. Pocock then stood down to be replaced by the younger man to whom he handed a promising and exciting side that would enjoy regular success over the next eight seasons. After retiring, Nick Pocock worked in insurance with Colin Ingleby-Mackenzie, which seemed a perfect match to those who had followed Hampshire – and eventually he succeeded the older man as another popular Hampshire President.

Poore, Brigadier General Robert Montagu (47, Amateur) born Co. Dublin, Ireland 20.3.1866, died Bournemouth 14.7.1938. He played for Hampshire from 1898-1906, although as a professional soldier he was not regularly available, but in 1899, between 12 June (his first match of the season) and 12 August, he enjoyed a two-month period as remarkable as any ever experienced by a Hampshire player. In that time, he played in nine Championship matches and scored 1,399 runs at 116.6, with seven centuries (then a Hampshire record for a season) including 304 v Somerset at Taunton, Hampshire's then highest innings, during which he and Wynyard added 411 for the sixth wicket, still a county record. He began the sequence with a century in both innings v Somerset at Portsmouth, the first for Hampshire anywhere, and the only instance ever on that ground. He also scored 29 & 71 for Hampshire v the Australians, and his only disappointment was that in two matches for the Gentlemen v Players he scored just 52 runs in three innings. His performances led to him being named as one of *Wisden's* Cricketers of the Year.

Prior to this, his first-class debut was for the Europeans in India in 1892/3; three winters later he was serving in South Africa and was selected *for* South Africa v England in all three matches that were later designated Tests, but scored only 76 runs at 12.66. In 1898, he played a fairly full summer for Hampshire, and scored 735 runs at 28.26, including his first two county centuries, while on his debut for the county, he 'carried his bat' with 49* (of 97) at Bath. After his extraordinary summer in 1899, he returned to Army duties in South America and South Africa, and with the two South African 'Boer' Wars imminent, played infrequently; it was not until 1906 age 40, that he scored his next and final century for the county, 129 v Sussex at Chichester. His final first-class matches were for the Europeans in India, in the two seasons before the First World War. He was a fine all-round sportsman and in his marvellous summer, he was also Best Man at Arms at the Royal Tournament. HS Altham (1957) described him as "a quiet, handsome man of magnificent physique ... (and) essentially a fast-wicket player". See also Jeremy Lonsdale (1992) *The Army's Grace*.

Porter, Rev. Albert Lavington (14, Amateur) born Croydon 20.1.1864, died Tiverton, Devon, 14.12.1937. He attended Malvern College, and played in the Freshman's Match at Cambridge University but not in first-class cricket there. He played in first-class cricket for Somerset (against Hampshire) in 1883, and in the same non-first-class fixture in 1886. From 1888-1899 he played in various matches in Hampshire, notably in the Portsmouth area. He played first-class matches for Oxford & Cambridge Universities Past & Present in 1890, and for Hampshire in one match v Derbyshire at Southampton in 1895, scoring seven.

Porter, Michael John (List A) born Poole, 21.4.1995. He has played principally for Dorset, since 2013, and for Hampshire 2nd XI in 2013 & 2014. In 2014, he played in one limited-overs match for Hampshire v Sri Lanka 'A'. The match was ruined by bad weather and he neither batted nor bowled. In the Southern League, he has played for Bournemouth, Hampshire Academy and Bashley.

Pothas, Nic (458) born Johannesburg, South Africa, 18.11.1973. Pothas was very much a batsman/wicketkeeper in the modern fashion. He played in South African domestic cricket in the 1990s, and for his country in three ODIs in 2000. He joined Hampshire in 2002 and played in the first team immediately, in that first season scoring 597 runs at 23.88 with a best of 99. In the following season, one of Hampshire's poorest, he increased the total to 809, the average to 44.94 and scored his first two centuries. Between then and 2009, he was a remarkably consistent batsman for the county, scoring 7,549 runs at an average of 43.88, statistically the best performance by a Hampshire wicketkeeper, and in addition, usually batting at number six, he frequently rescued difficult situations. His 17 centuries for Hampshire equals Neil McCorkell, with only occasional 'keeper' George Brown exceeding that number.

In his 132 matches for Hampshire, he held 375 catches and added 23 stumpings; a total of 398 dismissals at an average a fraction over three per match – the first Hampshire wicketkeeper to reach that figure, although it is revealing that his percentage of stumpings, just below six, was lower than any previous regular Hampshire wicketkeeper. By contrast 40% of Walter Livsey's dismissals were stumped. Interestingly in limited-overs cricket 20% of Pothas's dismissals were stumped, and he was an equally effective player in that format, scoring 2,770 runs at 35.97 with two centuries, sometimes opening the batting, notably in the 2005 C&G Trophy-winning side when he scored a century v Glamorgan, 73* v Yorkshire in the semi-final and 68 v Warwickshire in the Final. In 2009, he scored 35* as Hampshire won at Lord's again, v Sussex. When club-captain Mascarenhas was injured pre-season in 2010, Pothas deputised for him, until he too was injured, and gradually over that season and the next, Michael Bates replaced him, for what turned out to be a short-lived career. In addition to those records identified, Pothas retired holding the club's record of seven dismissals in an innings, and equalling ten victims in a match. He also equalled the county's record of five dismissals in a limited-overs innings, while he and Andy Bichel, added 257, setting the record for Hampshire's eighth wicket in first-class cricket v Gloucestershire at Cheltenham in 2005. Since leaving Hampshire, he has pursued a career in coaching with county and international sides.

Pothecary, Arthur Ernest ('Sam') (243) born Southampton 1.3.1906, died Iver, Bucks 21.5.1991. He was a batting all-rounder who bowled slow-left-arm and played in 271 matches for Hampshire from 1927-1946, scoring 9,477 runs at 23.34, with nine centuries and a best of 130. He took 52 wickets at 41.15, with best figures of 4-47. He was the nephew of SG Pothecary (below) and was nicknamed 'Sam' after him – despite the fact that his uncle's name was not Sam either. He came on to the Hampshire staff as a 'colt' and made his first-class debut in 1927, although the early seasons were quite difficult. Once established, he passed 1,000 runs in four seasons, 1933 and 1936-1938, and he scored nine centuries with a best of 130 v the New Zealanders at Bournemouth in 1937. Bowling slow-left-arm, he took 4-47 on debut v Surrey at the Oval, but took just a few wickets each season, 13 in 1930 being the most, and he never bettered those debut figures. He had a reputation as a fine cover fielder. During the war, he played some matches for London Counties and immediately following VE Day, played for Hampshire v a Southampton Police XI, who included some former Hampshire players. In that first non-first-class summer of peace time, he played other friendlies for Hampshire, and as 'Senior Pro', there were three Championship matches in 1946, while working as the groundsman at Southampton. He then moved to coaching, became a first-class umpire for ten years and became groundsman at RAF Uxbridge, finally retiring in 1975 after a lifetime in cricket.

Pothecary, Sidney George ('Sam') (172) born Southampton 26.9.1886, died Eastleigh 31.10.1976. He was a left-handed batsman and left-arm medium-pace bowler who played in 12 matches for Hampshire on either side of the First World War. He scored 103 runs in ten innings and took four wickets, including 3-43 v the Australian Imperial Forces at Southampton in 1919 (first-class). Also in 1919, he was given out 'caught' when a ball lodged in the top of his pads and was retrieved and claimed by the Gloucestershire wicketkeeper, but it was an incorrect decision – the ball was 'dead'.

Powell, Daren Brent Lyle (488) born Jamaica, 15.4.1978. He was a right-arm, fast-medium bowler who played in all three formats for the West Indies, and in addition to Jamaica and Gauteng, played for Derbyshire, Lancashire. In 2007, after playing in ODIs in England, he joined Hampshire, where he played in four first-class, and six limited-overs matches, including the FP Trophy Final v Durham – Hampshire's only Lord's Final defeat. He took 15 first-class wickets at 22.86 with a best of 4-8 at the Rose Bowl, as Hampshire beat Worcestershire.

Powell, Ernest Ormsby (Pre '95, Amateur) born Liverpool 19.1.1861, died Stafford 29.3.1928. He went to Charterhouse School where he captained the XI, and Cambridge University where he played two games of first-class cricket in 1883 & 1884. He also played first-class cricket for Surrey (1882), MCC, the Gentlemen of the South and Hampshire in 1884 & 1885. After Hampshire lost their first-class status, he continued playing for the county through the late-1880s. In 11 first-class matches for Hampshire he scored 759 runs at 39.94 with a best of 140 v Somerset at the Antelope in 1884, and in the same year, he scored 99 v Surrey at the Oval.

Powys, Walter Norman (Pre '95, Amateur) born Titchmarsh, Northamptonshire 28.7.1849, died Nottingham 7.1.1892. He was a fast, round-left-arm bowler who played for Cambridge University, MCC, other first-class sides and in 1877 & 1878, two matches for Hampshire, in which he took two wickets. For the University, he took 78 wickets at 11.88 with a best of 9-42 v MCC.

Prichard. There is some debate as to whether Hesketh Prichard's 'new' surname was hyphenated. He is included in this publication *with* the hyphen, under H, rather than P for Prichard, his original surname.

Prittipal, Lawrence Roland (452) born Portsmouth 19.10.1979. He was a right-handed batsman and occasional medium-pace bowler who made his Hampshire debut in limited-overs cricket in 1999, and in first-class cricket in the following season. He was the first Hampshire batsman to score a century at the new Rose Bowl, for the 2nd XI v Glamorgan 2nd XI in 2000, the last man to score a Championship century for the county at Northlands Road, v Derbyshire, and the last man to score a limited-overs half-century on that ground, in Hampshire's final game there v Nottinghamshire. He was clearly a player of promise, but like some of his contemporaries, struggled on the Rose Bowl pitches in the early years. He scored 975 first-class runs in 23 matches at 28.67, with nine wickets, in limited-overs matches, 498 runs at 12.45, with 19 wickets, and there were 13 matches in the T20. After leaving Hampshire, he played in the Southern League, and was one of two leading figures in the creation of Cage Cricket, a format aimed principally at young people in inner cities.

Prothero, Rowland (registered at birth as Roland) **Edmund** (Pre '95, Amateur) born Worcestershire, 6.9.1851, died Berkshire 1.7.1937. He played in four matches for Hampshire, in 1875, 1881, 1882 & 1883, scoring 57 runs at 11.40 and taking two wickets. While his first-class record was modest, his life was very interesting. He was a barrister and an MP, representing Oxford University during the war years; a Privy Counsellor, President of the Board of Agriculture & Fisheries and a Member of the Cabinet. He became Lord Ernle in 1919 and was President of MCC 1924-1925.

Proud, Roland Barton (292, Amateur) born Bishop Auckland, Co. Durham 29.9.1919, died Bishop Auckland, Co. Durham, 27.10.1961. He was a batsman who played at Winchester College and Oxford University, and after the war, for ten seasons with Durham, then a Minor County. In 1938 & 1939 he played in seven matches for Hampshire, with an average of 16.63 and a best score of 38* (& 28) v Derbyshire at Chesterfield on debut for the county; the first innings of 28 included four sixes. His highest first-class score of 87 (run out) came in the 1939 'Varsity' match, which Oxford won, and his final first-class match was for the Minor Counties v the West Indies at Lakenham in 1950.

Prouton, Ralph Oliver (320) born Southampton 1.3.1926, died Southampton, 12 September 2018. He was a wicket-keeper and right-hand batsman who played for Hampshire from 1949-1954, when he was one of a number of possible replacements for Neil McCorkell. In 1950 & 1951 he played for MCC during a period on the groundstaff at Lord's. In 52 first-class matches for the county he scored 982 runs at 14.44 and dismissed 97 batsmen, 13 stumped. His best score was 90, v Leicestershire at Portsmouth in 1953 when he added 161 with Cliff Walker and 81* with Reg Dare, rescuing Hampshire from 128-6. This innings was one of five half-centuries for the county. He played football for Arsenal and Swindon Town.

Q

Querl, Reginald Glenn (516) born Harare, Zimbabwe 4.4.1988. Glenn Querl attended Harrow School, while in Zimbabwe played for the national under-19 side and Matabeleland Tuskers. In England, he played club cricket for North Devon, limited-overs cricket for the Unicorns, and in 2013, he played for Hampshire 2nd XI, and once in first-class cricket for the county v Loughborough University, taking 1-20 & 0-27. During that season, his action was questioned, which led to a ban, and he seems to have played little cricket subsequently.

Quinton, Brigadier Francis William Drummond (15, Amateur) born Fyzabad, India 27.12.1865, died London 5.11.1926. He was a right-handed batsman and slow underarm bowler who attended Marlborough College and played in 45 first-class matches for Hampshire, from 1895-1900, having played in non-first-class games in the previous two seasons. He scored 2,178 runs for the county at 28.28 with two centuries, 178 v Leicestershire at Leicester in 1895, the county's first Championship century, and at the time Hampshire's highest maiden century, and 101* v Derbyshire at Derby in 1898. His brother (below) also played for Hampshire.

Quinton, James Maurice (24, Amateur) born Punjab, India 12.5.1874, died Reading 22.12.1922. He attended Cheltenham College and Oxford University, playing first-class cricket there in 1895 & 1896 (no 'blue'). He played in one Championship match for Hampshire in 1895, two more in 1896 and a final one in 1899. In those four matches, he scored 47 runs and bowling fast, took one wicket. He took his own life at the age of 48.

R

Raikes, Rev George Barkley (71, Amateur) born Norfolk 14.3.1873, died Shepton-Mallet, Somerset 18.12.1966. He attended Shrewsbury School and Oxford University, playing for three seasons and winning his 'blue' in the last two, 1894 & 1895. He was a useful batsman and good medium-pace bowler who played for his native Norfolk from 1890-1913, and, after being ordained in the Winchester diocese in 1898, for Hampshire in nine matches from 1900-1902. In the first season, he averaged over 40 but could play in only six matches; overall, he averaged 27.26 with the bat, scoring two half-centuries with a best of 77 v Yorkshire at Portsmouth in 1900, and taking 25 wickets at 30.24, including 4-30 at Derby in 1901. He was a good football goalkeeper, winning his 'blue', and playing for England.

Ransom, Victor Joseph (307, Amateur) born New Malden, Surrey 17.5.1917, died Esher, Surrey, 23.9.1988. A pace bowler, he played club cricket for Malden Wanderers and for the Club Cricket Conference before the war, and for the Royal Navy during it. In May 1947, he made his debut for Hampshire v Sussex at Portsmouth, and played in a number of matches over three seasons, with his last Championship match for Hampshire in July 1949. In total, he played in 34 matches for Hampshire, scoring one half-century, 58 v Gloucestershire at Portsmouth in 1949, and taking 88 wickets at 34.89 including five or more in an innings on three occasions with a best of 5-50 at Northampton in 1947. He played in two first-class matches for his native Surrey in 1950 & 1955, for their 2nd XI until 1961 and through that decade for the Forty Club.

Ravenscroft, Timothy John ('Tim') (List A) born Guernsey 21.1.1992. He was a batsman and occasional spin bowler, who played for the Hampshire age group sides, then for the Academy from 2007 and 2nd XI in 2011. In late August 2011, he opened the batting in one limited-overs match v Scotland in the CB40 competition, scoring five runs in a Hampshire victory.

Rawlence, John Rooke (270, Amateur) born Brockenhurst, Hants 23.9.1915, died Ascot, 17.1.1983. He was a right-handed batsman who went to Wellington School and Cambridge University, where he won a 'blue' for rugby but played no first-class cricket. In 1934, approaching his 19th birthday, he played two matches in a week for Hampshire, scoring 42 runs in his two innings. He played first-class cricket subsequently for the Army in 1938, and Combined Services v Glamorgan in 1950. He played regularly for the Army in non-first-class cricket.

Rayment, Alan William Harrington (315) born Finchley, 29.5.1928. He was a right-handed batsman and occasional bowler, who played club cricket in the London area, and from the end of the war played variously for Middlesex 2nd XI, London Counties, the Lord's XI and, on National Service, the RAF. His matches for the Combined Services included his first-class debut v Northamptonshire in June 1947, captained by AC Shirreff, also of Hampshire. In the 1940s, the Middlesex batting line-up, including Compton, Edrich and Robertson was very strong, and Rayment joined Hampshire in 1949, made his county debut, and playing for them in 198 first-class matches over ten seasons, scoring 6,333 runs at 20.36, with four centuries, 23 half-centuries and 19 wickets. He completed 1,000 runs in a season on two occasions. As a batsman, he was enterprising at the crease, and when fielding in the covers, quick on his feet, helped no doubt because with his wife he ran a dancing school in Southampton, and they often performed together. His maiden century was v Somerset at Portsmouth in 1952, while in the week of the Coronation in 1953, at Bristol, he scored 126, adding 246 with Cliff Walker for the fourth wicket. In 1955, at Weston-Super-Mare, his 104 came out of a Hampshire score of 245-7 declared, after Somerset had been bowled out for just 37. After retiring in 1958, he coached at Lord's and occasionally captained Hampshire's side in the new 2nd XI competition. He has led a fascinating and varied life since then, and at the start of the 2018 season he was, by virtue of his debut on 7 May 1949, Hampshire's 'senior pro' – the longest-serving of all their former professional players. See also the autobiography of his younger years *Punchy Through the Covers, 1928-1949.*

Raynbird, Robert (Pre '95, Amateur) born Whitchurch 29.6.1851, died Basingstoke 26.12.1920. He played for the Gentlemen of North Hampshire and also for the county in one first-class match v Kent at Tunbridge Wells in 1878, when he was dismissed without scoring in both innings, and took 0-15. His brother Walter (below) also played for Hampshire.

Raynbird, Walter (Pre '95, Amateur) born Basingstoke 1.6.1854, died Hackwood Park, Hants 6.5.1891. In his two matches for Hampshire in 1880 & 1881, he scored 25 runs at 8.33 and bowled briefly without taking a wicket.

Rayner, Oliver Philip (554) born Lower Saxony, Germany, 1.11.1985. Off-spinner Rayner played for Sussex from 2006-2011 and Middlesex since 2011. In 2018 he came to Hampshire on a short-term loan to cover Crane's injury and Dawson's selection for the England Lions. He failed to score in his two Championship innings and took five wickets in the two matches, including 4-54 v Yorkshire at the Ageas Bowl, before returning to Middlesex.

Read, Ernest George (105, Amateur) born Portsmouth 8.10.1873, died London 21.3.1921. He was the nephew of Dr. Russell Bencraft, and first played for Hampshire in non-first-class cricket in 1893 & 1894. He was a wicketkeeper and batsman although he only 'kept' in one of his three Championship matches for Hampshire – and dismissed no batsmen in any of the three games, while scoring 37 runs at 6.16. He played subsequently in four matches for Sussex in 1904 & 1906.

Redhouse, Harry (67) born Chatham, 27.3.1880, died 3.12.1959. We have no further information about his place of death, but a man of that name was registered in Portsmouth in January-March 1960. He played once for Hampshire v Lancashire at Old Trafford in 1900, where he scored 0 & 4, and took 0-13, in a heavy defeat.

Reed, Barry Lindsay (341, Amateur) born Southsea, Portsmouth, 17.9.1937. He was an opening batsman who attended Winchester College and played one match for Hampshire v Cambridge University in 1958, after which a combination of serious injury and business interests took him away from the first-class game until 1964 when he began playing for Hampshire 2nd XI; then in late August 1965, he came into the Hampshire side as they sought a partner for Roy Marshall to replace Jimmy Gray. There were three half-centuries in the four matches on his return, and from 1966-1970, until the arrival of Gordon Greenidge, he played regularly alongside Barry Richards. In 1966, 1967 & 1968, Reed passed 1,000 runs, scored consistently, and was capped, although there were only two first-class centuries, v Glamorgan (104) and Oxford University. There were two more against Minor Counties sides in the new limited-overs matches, among 900 runs at 36.00; he was also a fine cover fielder. He played no more first-class cricket after 1970, but in 1976 was a regular member of the county's 2nd XI, captaining the side, following the premature death of Geoff Keith. For some years, he was the coach of Hampshire's Colts and under-19 sides, and a number of those players went on to play for Hampshire's first team.

Reifer, Elvis Leroy (396) born Barbados 21.3.1961, died Barbados 26.8.2011. He was a left-arm pace bowler who came to Hampshire in 1984, to cover for Malcolm Marshall who was touring England, and after first choice Milton Small was called into the West Indies squad. Elvis Reifer had brothers who played cricket and there has been a view that he was not the player expected by Hampshire, not least because he had not played any first-class cricket before joining the county. It is not surprising that his performances did not match Marshall's, but he began by taking 4-43 v Cambridge University and overall took 49 first-class wickets at 35.93, and averaged nearly 20 with the bat, with a best of 47 v Somerset. In limited-overs games he took 19 wickets including 4-46 v Kent. On returning to Barbados, he played in one first-class and three limited-overs matches for Barbados.

Remnant, Ernest Richard (141) born Croydon 1.5.1881, died Harrow 18.3.1969. He was an all-rounder, bowling slow-left-arm, whose father GH, played in 42 matches for Kent. He made his first-class debut for Hampshire in May 1908 and played regularly through to 1921, with the exceptions of 1910, when he played only twice, and 1919 when he was still stationed in India. His first-class career, ended in early June 1922 after four matches in that final year. He scored his one first-class century, 115*, v Kent at Southampton in 1911 but played most often in the two seasons before the war. He was said to be a happy cricketer who would often sing as he ran in to bowl, and that might have worked particularly well in his last full season, 1921, when he took 46 wickets at 23.89 (38 in the Championship), including 8-61 at Colchester. He ended his career for Hampshire with 2,843 runs at 17.33 and 170 wickets at 27.35.

Renshaw, Simon John (432) born Cheshire 6.3.1974. He was a pace bowler and useful lower-order batsman who played for Northamptonshire and Essex 2nd XIs, Cheshire and the Combined Universities (York University), before joining Hampshire, where he played in first-class and limited-overs cricket from 1996-2000. He played for the county most often in 1997 & 1999 with a best bowling season of 1997, taking 37 wickets at 34.54. In that year, he played in 25 of his 49 limited-overs matches – overall there were 62 wickets, with a best of 6-25 v Surrey, again in 1997 – while in first-class cricket he took 91 wickets for Hampshire. In 2000, he played more often for the 2nd XI and captained Hampshire v Glamorgan 2nd XI in the first match played on the main Rose Bowl ground. He left Hampshire at the end of that season, playing for some years for Kibworth CC in Leicestershire.

Riazuddin, Hamza (492) born Hendon, 19.12.1989. He was a medium-pace bowling all-rounder who attended Bradfield College and played for England under-19s in 2008/9, by which time he had already made his first-class debut for Hampshire in one match v Somerset in May 2008. In the next two seasons, there were just two more matches against university sides, and then a run of four Championship matches in 2012 and one final first-class game v Loughborough University in 2013. In first-class cricket, he scored one half-century v Loughborough University in 2012, with best bowling of 5-61 (and 12*) as Hampshire won a tight game v Glamorgan by two wickets. He played more regularly in limited-overs cricket with 27 matches and 19 wickets, and 17 x T20 matches with 21 wickets, including 4-15 v the Windward Islands. Since leaving Hampshire he has played principally for Falkland in the Thames Valley League.

Rice, John Michael (364) born Chandler's Ford, Hants 23.10.1949. All-rounder John Rice was born in Hampshire, but raised in Surrey and was briefly on their groundstaff before moving to Hampshire in 1971, where he became a very flexible player, sometimes opening the bowling and sometimes the batting. He played in nine first-class matches in both 1971 & 1972, but there was just one Sunday League match in the Championship year of 1973 and a quiet season in 1974, before he established himself in 1975. In first-class cricket that year, he averaged 22.10 with the bat, and took 49 wickets at 26.65, but he made an even more important contribution to Hampshire's first Sunday League title – in all limited-overs matches that year he took 38 wickets at 13.86 at an economy rate below 3.5, and on a Sunday v Northamptonshire took 5-14 including Hampshire's first Sunday League 'hat-trick', then in the decisive match at Darley Dale, he took 4-14. In 1976, with Gordon Greenidge on tour he opened the batting in some Championship matches, while in the following year, his best bowling figures were 7-48 v Worcestershire, and in 1978 he played again in the Hampshire side that won the Sunday League v Middlesex at Bournemouth. In the first three years of the 1980s he took just 11 first-class wickets, becoming more important as a batsman, following the departures of Richards and Gilliat, and in 1981 he scored his two first-class centuries in consecutive matches. In the first at Hove he came in to face the second ball after opener Tim Tremlett was run out without facing from the first, and 'carried' his bat for 101*. Then he went to Edgbaston and scored 161*. Rice was also a fine slip fielder with 153 catches in 168 first-class matches, and his all-round skills and positive disposition seemed to fit him for a coaching career. He scored 777 runs in 1982 but was not re-engaged when in sight of a benefit, and he succeeded Vic Cannings as coach at Eton College, until he retired. He also worked closely with Barry Reed for some years coaching Hampshire's Colts and under-19 sides, helping to develop players including Chris Tremlett and Jimmy Adams.

Richards, Arthur Carew (107, Amateur) born Grays, Essex 20.2.1865, died Nottingham 29.11.1930. He was a batsman and slow bowler who played for Eton, and made his first-class debut, in August 1884, playing consecutive matches v Sussex (scoring 40, taking 3-45) and Somerset (47). There were no more wickets, and while he played some non-first-class games for the county, and for MCC, he did not play again until one match in each of 1903 and 1904, scoring a total of 11 runs.

Richards, Barry Anderson (357) born Durban, South Africa 21.7.1945. Barry Richards signed for Hampshire under the new instant registration rule in 1968 and when he left mid-way through the 1978 season he had played in 204 first-class matches for the county, scoring 15,607 first-class runs at 50.50. Only CB Fry, who played in just 44 matches, has a higher average for Hampshire (58.90) but those figures can only suggest, without revealing, the quality of Richards' batting – some consider him the finest natural batsman who ever played for the county. John Arlott (1979) began a brief appreciation of him by stating quite simply, "Barry Richards is a great batsman". Few who saw him, would dissent from that view, yet unlike the majority of 'great' players, he achieved what he did, despite his immense frustrations at being largely excluded from Test cricket for political reasons, and despite admitting frequent boredom with the treadmill of county cricket in those days. There were times when he seemed less than fully engaged, but on others he was a batsman of astonishing skill and elegance.

He played in just one Test series, in South Africa v Australia in 1969/70, when he scored 29, 32, 140, 65, 35, 81 & 126 – an average of 72.57 – while in November

1970, he scored 356 in 372 minutes for South Australia v Western Australia (with four Test bowlers). That was his one season playing domestic cricket in Australia although he spent some English winters playing at home for Natal, for whom he first played in 1964. At Hampshire, he had a slightly hesitant start, but then scored over 2,000 runs in the first season, including 206 v Nottinghamshire, whose attack was led by Garry Sobers. For his performances in 1968, he was nominated as one of *Wisden's* Cricketers of the Year. It sometimes seemed that context and opposition motivated him; in August 1972, in a quarter-final v 'one-day kings' Lancashire he scored 129 in a losing cause, with the next highest score 28; in 1973, with a title to win, there were four Championship centuries (240 at Coventry) yet perhaps his finest display came in a low-scoring match between first-place (Hampshire) and second (Northamptonshire) at Southampton. After Hampshire dismissed their opponents for 108, Richards scored 45, resisting the wiles of Bishen Bedi (6-69) in securing a lead of 59, then, needing just 90 to win, Bedi took two more wickets as Hampshire fell to 16-2 and 49-3, but Richards, with 37*, took them to the key victory.

As Champions, they opened the following season with the then traditional match at Lord's v MCC, and on a freezing April day, Richards scored 189, dismissed with the score 249-6, in an astonishing display, which ASR Winlaw (*Daily Telegraph*) described as "full of grace and majesty". In 1975 Jeff Thomson led the Australian attack at Southampton and Richards scored 96 (of 156-2) and 69, retired hurt. It sometimes seemed he had a point to prove. In three Championship matches he 'carried his bat', in 1969 v Northamptonshire, in 1974 with 225* at Trent Bridge and in 1975 v Middlesex. There might be many more facts and figures, but Richards' quality went beyond that. He reached 1,000 runs for Hampshire in every season from 1968-1976 and played in the two Sunday League title-winning sides of 1975 and 1978, but by the latter he had had enough. He played a Championship match at Leicester in late June 1978, and in July four limited-overs games, including another last one at Leicester and then he was gone. He was no longer motivated to play county cricket, perhaps affected by the artificial, but nonetheless challenging World Series matches in Australia, in which he averaged 79.14. The end was very sad for Hampshire fans, but the memories are indelible. When he was not batting, he was a very fine slip fielder, with 264 catches in 204 matches, one of the county's highest percentages, and he could bowl off-spin very effectively although rarely inclined to do so; he took 46 wickets at 36.41 for Hampshire with a best of 7-63 v a Rest of the World side. He played in South Africa for a few more years, became an intelligent commentator, and returned to Hampshire as their President from 2007-2009,

Richards, Cyril James Ridding (25, Amateur) born Andover 14.7.1870, died Scotland 27.10.1933. He was a batsman who went to Lancing College and Oxford University, although played in no first-class matches there. He played in non-first-class cricket for Hampshire from 1889-1892, then in September

1895 one Championship match v Surrey at the Oval, scoring 43 & 5 in an innings defeat. He played subsequently for Shropshire.

Ridding, Rev. Charles Henry (Pre '95, Amateur) born Winchester 26.11.1825, died Fareham 13.3.1905. He was a batsman who attended Winchester College and Oxford University where he played first-class cricket, winning his 'blue' in five years, 1845-1849. In 1861, before the formation of the County Club, he played a first-class match for Hampshire v MCC but was run out twice, for four and two. In 1864, he played for Hampshire in the club's first season, v Sussex at Hove, scoring 7 & 10. In the following season, he played for Hampshire in one non-first-class match v Buckinghamshire, and was again run out twice!

Ridley, Alfred Bayley (Pre '95, Amateur) born Hollington House, Hants, 14.12.1859, died London, 26.3.1898. He was an all-rounder who went to Eton and played two first-class matches for Hampshire in 1884 (v Kent) & 1885 (v Derbyshire), scoring 43 runs at 10.75 and taking two wickets. He also played for MCC and I Zingari. His older brother (below) also played for the county.

Ridley, Arthur William (Pre '95, Amateur) born Hollington House, Hants 11.9.1852, died London 10.8.1916. He was an all-rounder who bowled underarm lobs, playing at Eton and Oxford University with a 'blue' in four years, 1872-1875. As Oxford's captain in that last year, Cambridge needed 175 to win and were 161-7 when Ridley brought himself on, took two wickets (2-16) and his side won by six runs. In that same year, he first played for Hampshire v Sussex at Hove, scoring 54 and taking 6-35 and 6-38, including Hampshire's first 'hat-trick'. He was described in Lillywhite's Companion as "one of the best cricketers of the day" and "probably the best slow under-hand bowler since the time of Clarke". He played in representative matches for the Gentlemen v Players, MCC and others, as well as once for Kent v England as a 'given man' in 1877. He played in ten matches for Hampshire, but after one game v MCC in 1878, business took him to London, and he then played for Middlesex in 16 matches from 1882-1885. For Hampshire, he scored 558 runs at 29.36, with one century v Kent at Faversham, which set a record since it included not one boundary. He also took 68 wickets, including 7-46 v Derbyshire at the Antelope in 1877. HS Altham (1957) suggested he was Hampshire's "most distinguished cricketer" of the period, noting that his all-round skills included being a "superb fielder" and "the last" of the original line of lob bowlers.

Rimell, Anthony Geoffrey Jordan (306, Amateur) born Punjab, India 29.8.1928, died Berkshire 18.10.2007. He was an all-rounder who attended Charterhouse and Cambridge University, winning his blue in 1949 & 1950. He made his first-class debut in a friendly, fund-raising match v Surrey at Kingston in late August 1946, scoring 27 & 42*, but played only once more for the county, in his final first-class match v Worcestershire at Dudley in 1950, taking 1-52 & 0-13, scoring 8 & 5. The only record of his cricket after that, is one match for MCC in 1964

Rimmington, Nathan John (527) born Queensland, Australia, 11.11.1982. He was a pace bowler and useful batsman who joined Hampshire briefly in 2014. He played in one T20 match, without scoring or taking any wickets, and one Championship match at Chelmsford, a top-of-the-table Division Two game v Essex. He came in with Hampshire 97-7 and hit 65*, adding 115 with Wheater, and taking them to 246. He then took 2-46, but was dismissed without scoring and did not bowl as Essex won by two wickets. He played for Queensland, Western Australia, Perth Scorchers and Melbourne Renegades in the 'Big Bash', Kings XI Punjab in the IPL, and Derbyshire, T20 in 2015.

Roberts, Anderson Montgomery Everton ('Andy') CBE (371) born Antigua 29.1.1951. Andy Roberts was a fast bowler who played for the Leeward Islands from 1970, and came to Hampshire in 1973 when, not qualified for the Championship, he played just in one match v his fellow countrymen at Southampton. He took only one wicket, but injured the opening batsman Camachao, putting him out of the tour. At the end of that season, Hampshire had to choose a second overseas player between O'Sullivan who had just played a major part in bowling them to the title, and Roberts, whose pace in 2nd XI cricket was often fearsome. They chose Roberts, and in 1974 he probably bowled faster than anyone else before or since, for the county. In what was surely the unluckiest season in their history, the rain consigned Hampshire to runners-up by just two points, but in that season Roberts took 119 wickets at just 13.62, six times taking five or more in an innings – ironically his best of 8-47 at Cardiff, came in what can now be seen as a crucial late season, improbable defeat. He also took 7-45 at Hove, while his match figures of 9-39 v Kent at Basingstoke, included putting Cowdrey out of the match. For his performances in 1974, he was nominated as one of *Wisden's* Cricketers of the Year.

In 1975, and again in 1979, he was in the West Indies sides that won the first two World Cups, and in 1976 he toured England, so there were fewer Championship matches, after this, and in 1975 he missed the successful conclusion to Hampshire's Sunday League campaign in Derbyshire. In 1977, his first-class average was still below 20 but there were fewer wickets, and during the unrest caused by World Series cricket, in which he took 50 wickets, he became disenchanted with county cricket. In July 1978, as Barry Richards announced his retirement from Hampshire, Andy Roberts asked to take a break, but the request was refused, so he too left the county, during the season when they would win their second Sunday League title. He returned to county cricket with Leicestershire in 1981. He took 202 Test wickets for the West Indies in just 47 games, and for Hampshire his 244 wickets in just 58 games came at an average of 16.70, the lowest by any regular bowler in the county's history. There were also 104 limited-overs wickets at 13.65. He was for many years the groundsman at the Antigua Recreation Ground, and was knighted by the Antiguan Government.

Roberts, Michael David Tudor (517) born Oxford, 13.3.1989. He was a batsman who came to Hampshire in his mid-twenties after some success with Berkshire. In 2013, he played in six first-class matches, scoring 159 runs at 19.87 with a best of 44 v Gloucestershire. He played in four limited-overs matches with an average of 27.66.

Robinson, Oliver Edward (List A) born Margate 1.12.1993. He is a bowling all-rounder who played initially for Yorkshire, but left under a cloud, and appeared in one rain-ruined limited-overs match for Hampshire v Sri Lanka 'A' in 2014 in which he bowled four overs without taking a wicket. He moved on to Sussex, where he has played with some success.

Robson, Charles (8, Amateur) born Kilburn, 20.6.1859, died Abingdon, Berks, 27.9.1943. In the early 1890s he played for Middlesex and MCC, before joining Hampshire when they were admitted to the Championship in 1895. He began as their wicketkeeper, then in 1900 took over as captain, their third in the first six Championship years, and gradually handed over behind the stumps to Jimmy Stone. Hampshire finished last in 1900 and 1902, and Robson passed the captaincy to EM Sprot, playing just a few games in 1903 & 1906, while also appearing for London County, the Gentlemen and other sides. In 129 matches for Hampshire he scored 3,299 runs at 15.27, dismissing 202 batsmen (37 stumped). HS Altham (1957) described him as "an exceptionally good captain … a fine judge of the game and … (with) the personality and serenity to weather adverse fortune", of which there was quite a bit in those years at Hampshire.

Rock, David John (377) born Portsmouth 20.4.1957. He was right-handed batsman who was an outstanding schoolboy cricketer at Portsmouth Grammar, touring India and representing MCC Schools at Lord's. He played in Hampshire's 2nd XI from 1974 and two years later made his Championship debut, age 19, v Surrey at the Oval. He scored few runs in his first six matches, but in July 1977 reached his maiden century, 114 (& 45) at Leicester, sharing a century partnership with Greenidge. In the next match, he opened with Richards and scored 91 v Sussex at Southampton and it seemed his undoubted promise would be realised – especially when he scored another century v Nottinghamshire at Basingstoke. He finished that season with an average of 23.89 and scored two limited-overs half-centuries, but his form declined in the next two seasons when he played very few limited-overs games and averaged under twenty in first-class cricket. There was one more century at Nuneaton in 1979, but after reporting back pre-season in 1980, he retired from county cricket without playing further. He played a little club cricket back in Portsmouth, but turned his back on the game in his twenties.

Rogers, Herbert James (165) born Frimley, Surrey 6.3.1893, killed in action, Somme, France, 12.10.1916. He was a left-handed batsman who came from a cricketing family, including NH Rogers (below). He toured Ireland with

Hampshire in 1911, before playing in seven first-class matches for Hampshire from 1912-1914, but scored only 69 runs at 5.75 with one wicket. He was planning to qualify to play for Worcestershire, but enlisted in 1914, and was killed the following year. His name appears on the Honours Boards at Hampshire, and Worcestershire.

Rogers, Neville Hamilton (298) born Cowley, Oxford 9.3.1918, died Southampton 7.10.2003. Batsman Neville Rogers, was the son of 'Brusher' Rogers, a notable Oxfordshire Minor Counties cricketer. Neville came to Hampshire in 1939 as a promising 21-year-old, to spend a year qualifying by residence, but because of the war did not play first-class cricket until 1946, when on debut, he scored 90 v Worcestershire at Portsmouth. Until the availability of Roy Marshall in 1955, Rogers was the cornerstone of the inconsistent Hampshire batting, and while he was selected as twelfth man for England, and played in Test Trials, it might be that he sacrificed aspects of his game to suit the needs of his team – he never played at the higher level.

John Arlott (1956) described him as "craggy – tough perhaps – but something near to being a master craftsman of defensive batting". He scored just under 700 runs in 1946 at 16.97, but thereafter passed 1,000 runs in nine consecutive seasons, before an offer of employment led to his retirement after the 1955 season. His best year was 1952, with over 2,000 runs, although in the previous season, five centuries included his best of 186 v Gloucestershire at Portsmouth. There were 26 centuries in those last nine seasons, and three times in 1953 & 1954 he carried his bat for the county – in 1954 he added to two occasions for Hampshire, the same feat for MCC v Surrey, and for an England XI v the Pakistanis at Hastings, setting an English record of four in one season. In 1955, with Marshall, Gray and Horton establishing their top three positions, Rogers moved down to number five and for the first time played in a strong side, as Hampshire finished in an unprecedented third place. When Desmond Eagar was injured in the run-in, Rogers' county career ended with him captaining them in the last Championship five matches, winning four and drawing one. He hoped for another three-year contract and a benefit but only one year was proposed, so he took the offer of employment, and a testimonial in 1956. He played in Southampton with Trojans CC, and in later years, worked alongside his friend Jimmy Gray who was then Hampshire's Cricket Chairman. On Rogers' retirement, Arlott described him as "among the county's greatest players".

Roper, Colin (338) born Bridport, Dorset 25.7.1936. Wicketkeeper Roper played for Hampshire's 2nd XI from 1955-1958, when Bryan Timms took his place as understudy to Leo Harrison. In 1957, he played in one first-class match v Oxford University, scoring seven in his one innings and taking one catch in a drawn match. Through the 1960s, he played Minor Counties cricket with his native Dorset

Roper, Donald George Beaumont (310, Amateur) born Botley 14.12.1922, died Southampton 8.6.2001. In 1947, he played in one match v Cambridge University at Portsmouth, scoring 30 & 0 in a drawn match. In the 1950s he played club cricket for Southgate CC, but he was better known as a footballer. He played for Southampton, was transferred to Arsenal and played in their team that won the league title in 1947/8, and their Cup Final defeat in 1952. In 1957, he re-joined Southampton and finished his career with Weymouth.

Rossouw, Rilee Roscoe (546) born Orange Free State, South Africa 9.10.1989. He is a left-hand batsman who has played for South Africa in the two 'white ball' formats and joined Hampshire in 2017, on a three-year Kolpak contract. In his second Championship match, while carrying an injury, he played a superb innings of 99 v Middlesex at the Ageas Bowl, and at Taunton an even more astonishing limited-overs innings of 156, but otherwise he struggled, with just one other half-century in all games and that in the T20. In that first season, he scored 253 first-class runs, 196 limited-overs runs, and 255 runs in T20. 2018 was a similarly mixed season, with a Championship century at Old Trafford but fewer than 500 Championship runs, and an average of under 20 in the T20 competition. He did nonetheless score two centuries and 90 in the Royal London Cup and his 125 v Kent in the successful Lord's Final brought him the Man-of-the-Match award. 2019 will be the last year of his initial contract and he remains something of an enigma to Hampshire followers.

Rouse, Adam Paul (519) born Harare, Zimbabwe 30.6.1992. Although born in Zimbabwe, wicketkeeper Rouse went to school in Winchester and Alresford and played for England under-19s in 2010. He played for Hampshire's age group sides, their Academy from 2007 and the 2nd XI from 2008, but he was always competing with Michael Bates to succeed Nic Pothas. In 2013, he played a Championship match at Canterbury, as a batsman, by which time Adam Wheater was behind the stumps, while Rouse also played in one limited-overs match v Bangladesh 'A'. He left Hampshire and played briefly for Gloucestershire, before joining Kent, where he has played more regularly.

Russell, HF (Pre '95, Amateur) we have no further details of name or dates of birth/death. He played in one match v Surrey at the Oval in 1884, scoring 1 & 10 in a defeat. In 1891, he played in a non-first-class match for the county v Staffordshire, scoring six runs in his two innings.

Russell, William Cecil (52, Amateur) born Victoria, Australia 25.4.1866, died Etchingham, Sussex 9.5.1929. He went to Eton, and in 1898, played in one Championship match for Hampshire v Yorkshire at Huddersfield, scoring 2 & 5 in an innings defeat. In 1900, he played for the Minor Counties v MCC at Lord's, scoring 30 & 1 and taking 3-91 & 1-65.

Rutherford, Arnold Page (166, Amateur) born Highclere, Hants 2.9.1892, died Weybridge 23.7.1980. He went to Repton, and was the younger brother of JS (below) who played for Hampshire in 1913. Arnold played once in 1912, age 19, v Cambridge University, scoring 18 in his only innings.

Rutherford, John Seymour (177, Amateur) born Highclere 27.2.1890, died Oxford, 14.4.1943. He went to Repton, and was a right-handed batsman and medium-pace bowler, who played eight matches for Hampshire in 1913, scoring 128 runs with a best of 33* v Warwickshire. He took three wickets.

Ryan, Francis Peter (200) born United Provinces, India 14.11.1888, died Leicester, 5.1.1954. He was a slow-left-arm bowler, who played mainly for Glamorgan, but in 1919 & 1920 he played in 23 matches for Hampshire, taking 63 wickets at 26.09, then spent one year in the Lancashire Leagues, before coming to the notice of Championship newcomers Glamorgan. In all first-class cricket, he exceeded 1,000 wickets, with 100+ in four seasons for Glamorgan, so he was obviously a fine bowler, although he had a reputation for eccentric behaviour, a temper, and a fondness for a drink. On five occasions Ryan took five or more wickets in an innings for Hampshire, with a best of 7-60 v Sussex at Portsmouth in 1919. Against Somerset in 1919, he took 10-64 in the match at Weston-Super-Mare, despite which, Somerset won. John Arlott (1957) reported the commonly-held belief that he was born in the USA, but this was subsequently corrected.

S

Sainsbury, Peter James (332) born Chandlers Ford 13.6.1934, died Chandlers Ford 12.7.2014. Peter Sainsbury was Hampshire to his core, and in a career as player and coach that spanned the best part of 40 years, became, not least by hard work, one of the greatest of Hampshire's home-grown player. He impressed as a schoolboy in Southampton, played for the Club & Ground by 1951, went to National Service in 1953-4, playing for the army, and made his first-class debut for the county in June 1954, thereafter playing regularly to the end of the season. His breakthrough came in 1955 when, following the departures of the three senior spinners, Knott, Hill and Dare, he formed with Burden a key part of the attack that took Hampshire to third place for the first time. Sainsbury famously dismissed Len Hutton twice on his 21st birthday in a victory at Bradford, and took 102 wickets at 18.05, including 7-25 v Essex at Southampton. He also scored over 500 runs and impressed with his all-round fielding, particularly at short leg. He held 601 catches in his 593 matches, one of the few Hampshire players to catch more than one per match.

After his success in 1955 he went to Pakistan with the MCC, a side somewhat like today's Lions, where he took 16 wickets, at no great cost. There were fewer wickets in the next two English seasons, and it is interesting to note that in the wet summer of 1958, on uncovered pitches he took 71 at 19.98, whereas in the following hot, dry summer, and an experiment with covering, his 60 wickets cost 27.75. On the other hand, he scored more runs in 1959 as his batting average went from 23 to 30. From 1960-1964 and again in 1967, he passed 1,000 runs and it was not until 1969, when teams played just 24 matches, that he dropped below 800 in a season. In 1961, as Hampshire won the Championship, he took 54 wickets to add to his highest aggregate of 1,533 runs at 30.05, and it was his dismissal of Derbyshire's Bob Taylor at Bournemouth that brought the title. There were fewer wickets each year in the mid-late 1960s, when Hampshire fielded their fine pace attack of Shackleton, White and Cottam, but he had a marvellous year in 1971 falling just 41 runs short of his 1,000 runs and the 'double', alongside 107 wickets at 17.51. It should have brought him nomination as one of *Wisden's Cricketers of the Year,* but he had to wait until 1974, in recognition of his contribution to Hampshire's second title – 53 wickets at 17.83, and 758 runs at 34.45.

By then he had performed well in Hampshire's early adventures in limited-overs cricket. In their fourth Gillette Cup match, v Norfolk in 1965, he top-scored with

76, and returned figures of 13-3-30-7. In his first matches in the new Sunday League in 1969, limited to eight overs, he took 3-31, 2-24, 1-20, 3-33, and 1-29, then to end the season, 4-23 and 4-37 as Hampshire finished runners-up to Lancashire. In 1975, they went one better, and Sainsbury was there again with 20 wickets and 295 runs. He played for one more year before retiring to become coach, and during his time, Hampshire won two more Sunday titles, and their first Lord's Final. For Hampshire, Peter Sainsbury scored 19,576 first-class runs, placing him eighth in their all-time list, and he was fifth with 1,245 wickets, to which he added 2,079 limited-overs runs (23rd) and 202 wickets (8th). Only three men have exceeded his grand total of wickets in all formats. John Arlott (1979) said of him that "there has never been a keener cricketer than Peter Sainsbury … he has the complete air of enthusiasm" and "he gives every ounce of his being to each moment of play, but … he is utterly fair: one of cricket's idealists".

Salisbury, Matthew Edward Thomas (548) born Chelmsford 18.4.1993. He played for the Cambridge University MCC side 2012-2013, and for his native Essex in 2014 and 2015. In 2017, he played in three first-class matches for Hampshire, and on debut v Warwickshire took a wicket with his first ball for the county and a second in that first over. In his three matches, he took eight wickets with a best of 3-65 v South Africa 'A'.

Sammy, Darren Julius Garvey (T20) born St Lucia 20.12.1983. Darren Sammy played for the West Indies in all formats of the game, sometimes as captain. In 2016, he played for Hampshire in the T20 tournament, scoring 70 runs at 14.00 and taking six wickets at 21.00.

Sandeman, George Amelius Crawshay (181, Amateur) born London, 18.4.1883, killed in action, Zonnebeke, Belgium 26.4.1915. He attended Eton where he was a notable bowler, and Oxford University but played no first-class cricket there. In June 1913, age 30 he played in three matches for Hampshire, and his final first-class match was for MCC in 1914. For Hampshire, he scored nine runs and took three wickets. He was a partner in the wine company Sandeman & Sons, and also Squire of Fonab, Perthshire. He was called to the Bar in 1913, but died in the second battle of Ypres.

Savident, Lee (439) born Guernsey, 22.10.1976. He was a medium-pace all-rounder, who played for Guernsey, and from 1995 in the Southern League for Old Tauntonians, playing in 2nd XI games for Hampshire from 1994. In late 1997, he played for Hampshire in three Championship and three Sunday League matches. He struggled at times with injuries, and apart from two further Sunday League games in July 1998, did not play for the first team again until 2000, when there were three limited-overs matches and one last Championship game. In first-class matches, he scored 32 runs and took four wickets, while in the shorter form, there were 94 runs at 18.80 and six wickets, including 3-41 v Middlesex at Lord's on debut in 1997. He played subsequently for the

Hampshire Cricket Board, Dorset, and in the Southern League for various sides including Portsmouth, Totton and Burridge.

Schofield, James Edward Knowle (455) born Blackpool, 1.1.1978. He was a pace bowler who played in schools and university representative cricket, for Worcestershire's age group sides and their Cricket Board XI, and for other 2nd XI sides. In 2001, he played for Hampshire's 2nd XI and in late July, made his first-class debut v the Australians as Hampshire beat the tourists for the second time. On the first morning, Schofield (3-25) took a wicket with his first ball, helped reduce them to 23-5 and 97 all out, and he was batting when Hampshire clinched the victory with just two wickets to fall. He played two more Championship matches in August of that year and returned to Worcester for his one limited-overs match (1-21). There was one last Championship game v Surrey at the end of the 2002 season and he finished with 19 first-class wickets at 25.10, with a best of 4-51 v Worcestershire in 2001. He played Southern League cricket with BAT.

Scott, Richard John (407) born Bournemouth 2.11.1963. He was a left-handed batsman, and occasional bowler, who played for Dorset from 1981 when he also appeared for the first time with Hampshire's 2nd XI. He played regularly for them from the following season but was on the county's staff at the time of the Smith brothers, Greenidge, Nicholas, Terry, James, Jesty and competing with Middleton and Hardy for a place. He played first v Oxford University in 1988, then in the Portsmouth week of that year, when he failed to score in his three innings. To their credit, Hampshire persevered and in his next match at Eastbourne he top-scored with 58 in the second innings, followed by 41 at Leicester and then 107* v the Sri Lankans, and 40 at Taunton and 56 v Sussex at Southampton. After the nightmare start, he scored 362 runs in ten first-class innings, and he played quite regularly in the next two seasons, but in 1990 another left-hander, David Gower, joined Hampshire, and Cox and Wood were pressing for places, so Scott moved to Gloucestershire where he played in 45 first-class matches. For Hampshire, he scored 917 runs at 21.83 and took five wickets, and he enjoyed some success in limited-overs cricket with 976 runs at 29.57 with seven half-centuries and a very fine 116* v Yorkshire in a Sunday League match at Southampton in July 1989, when Hampshire, chasing 180 to win, were 24-3, until Scott took them to victory. He left Gloucestershire after the 1993 season and returned to Dorset, and Bournemouth in the Southern League, then became coach at Middlesex, winning the Championship in 2016.

Scott, William Ernest Newnham (245, Amateur) born Isle of Wight 31.5.1903, died Isle of Wight 6.8.1989. He was an all-rounder who played in five Championship matches for Hampshire in June 1927, scoring 102 runs and taking four wickets. He played for the South of England Club Cricket Conference, and Lymington.

Sexton, Andrew John (449) born Southampton 23.7.1979. In his teens, he played for Wimborne, and then for Dorset. In 1998, he scored 84 for the MCC Young Cricketers v Hampshire 2nd XI, and in the following year, first played for Hampshire 2nd XI. In mid-summer 2000, he played in four first-class matches for the county, scoring 36 on debut v Durham at Basingstoke in an innings victory, in which no Hampshire batsman reached 50. It remained his highest score. In the same year, he played in two Nat West Trophy matches for Dorset, and subsequently for some years, for Bashley in the Southern League.

Seymour, Alfred (Pre '95, Amateur) born Brussels, Belgium 16.2.1843, died Folkestone 31.1.1897. He attended Rugby School but was not a member of the XI. During the 1860s he was a professional soldier and just months before retiring, in 1869, he played one first-class match for Lancashire at Hove, scoring 20 & 25. He played one further match, for Hampshire *against* Lancashire in 1870, scoring 2 (run out) & 0.

Seymour, Charles Read (Pre '95, Amateur) born Hartley Wintney, Hants 6.2.1855, died Winchester 6.11.1934. He was a batsman, who attended Harrow School and Oxford University, where he won a 'blue' for Royal Tennis, but played no first-class cricket. He made his first-class debut for MCC in 1879, and then played in 15 first-class matches for Hampshire from 1880-1885, continuing to play for Hampshire after they lost their first-class status. For Hampshire, he scored 481 runs at 18.50, with two half-centuries, 77* v Surrey at the Antelope in 1883, and 57 v Somerset at Taunton in 1882. The innings v Surrey was the first occasion on which a Hampshire opening batsman 'carried his bat'. He played club cricket for Esher, and was a barrister and JP.

Shackleton, Derek (312) born Todmorden, Yorks 12.8.1924, died Canford, Dorset 28.9.2007. By a number of statistical measures, pace bowler Derek Shackleton was the greatest of all Hampshire bowlers. He took 2,669 first-class wickets for the county at 18.23 and over 20 consecutive seasons took more than 100 first-class wickets. No other bowler has ever achieved that latter feat, and his 2,857 wickets in all first-class cricket places him eighth on the all-time list – and the only one of those eight to have played all his cricket post-war. While it is entirely reasonable to argue that any judgement of 'greatness' must place Hampshire's overseas Test bowlers Warne, Marshall and Roberts, above Shackleton, he shares with the latter two, a career average for the county below 20, which no other regular bowler has achieved. He is also the only one of those three to have bowled Hampshire to a Championship title.

There is no doubt that he benefitted from playing in a period which, through the twentieth century and beyond, most favoured the bowlers, with uncovered pitches and outgrounds, and in the damp summers of say, 1956 or 1958 his record was considerable – in 1956, 140 wickets at 16.34, or 1958 when

Hampshire were runners-up, 165 at 15.44. But things were not substantially different in the blazing hot summer of 1959, when English cricket began a brief experiment with covering – certainly his average rose to 21.55 but there were still 148 wickets as he passed his 35th birthday, and two years later 158 wickets at 19.09 as Hampshire won the title for the first time. On that key afternoon at Bournemouth, 'Shack' bowled one of his great spells; in a game which the batsmen had largely dominated, he took 6-39 v Derbyshire in 24 overs and Hampshire were Champions. There were other remarkable performances – 9-77 at Newport in 1953; one year later, at Worthing he bowled *unchanged* for figures of 54-29-60-4; in the sunny summer of 1955, he took 8-4 v Somerset at Weston-Super-Mare; there was 9-59 at Bristol in 1958; on a Friday afternoon at Portsmouth in 1960, Warwickshire were 200-4, batting out for the draw, and in no time, 206 all out; Shackleton 9-30, his best figures.

In 1963, he enjoyed the longest spell of his brief Test Match career against Worrell's West Indians and his best moment at that level, taking three wickets in four balls at Lord's on the Friday morning, on a ground where he liked to bowl. Perhaps he was not quite a Test-class bowler, particularly overseas, but three times he was selected for a single Test of a series early in his career, then ignored for 12 years in his prime, and only as he reached his 39th birthday did he play consecutive Tests. He retired after the 1968 season, but returned for the first two years of the Sunday League – in 1969, taking 17 limited-overs wickets with an economy rate of 2.31. He also returned for one final Championship match that year, v Sussex at Portsmouth, and in 47.5 overs had match figures of 7-95. For his performances in 1958, he was nominated as one of *Wisden's* Cricketers of the Year.

'Shack' was never a fast bowler, but one with extraordinary patience and accuracy – after he retired it was discovered that he was blind in one eye, and one of his colleagues suggested this enabled him to see as if down the sights of a gun. Whether true, he generally hit the spot. He was a useful lower-order batsman, particularly in his early years, and scored 17 half-centuries for Hampshire at an average just below 15; he also top-scored for England on his Test debut. After retiring, he umpired a little, coached a little, and returned to the club for the opening of the Members' Bar in his name. For those of a certain generation, he is still remembered with the greatest fondness as the archetypal craftsman county bowler. John Arlott (1958) suggested he was "essentially a cricketer's cricketer: he impresses the best batsmen, far more than many bowlers who look more spectacular from the ring", adding "it is doubtful if any single player has done quite so much for any county in the last ten years". And he still had another ten years to play.

Shafayat, Bilal Mustapha (513) born Nottingham 10.7.1984. He was a right-handed batsman who played for England under-19s and his native Nottinghamshire from 2001-2005, then for Northamptonshire 2005-2006, (and in limited-overs cricket for them in 2011) returning to Nottinghamshire until

2010. In 2011, he played some matches for Hampshire 2nd XI, including 219* on debut v Glamorgan 2nd XI, and in May 2012 he made his first-class debut for Hampshire v Derbyshire at the Ageas Bowl, scoring 93. There was one more half-century in eight matches in which he scored 289 runs at 28.90. He played for Hampshire in one limited-overs match, their successful CB40 semi-final at Hove, but did not bat. He played subsequently for Shropshire, and for Habib Bank in Pakistan.

Shah, Owais Alam (T20) born Karachi, Pakistan 22.10.1978. Batsman Owais Shah, played for England in all three formats, for Middlesex from 1996-2010, for Essex from 2011-2013 and for a number of overseas teams. In 2014 & 2015, he played for Hampshire in their T20 sides. He scored three half-centuries and averaged 31.00, playing twice in Finals Day, in Hampshire sides that lost semi-finals to Lancashire.

Shahid Afridi (List A/T20) born Pakistan 1 March 1980. He has played for many teams, including Pakistan in all three formats. In England, he played for Derbyshire, Kent and Leicestershire before joining Hampshire to play in the T20 tournament in 2011. He returned to play in that competition from 2015-2017, and also played in one limited-overs match for the county in 2016. His highest T20 score for Hampshire is 101 v Derbyshire in 2017 and his best bowling (from 41 wickets) 5-20 v Gloucestershire in 2011.

Sheldrake, Edgar Francis Talman (Pre '95, Amateur) born Aldershot, 18.1.1864, died Surbiton 14.12.1950. He was a batsman and fast bowler, who played in three first-class matches for Hampshire in 1884 & 1885, scoring 52 runs at 10.40 and taking one wicket.

Sheppard, Jack David (List A) born Salisbury 29.12.1992. He was a pace bowler who played for Hampshire's age group sides, England under-19s, and Hampshire 2nd XI, from 2010. In 2013, he played in one limited-overs match for Hampshire v Bangladesh 'A', and took 2-49 in a Hampshire victory by eight runs. He played for South Wilts in the Southern League, and in recent years for Ealing in the Middlesex League.

Sheppard, Thomas Winter (125, Amateur) born Havant, Hants 4.3.1873, died Scotland 7.6.1954. He changed his name to TW Sheppard-Graham in 1919, and was the great-uncle of the Sussex and England cricketer, DS Sheppard. He was a right-handed batsman who played once for Hampshire in 1905 in a rain-affected, drawn match v Yorkshire at Hull, scoring 17. Four years later he played one match for Worcestershire (22 & 14). He played also for MCC, Free Foresters and the Army, including one non-first-class match *against* Hampshire at Aldershot.

Shield Ian Noel Ridley (293, Amateur) born Hertfordshire, 24.12.1914, died Petersfield, Hants 22.2.2005. He attended Rugby School and played for

Hampshire's Club & Ground and 2 XI sides from 1937. In 1939, he played in four Championship matches, scoring 16 runs and taking four wickets. He played also for the Hampshire Hogs and the 40 Club.

Shine, Kevin James (408) born , Bracknell, 22.2.1969. He was a pace bowler who played for his native Berkshire, and for Hampshire 2nd XI from 1985. He made his first-class debut in 1989, playing in two matches, with a few more in 1990 then 38 wickets in 1991, and 40 at 32.25 in 1992 – his most success-ful season for Hampshire, including a hat-trick and 8-47 v Lancashire at Old Trafford. Sadly, this did not signal his breakthrough, and after one more year, he moved to Middlesex for two seasons, then to Somerset from 1996-1998, where he was capped and took 55 wickets in 1997. His career ended after the 1998 season but he coached at Somerset and then with England, and still leads the pace-bowling coaching for the ECB. For Hampshire, his 119 first-class wickets cost 38.28, and there were 15 limited-overs wickets.

Shirley, William Robert de la Cour (219, Amateur) born London, 13.10.1900, died Bognor Regis 23.4.1970. He was an all-rounder who played at Eton, Middlesex Colts and the MCC. In 1922, he played in a first-class match for Free Foresters v Cambridge University, then quite regularly for Hampshire for three seasons, with a few games in 1925, at the end of his first-class career. From the age of 17, he suffered a number of serious accidents which inhibited his first-class career, but in 1924, he played also at Cambridge University, winning his 'blue'. Arlott (1957) suggested that at another county, given more opportunities with bat and ball "he might … have been a very valuable county cricketer". In 49 matches for Hampshire, he scored three half-centuries at 17.54, with a best of 90 v Glamorgan at Southampton in 1922, and took 52 wickets.

Shirreff, Alexander Campbell (301, Amateur) born Ealing 12.2.1919, died Kent 16.12.2006. He attended Dulwich College. During the war, he was a squadron-leader in the RAF and remained there, enabling him to play for the Combined Services, sometimes as captain, from1946-1957. He won his 'blue' at Cambridge University in 1939, when he played also for Surrey 2nd XI, then in 1946 & 1947 he played for Hampshire when available. In 1948 & 1949 he played in first-class cricket only for the Combined Services, and from 1950-1956 for Kent, and in 1958 was player-coach at Somerset. In 12 matches for Hampshire he scored 387 runs at 21.50, with a best of 77* v Essex at Westcliff-on-Sea in 1946, and took 13 wickets at 56.23.

Shutt, Herbert (133) born Ardwick, Lancs 3.9.1879, died Whitehaven, Cumberland 19.11.1922. He was an opening bowler who played most of his cricket in the north of England, but in 1906 played in four matches for Hampshire, scoring seven runs in two completed innings, and taking eight wickets at 28.87, with a best of 4-29 v Somerset at Taunton in a Hampshire victory.

Simpson, Valentine (Pre '95, Amateur) born London 15.8.1849, died Fareham 2.11.1915. In 1885, he played for Hampshire v Kent at Southampton, scoring 7 & 3 in a defeat.

Smith, Christopher Lyall ('Chris') (386) born Durban, South Africa, 15.10.1958. Smith played for his native Natal from 1979-1983 and at the age of 20 played in one first-class match for Glamorgan. In the following season he joined Hampshire, as an overseas player, replacing Greenidge who was on tour, and scored over 1,000 runs at 31.75, with three centuries. He stayed, qualifying by residence, and playing whenever Greenidge or Marshall was not available, until 1983 when he played a full season, scored 1,923 runs at 53.41 and won a place in the England side. For his performances that season, he was nominated as one of *Wisden's* Cricketers of the Year. He was never an established Test batsman but in eight matches he scored 392 runs at 30.15, with a best of 91 in New Zealand. In county cricket, he was one of the most consistent players, passing 1,000 runs in every full season from 1983-1991, while his 41 centuries for the county have only been exceeded by four men. In total, he scored 15,287 first-class runs for Hampshire at 46.63, with a best of 217 v Warwickshire at Birmingham in 1987, when he shared with Paul Terry, Hampshire's record opening first wicket partnership of 347. In 1991 he scored centuries in both innings v Sussex at Hove. He added 6,301 limited-overs runs at 42.57 with 11 centuries, and was an occasional off-break bowler, who took 44 first-class wickets including 5-69 v Sussex at Southampton in 1988 . He played in the 1986 Sunday League Champions side, and the team that won the B&H Cup at Lord's in 1988, but having played in the winning Nat West semi-final at Birmingham in 1991 he surprised everyone by leaving in August to take up an administrative post with the Western Australia Cricket Association. He settled in Australia, becoming a successful businessman.

Smith, Hamilton Augustus Haigh, also known as Haigh-Smith (148, Amateur) born Isle of Wight 21.10.1884, died London 28.10.1955. He attended Marlborough College and was a fine all-round sportsman, playing rugby for Barbarians (later President) and Hampshire, and hockey for the county, as well as cricket. In 1909 (and 1911) he toured Ireland with Hampshire, and in 27 first-class matches for the county scored 327 runs at 10.54, and took 14 wickets at 41.00

Smith, Robin Arnold (392) born Durban, South Africa, 13 September 1963. Robin Smith was quite simply one of the finest batsmen ever to play for Hampshire, and other than Kevin Pietersen, he played for England while with Hampshire, more times than any other player. Over his career which ran from 1982-2003, and despite Test Match commitments, he passed 1,000 runs in 11 seasons; initially in his first regular season in 1985, and the last in 1999 at an average of 42.69 – very similar to his final first-class average. There were fewer runs, in the new millennium, although in 2001 he scored a century and led Hampshire to victory against the Australians. In 2003, he struggled with hamstring problems and missed six weeks, returning at Durham in late August, followed by Taunton where the injury recurred while batting. He returned to the crease with Adams as his runner, and reached a half-century, finishing 56* when the innings closed. It seemed likely that his career might be over and despite a desperate wish to continue playing, that was the case. It felt unfair that there was to be no fine farewell in front of his own supporters at the conclusion of such a great career, but the bravery of that final innings was typical of a man who for his adopted country took on the might of the West Indies pace men as effectively as anyone.

It was not merely the quantity of runs scored by Smith but the entertaining way in which he led every assault and gave confidence to the lesser players around him. He was also a thoroughly nice, man; despite his impressive physique, there was always something about him of the schoolboy who had posed for Barry Richards' coaching book in the 1970s. The figures tell something of the story with 4,236 runs at 43.67 in 62 Test Matches and nine centuries – only Gower of his regular England contemporaries ended with a higher average – and there was a strong feeling that his Test career ended prematurely. For Hampshire, there were 18,984 runs at 42.09 with 49 centuries in 307 matches, and his best of 209* v Essex in 1987 came after Hampshire were reduced to 5-3. He was as effective in limited-overs games, playing significant innings in his three Lord's Cup Finals and scoring 12,034 runs for Hampshire and 2,419 runs for England with four centuries including a magnificent 167* v Australia which remained the country's highest innings until very recently. For Hampshire, his total of over 30,000 runs in all formats puts him behind just Mead and Marshall, who both played many more games. *Wisden* chose him as one of their Cricketers of the Year in 1990.

Given the extent of his experience, it is unsurprising that, like his England contemporaries Gooch, Stewart, and Gatting he captained his county, although the circumstances in 1998 when he took over from John Stephenson were as much crisis as natural choice. Despite this, he led Hampshire to 6th and 7th in the Championship and to a semi-final in the Nat West, although they lasted only one season in the top league when two divisions were introduced in the Sunday League in 1999. In the same year, they qualified for Division One when the Championship followed suit, but even with the addition of Warne and Mullally, they were relegated the following season. Smith led them straight back up in 2001, when he was the first captain at the brand-new Rose Bowl; sadly, they went down again in 2002, and were perhaps the first 'yo-yo' side. He played his final year under John Crawley's brief period in charge, and has since moved to Australia.

Smith, Thomas Michael (224, Amateur) born London 16.5.1899, died Taunton 17.11.1965. He was a batsman who played in nine matches for Hampshire in 1923 & 1924, scoring 89 runs in 10 completed innings. In the late 1920s, he played in non-first-class matches for European sides in Nigeria and the Gold Coast.

Smith, William Rew ('Will') (524) born Luton 28.9.1982. He is a batsman and occasional off-spin bowler who played for Durham University, Nottinghamshire and Durham, before joining Hampshire in 2014, where he played for four years, before returning to Durham. In 2014, he passed 1,000 runs for the first time in his career (51.60) as Hampshire won promotion, and he was only just short of that total in the following year. There were fewer runs in 2016, but a fine innings of 210 as stand-in captain v Lancashire at the Ageas Bowl. He played in just one Championship match in 2017, mainly captaining the 2nd XI. He was a useful all-rounder in limited-overs cricket, especially in T20 matches, taking 35 wickets in three seasons, but again there were no 'white ball' matches in 2017. He was a very cheerful, popular cricketer.

Smoker, George (Pre '95) born Ovington, Hants 30.12.1856, died Alresford, Hants, 23.5.1925. He played in a Hampshire 'Colts' trial match in May 1885, and in the following month in matches v MCC and Derbyshire, scoring 17 runs at 5.66. His son HG (below) also played for Hampshire.

Smoker, Henry George (87) born Hinton, Hants 1.3.1881, died Cheshire 7.9.1966. He was a pace bowler and left-handed lower order batsman, who played in 31 first-class matches for Hampshire from 1901-1907, scoring 334 runs at 9.54 and taking 33 wickets at 22.21 with a best of 7-35 v the South Africans at Southampton in 1907. In the Championship, his best was 6-63 v Kent in the same year, on the same ground. From 1909, he played for many years for Cheshire, and in 1912 & 1913, in the Lancashire League for Colne.

Soames, Henry (Pre '95, Amateur) born Brighton 18.1.1843, died Salisbury 30.8.1913. He had a brother who played for Sussex, while he played for Brighton College, then the Gentlemen of Sussex, followed by the Gentlemen of Hampshire. He played in one first-class match for Hampshire v Kent at Southborough in 1867, scoring 2 & 52 (top score) in a match that Kent won by nine wickets. In the 1870s, he played matches for the Royal Artillery XI.

Soames, Oliver Courtenay ('Ollie') (555) born Kingston-upon-Thames 27.10.1995. Opening batsman Soames attended Cheltenham College and Loughborough University, playing two first-class matches for the latter in April 2018. He played one match for Hampshire 2nd XI in September 2017 and further games in 2018, after which he played in the last four Championship matches with a best of 29 in the final match v Lancashire. He then signed a two-year contract.

Soar, Thomas ('Tom') (9) born Whitemoor, Nottinghamshire, 3.9.1865, died Carmarthenshire, Wales 17.5.1939. Tom Soar was a pace bowler and useful lower-order batsman who came to Hampshire after failing to win a contract with his home county, played for Hampshire in non-first-class matches from 1888, and in 101 first-class matches from 1895-1904. HS Altham (1957) described him as "a fastish and stout-hearted bowler … (who) was for some years, groundsman and rendered loyal service at a crucial time in our history". On first-class debut at Taunton in their famous inaugural Championship match, which Hampshire won after following-on, he took 4-89 and 7-71 – the latter remains Hampshire's best figures by a man making his first-class debut. He took seven or more wickets for Hampshire on six occasions, the best 8-38 v Essex at Leyton in 1896. In the Championship, his best season was the first, 1895, when he took 89 wickets, usually sharing the load with Harry Baldwin. He took 53 first-class wickets the following year, 31 in 1897 but missed almost the whole of 1898 injured; after that his figures were more modest, although never more expensive than the mid-twenties, and his career ended with 323 wickets at 23.82 and five half-centuries. He was briefly a coach at Winchester College, and then moved to Wales, coaching at Llandovery College for the rest of his life, while, in his forties, playing some Minor Counties matches for Carmarthenshire.

Sohail Tanvir (518) born Rawalpindi, Pakistan 12.12.1984. He is a left-arm pace bowler who played in all three formats for Pakistan and for many other sides around the world. In 2013, he played as an overseas player for the second part of the season, replacing George Bailey. In four first-class matches, he took 10 wickets at 34.80, in six limited-overs matches, 17 wickets at just 12.17 with a best of 4-29 v Essex at the Ageas Bowl, and in nine T20 matches, nine wickets.

Southern, John William (374) born London 2.9.1952. He was a tall, orthodox slow-left-arm bowler who played for Hampshire 2nd XI from 1972, and in nine seasons from 1975-1983, played mainly in first-class matches, taking 412 wickets for Hampshire at 29.81. On 17 occasions, he took five or more wickets in an innings with a best of 6-46 v Gloucestershire at Bournemouth, bowling Hampshire to victory in his fifth match. He was a useful tail-end batsman, scoring 1,653 runs at 15.30 with three half-centuries; in 1978 he set a county record reaching 51*v Gloucestershire at Bournemouth with just 12 strokes. In 25 limited-overs matches took 14 wickets. He played Southern League cricket with Deanery before moving to New Zealand.

Southerton, James (Pre '95) born Petworth 16.11.1827, died Mitcham, Surrey 16.6.1880. He was a fine all-round cricketer who played for England in two Test Matches in 1876/7, in his 50th year, and remains England's oldest debutant. He moved counties and in one season played for Surrey, Sussex *and* Hampshire – he played for Sussex *against* Hampshire in the latter's inaugural county match at the Antelope in July 1864, but did not bowl. For Hampshire, he played in 12 matches from 1864-1867, scoring 200 runs at 10.00 and taking 63 wickets; nine times taking five or more in an innings, including a best of 7-45 v Surrey at the Antelope in 1865 – the county club's first victory in a first-class match, in their second season.

Sparrow, Adolphus James (94) born Gosport 10.5.1869, died Kent, 6.9.1936. He played in one match v Leicestershire at Southampton in 1902, but was dismissed after scoring one run.

Spencer-Smith, Gilbert Joshua (Pre '95, Amateur) born Brooklands, Hants 17.12.1843, died Bursledon, Hants 7.2.1928. He went to Eton and played for Hampshire in one match v Sussex at Hove in 1864, scoring 11 & 9. In the following year, he was playing in non-first-class Army matches. His twin brother Orlando played once for Hampshire (below)

Spencer-Smith, Rev. Orlando (Pre '95, Amateur) born Brooklands, Hants 17.12.1843, died Swanwick, Hants 23.11.1920. He went to Eton and Oxford University, winning his 'blue' in 1866, when he also played for Hampshire v MCC, scoring 14 & 39 (top score) in a narrow defeat by 11 runs. He played in non-first-class matches for the Gentlemen of Hampshire and the Gentlemen of Dorset.

Spens, Major General James (Pre '95, Amateur) born Subathoo, India 30.3.1853, died Folkestone 19.6.1934. He played at Haileybury School and in first-class cricket for MCC, and Hampshire in one match v Kent in 1884, scoring 60 on debut. He then played in nine more for the county, from 1897-1899, scoring 546 runs at 28.73, with two more half-centuries and 118* v Gentlemen of Philadelphia at Bournemouth in 1897. His best Championship score was 74 v Somerset at Portsmouth in 1899. He played also for various sides including MCC, Free Foresters, the Army and United Services, Portsmouth. For the latter, on their home ground, he scored 386 v the Nonedescripts XI, believed to be the highest innings recorded in the county.

Sprinks, Henry Robert James (240, Amateur) born Alexandria, Egypt 19.8.1905, died Bramshaw, Hants 23.5.1986. He was a fast-bowler who played in 21 first-class matches for Hampshire, one v Essex in 1925 and then 13 in 1928 and seven in 1929. He took 29 wickets with a best of 4-56 v Warwickshire at Edgbaston in 1929.

Sprot, Edward Mark (54, Amateur) born Edinburgh, Scotland 4.2.1872, died Farnham, Surrey 8.10.1945. He went to Harrow but did not play in the XI, and while still in the army, he made his Hampshire debut in 1898 in one match v Cambridge University, top-scoring with 21 & 56, in totals of 72 & 120 all out (Jessop 12-67). He did not play again until the following season, when he played in five Championship matches, and began playing regularly in the poor Hampshire side of 1900, scoring his first century, 103* v Warwickshire – there would be eleven more three-figure innings between 1900-1911 and one last one at the Oval in 1914, his final season with the county. In 1905, he scored 1,206 runs at 41.58, the best average of four seasons in which he reached four figures. In 1903, he took on the Hampshire captaincy, and while he could not immediately arrest their occupation of last place in the Championship, with the arrival of the great professionals, Hampshire's cricket improved from 1906 (eighth), finishing sixth in 1910 & 1912 – when they beat the Australians. In 1908, he was praised for what was then an unusual and inspired piece of captaincy. Declarations were uncommon when he closed Hampshire's innings 24 runs behind Northamptonshire, and gave the ball to the great batsman Phil Mead who took 7-18 in a score of 60 all out. Sprot then scored 62* as Hampshire won. In 1911, his century in 45 minutes v Gloucestershire was, and remains, Hampshire's fastest, while in 1914, Sprot's side finished fifth, their highest until 1955, although by the end of that season he often handed leadership to the pace bowler Jaques who was killed at the front in 1915. With cricket to resume in 1919, Sprot, by then 46, told the county he would not return, and Tennyson took charge. Sprot scored more than 12,000, often lively runs for Hampshire at 28.80, was a fine field, and an excellent leader; there were also 54 wickets, including 5-28 v Sussex at Portsmouth in 1900. He retired, to fish, draw, paint and play the piano; he was also a keen shot and played, billiards, rackets and golf. HS Altham (1957) described him as "a fine field … (and) natural hitter … who played each game with optimism and zest …and made the game enjoyable both for his own side and the opposition".

Steele, David Aubrey (21, Amateur) born Southampton, 3.6.1869, died Caterham, Surrey, 25.3.1935. He was a slow-bowling all-rounder, who played in non-first-class matches for Hampshire from 1886, in the early 1890s played for Scotland, and from late July 1895-1906 in 163 first-class matches for Hampshire. As a batsman, he rarely averaged above the mid-teens, but in five of his seasons he scored six half-centuries including a best of 80 v Leicestershire at Bournemouth, in 1899. As a bowler, his best seasons were from 1896-1899 during which he took 96 wickets, with a best of 5-32 v Somerset at Portsmouth in 1897. He scored 3,418 runs for the county and took 135 wickets.

Steele, Rev. John William Jackson (286, Amateur) born Cheshire 30.7.1905, died Devon 29.3.1990. He was a pace bowler and useful lower-order batsman, who played for the Army from 1933, including two first-class matches v the two major universities in 1938 & 1939. In those two seasons, he played also in 17 first-class matches for Hampshire, scoring 406 runs at 16.91, and taking 57 wickets at 26.64. He took five or more wickets in an innings on three occasions, with a best of 6-62 v Warwickshire, at Portsmouth in 1939. John Arlott (1957) suggested he was "a very real asset" with "brisk" pace and "consistent … length and direction, while moving the ball either way off the seam".

Stephenson, George Robert ('Bob') (359) born Derby 19.11.1942. Wicketkeeper Bob Stephenson joined Hampshire in an emergency at the start of the 1969 season after 28-year-old Bryan Timms left unexpectedly to pursue a business career – and play occasionally 'freelance' for Warwickshire. At that point, Hampshire had no regular reserve wicketkeeper and Stephenson, the son of an England football international, was one of the last generation of cricketers who also played football; in his case for Derby County, Shrewsbury, and Rochdale. He played cricket in the Lancashire League while with Rochdale, then for Derbyshire as understudy to Bob Taylor, but was never likely to replace Taylor and after just nine first-class matches in 1967 & 1968, the invitation to join Hampshire, guaranteed him a first team place, which he held from 1969-1980. By then, he had played in 263 first-class matches for Hampshire and batting pragmatically in the late middle order scored 4,566 runs at 16.48, with one century, 100* at Taunton, and 625 dismissals – 75 of them stumpings. His 80 victims in 1970 is the third highest total for the county in one season and in 1971, when Peter Sainsbury dismissed more than 100 victims, Stephenson stumped 17 batsmen. In 1972 and 1974 he was the country's leading wicketkeeper, and he was second in 1975. There were 65 dismissals in 1973, a significant contribution to the Championship title, and in 1975 and 1978 he 'kept', as Hampshire won two Sunday League titles; overall, he had 249 victims in 237 limited-overs matches.

Bob Stephenson was Hampshire's representative on the developing Professional Cricketers Association, and he served as Gilliat's deputy before his appointment as captain. In that one season, Hampshire finished 12th, a respectable performance given the transitional time, but he was disappointed to be replaced by Pocock, feeling that he could have done much to bring through the less experienced man. He returned 'to the ranks' as Hampshire finished bottom for the only time since 1905, and by the time the final table was published, Bobby Parks had replaced him at the start of his career. Stephenson's last match, in early August, was against the touring Australians at Southampton; Jeff Thomson got him without scoring in the first innings and in the second Stephenson arrived at number 10 with Hampshire facing an innings defeat. The Australians won, but they had to bat again because Stephenson scored 65 before Lillee ended his career. That final innings was typical of his professionalism, his determination and resilience and he moved into a long career teaching and coaching in Hampshire.

Stephenson, John Patrick (426) born Stebbing, Essex, 14 March, 1965. Batting all-rounder John Stephenson was one of a number of 'graduates' of Felsted School who played professional cricket at Essex, and he played for his native county for ten seasons, including a single Test Match appearance, before he joined Hampshire in 1995. Mark Nicholas was in his final season as captain and it was no surprise when Stephenson deputised for him in mid-August v the West Indians, and then became captain from 1996. It was however a difficult transitional period for the county, and Stephenson only held the post for two years, before reverting to a playing role. He left Hampshire after the 2001 season and returned to Essex for three seasons before taking over as Head of Cricket at the MCC.

In his full first-class career, he scored 14,773 runs at 32.39 with 25 centuries and took 396 wickets at 32.55, to which he added 7,252 limited-overs runs and 270 wickets. That is the record of a very good county all-rounder, although at Hampshire his batting average dropped to the mid-20s (six centuries), and playing in a side with a generally weak attack, he was often more effective with the ball, with a best return of 7-51 v Middlesex in 1995. In his two seasons as captain he took 73 wickets and scored 1,395 runs. In 1996 Hampshire finished 14th in the Championship, 15th in the Sunday League, failed to qualify for the knock-out stages in the B&H Cup and beat Norfolk and Worcestershire in the Nat West Trophy before losing to Essex. The debut of 'Dimi' Mascarenhas late in the season is in retrospect the brightest feature. In 1997, Hampshire finished in the same places in the two tables despite the magnificent form of their overseas player Matthew Hayden, beat only Cambridgeshire in the Nat West Trophy and again failed to progress in the B&H Cup. Off the field the club was preoccupied with the complex business of funding the new stadium, while English cricket began a dramatic reorganisation, with the creation of two divisions in the Championship, annual tinkering with the formats of the old limited-overs tournaments and under-achievement by the England side. In such circumstances, it is unsurprising that Stephenson inherited a difficult task but one that he always approached with politeness and a determination to lead from the front, batting and bowling, whatever the consequences. These qualities appear to have served him very well in his career at Lord's – not the first former Hampshire player to progress to 'Headquarters'.

Stevenson, Keith (380) born Derby 6.10.1950. Stevenson was a pace bowler who played for his native Derbyshire from 1974-1977, taking 98 first-class wickets at 30.58. He joined Hampshire in 1978 as they rebuilt their attack after the departures of Herman, Mottram and Roberts, and with the relatively unknown Malcolm Marshall playing for the West Indies in England in 1979, and 1980. Stevenson was a reliable county bowler for Hampshire, taking 257 wickets in 99 matches at 29.33, and on 12 occasions taking five or more wickets in an innings with a best of 7-22 v Oxford University in 1979. His best Championship return for Hampshire was 6-73 v Sussex at Hove in 1978, his best season was 1979, with 69 wickets; he passed 50 in the next two seasons, played little in 1982, and ended his career in 1983. He took 79 limited-overs wickets at an economy rate just over four. He was an unremarkable batsman with a top score in all first-class cricket of 33, and in limited-overs of 14.

Stevenson, Ryan Anthony (537) born Torquay 2.4.1992. He is a pace bowler who played for Devon and joined Hampshire in 2015, making his first-class debut v Durham, and playing in three key games at the end of 2015, as Hampshire fought successfully to avoid relegation. In that first brief period, he had a top score of 30, and took three wickets, but has subsequently suffered from a serious back problem, playing three limited-overs games in 2016 (two wickets) and only one more first-class match, in 2017, v Cardiff University. In 2018, he played in 10 T20 matches

Stewart, Maj-Gen Sir Herbert (Pre '95, Amateur) born Sparsholt, Hants 30.6.1843, died of wounds following the battle of Abu Klea, Sudan, 16.2.1885. He was a wicketkeeper who went to Winchester and in 1869 played in four first-class matches, three for MCC and for Hampshire against MCC, scoring 0 & 1 and holding one catch. His brother WA (below) played twice for the county. There is a memorial to him as a soldier, in Hans Place, London.

Stewart, Rev. William Anthony (Pre '95, Amateur) born Sparsholt 19.5.1847, died Twyford Lodge 31.7.1883. Like his brother (above) he was a wicketkeeper, who went to Winchester and Oxford University where he won his 'blue' in 1869 & 1870. He played twice for Hampshire v MCC, in 1869 and 1878, scoring 10 runs at 3.33, and dismissing four batsmen.

Steyn, Dale Willelm (553) born Northern Province, South Africa 27.6.1983. South African fast bowler Dale Steyn has been one of the outstanding international bowlers of the 21st century, with more than 400 Test Match and nearly 200 ODI wickets by the close of the 2018 season, during which he played for Hampshire. During the following winter he became South Africa's highest Test Match wicket taker. At Hampshire in 2018, he replaced fellow-countryman Hashim Amla as the county's overseas player and in five Championship matches headed the averages with 20 wickets at 19.10. He played in the last three Royal London Cup matches, including the Lord's Final, taking three wickets, and added five wickets in four T20 matches.

Stokes, Mitchell Sam Thomas (List A/T20) born Basingstoke 27.3.1987. He was a batsman who played for Berkshire, England under-19s, Hampshire 2nd XI, and from 2005-2007, for the county in limited-overs and T20 matches. In five limited-overs matches he scored 53 runs, and in 14 T20 matches 179 runs with a best of 62 in 2006, v Middlesex at the Rose Bowl, sharing an opening partnership of 122, with Michael Carberry. He played subsequently for Wiltshire.

Stone, James ('Jimmy') (81) born Southampton 29.11.1876, died Maidenhead, Berkshire 15.11.1942. Wicketkeeper Jimmy Stone was the first local-born professional player to establish himself in the side, making his debut in 1900, and replacing Charles Robson regularly from 1902. In addition to his wicketkeeping, he sometimes played as a batsman, and from 1911-1913, passed 1,000 runs in each of three seasons. He established his credentials as a batsman scoring 174 v Sussex at Portsmouth in 1905, which remained his highest score, and one

S

of five centuries for the county. In 274 matches for Hampshire he dismissed 474 batsmen, almost 25% of them stumped. In 1914, Walter Livsey came into the side and Stone seemed to retire from first-class cricket during the war, but he moved to South Wales, played club cricket for Briton Ferry Town CC and then for Glamorgan from 1922-1924 in their first years in the Championship. In 1923, he returned to Southampton with his new county and scored 37 & 81. He was a first-class umpire from 1925-1934.

Streak, Heath Hilton (427) born Bulawayo, Zimbabwe 16.3.1974. Pace bowler Heath Streak played in 65 Test Matches and 187 ODIs for Zimbabwe and in 1995, spent one season as Hampshire's overseas player, while Winston Benjamin was touring with the West Indies. For Hampshire, he played in 19 first-class matches, taking 53 wickets at 30.73, with a best of 4-40, and hit one half-century, with an average of 15.12. In 21 limited-overs matches he took 33 wickets at 26.60 and an economy rate of 5.28. He played subsequently for Warwickshire, and after he retired worked as a commentator and a coach, at one time with the Zimbabwe side.

Studd, Brig-Gen Herbert William (56, Amateur) born Tidworth House, Wiltshire, 26.12.1870, died London, 8.8.1947. He was one of six brothers all of whom played cricket including GB who played in four Test Matches and RA (below) who also played for Hampshire. HW went to Eton, played for some years for the Household Brigade, and in the early 1890s, for Middlesex and MCC. In August 1898, he played in four Championship matches for Hampshire, scoring 217 runs at 31.00, with a best of 60 v Sussex at Portsmouth.

Studd, Reginald Augustus (16, Amateur) born Tidworth House, Wiltshire 18.12.1873, died Northampton 3.2.1948. He went to Eton, made his first-class debut for MCC in 1894, and at Cambridge University won his 'blue' in 1895, when he played in three matches for Hampshire. He scored 169 runs at 28.16, with a best of 93 (& 37) v Sussex at Hove, two weeks after he had scored 96* for Cambridge University against the same county on the same ground. In September 1895, he played on Staten Island v All New York and in Canada with F Mitchell's XI.

Style, Sir William Henry Marsham (Pre '95, Amateur) born Bicester House, Oxfordshire 3.9.1826, died Folkestone 31.1.1904. He was a wicketkeeper and lower-order batsman who went to Eton, and Oxford University, but did not play first-class cricket there. In 1865, he played for Hampshire v Surrey at the Oval, scoring 0 & 1 in a defeat by an innings and 221 runs.

Sutcliffe, James Frederick (164) born Medway, Kent 12.12.1876, killed in action, Gallipoli 14.7.1915. He enlisted in the Royal Marines in 1895, and from 1909 was stationed at Eastney Barracks, Portsmouth. He was described as one of the great enlisted cricketers – in 1907, while at Deal, he scored 1,154 runs and took

221

76 wickets – although the full Royal Navy XI seemed to prefer to select officers. When he did play for them, he had some success, notably v the Gentlemen of Sussex at Lewes in August 1911, when he took 11 wickets in the match and scored 32*. In the same month, he played once for Hampshire at Worcester, scoring 16 & 8, although Hampshire then travelled back to Portsmouth to play Yorkshire, but Sutcliffe was not retained on his home ground. He was a regular member of church choirs in Portsmouth and is remembered on a memorial cross in Portsmouth Cathedral.

Sutherland, Thomas (57) born England 17.2.1880 we have no further details of his birth or death. He was a fast bowler who played once for Hampshire v Warwickshire at Southampton in 1898 taking 6-111, and then in seven Championship matches, plus v the Australians, in the following season, although he took only five more wickets.

Sykes, Ernest Castle (28) born Sheffield 31.5.1869, died Bolsover, Derbyshire 30.11.1925. 1896. He played in one match as a wicketkeeper for Hampshire, v the Australians in 1896, scoring 0* & 5*. In the following year, he played for Yorkshire Colts v Nottinghamshire Colts.

T

Tate, Edward (53) born Lyndhurst 30.8.1877, died Malvern, Worcs 4.1.1953. He played for Hampshire between 1898-1902, and during the same period played regularly for MCC – many of those matches, non-first-class. For Hampshire, he played in 29 matches, scoring 256 runs at 7.11 and taking 56 wickets at 31.03, with a best of 8-51 in 1898 in a victory v Somerset in Hampshire's first-ever match at Bournemouth. From 1911-1923 he played for Devon.

Tate, Frederick (Pre '95) born Lyndhurst 6.6.1844, died Lyndurst 24.4.1935. He was the brother of HW (but not Edward, despite shared place of birth?). For Hampshire, he played in two matches in 1870 and two more in 1876, and his most successful time was with the ball in 1870, taking 13 wickets at 10.69, with a best of 6-63 v Lancashire at Old Trafford, and 5-46 in the return at the Antelope. He scored few runs, and took no wickets in 1876. He played also for the Gentlemen of Hampshire and Huntingdonshire in non-first-class matches.

Tate, Henry William (Pre '95) born Lyndhurst 4.10.1849, died Richmond, Surrey 9.5.1936. He played in 29 first-class matches for Hampshire from 1869-1885, against just four opponents, Derbyshire, Kent, Sussex and MCC, scoring 499 runs at 11.08, with 96 wickets at 18.16. His one half-century of 61*, and his best bowling of 6-51 came v Kent at the Antelope in 1878, despite which, Kent won. He took five or more wickets in an innings on six occasions.

Tayler, Robert Frederick (Pre '95, Amateur) born Wendover, Bucks 17.3.1836, died Woking, Surrey 1.1.1888. In the 1860s he played in various non-first-class matches, and in 1865, in three first-class games for the Gentlemen of Kent, and Kent. In 1866, he played twice for Hampshire, v Surrey and MCC, scoring 68 runs at 17.00 with a best of 42 v Surrey at the Oval

Taylor, Bradley Jacob (521) born Winchester 14.3.1997. He is an off-break bowling all-rounder who played for Hampshire's age group sides, and, from 2013 age 16, Hampshire 2nd XI. In August 2013, he made his debut for the county in Championship and limited-overs matches, and in the former, he took 4-64 v Lancashire at Old Trafford, still his best figures. In the following year, he made his T20 debut; in all three cases setting the record as Hampshire's youngest debutant. In 2014 & 2015 he played for England under-19s in all formats, but despite his early county debuts, he has struggled with ankle injuries since, although he played in the first seven Royal London Cup matches in 2018, scoring two half-centuries to which he added the team's best economy rate of under five. His best bowling in limited-overs matches, 4-26, came in February 2018, in the Caribbean Regional Super 50.

Taylor, Billy Victor (471) born Southampton 11.1.1977. On 6 June 2000, Hampshire-born pace bowler Billy Taylor, bowled the first ball at Hampshire's new ground, the Rose Bowl, but for Sussex 2nd XI against Hampshire 2nd XI. He played for Sussex from 1999-2003, including their Championship title in that last year, then joined Hampshire, where he played from 2004-2009. In the Championship, he took 6-45 v Gloucestershire, in April 2005, bowling Hampshire to victory, and in May 2006, 6-32 v Middlesex which included the first hat-trick at the Rose Bowl. He was a regular player for both counties in limited-overs matches; for Hampshire, he took 73 wickets at 29.58, with an economy rate of 4.6, and he took 30 wickets in T20 matches at almost the same average. His batting was unremarkable but, in 2004, he hit 40 v Essex in a 61-run 10th wicket partnership with Alan Mullally. He was very popular with the supporters; since retiring he has become an umpire, in recent years in first-class and Women's International matches.

Taylor, George Rammell (277, Amateur) born Havant, Hants 25.11.1909, died Romsey 21.10.1986. He attended Lancing College, played one match for Hampshire v Lancashire at Southampton in 1935, scoring 0 & 21, after which he continued to play for the 2nd XI and Club & Ground sides. In 1939, he was asked to captain the side, Hampshire's fourth captain in five years. His performances were modest, in 24 matches he scored 306 runs at 9.27, with a best of 41 v Lancashire at Southampton in a total of 434, despite which Lancashire won by six wickets. Hampshire finished in 15th place, winning three matches, including their traditional Bank Holiday game at Canterbury, which was Taylor's last county game – Giles Baring led them for the last six matches. He played in a services match at Lord's in 1943.

Taylor, John Denis (311) born Ipswich, 18.2.1923, died Southampton 14.3.1991. He was a batsman who played in four first-class matches for Hampshire, two in 1947 and two in 1949, scoring 76 runs at 15.20. He made his debut v Lancashire at Bournemouth in the county's first tied match. In 1949, he played regularly for the 2nd XI in the Minor Counties competition, with two half-centuries, and a best of 76 v Kent 2nd XI.

Taylor, Michael Norman Somerset ('Mike') (368) born Amersham, Bucks 12.11.1942. Bowling all-rounder Mike Taylor played for his native Buckinghamshire from 1961, and in the following year made his debut for Nottinghamshire 2nd XI. He made his first-class debut for them in 1964 and played there until 1972, when he was not offered a new contract, despite playing in 230 matches with a batting average of 18.01 and 522 wickets at 27.88. In that final season, he played in a Gillette Cup match against Hampshire at Trent Bridge, taking 2-39 in 12 overs and top-scoring with 58, and when they learned of his release, Hampshire signed him. He had an immediate impact, for in 1973 he took 64 first-class wickets at 21.71, and scored 507 runs at 24.14, to help his new county to the title. His bowling figures were even better in 1974 when they were foiled by the weather in the search for a second successive Championship, and through the 1970s he proved himself one of the best of Hampshire's signings from another county. In addition to his fine medium-pace bowling he scored his first century for the county in 1977, and there was another in 1978. In that season, age 35, he was a member of the Hampshire side that won the Sunday League, as he had been in 1975. He retired at the end of the 1980 season and became Hampshire's Assistant Secretary and then Marketing Manager, not least during the demanding 1990s in the move to the Rose Bowl. He took 308 first-class wickets for Hampshire at 24.21, plus 162 limited-overs wickets at 25.70 and an economy rate below four runs per over. He retired from the office in 2002, after 30 years with his 'new' county. His twin brother Derek was a wicketkeeper with Surrey and Somerset.

Tennyson, Lionel Hallam (186, Amateur) born London, 7.11.1889, died Bexhill-on-Sea, Sussex 6.6.1951. The Hon LH Tennyson succeeded as 3rd Baron Tennyson in 1928. He was the grandson of the famous Victorian poet and went to Eton and Cambridge University although he played no major cricket there. In his biography, Alan Edwards offers an explanation which would describe one aspect of Tennyson's life very well, suggesting that he "found all the temptations of Cambridge too hard to resist. The racecourses of Newmarket were just up the road. London was still conveniently near. There were shooting parties at country houses in the locality". He did not take his degree, but became an officer in the Coldstream Guards and played cricket for the Army. His achievements there brought him a first-class debut for MCC v Oxford University, and with 110 in the second innings, became the only Hampshire cricketer *ever* to score a century on first-class debut. Stationed in Aldershot, and with a family home on the Isle of Wight, he was invited to play for Hampshire, in his second match scored 116 v Essex and in the next, 111 at Trent Bridge. His exploits in that first season brought him the accolade as one of *Wisden's* Cricketers of the Year, and he toured South Africa in the winter playing in all five Test matches,

He was able to play very little in 1914, before the war intervened. By contrast with his 'playboy' image, he saw action at the front throughout the war, evidently heroically despite a lack of decorations, and he was wounded and sent home on three occasions. Despite his lively, optimistic personality, he documented the horrors of his experiences in the trenches in some detail, and by the war's end he had lost two brothers, and his mother, with whom he was close. He accepted the task of captaining Hampshire and held the post from 1919-1933, after which he played occasionally until the end of the 1935 season. He formed a strong relationship with his fine professionals and from 1921-1926 Hampshire only once slipped below seventh. Against Yorkshire at Sheffield in

1921 he bowled an extra ball after his opponents had won, to allow Oldroyd on 99* to reach his century – it is recorded in *Wisden*, but deleted by *Cricket Archive*. In 1922, he led Hampshire to what is probably still the most remarkable victory in Championship history, after Warwickshire had bowled them out for 15, and in his first-class career he scored 19 centuries, while one wit suggested he had never quite learned to live in the twentieth! Phil Mead likened him to a "big boy".

In 1921, after Australia had beaten England in the first two Test Matches he was invited to take on the captaincy, after CB Fry, who withdrew injured, recommended him. In the first match at Leeds he lost Hobbs to illness, unable to bat in either innings; then Tennyson split his hand in the field, used a boy's bat, and scored 63 & 36 one-handed. England lost again but he arrested that sequence in the final two Tests, having brought in two of his men, Mead and Brown, but he never played for England again. He played in 347 first-class matches for Hampshire, scoring 12,626 runs at 23.68, with a best of 217 v the West Indians in 1928. In that year, and previously in 1922 and 1925, he passed 1,000 runs. As an occasional and somewhat unpredictable fast bowler he took 43 wickets for the county. His first-class career ended with his own side touring India in 1937/8. He holds the record for the most matches as Hampshire's captain – 323. He wrote two autobiographies; see also Alan Edwards (2001) *Regency Buck: The Life & Times of a Cricketing Legend;* the first part of the title comes from John Arlott (1957) who said of him also that "as a cricketer he often exhibited, and sometimes justified, a remarkable optimism in face of probable defeat".

Terry, Sean Paul (512) born Southampton 1.8.1991. A batsman, he was born in Southampton, the son of Paul Terry (below) but raised in Australia. He spent summers in Hampshire when his father was coach and played for Hampshire's age group sides. In 2011, he played for MCC Young Cricketers, and then Hampshire 2nd XI, and in 2012 made his debut for the county in first-class cricket. He played in a few matches for Hampshire over four seasons, without establishing himself, scoring 440 runs in 11 matches at 29.33 with five half-centuries, adding two more in eight limited-overs matches. In 2016, he played for Northamptonshire, and for Ireland in ODIs and IT20s, and in 2017 for The Hills CC in Ireland, and for Ireland 'Wolves'.

Terry, Vivian Paul (382) born Osnabruck, Germany, 15.1.1959. Paul Terry went to Millfield School and captained the England Schools side touring India in 1977. He played for England in their under-19 sides in 1977 & 1978, by which time he was also playing for Hampshire 2nd XI, and in 1978 he made his first-class debut for the county. For five years, he played occasionally in the first team but in 1983, established himself, passing 1,000 first-class runs, with 467 in limited-overs matches and in 1984, there were more runs and higher averages in both formats which won him a Test Match call-up against the fearsome West Indies pace attack. On debut for England, at Leeds he scored 8 & 1 as West Indies won by eight wickets, in the next at Manchester, his arm was broken by a ball from Winston Davis. He returned to bat one-handed, allowing Alan Lamb to reach his century, but was absent as England lost by an innings, and his Test career was over. For more than ten years however, he became a key batsman in Hampshire's powerful top-order, and while they could not better runners-up in 1985, he was a member of the sides that won trophies in 1986, 1988, 1991 & 1992. In 288 first-class matches for the county he scored 16,134 runs at 36.50 with a best of 190 v the Sri Lankans in 1988. In the Championship, his best was 180 at Derby in the following year, while in 1987, with Chris Smith, he broke his own first wicket record for Hampshire (with Greenidge), posting 347 at Edgbaston v Warwickshire. In 1994 he carried his bat, scoring 141* v Yorkshire at Headingley, while in limited-overs cricket, he scored 8,622 runs with 12 centuries, none more important than his 109 at Chelmsford in 1988, when after 25 years, Hampshire won a cup semi-final at last. During one season with Hampshire Colts he was their leading wicket-taker, yet despite being a fine all-round sportsman he did not take a first-class wicket, but he was a superb fielder – perhaps Hampshire's finest all-rounder, equally at home catching at slip or in the covers. The end of his Hampshire career in 1996 was a disappointment to him, but he moved to Australia and established himself as a coach. With a new regime, he returned to his old county in that capacity for a few years in the new century and his son (above) followed him to Hampshire.

Thompson, Hugh Reginald Patrick (329, Amateur) born Scunthorpe 11.4.1934. He was an off-break bowler, who went to Cheltenham College and age 19, made his debut for Hampshire v Oxford University in 1953. He played in the same match in the following season, and in a non-first-class match v the Army. In the first-class matches, he took two wickets and scored 16 runs.

Thorburn, Mark (466) born Bath 11.8.1978. In 1999, he played for Gloucestershire 2nd XI, and in 2001 & 2002, in five first-class matches for Durham University. He played for Hampshire 2nd XI in 2003, and in one first-class match, v Oxford University when he did not bat, but took 2-53, & 1-67. He played subsequently for Essex and Somerset 2nd XIs, and for Somerset Cricket Board in the Minor Counties Trophy. He worked for Gloucestershire as an analyst.

Thorne, Robert (Pre '95, Amateur) born Southampton 1.3.1860, died Southampton 11.2.1930. He played in two matches v Sussex in 1883, opening the batting, but scored just nine runs.

Thornely, Dominic John (483) born New South Wales, Australia 1.10.1978. He was a batsman and occasional medium-pace bowler who played for Australia under-19s and Australia 'A'. In 2005, he played for Surrey, and in 2006 for Hampshire as an overseas player. He played in 15 first-class matches, scoring 759 runs at 34.50 with six half-centuries, and was particularly effective in limited-overs games with 485 runs at 44.09, including 107* v Kent at the Rose

Bowl, when he also took 2-43, despite which Kent won from the last ball. He took 22 first-class wickets for the county, and there was a best T20 innings of 50* v Middlesex, and 4-22 v Kent. He played subsequently for Mumbai Indians in the IPL, and back in Australia.

Thresher, Phillip (Pre '95, Amateur) born Hamble, 1.3.1844, died London 11.4.1883. He went to Winchester College, playing in the XI, and then for the Gentlemen of Hampshire, and also for the Gentlemen of West Kent. In 1865, 1866 & 1869 he played in five games for Hampshire, three v MCC, scoring 93 runs, with a best of 47* v MCC in 1869 – Hampshire's highest score of the season. He took one wicket.

Thursfield, Martin John (416) born Co. Durham 14.12.1971. He was a pace bowler, who played for an England under-19 side and for Middlesex at the start of the 1990s. He moved to Hampshire in 1991 and played there to 1996. He played in one first-class match in 1992, there were two more in 1993 then more regular appearances in 1994, when he took 17 wickets including his best of 6-130 v Middlesex. There were fewer games in following years and in 1997 he played briefly with Sussex. He played in 31 limited-overs matches for the county, with 23 wickets, and a best of 3-31. He played for the Hampshire Cricket Board, then for Durham Cricket Board.

Timms, Bryan Stanley Valentine (343) born Ropley, Hants 17.12.1940. As a young man, wicketkeeper Timms served an 'apprenticeship' with Leo Harrison who he was destined to succeed in the early 1960s. At 18, he played for Hampshire in the first year of the 2nd XI Championship in 1959, and in two first-class matches against the two University sides. Harrison was injured in 1960, and Timms played in 17 county matches with 38 dismissals and 224 runs. In 1961, as Hampshire chased their first title he came into the side again to cover injury, before Ingleby-Mackenzie took the gloves, allowing the selection of an extra batsman or bowler. There were six matches in 1962, then Harrison retired and for six seasons Timms was Hampshire's wicketkeeper, although Ingleby-Mackenzie was briefly preferred in the Gillette Cup. In 208 first-class matches for the county, Timms scored 3,236 runs at 15.70 and dismissed 462 batsmen (60 stumped) – in 1964 his six victims in an innings v Leicestershire at Portsmouth equalled the then Hampshire record. Although still only 28, he decided to retire before the 1969 season to concentrate on business, although Warwickshire approached him to cover for AC Smith when absent on duty as a Test selector. He did not join their staff or play 2nd XI cricket for them, but for three years played in 24 first-class and seven limited-overs matches.

Tolfree, Edward (134) born Southampton 12.7.1881, died Southampton 20.3.1966. He made his first-class debut for Hampshire v the West Indians in 1906, played one Championship match in 1907, two in 1909 and finally, one in 1919. In those five matches, he scored 53 runs at 8.83, and took two wickets.

Tomlinson, James Andrew (459) born Winchester 12.6.1982. James Tomlinson was in every sense a first-class Hampshire bowler, he played almost wholly in first-class cricket, he displayed a first-class attitude as a thoughtful and hard-working player, and he was essentially a bowler, who rarely looked at home in the field, although there were occasionally fine moments as a batsman – often at number 11. He bowled left-arm fast-medium, and after school in Andover played for Hampshire under-19s, Wiltshire, South Wilts in the Southern League, and at Cardiff University, and for the British Universities side. In 2001, he made his debut for Hampshire's 2nd XI, and in the following season made his debut for the county. For five years, he played in a few games, then in 2008 came the breakthrough, with his county cap and 67 wickets at 24.76, including 8-46 at Taunton, which remained his best figures. Over seven seasons he was an important member of Hampshire's first-class attack, in 2010, taking six wickets in a key game at Canterbury, helping Hampshire to avoid relegation. In 2011, his one year of less frequent appearances, Hampshire were demoted, then in 2014 he took 47 wickets at 25.85, including 6-48 at Cardiff, on the day that Hampshire clinched the Division Two title. For much of his career, Hampshire enjoyed greatest success in the 'white ball' formats, with trophies in 2005, 2009, 2010, & 2012 (two) but these occasions were denied to him, as he played in just 34 limited-overs and two T20 matches. Sadly, after some years without that fixture, in 2015, Hampshire went to Lord's to play Middlesex in a Championship fixture but he was omitted and in the following year the fixture was switched to Northwood. It was his final county match, and he never got to play at 'Headquarters'. He played in 127 first-class matches for Hampshire and took 380 wickets at 31.61, and while he scored just one first-class half-century, that innings of 51 v Gloucestershire at the Ageas Bowl in 2014, came in a partnership of 115 with David Balcombe – the highest ever for the county by their numbers 10 & 11 batsmen. In 2010, elevated to number 10, he scored 42, accompanying Sean Ervine in a partnership of 230 v Somerset. He was always a very popular and intelligent player, and has moved naturally into coaching with the task of bringing through a new generation of Hampshire cricketers.

Topley, Reece James William (540) born Ipswich 12.2.1994. Left-arm pace bowler Topley played for his father's county, Essex from 2011-2015 before joining Hampshire in 2016. He made his debut for them v Warwickshire and seemed to start well, recording his highest score (15) but suffered a hand injury and could not bowl. He then developed a back problem, and played no more first-class cricket for a year. After two matches early in 2017, he was injured again, and in 2018, decided to play only in 'white ball' cricket. He played in six Royal London Cup matches including the semi-final, taking seven wickets, but was frustrated when Dale Steyn was preferred for the Final. He had by then played in three 50-over matches for the England Lions but two days after the Final he played again and broke down after four overs, bringing his season to an end. He left Hampshire at the end of the season. During his three-year Hampshire career he played in three first-class matches (two wickets), 11 limited-overs matches (16 wickets), and seven T20s (seven wickets). While with Essex, he took 16 wickets for England in ten ODIs.

Toynbee, Geoffrey Percy Robert (171, Amateur) born London, 18.5.1885, killed in action, Belgium 15.11.1914. Renshaw (2014) reports that he played in the Winchester XI, scored many runs at Sandhurst and also in military matches including a century in both innings in a match at Aldershot. He played one first-class match for the MCC, and two for Hampshire in 1912, but scored just 18 first-class runs.

Toyne, Stanley Mease (124, Amateur) born Bournemouth 13.6.1881, died Hertfordshire 22.2.1962. He went to Oxford University but played in no first-class cricket. He played for Hampshire v Yorkshire at Bournemouth in 1905, scoring 1 & 9, and 23 years later played a first-class match for MCC v Ireland. His nephew HD Hake also played for Hampshire. Toyne was a schoolmaster and published historian.

Tremlett, Christopher Timothy ('Chris') (451) born Southampton 2.9.1981. Pace bowler Chris Tremlett was the son of Hampshire's TM Tremlett (below), and the grandson of MF Tremlett (Somerset & England). Hampshire have a poor record of producing their own fast bowlers and Chris Tremlett is probably the finest, although his Hampshire career never quite fulfilled the considerable promise of his early years. He played in Hampshire's age-group sides, for England under-19s and in the Southern League with Hursley Park. In July 2000, age 18, he made his first-class debut v New Zealand 'A' at Portsmouth, took a wicket with his first ball, and returned figures of 13-6-16-4. One year later he made his Championship debut and took 20 wickets that season, plus 22 in limited-overs matches. From that point, he was usually a regular choice for Hampshire, although this was often a matter of fitness, as he never played in more than 11 first-class matches in a season until 2008, when there were 13. In 10 seasons with Hampshire, he played in 84 matches, taking 264 wickets at 28.55, on seven occasions taking five or more wickets in an innings, with a best of 6-44 v Sussex at Hove in 2005. In that year, he took a 'hat-trick' at Trent Bridge, and was also a member of the Hampshire side that won the C&G Trophy, and he was at Lord's again for a second trophy in 2009. In 2005, he took 48 first-class and 35 limited-overs wickets, in both cases his best season returns, and after this he played far less in the shorter forms – at Hampshire relatively little in the T20. In that season, he also played for England for the first time in ODIs – there would 15 such games and 15 wickets, and two years later, during the winter's World Championship, he played in his one IT20. Most significantly however, he made his Test Match debut v India at Lord's in 2007, playing in all three Tests, although it was more than three years when his next opportunity came, on the tour of Australia, where in the fifth Test at Sydney he took 3-79, including the final wicket, as England won the 'Ashes'. In the following summer, he played in the series v Sri Lanka, and in the inaugural Test Match at the Rose

Bowl he won the 'Man of the Match' award for his 6-48, although by then he had left Hampshire, and from 2010, played for Surrey. In total, he played in 12 Test Matches, over seven years and took 53 wickets at 27.00. He was a useful lower-order batsman averaging just below 18 in first-class cricket with a best of 90. He retired at the end of the 2015 season.

Tremlett, Timothy Maurice (376) born Wellington, Somerset 26.7.1956. His father played for England and captained Somerset, where Tim Tremlett was born, but the family moved to Hampshire, and he played for the 2nd XI in 1973, just before his 17th birthday. He was principally a medium-fast bowler in his early career, and in July 1976, made his first-class debut at Hove. It would be another year before his next Championship game, at Cardiff, but he began appearing in Hampshire's limited-overs sides, and in 1978, as the departures of Richards and Roberts disrupted Hampshire's season, he held his place in the side, playing in the match v Middlesex at Bournemouth as Hampshire clinched their second Sunday League title. When Richard Gilliat retired and the promising David Rock departed, Tremlett sometimes stood in as an opening batsman, in the early 1980s, and while he was predominantly a very fine county bowler, his Hampshire career brought 3,815 first-class runs at 21.31 with 18 half-centuries and one century, 102*, returning to Taunton in 1985, where he shared with Kevan James what was then Hampshire's record eighth-wicket partnership of 227. In 1980 he 'carried his bat' with 70* v Leicestershire at Southampton.

But it is for his bowling that he will be remembered, particularly and mostly as first-change in the 1980's attack led by Marshall, in the decade when covered pitches became the norm. Had he bowled 20 or 30 years earlier he might well have opened regularly and taken considerably more wickets, but his record was nonetheless admirable. In a reduced programme of Championship matches he took 63 in 1983, followed by 71, 75, 43, and 72 in successive seasons. The latter was 1986 when his accuracy and control also made him Hampshire's leading bowler as they won their second Sunday League title – he took 26 wickets at 18.00. In 1988, he suffered injury problems which would eventually curtail his career, and meant he missed Hampshire's first Lord's Final. By the next Final, he had joined and then succeeded Peter Sainsbury as Hampshire's coach, before moving to Director of Cricket, and he is still at the club, after 45 years, in his capacity as Cricket Secretary. He took 445 first-class wickets for Hampshire at 23.44, and 252 in limited-overs matches, and he won selection on tours with the England Counties and 'B' sides – the equivalent of today's Lions. He was known as 'Trooper', a reference to his immaculate appearance, and bearing, but he has too a mischievous side, and a sense of humour which often surfaced in the dressing room.

Tubb, Samson (or Sampson) (Pre '95) born Broughton, Hants 11.10.1840, died Portsmouth 27.1.1891. He played for Devon and Wiltshire, then in ten matches for Hampshire from 1864-1867. He scored 170 runs with a best of 24*, and took 37 wickets at 20.16, including 7-32 v Surrey at the Antelope in 1865; the Hampshire club's first victory in their second season, after six successive defeats. He appeared in nine-first-class matches for the Players of Hampshire the United South of England XI, and other sides.

Tuck, James Jeffry (Pre '95) born Ringwood 3.6.1853, died Devizes 20.1.1918. He played for Aldershot Division in the 1870s, and for Hampshire in nine matches from 1877-1882, scoring 176 runs and taking two wickets. He suffered a football injury in the winter of 1882/3 and played no more cricket, but became an umpire from 1886-1899.

Tulk, Derek Thomas (335) born Southampton 21.4.1934. In the early 1950s, medium-pace bowler Derek Tulk played at Taunton's School, Southampton, and subsequently for Old Tauntonians CC. From 1956-1958, he played for Hampshire 2nd XI and in county friendly matches, and in June 1956, he made his first-class debut v Gloucestershire at Southampton. In the following year played in one first-class match v Cambridge University at Bournemouth. With the exception of one 2nd XI Championship match for the county a decade later, he returned to local cricket, playing into the late 1980s with OTs and the Forty Club. His sons and grandson all played local cricket, and son Ian has worked at the Ageas Bowl for some years.

Turner, David Roy (354) born Corsham, Wilts 5.2.1949. David Turner played for Hampshire in 24 consecutive seasons, which, with the impact of the First World War on certain players, is the longest unbroken run in their history. He is also the only Hampshire cricketer to have been in sides that won the Championship, Sunday League and a Lord's Final. Hampshire were not the only county who sought to sign the promising young left-hander but he came to the county, making his first-class debut in August 1966, when just 17. He was not a regular member of the side in the early seasons, but in August 1969, scored 181* at the Oval, still Hampshire's highest maiden century in a Championship match. In the next two seasons, he passed 1,000 runs with more centuries, and in mid-May, 1972, he impressed the touring Australians, taking 131 off their attack, including Lillee, at Southampton. He was spoken of as a Test prospect, but a few weeks later at Basingstoke retired hurt with an eye injury from a short ball, which seemed to dent his confidence. He was nonetheless back in the side as an ever-present with 1,000 runs as Hampshire won the title in 1973 – from then until he retired in 1989, he continued to score runs in both formats and by the end he had passed 1,000 runs in nine seasons. With the covering of pitches in his later years, his average rose into the 40s, and to 49.18 in his 'Indian Summer' of 1987 – for Hampshire he finished with 18,683 first-class runs and 27 centuries. He scored almost 10,000 limited-overs runs for Hampshire, and fittingly was at the wicket with his captain when Hampshire won their first Lord's Final in 1988. He was also a very fine out-fielder with a fierce accurate throw, and while he was no bowler, in the 1960s, when the authorities briefly revived single-wicket competitions among county cricketers, he, rather than Hampshire's all-rounders or big-hitting bowlers, was the county's champion in 1967 & 1968. In addition, in 1981, he took a hat-trick in a limited-overs 'Lambert & Butler's' tournament. He retired to take over the family shoe business, back home in Wiltshire.

Turner, Francis Gordon (167, Amateur) born London 1.3.1890, died Deal, Kent 21.11.1979. He was a batsman and leg-break bowler who went to Westminster School and Cambridge University, but played no cricket there. He played once for Hampshire v Cambridge University in 1912, scoring 14. He played in a number of non-first-class matches for MCC.

Turner, Ian John (411) born Denmead, Hants 18.7.1968. Ian Turner was a Hambledon cricketer; his father 'Topsy' was a leading player with the club for many years, and Ian played for them for decades, sometimes as captain. Ian played for Hampshire 2nd XI from 1988-1993, making his first-class debut v Glamorgan at Southampton in 1989. His best season was 1992 when he took 19 wickets, including 5-81 v Essex at Chelmsford, but there was competition for spin bowling places at this time with Maru, Udal and Flint also playing. Turner played fewer games in 1993, and his career ended with 54 first-class wickets at 36.38. He played in 17 limited-overs matches, taking 16 wickets.

U

Ubsdell, George (Pre '95) born Southampton, 4.4.1845, died Liverpool 15.10.1905. Wicketkeeper Ubsdell played in 15 matches for Hampshire from 1864-1870. His batting record was modest (average 6.80), although with Henry Holmes, he shared in Hampshire's first century partnership v Sussex at Hove in 1864. As a wicketkeeper his 17 dismissals, included no fewer than 13 stumpings – including a county record of five in one innings v Surrey at the Antelope. Edwards (2014) tells us that this was the first such instance, and has only been equalled twice since – extraordinarily it was Ubsdell's first match behind the stumps. In the early 1870s, when Hampshire played no first-class matches, he was a professional at various clubs in Surrey, Kent, Exeter and Liverpool. He moved to Liverpool, and was Head Groundsman at Liverpool CC's ground at Aigburth.

Udal, Shaun David (409) born Cove, Hants 18.3.1969. Off-spinner Shaun Udal was one of Hampshire's finest Hampshire-born, home-grown cricketers. He came from a cricketing family and played for Hampshire Colts and 2nd XI from 1987. In 1989, he made his debut in the Championship and limited-overs matches, and in the following season he took 22 wickets in seven first-class games, plus 32 in 26 limited-overs matches, although it was not until 1992 that he played regularly in the Championship. He played in Hampshire's two Lord's trophy-winning sides in 1991 & 1992, while in 1992 he took 8-50 v Sussex at Southampton, which remained his best first-class figures. In four domestic first-class seasons, 1992-1995, he took 256 wickets, plus 105 in limited-overs, after which for a few years, his figures declined a little, with the exception of 39 limited-overs wickets at 22.56 in 1997. Between 1994 & 1995, he was in the England squad for the first Test after South Africa's re-admittance, but was omitted from the final XI, and toured Australia without winning a 'cap', although he had played in ten ODIs, taking eight wickets, after which it seemed his international hopes had gone.

He was a very useful late middle-order batsman, with a number of half-centuries, and his best score of 117* v Warwickshire at Southampton in 1997. In the new millennium, he found himself sometimes competing for a place with Shane Warne, but took wickets regularly again, particularly in 2005, when, with Warne playing in the 'Ashes' series, there were 44 first-class and 31 in limited-overs matches, and at Lord's in the C&G Final, deputising for Warne, he became the first Hampshire-born player to captain the county to a Trophy. In the following winter of 2005/6, he was selected to tour Pakistan and India with England, and when he played in three Tests in Pakistan, taking three wickets, he was the first Hampshire-born, Hampshire player to represent England for well over a century (AJL Hill). He was not selected in India until the third and final Test, when he took 1-53, and, then, with India chasing 313 to win, 4-14, as they were dismissed for 100. It was his last international appearance but a fine way to finish. He retired from Hampshire at the end of the 2007 season, having played in 250 first-class matches with 6,496 runs and 708 wickets – the latter placing him 11th in Hampshire's all-time list – to which he added, 2,503 limited-overs runs and 407 wickets, and 25 T20 wickets – he is one of only ten men to have taken more than 1,000 wickets in all forms for Hampshire. He returned to county cricket for three years with Middlesex, and in 2008 was in their side at the Rose Bowl, as they won the T20 Final. He played for Berkshire in the Minor Counties, and has worked for Sky Sports on their commentary teams.

Underdown, George (Pre '95, Amateur) born Petersfield 12.5.1859, died Petersfield 29.5.1895. He made his first-class debut for the United XI v the Australians at Chichester in June 1882, scoring 4 & 0 in a large innings defeat. Six weeks later he made his Hampshire debut principally as a batsman, and appeared in nine first-class matches from 1882-1885, scoring 227 runs at 14.18 with one half-century, 63 v Somerset, on county debut.

Utley, Father Richard Peter Hugh OBE (244, Amateur) born Havant 11.2.1906, died Ampleforth, Yorkshire 28.8.1968. He was a very effective fast bowler who in 1927 & 1928 played first-class cricket for the Gentlemen, the RAF and, in 27 matches, for Hampshire. He scored few runs (average 6.56) but took 79 wickets for the county at 26.32. In 1927, he took 6-71 v Essex in 1927, and in the following year 12-140 in the match v Warwickshire at Bournemouth, including wickets with the third and fourth balls of the match. He also took 6-40 v Middlesex at Lord's. He was then a 22-year-old Pilot Officer in the RAF, with the chance of more county cricket ahead, but since being educated at Ampleforth he had wanted to take holy orders and this he did – returning eventually to his old school as a master. He played no more county cricket, although he ran cricket at the school, eventually with Stuart Boyes as coach, and played in minor matches throughout his life.

V

Vaas, Warnakulasuriya Patabendige Ushantha Joseph, Chaminda (468) born Mattumagala, Sri Lanka 27.1.1974. He was a left-arm pace bowler, who played in all formats for Sri Lanka, taking 355 wickets in 111 Tests, and 399 ODI wickets. In 2003, he played for Hampshire in three first-class matches, taking eight wickets at 38.75, and in eight limited-overs games he took nine wickets. In England, he played also for Middlesex, Northamptonshire and Worcestershire.

van der Gucht, Charles Graham ('Charlie') (447) born London 14.1.1980. He was a slow-left-arm bowler who attended Radley College and played first-class cricket for Durham University. He played in limited-overs and Minor Counties cricket for the Hampshire Cricket Board, and in 2000 played one first-class match for Hampshire v the Zimbabweans, taking 3-75. He was badly injured in a road accident and never regained sufficient fitness to play first-class cricket successfully – his final 2nd XI match was in July 2003. He played subsequently for Radley Rangers and MCC.

Vince, James Michael (499) born Cuckfield, Sussex 14 March 1991. When James Vince finally retires, he will be remembered as one of the most elegant batsmen to have played for Hampshire, perhaps the most elegant ever to have come through the county's age group and 2nd XI sides. Whether he will be remembered as one of the greatest Hampshire batsmen remains to be seen, even nine years after his debut, but since he is still in his mid-twenties, it remains a possibility. At the end of the 2018 season, he had scored 8,256 first-class runs for Hampshire at a fraction under 40, with 22 centuries, some of the highest class. Late in 2010, he and Adams set a (then) partnership record v Yorkshire at Scarborough with 19-year-old Vince contributing 180, his maiden century. There were nine more in the next three years, and four in the promotion year of 2014, including 240 v Essex in a victory that would be crucial at the season's end. In that second division season, he scored 1,525 runs at 61.00, but in the first three seasons in the higher division, he averaged in the low thirties with just five centuries, before in 2018 he came very close to reaching four figures again and perhaps only missed out in a difficult late season run after he suffered a very unpleasant bout of food poisoning.

As a captain, he led the T20 side in 2014, added the limited-overs side in 2015, and became club captain in 2016, although in 2017, George Bailey took over in the Championship. By this time, Vince was being selected at times for England in all three formats, albeit with mixed results. At the conclusion of his international appearances following the winter of 2017/18 he had played in 13 Tests with a best of 83 in Australia, and a final innings of 76 v New Zealand, and an average of 24.90. There were also five LOIs with one half-century, and seven IT20s at an average of 27.71. As club captain, he had a difficult first season, which concluded with him being run out for 92 in the defeat v Durham that seemed to condemn Hampshire to relegation. They were reprieved, but in 2017 under Bailey, they struggled – and survived – again - thanks not least to a last day obdurate innings by Vince. They were not one of the stronger sides in 2018, but they did at least avoid final day traumas. Following the double of 2012, they made little impact in the longer form of 'white ball' cricket for a few years, although often reaching T20 Finals Day. In the 2017 semi-final, Vince top-scored with 56 from 50 balls but Hampshire fell short again. Whatever Hampshire's fortunes In the shorter forms, Vince's performances have been of the highest quality; in 2017, leading from the front, he scored 476 limited-overs runs at 68.00, adding 542 runs in the T20 at 38.71 and his 50-overs score of 178 v Glamorgan at the Ageas Bowl took him beyond Gordon Greenidge as the highest limited-overs innings for Hampshire. Then in 2018 he had his first experience of leading Hampshire to a trophy, scoring over 500 runs in the Royal London Cup with two centuries including a superb 171 in the semi-final v Yorkshire. Although principally a batsman, he bowls occasional medium pace, with a few wickets in each format, and has even kept wicket in an emergency.

Voges Adam Charles (T20) born Western Australia 4.10.1979. Batsman Adam Voges played in all three formats for Australia, and in England for Nottinghamshire and Middlesex. In 2007, he played in seven T20 matches for Hampshire, scoring 106 runs at 17.66 with a best of 66* in a rain-reduced match v Sussex at the Rose Bowl, despite which Sussex won by nine wickets.

W

Wainwright, David John (544) born Pontefract, Yorkshire 21.3.1985. He was a slow-left-arm bowler who played for Yorkshire and Derbyshire. Towards the end of the 2016 season, having retired, and with Hampshire fighting to avoid relegation, he was called into the Hampshire side for one Championship match at Taunton. He scored 35* and took 2-112.

Waldron, Alan Noel Edwin (313, Amateur) born Southsea, Portsmouth 23.12.1920, died Richmond, Surrey, 2.9.1999. He was an Army officer, and prisoner-of-war in Germany from 1942. In June 1948, he played in two first-class friendly matches for Hampshire at a week in Aldershot, and a few weeks later played twice for the Combined Services against county sides. For Hampshire, he scored 52 against the Combined Services, and took three wickets overall. He was awarded the MC in November 1945.

Walker, Clifford ('Cliff') (316) born Huddersfield, 27.6.1919, died Huddersfield 3.12.1992. He was a batsman and medium-pace bowler who played for his native Yorkshire in 1947 & 1948, scoring 91 v Hampshire in 1947. In 1949, he moved to Hampshire and played there until early in 1954 when following a family bereavement, he asked to be released from his contract to return home to work in the family's cinema business. From 1949-1951 and in 1953, he passed 1,000 runs and scored eight centuries with a best of 150* v Gloucestershire in 1953 at Bristol, sharing a partnership of 246 with Alan Rayment. He took 51 first-class wickets, occasionally opening the bowling, with a best of 5-40 v Combined Services in 1949.

Walker, Donald Frederick ('Hooky') (281) born London 15.8.1912, killed in RAF bomber flight over Holland 18.6.1941. He was a batsman who played at King's College School, Wimbledon and for Surrey 2nd XI in the Minor Counties Championship in 1933. He joined the RAF as a Pilot Officer and played for them, but his home was in Bournemouth and he played for Hampshire Club & Ground in 1936. In May 1937, he made his first-class debut for Hampshire at Old Trafford, and thereafter played regularly for three seasons before first-class cricket ceased. He passed 900 runs in the first two seasons and scored his maiden century v Sussex at Portsmouth in 1937, in the process sharing Hampshire's record 5th wicket partnership with Gerry Hill, which still stands. In 1939, he passed 1,000 runs at 28.72 and added three more centuries, including his best of 147 at Trent Bridge. John Arlott (1957) called him a "lively, amusing" man whose "chief merit as a batsman lay in his immense speed of footwork". He was a fine slip-fielder and in the winter, was a squash professional in Bournemouth. He was also a good rugby player who captained Dorset, and an RAF side.

Walkinshaw, Frank (Pre '95, Amateur) born Hong Kong, 28.2.1861, died Bramley, Hants 14.7.1934. He played in three matches for Hampshire in 1885, scoring 15 runs. After Hampshire lost their first-class status he continued to play for them, and for the MCC and other sides.

Wallace, Nesbit Willoughby (Pre '95, Amateur) born Nova Scotia, Canada 20.4.1839, died Guildford 31.7.1931. He played for the Gentleman of the South in 1861, and Gloucestershire in 1871, before playing in two first-class matches for Hampshire in 1884, scoring 57 runs in four innings. In the following season, he played in his final first-class match for MCC against Hampshire. In minor cricket, he played for many sides, over 40 years, including Portsmouth Borough, the Green Jackets, MCC, Combined Services and the Gentlemen of Hampshire.

Walton, Francis (Pre '95, Amateur) born England 1832, died Surbiton, Surrey 14.7.1871, we have no further information about his birth. He played in three matches for Hampshire, one each in 1864, 1865 & 1866, scoring 55 runs and taking six wickets, including 3-48 v Middlesex on debut at Islington. He played regularly for the Gentlemen of Hampshire.

Ward, Albert Paine (214) born Highgate 9.11.1896, died Jersey 5.3.1979. He was a fast bowler who played v Lancashire at Southampton in 1921, scoring 6 & 5* and taking 0-29 & 1-28.

Ward, Rev. Charles Gordon (40, Amateur) born Braughing, Hertfordshire 23.9.1875, died South Ormsby Hall, Lincs 27.6.1954. He was a batsman from a cricketing family, who made his first-class debut for Hampshire in May 1897, then played three more games that year in August. He played a few more matches in each of the next three years but with little success – in 14 matches he scored 186 runs at 8.08 with a best of 30, and took two wickets at 67.50. He played Minor Counties cricket subsequently for Lincolnshire and Hertfordshire.

Ward, Herbert Foster (10, Amateur) born London 24.3.1873, died Winchester 6.6.1897. He played for Hertfordshire in the early 1890s, and was a regular member of the Hampshire side in their first two years in the County Championship, playing in their first match at Taunton where he (71) and Bacon added 131 in the follow-on, setting Somerset a target that proved beyond them. In 33 matches, he scored 1,344 runs at 22.03 with two centuries and a best of 113 v Derbyshire at Southampton in 1896, and took 19 wickets, all in 1896, at just under 30 each, including 4-17 v Sussex at Hove. In late May 1897, he played v Lancashire at Southampton, scoring 40 & 39 but was taken ill and died age 24, two weeks later. Some reports have suggested he was affected by sun-stroke, but it was typhoid fever.

Ward, John (Pre '95, Amateur) we have no information about his birth or death. He was a fast, round-arm bowler, who played in one match for Hampshire v Kent at Canterbury in 1877, scoring 14 runs and taking 0-77.

Ward, Merrick de Sampajo Cecil (247, Amateur) born Belgravia, London 15.7.1908, died Bath 13.2.1981. He went to Eton, where he played in the XI in 1926 & 1927 and also in representative school games at Lord's. He played in five matches for Hampshire in 1927-1929, scoring 141 runs at 15.66 with a best of 48 v Kent in 1928, when he captained Hampshire in the absence of Tennyson, days before his twentieth birthday.

Warne, Shane (448) born Victoria, Australia 13 September 1969. Leg-break and googly bowler Shane Warne was quite simply one of the greatest bowlers the world has known, and one of the great cricket 'characters' – although this led sometimes to difficulties with the authorities. He was also a charismatic and highly influential captain at Hampshire as they rebuilt in the first decade of the new century and from 2004, when he took over and led them to promotion they enjoyed eight seasons of regular successes, after a gap of 13 years. It is an odd fact that while Warne is rightly credited with contributing so much to the achievements of those teams and players, he never actually captained Hampshire to a trophy. He came closest in 2005, when he spent much of the summer preoccupied with the matter of an Ashes Test series in England, while his team won a Lord's Final under his deputy, Shaun Udal. When he returned to the Championship team he took them to second place, but was left fuming when a Kent declaration in bad weather gave Nottinghamshire the opportunity to win the match and the title, with one game remaining. Coincidentally, that final game was between the top two at the Rose Bowl where Hampshire posted their record total and hammered the new Champions by an innings.

The initial signing of Warne was a coup for the old Members Committee, initiated during the 1999 World Cup, and he arrived in 2000 having been named by *Wisden* as one of the Five Cricketers of the (20th) Century. He began by helping Hampshire to the B&H quarter finals but they were well beaten in Cardiff and while Warne took first-class wickets consistently – 70 at 23.14 – the batting failed too often, Hampshire were relegated, and Warne returned to Australia and Test cricket. But the new Chairman Rod Bransgrove persuaded Warne to return as captain in 2003, until a world-wide, one-year ban prevented that, and he came finally in 2004, after which, when international calls permitted, he spent four years at Hampshire, not merely taking wickets and captaining the side, but doing so in the most entertaining manner, while initiating a significant cultural shift at Hampshire. In his five seasons, he played in 66 first-class matches for the county, scoring just over 2,000 runs, including the only first-class centuries of his career, and he took 276 first-class wickets at 25.58; 18 times taking five or more wickets in an innings. There were also 71 limited-overs matches, with 120 wickets at just 19.72 each, although he tended to avoid the new T20, playing just twice.

As a captain, he sometimes wore his emotions on his sleeve which translated into delight and disapproval. He was happy to have nine slips and gullies or to bowl 'doubtful' deliveries if he found opposing teams resisting the pursuit of victory and entertainment, but while this mischievous approach amused spectators, it could disguise the fact that he was one of the most intelligent cricketers, and quite brilliant when working with youngsters who showed promise. Despite his huge international successes, with over 700 Test Match wickets, his commitment to Hampshire was never in doubt. One of his difficulties with the authorities led to him losing the Australian vice-captaincy and he was never appointed captain of his country. Most who saw him in action at Hampshire remember him with great fondness, and would subscribe to the common view that he was the finest captain that Australia never had.

Wasim Akram (462) born Pakistan 3.6.1966. He played for Pakistan in 104 Test Matches and 356 ODIs, and in England for Lancashire from 1988-1998. His final matches for Pakistan were in the 2002/3 season, but in the following summer he joined Hampshire as a late replacement for the suspended Shane Warne. In the event, he played in just five first-class matches for Hampshire, plus nine limited-overs and all five T20s in that competition's first season, but he left before the season ended.

Wassell, Alan Robert (339) born Fareham 15.4.1940. He was a slow-left-arm bowler who first played for Hampshire's 2nd XI age 16 in 1956, then in 1957 & 1958 in first-class matches v Cambridge University and at the end of the latter season, when Hampshire finished runners-up, he made his Championship debut v Derbyshire at Bournemouth. There were a few more games in 1959 & 1960, then in June 1961 he came into the side and held his place as Hampshire clinched the title for the first time, taking 66 wickets in all matches at 25.06, with a best of 7-87 (and 5-76) v Surrey at Bournemouth, and on three other occasions taking five wickets in an innings, including the second day of the title-winning match v Derbyshire at Bournemouth. In that famous match he bowled 93.3 overs, or 561 balls, which remains a Hampshire match record. He was similarly effective in 1962 & 1963, when he was capped, with 130 wickets at a similar average, but in 1964 he played fewer matches and took fewer wickets, as Bob Cottam came into the side to bowl alongside Shackleton & White, with Peter Sainsbury a regular choice for his all-round abilities. By 1965, those four men bowled 80% of Hampshire's first-class overs, and while Wassell bowled more than the other young spinners, Wheatley, Caple and Keith, their opportunities were limited. He took 29 wickets, including a best of 6-54 v Somerset at Bournemouth, and eight in the match v the South Africans, but in 1966 he played in just three matches, and only one in the Championship, in August, and took just five wickets, as the younger spinners were given more opportunities. Hampshire, seeking to make economies, released Wassell at the age of just 26. In 121 matches, he scored 1,207 runs with one half-century v Lancashire in 1962, and took 317 wickets at 27.05. He still played some matches for Hampshire 2nd XI, and for Gosport for many years, including the 1980 Club Championship Final v Moseley at Lord's, as well as representative matches for Southern League sides.

Watson, Arthur Lacon (Pre '95, Amateur) born Isle of Wight, 27.8.1866, died 28.6.1955. He went to Winchester College and Cambridge University where he played in one first-class match in 1888. Three years earlier, he played for Hampshire against Sussex at Southampton, scoring 22 & 0. He continued to play for Hampshire after that, and for MCC, in non-first-class matches.

Watson, Ian Ronald (372) born Teddington, Middlesex 9.6.1947. Opening batsman Watson holds a record that might be unique in English first-class cricket; he played in just three first-class matches for three different county sides – although none in the Championship. In 1969, he played for Middlesex v Oxford University, in 1971, for Northamptonshire against the same opponents, and in 1973, for Hampshire v the West Indians at Southampton. He played for many years for Deanery and in Southern League representative sides, and more recently for Hursley Park. In the Hampshire Cricket Society Newsletter for March 2018, Alan Edwards reported that Watson, age 70, scored a century for Hursley Park 4th XI in 2017, and in the following winter represented England's Over-70 side v the Australians in the first 'Test'.

Watson, Shane Robert (472) born Queensland, Australia, 17.6.1981. All-rounder Watson represented Australia in all three formats, playing in 59 Test Matches. He played for many domestic sides around the world, including Hampshire in 2004 & 2005. He made his first-class debut v Somerset at the Rose Bowl, scoring 112* – one of six debutant centurions for Hampshire, although all had played first-class cricket previously elsewhere. In 2005, he scored 203* v Warwickshire at the Rose Bowl. He played two limited-overs games for Hampshire in 2004, then in 2005, began with 132, leading an impressive run chase in a C&G quarter-final at the Oval, and was a member of the side that won that competition v Warwickshire at Lord's, scoring 25 and taking 3-34. He played in five T20 matches for Hampshire in 2004 and scored 97* in the last of them, v Kent at the Rose Bowl

Watts, Alfred William (Pre '95, Amateur) born Southampton 5.4.1859 we have no definite information about his date or place of death but it might be Christchurch, 9.1949. He played for the Gentlemen of Hampshire in 1879 and St Luke's (Southampton) v the Australians in 1880. In 1882, he played twice for Hampshire, v Somerset and MCC, scoring 26 runs at 8.66, and taking two wickets at 21.00. In 1886, he played in a non-first-class match for Hampshire v Norfolk.

Weatherley, Joe James (539) born Winchester 19.1.1997. He is a batsman and occasional off-break bowler, who played for Hampshire's age group sides, the Academy, and the 2nd XI from 2014. He played for England under-19s in the following winter, and in 2015, made his first-class debut v Cardiff University, scoring 83 – one of the higher scores for Hampshire on first-class debut. A few weeks later he made his Championship debut in Division One v Middlesex at Northwood, then in 2016 went on loan to Kent, where he played in five Championship matches, with a best score of 36. He returned to Hampshire, and in September 2017, he played in three further Championship matches. In 2018 he reached three figures in the Championship for the first time (126*) at Old Trafford, and also in the Royal London Cup v Kent at the Ageas Bowl. For Hampshire, to the end of 2018, he has played in 18 first-class matches, 19 limited-overs and 11 in the T20 competition with a best of 43 v Glamorgan at the Ageas Bowl in 2016. He plays for St Cross in the Southern League.

Weaver, Phillip Humphrey Peter (288, Amateur) born Kaimpong, India, 12.3.1912, died Poole, Dorset 28.6.1991. He went to King's School, Bruton, and played in two matches for Hampshire in 1938, scoring 55 runs in three innings. He played also for the Club & Ground, 2nd XI and Bournemouth CC. He played hockey for England.

Webb, Arthur Stuart (17) born Bridge, Kent 6.8.1868, died Briton Ferry, Wales 3.12.1952. He was a batsman and occasional medium-pace bowler, who played for Hampshire regularly between 1895-1904. His best season was in 1901, when he passed 1,000 runs at 34.00, with nine half-centuries. He scored two centuries in his career, with a best of 162* v Surrey at Southampton in 1904. For Hampshire, there were 5,475 runs in 149 first-class matches and 22 wickets. He played in Wales subsequently, as an amateur, including his last first-class match, which was for South Wales v the South Africans in 1912.

Webb, Dr Hubert Eustace (333, Amateur) born Rajasthan, India 30.5.1927, died 8.11.2010 (place of death unknown). He was a batsman who went to Winchester College and Oxford University, where he played from 1946-1948, winning his 'blue' in the final year, when he scored 145 in the victorious side who won by an innings - his score was then the eighth highest for either side in the 'Variety' Match since 1919. In 1954, he played in a number of matches for the Army, and also for Hampshire in one match against his old University, scoring 16 & 11.

Whalley-Tooker, Edward (Pre '95, Amateur) born Wem, Shropshire 15.1.1863, died Hambledon 23.11.1940. He went to Eton, without playing in the XI, and was a right-handed batsman who played twice for Hampshire v Sussex, at the Antelope in 1883, and at Hove two years later, scoring 14 runs in four innings. In 1908, he played in a third and final first-class match for Hambledon v England, in the only match of that status played on Broadhalfpenny Down. He played a central role in the Hambledon Club, from his election as captain in 1896, and in the renovation of the Hambledon ground which had been ploughed for farming in the nineteenth century. Jenkinson (2000) noted that he remained influential in the famous club for 40 years, and that "there was little that went on in and around Hambledon in which (he) was not involved".

Wheal, Bradley Thomas James ('Brad') (533) born Durban, South Africa 28.8.1996. Pace bowler Brad Wheal was brought to England by Hampshire's then coach Dale Benkenstein in 2015, and he made his debut that season in first-class cricket, with limited-overs and T20 matches in the following year. Through his mother he has a qualification for Scotland and has represented them since the winter of 2015/16. He suffered injury problems in the 2018 season, at the end of which he had played in 25 first-class matches for Hampshire, with 56 wickets including a best of 6-51 v Nottinghamshire at Trent Bridge in 2016. He has taken 18 limited-overs wickets for the county and another six in the T20. In 2015, he played Southern League cricket for Havant.

Wheater, Adam Jack Aubrey (515) born Leytonstone, Essex 13.2.1990. Wheater is a wicketkeeper batsman who played for England under-19s, and for Essex where in a Championship match against Hampshire in 2012, he scored 98 from 111 balls to take Essex within three runs of winning the game. With his way into the Essex side blocked by James Foster he joined Hampshire, replacing Michael Bates – not always a popular choice among supporters, yet he performed effectively. In 56 first-class matches, he scored 2,760 runs at 36.80, with seven centuries, and there were two more at a similar average in limited-overs games. But after more than a century of Hampshire having regular long-serving wicketkeepers, the retirement of Pothas led to a period of frequent changes, and by 2016, Wheater found himself playing as a batsman, while McManus came into the side as wicketkeeper. Before the end of that season he returned to Essex.

Wheatley, Keith James (352) born Guildford 20.1.1946. All-rounder Wheatley was an off-break bowler who played at Lord Wandsworth College, in north Hampshire and played his first match for Hampshire's 2nd XI in September 1962, age 16. He played regularly from 1963, and in July 1965 made his first-class debut in a week at Bournemouth. He played quite regularly in 1966 when the authorities introduced a limit in a number of matches of 65 overs in each first innings. The consequence for Wheatley was that while playing in 10 of the 12 restricted matches, he batted just five times and never bowled in a first innings. Some games had ludicrous conclusions – for example, Hampshire dismissed Glamorgan for 167, had their innings closed at 191-5, yet lost by 45 runs (Wheatley 3-30). He played in 20 matches in 1967, scoring his first two (of six) half-centuries and while there were fewer matches in 1968, he took 4-1 v Glamorgan at Southampton. This was one of six occasions, when he took four wickets in an innings, but never five, while his highest score of 79* came in 1969 v Kent at Maidstone. He played in ten limited-overs matches, seven in 1970, but never bowled, and at the end of that season he left the club. Many years later, he succeeded Mike Barnard, in organising the annual reunion of Hampshire's players.

Wheeler, Walter Charles (Pre '95) born Isle of Wight 30.12.1841, died London 10.10.1907. He was a round-arm medium-pace bowler, lower-order batsman and good fielder who, in the 1860s, played for the Isle of Wight and Hampshire Colts, then in one match for Middlesex in 1873, five for Surrey in 1875, and three for Hampshire in 1878 & 1880. For the county, he scored 35 runs at 7.00, and took six wickets, all in one innings, with figures of 6-133 v Kent at Tunbridge Wells in 1878, in a total of 405. Kent won by an innings.

Whitaker, Paul Robert (425) born Keighley, Yorkshire 28.6.1973. He was a left-handed batsman and occasional off-break bowler, who was with Derbyshire from 1991 without playing first-class cricket, before he moved to Hampshire in 1994. He made his first-class debut in September of that year at Leicester, scoring 94 in the second innings, which remains the highest innings for Hampshire, by a player making his first-class debut. In the next two seasons, he played in 25 first-class matches, with an average just short of 30, and including his only century, 119 v Worcestershire at Southampton, but there were fewer games in the next two years and having played in New Zealand for Central Districts in 1995/6, he moved there. He scored 1,734 runs for Hampshire at 30.42 and took 13 wickets. In limited-overs matches, he played in 54 games with an average of 17.60 and a highest score of 97, also v Worcestershire at Southampton and he took 18 limited-overs wickets for the county.

Whitcher, William (Pre '95) born Emsworth, Hants 1832, died Southampton 9.3.1910. He played two matches for Hampshire, in 1864 & 1867, scoring 27 runs at 13.50 and taking 0-30. He played in various non-first-class matches, including for the East Hants Club v Australian Aborigines in Southsea in 1868.

White, David William (340) born Sutton Coldfield, Warwickshire 14.12.1935, died Pulborough, Sussex 1.8.2008. David White, always known as 'Butch', was the archetypal fast bowler in physique, attitude and performance. He played cricket for various Warwickshire sides in the early 1950s, then, while on National Service, was seen by Hampshire and invited for a trial in 1957, playing in friendly matches, mostly for the 2nd XI, and one first-class match v Cambridge University at Bournemouth, when he took 3-78. Fellow pace-bowler Malcolm Heath enjoyed his best season opposite Derek Shackleton in 1958, and Vic Cannings was still playing in his penultimate season, but White took 29 first-class wickets at 19.96, and a similar number in 1959, albeit more expensively on covered pitches in a hot summer. He established himself as Shackleton's opening partner in 1960 with 124 wickets at 19.10 and passed 100 again in 1961, contributing significantly to the Championship title success, including 7-61 v Nottinghamshire at Southampton. His batting was rarely as effective as it might have been, he batted like the tail-end fast bowler he was, but in one key victory v Gloucestershire at Portsmouth he hit a rapid 33* after Hampshire slumped from 146-4 to 162-8, and in the previous season he hit 28 runs in one over from Dan Piachaud of Oxford University. In his career, there were five half-centuries with a best of 58* v Essex at Portsmouth in 1963, and he liked that ground with its fast, hard pitches and the heaviest of rollers, taking 9-44 there v Leicestershire in 1963.

On their way to the title in 1961, Hampshire won another crucial game at Portsmouth in August. Following a frustrating draw v fellow challengers Middlesex, they met Sussex in the second match of the traditional 'week,' and very late on the second evening, in autumnal weather this game too was drifting, with Sussex on 179-4, almost 150 ahead. Then 'Butch' took a hat-trick, had a man dropped from the fourth ball, got him at the end of the over and Sussex closed on 179-8. They added one run the following morning – White 5-21 – and Hampshire won by six wickets. In the following season, he went to Hove for a second hat-trick, which might have expunged some of the bad feelings after he was called for throwing there in 1960 – the only occasion in his career, and a ludicrous consequence of a certain hysteria at the time.

With Tyson gone, and Trueman and Statham nearing the end, 'Butch' White should have been a serious candidate for Test selection but his only taste came in 1961/2 when he toured India and Pakistan, struggled unusually with injury, and felt he was not well-handled. He was only in his mid-twenties, but with four Test wickets at 29.75 his England career was over. This was at least to Hampshire's advantage as they went through the 1960s with their finest pace trio of Shackleton, White & Cottam. 'Butch', still recovering from the winter injury, took fewer wickets in 1962, but for the next seven seasons there were never less than 86, with 100 in a season four times, and only in the early 1970s did injury takes its toll and the figures decline. In 315 first-class matches for Hampshire he took 1,097 wickets at 23.36 – only five men have taken more – and on 56 occasions he took five or more in an innings. In 52 limited-overs matches, he took 90 wickets at under 20 each and an economy rate of 3.68. In 1972, he went to Glamorgan for one season, playing in eight limited-overs matches. John Arlott (1979) said of him that "he can only play cricket one way – as hard as he can".

White, Giles William (424) born Barnstable, Devon 23.3.1972. He was principally an opening batsman and occasional leg-break bowler who played for his native Devon from 1988, briefly for Somerset (1991-1993) and Combined Universities, before joining Hampshire in 1994, making his debut in July. He played fairly regularly for eight seasons, and in 1997 & 1998 averaged over 40, with 1,211 runs in 1998, including four centuries, and a best of 156 v the Sri Lankans – in the Championship, his best was 145 v Yorkshire at Portsmouth in 1997. On the same ground in 2000, Hampshire's last game there, he carried his bat for 80* in a defeat by six wickets. He took 11 wickets with his leg-breaks for Hampshire, most amusingly perhaps in that same match v Kent, when after Dravid had scored a marvellous hundred, resisting the wiles of Warne, White came on and dismissed him. He took 3-23 v Nottinghamshire at Trent Bridge in 1999. He had a reasonable batting record in limited-overs cricket with 2,346 runs at 21.72, fifteen half-centuries, and a best of 76 v Glamorgan at Southampton in 1998. In the same year, he played a valuable innings of 69 v Middlesex at Lord's, in a winning Nat West quarter final. His career ended after the 2002 season but he returned to Hampshire in a coaching role and in 2008, replaced Paul Terry as the Cricket Manager, since when he has moved up to become Director of Cricket. In these roles, he has been particularly successful in 'white ball' cricket, with trophies in 2009, 2010 and two in 2012.

White, William Nicholas (104, Amateur) born London 10.9.1879, died Devon, 27.12.1951. He was a batsman who went to Malvern College, and played in junior sides in Surrey and Hampshire. He made his first-class debut for Hampshire in 1903, then between 1903-1906 played for Barbados, and in 1906 for the Army against Hampshire. As a soldier, he played a number of matches for the Army and Combined Services and in 1907 began playing more regularly for the county, eventually appearing in 61 first-class matches, scoring 2,827 runs at 27.44 with two centuries including a best of 160* (& 70) at Gloucester in 1909. That was his best season with 873 runs at 34.92. He played just one Championship match in 1914 and after the war, his three first-class matches were services games. His son, GW, played first-class cricket for the Army.

Wild, Tom (Pre '95) born Southampton 4.11.1855, died Southampton 2.5.1921. He was a batsman who played in two first-class matches for Hampshire at the Antelope in 1880, v MCC and Sussex, scoring 40 runs at an average of 13.33.

Wild, William (Pre '95) born Thornecombe, Dorset 21.2.1846, died Norwich 7.1.1891. He was a batsman and fast round-arm bowler, who played for Hampshire Colts from 1863-1877, and in that latter year in one first-class match for the county v MCC, scoring 8 & 2* and taking 0-11.

Wilder, George (150, Amateur) born Stansted Park, Sussex 8.6.1876, died Las Vegas, USA, 10.6.1948. He went to Eton and then played in six first-class games for Sussex (1905-1906) and once for the England XI v Hambledon at Broadhalfpenny Down in 1908. In the following year, he played in a Championship match for Hampshire v Derbyshire at Southampton, scoring 0 & 13 and taking 3-14 & 0-11. The authorities ruled that he was not properly qualified, and he did not play again.

Willes, Canon Edmund Henry Lacon (Pre '95, Amateur) born Hythe, Hampshire 7.7.1832, died Monk Sherborne, Hants, 9.91896. He was a fast, round-arm bowler, who went to Winchester College and played for the county in 1850 prior to the formation of the county club, and for Oxford University from 1851-1854, captaining in 1852 & 1853, and winning his 'blue' in the last three years.

He played first-class matches for teams in Kent & Surrey in the 1850s, then in 1865 in one first-class match for Hampshire CCC v Middlesex at Islington, scoring 0 & 1*, and taking 0-7. In the following year, he played for MCC against Hampshire, scoring 48 in an innings victory for MCC. He continued to play in non-first-class matches for MCC, and also played for Oxfordshire and pre-first-class for Northamptonshire and Warwickshire.

Williams, George Edward (113, Amateur) born Aldershot, probably 1880, but we have no further information about birth or death. He played in one first-class match for Hampshire v Somerset at Taunton in 1904, scoring 15 & 1, run out in both innings, as Somerset won by 222 runs. He played subsequently for Berkshire.

Willoughby, Frederick George (Pre '95) born Edinburgh, Scotland 25.2.1862, died Eastleigh 16.4.1952. He was a left-arm pace bowler who played in eight Championship matches for Hampshire in 1885, taking 25 wickets at 22.56, with a best of 4-39 (& 4-42) v Somerset at Taunton. In 1886, he continued playing for the county in non-first-class matches, but from 1890 played in similar games for Worcestershire, and in 1895 he played a Minor Counties game for them v Hertfordshire at Watford. He was also a first-class umpire.

Wilson, Thomas Henry (Pre '95, Amateur) born Cheltenham 10.6.1841, died Argentine 31.1.1929. He was a wicketkeeper who went to Harrow and made his first-class debut for MCC against Hampshire in 1869 – he played also in non-first-class matches for Huntingdonshire, Lincolnshire and Northamptonshire, and in two first-class games for Hampshire in 1870, scoring 15 runs, with one stumping.

Wood, Alfred Herbert (91, Amateur) born Portsmouth 23.4.1866, died Southsea, Portsmouth 19.4.1941. He went to Portsmouth Grammar School (PGS) then taught there, before becoming Secretary to Sir Arthur Conan Doyle. The two men played local cricket together for Portsmouth Borough, and Wood went to Oxford University, but only played minor cricket there. He played in non-first-class cricket for Hampshire in the 1890s and in one first-class match v Somerset at Portsmouth in 1901, scoring 11 in each innings. He played later for MCC and Sussex Martlets. There is a suggestion that he was Conan-Doyle's inspiration for Dr Watson.

Wood, Arthur Hardy (Pre '95, Amateur) born Alton 25.5.1844, died Hove 10.7.1933. He went to Eton and played matches for the Gentlemen of Hampshire and MCC. He made his first-class debut at Old Trafford in 1870 and played in Hampshire's two games v Lancashire that year, then again from 1875. In 1883 he was appointed captain, holding that post in their three years of first-class cricket, before they were demoted from 1886-1894. He played in 28 first-class matches for the county, scoring 849 runs at 18.45, with a best of 82 v Sussex, in 1882, and five other half-centuries. He was President of Hampshire in 1887. In the 1870s, while living at Winchfield House, he opened a new cricket ground there, for country house matches, and he was secretary of the Hampshire Hunt.

Wood, Christopher Phillip ('Chris') (504) born Basingstoke 27.6.1990. From 2006-2010, Hampshire gave first-class debuts to seven young cricketers, who had come through their age-group sides: David Griffiths, Liam Dawson, Hamza Riazuddin, James Vince, Danny Briggs, Michael Bates, and Chris Wood. Of those seven, Dawson and Vince have become key members of the first team, and have played for England; otherwise only left-arm pace bowler Wood, who played for England under-19s, remains, although largely as a result of injury he has played very little first-class cricket, with 13 matches in the past five seasons - and only 10 in the Championship. He is however an effective 'white ball' bowler, having played in 75 limited-overs matches plus 108 in the T20, during a period when Hampshire have enjoyed some success, He played in the Hampshire side that won the T20 in 2010 and was a member of the 'double' winners of 2012. During 2018, he became the only bowler to have passed 100 wickets for Hampshire in all three formats and was awarded his county cap. He is a useful lower-order batsman with 1,326 first-class runs at 23.67 including a century at Leicester in 2012 and six half-centuries. He signed a new contract at the end of 2018.

Wood, Julian Ross (410) born Winchester, 21.11.1968. He was an enterprising left-handed batsman, who played for Hampshire 2nd XI from 1988, and in June of the following year, age 20, began playing regularly in Championship and limited-overs matches. In that first season, he scored 588 runs at 36.75 with four half-centuries and a best of 96 at Northampton in his third game. He also scored his first limited-overs half-century, 66 v Nottinghamshire, but he returned in 1990 to find that Hampshire had signed a new left-hander, DI Gower, and there were fewer opportunities for him. In the next four seasons, he played in just 15 first-class matches, with one more half-century, although he played more often in limited-overs matches, scoring three more half-centuries with a best of 92* again v Northamptonshire in 1993, his last season of county cricket. He played regularly with Berkshire from 1994-2006 and with Hungerford in the Southern League, and later Basingstoke & North Hants, while developing his coaching career.

Wood, Sir Matthew (Pre '95, Amateur) born Isle of Wight 21.9.1857, died London 13.7.1908. he was a batsman and underarm bowler who went to Winchester College and played one match for Hampshire at Derby, age 18, in 1876, but batted in the tail, made a 'pair', and did not bowl. He played non-first-class cricket for Essex and MCC.

Wood, Maxmillian David Francis DSO (135, Amateur) born Maharashtra, India 22.2.1873, killed in action, Gallipoli, 22.8.1915. He was a pace bowler who went to Wellington College, and Sandhurst, where he played cricket. He played first-class cricket in India for the Europeans, from 1897-1902, then in 1907, in one match for Hampshire v Yorkshire at Bradford, scoring 5 & 4. He played in two further university matches for HDG Leveson-Gower's XI.

Woodroffe, Kenneth Herbert Clayton (174, Amateur) born Lewes, Sussex 9.12.1892, killed in action, Neuve Chapelle, France 13.5.1915. He went to Marlborough College, captaining the XI in 1912. He was a fast bowler who played in two matches for Hampshire, age 19 & 20, taking eight wickets at 27.00 with a best of 5-33 v the South Africans on debut. He played for Cambridge University in 1913 & 1914, winning his 'blue' both years, and in two matches for his native Sussex in 1914, taking 6-43 v Surrey.

Wootton, James (19) born Sutton-at Hone, Kent 9.3.1860, died Leytonstone, 21.2.1941. He was a left-arm pace bowler and good slip field, who played in 115 first-class matches for Kent from 1880-1890, but from 1891-1912 he was cricket coach at Winchester College, and in 1895 he played his first matches for Hampshire. He re-appeared in 1896 & 1900, playing in 24 matches overall, with 69 wickets at 27.05, and 391 runs at 12.61 with one half-century, 53 v Somerset at Southampton in 1896. On five occasions, he took five wickets in an innings for the county, with a best of 5-37 v Leicestershire at Portsmouth in 1895. In all first-class cricket, he took 761 wickets at 18.16.

Worrell, Lawrence Roosevelt (361) born Barbados 28.8.1943. He was an off-break bowler and cousin of the great West Indian captain, Sir Frank Worrell. He joined the British Army and played cricket for them from 1964. In 1969 he played for Dorset, and made his debut for Hampshire 2nd XI, playing regularly for them for the next four years. He made his first-class debut, for Hampshire v the New Zealanders at Southampton in 1969, then in 1971, played v Oxford University and the Pakistanis before making his Championship debut. He then played regularly through that season, and during the first half of the following season, but his last game came at the start of July 1972. He took 65 wickets for Hampshire at 32.55, with a best of 5-67 v Leicestershire at Southampton in 1971, when he took 52 wickets. In the same year, he scored his one half-century, 50, at Canterbury. He played in one limited-overs match but did not bowl.

Wright, H W (Pre '95) we have no further information about his names or dates/places of birth & death. He played in one first-class match for Hampshire v MCC in 1885, taking 1-70, and scoring 0 & 12 in an innings defeat. He played in three non-first-class matches for the county in the next two seasons.

Wyatt, Francis Joseph Caldwell (123, Amateur) born Madras, India 10.7.1882, died Chichester 5.5.1971. He was a medium-pace bowler and lower order batsman who made his first-class debut for the Gentlemen in 1904, and for Hampshire v the Australians in 1905, while in the winter of 1906/7 played in South Africa for Orange Free State. He also played in first-class and other matches for the Army from 1903-1927. In 1906, he played in four Championship matches, another four in 1908, plus one v MCC, and in 1919 a final game for Hampshire v Yorkshire at Southampton. He took 44 wickets at 21.25, four times taking five wickets in an innings with a best of 6-31 v Somerset (9-91 in the match) at Bath in 1908, scoring 73 runs at 5.61

Wynyard, Edward George (11, Amateur) born Uttar Pradesh, India, 1.4.1861, died Beaconsfield, Bucks 30.10.1936. He went to Charterhouse School and St Edward's Oxford, and first played for Hampshire age 17 in 1878. He was a fine batsman, a useful, if occasional bowler and a very talented all-round sportsman, who played for Old Carthusians when they won the FA Cup in 1881 and also performed with distinction in rugby and 'winter' sports. In his twenties, he was in the King's Liverpool Regiment and he remained in the Army which affected his first-class cricket career, despite which he played in 154 first-class matches between 1878-1912, including 71 for Hampshire, in which his 4,322 runs came at 34.57 with seven centuries. There were two double centuries, 268 at Southampton v the powerful Yorkshire side of 1896, one of his three centuries for Hampshire in a first-class season when he scored 1,038 runs at a fraction below 50. There were also 1,281 runs at 41.32 in 1899, when he scored 268 at Taunton in 1899, and with his fellow Army officer RM Poore, added 411 for the sixth wicket, which remains a record. That was the one season in which he completed 1,000 runs for Hampshire, and while he played some first-class cricket through the first 13 seasons of the twentieth century, Army duties, not least in the South African 'Boer' wars, and other commitments ensured he was never a regular player again. He was the county's captain from 1896-1899, but for the same reasons had to pass that on to Charles Robson. In 1896, he played for England v Australia at the Oval and ten years later in two Test Matches in South Africa but he scored only 72 runs in his six innings. In non-first-class matches, he played for MCC and went on a variety of overseas tours to the West Indies, South Africa, Philadelphia, and Egypt. His last recorded match was for MCC v Lord's & Commons at Lord's in 1931 age 70. HS Altham (1957) described him as "a man of arresting presence and strong personality". See also: Keith Warsop (2004) *EG Wynyard: His Record Innings-by-Innings*.

Y

Yaldren, Charles Henry (168) born Southampton 8.12.1891, killed in action at the Somme, France, 23.10.1916. He played in one drawn match for Hampshire v Cambridge University at Southampton in 1912, in which he was run out for eight, and took 1-52, one of eight bowlers, as the University scored 484 (& 0-8).

Yasir Arafat, (List A/T20) born 12.3.1982 in Pakistan. Pace bowler Yasir Arafat played international cricket for Pakistan in all three formats and for various domestic teams there, as well as for a number of county sides. He joined Hampshire to play in 'white-ball' cricket in 2015 and in the following season went on loan to Somerset. In 2015, he played in six limited-overs matches (BB 3-56) and 16 x T20s (BB 4-37 v Somerset).

Yates, Humphrey William Maghull (154, Amateur) born Eccles, Lancashire, 25.3.1883, died Johannesburg, South Africa 21.8.1956. He attended Winchester College and played for Lancashire 2nd XI and in first-class cricket for the Army, and Army & Navy Combined XIs. From 1910-1913, he played in 13 first-class matches for Hampshire, scoring 242 runs at 15.12 with one half-century, 65*, on his county debut v Worcestershire in 1910. He moved to South Africa and from 1945-1956 was the scorer with Transvaal.

Young, Charles Robertson (Pre '95, Amateur & Professional) born Dharwar, India 2.2.1852, died Bolton 12.4.1913. He was a left-handed batsman and left-arm medium pace bowler who played in non-first-class matches for various sides in Hampshire, before making his first-class debut for the county v Kent at Gravesend on 13 June 1867 when he was just 15 years and 131 days old. Until the 21st century, he was believed to be appropriately named, as the youngest man to play for a first-class county, and while in 2011, Yorkshire fielded Barney Gibson, age 15 years & 27 days, that was v Durham University, so Young's record remains for an inter-county match. It was Gibson's only first-class match. On his debut, Young scored 20* and took one wicket, and he played three matches in that first month, but he then became a professional in Scotland and nearer home, for Stubbington. He next played for Hampshire, ten years after his debut, and played regularly until Hampshire lost their first-class status after the 1885 season, after which he continued to play for the county in non-first-class matches until June 1890. He played in 38 first-class matches for Hampshire, with a highest score of 48 and took

149 wickets – including in three games, 10 wickets in the match. His best bowling was 7-19 (& 4-52) v MCC at the Antelope in 1882, Hampshire winning by an innings. In 1887 & 1888 he stood as an umpire in first-class matches at Cambridge University.

BIBLIOGRAPHY, REFERENCES & OTHER SOURCES

Hampshire Handbook: I have referred extensively to the publication, which under that title has been published since 1950, notably to individual profiles written by John Arlott including Neville Rogers in the 1956 Handbook plus Charlie Knott & Leo Harrison (1957), Desmond Eagar & Derek Shackleton (1958), Vic Cannings (1959), Jimmy Gray (1960), Roy Marshall (1961), Colin Ingleby-Mackenzie (1962), Arthur Holt & Malcolm Heath (1963), Mervyn Burden (1964), and Peter Sainsbury (1965).

Stephen Saunders published (1997) *Cricket in Hampshire: A Bibliography* and (2010) *Cricket in Hampshire: An Updated Bibliography* which offer a comprehensive list of all publications about Hampshire cricket to that date.

Otherwise, apart from various years of *Wisden Cricketers' Almanack*, my main sources, and references in the text are as follows:

ACS, 1982, *Hampshire Cricketers 1800-1982*

Allen D & Saunders S, 2013, *150 Not Out: Hampshire County Cricket 1863-2013*

Altham HS, Arlott, J, Eagar EDR, Webber R, 1957, *Hampshire County Cricket: The Official History*, Phoenix Books

Arlott J, 1957, see Altham *et al* (above)

Arlott J, 1980, *John Arlott's Book of Cricketers*, Readers' Union

Arlott J, 1958, *John Arlott's Cricket Journal*, Heineman

Ashley-Cooper FS, 1924, *Hampshire County Cricket*, George W May

Bailey P, Thorne P, & Wynne-Thomas P, 1984, *Who's Who of Cricketers*, Hamlyn

Brooke R, 1991, *A History of the County Cricket Championship*, Guinness

Chalke S, 2015, *Summer's Crown: The Story of Cricket's County Championship*, Fairfield Books

Doggart H (editor), 1967, *The Heart of Cricket: A Memoir of HS Altham*, Hutchinson

Edwards A, 2014, *Hampshire Cricket Miscellany*, Pitch Publishing

Edwards A, 2014, *Hampshire's First Eleven: 1864*, Hampshire Cricket Heritage

Edwards A, 2001, *Lionel Tennyson: Regency Buck*, Robson Books

Hampshire Cricket Society, 1983, *Milestones of Hampshire Cricket*

Hayes D, 1993, *Famous Cricketers of Hampshire,* Spellmount

Isaacs V, 1997, *Hampshire County Cricket Club: First Class Records 1864-1996*

Isaacs v & Allen D, 2000, *Malcolm Marshall: Famous Cricketers Series,* ACS

Jenkinson N, 2012, *CB Llewellyn: A Study in Equivocation,* ACS

Jenkinson N, 1993, *CP Mead: Hampshire's Greatest Run-Maker,* Paul Cave

Jenkinson N, Allen D, Ricquier, 2003, *100 Greats, Hampshire County Cricket Club,* Tempus

Jenkinson N, 2001, *Here's the Hambledon Club!* Downend Books

Jones P, 2014, *A Torch in Flame,* Natula Publications

Lonsdale J, 1992, *The Army's Grace: The Life of Brigadier General RM Poore,* Spellmount

Murrell, RJ, 2008, *Hampshire Cricket 'Top Tens',* Hampshire Cricket Heritage

Murtagh A, 2016, *Test of Character: The Story of John Holder,* Pitch Publishing

Parker E, 1924, *Hesketh Prichard: A Memoir,* Fisher Unwin

Renshaw A, 2014, *Wisden on the Great War,* John Wisden

Sandiford KAP, 2005, *Roy Edwin Marshall: Famous Cricketers Series,* ACS

Sweetman S, 2012, *HV Hesketh-Prichard: Amazing Stories,* ACS

Warsop K, 2004, *EG Wynyard: Famous Cricketers Series,* ACS

Webber R, 1958, *The County Cricket Championship,* Sportsman's Book Club.

Wynne-Thomas P, 1988, *The History of Hampshire County Cricket Club,* Helm

ON-LINE:
http://www.cricketarchive.com/
http://hampshirecricket.net/
https://hampshirecrickethistory.wordpress.com/